CLIMATE CHANGE AND MARITIME BOUNDARIES

Coastal States exercise sovereignty and sovereign rights in maritime zones, measured from their coasts. The limits to these maritime zones are bound to recede as sea levels rise and coastlines are eroded. Furthermore, ocean acidification and ocean warming are increasingly threatening coastal ecosystems, which States are obligated to protect and manage sustainably. These changes, accelerating as the planet heats, prompt an urgent need to clarify and update the international law of maritime zones. This book explains how bilateral maritime boundaries are established, and how coastal instability and vulnerable ecosystems can affect the delimitation process through bilateral negotiations or judicial settlement. Árnadóttir engages with core concepts within public international law to address emerging issues, such as diminishing territory and changing boundaries. She proposes viable ways of addressing future challenges and sets out how fundamental changes to the marine environment can justify termination or revision of settled maritime boundaries and related agreements.

Snjólaug Árnadóttir is a Lecturer at Reykjavik University and member of the International Law Association Committee on International Law and Sea Level Rise.

Climate Change and Maritime Boundaries

LEGAL CONSEQUENCES OF SEA LEVEL RISE

SNJÓLAUG ÁRNADÓTTIR
Reykjavik University

CAMBRIDGE
UNIVERSITY PRESS

CAMBRIDGE
UNIVERSITY PRESS

Shaftesbury Road, Cambridge CB2 8EA, United Kingdom

One Liberty Plaza, 20th Floor, New York, NY 10006, USA

477 Williamstown Road, Port Melbourne, VIC 3207, Australia

314–321, 3rd Floor, Plot 3, Splendor Forum, Jasola District Centre, New Delhi – 110025, India

103 Penang Road, #05–06/07, Visioncrest Commercial, Singapore 238467

Cambridge University Press is part of Cambridge University Press & Assessment, a department of the University of Cambridge.

We share the University's mission to contribute to society through the pursuit of education, learning and research at the highest international levels of excellence.

www.cambridge.org
Information on this title: www.cambridge.org/9781009048620

DOI : 10.1017/9781009047906

First published 2022
First paperback edition 2025

A catalogue record for this publication is available from the British Library

ISBN 978-1-316-51789-5 Hardback
ISBN 978-1-009-04862-0 Paperback

Contents

Acknowledgements

This book is the culmination of a project spanning the past seven years. It began when I studied coastal instability at the Rhodes Academy of Oceans Law and Policy and enrolled, shortly thereafter, as a doctoral candidate at the University of Edinburgh. I had the good fortune of being supervised by Professor Alan Boyle, and he has been my greatest source of inspiration throughout this journey. I graduated from the University of Edinburgh in 2018 and have since taught public international law, international environmental law, law of the sea and a preparatory course for the Philip C Jessup Moot Competition at the University of Iceland and Reykjavik University. I have been a visiting scholar at the Netherlands Institute for the Law of the Sea and at the University of British Columbia. I am currently a postdoctoral fellow and lecturer at Reykjavik University and a member of the International Law Association Committee on International Law and Sea Level Rise.

I am in constant awe of the ocean. I have lived in close proximity to it my whole life and, every day, I see the surging waves of the Atlantic Ocean from my home office. The idea to write a book about sea level rise actually arose when I lived (as an exchange student) in a cabin at the seafront of the small island Styrsö, Sweden, where I often felt that the waves were too imposing. The other thing that piqued my interest was a sentence in a law of the sea textbook indicating that the consequences of sea level rise for maritime boundaries were unknown. This book aims to shed light on some of those consequences.

I am particularly grateful to Professor Alan Boyle for his uniquely thought-provoking input and the wealth of scholarly work and case law he contributed to and which informed my research. I have also enjoyed discussions with other wonderful scholars, and I am deeply grateful to all of them. I would particularly like to mention the following, who gave me insightful comments at various stages and helped me approach the issues from new perspectives. In alphabetical order: Professor Michael Byers, Professor Robin Churchill, Professor Alex Oude Elferink, Professor James Harrison, Judge Tómas Heiðar, Dr Massimo Lando, Professor Bjarni Már Magnússon, Dr Kasey McCall-Smith, Dr Andreas Østhagen, Professor

Clive Schofield, Professor Alfred Soons, Professor Davor Vidas and Dr Aron Westholm. I also want to thank all the esteemed members of the ILA Committee on International Law and Sea Level Rise for intriguing discussions.

Many others have supported and inspired me while I have worked on this project. The friends I made in Edinburgh had a profound impact on me and some will have a place in my heart forever more. My family has also been incredibly supportive. My partner (the artist), my mother (the French horn player) and my father (the Director of the Office of the President of Iceland) have diligently read my work and are now well-versed in public international law! Thank you all from the bottom of my heart.

Table of Cases

(in reverse chronological order by jurisdiction)

INTERNATIONAL COURT OF JUSTICE

Maritime Delimitation in the Caribbean Sea and the Pacific Ocean *(Costa Rica* v. *Nicaragua)* and Land Boundary in the Northern Part of Isla Portillos *(Costa Rica* v. *Nicaragua)* (Judgment) [2018] ICJ Rep 139.

Maritime Delimitation in the Indian Ocean (*Somalia* v. *Kenya*) (Preliminary Objections) [2017] ICJ Rep 1.

Questions of the Delimitation of the Continental Shelf between Nicaragua and Colombia beyond 200 Nautical Miles from the Nicaraguan Coast (*Nicaragua* v. *Colombia*) (Preliminary Objections) [2016] ICJ Rep 1.

Whaling in the Antarctic (*Australia* v. *Japan*: *New Zealand intervening*) (Merits) [2014] ICJ Rep 226.

Territorial and Maritime Dispute (*Nicaragua* v. *Colombia*) (Judgment) [2012] ICJ Rep 624.

Pulp Mills on the River Uruguay (*Argentina* v. *Uruguay*) (Judgment) [2010] ICJ Rep 14.

Maritime Delimitation in the Black Sea (*Romania* v. *Ukraine*) (Judgment) [2009] ICJ Rep 61.

Sovereignty over Pedra Branca/Pulau Batu Puteh, Middle Rocks and South Ledge (*Malaysia/Singapore*) (Judgment) [2008] ICJ Rep 12.

Territorial and Maritime Dispute between Nicaragua and Honduras in the Caribbean Sea (*Nicaragua* v. *Honduras*) (Judgment) [2007] ICJ Rep 659.

Application of the Convention on the Prevention and Punishment of the Crime of Genocide (*Bosnia and Herzegovina* v. *Serbia and Montenegro*) (Judgment) [2007] ICJ Rep 75.

Case Concerning Armed Activities on the Territory of the Congo (*Democratic Republic of Congo* v. *Uganda*) (Judgment) [2005] ICJ Rep 168.

Legality of the Use of Force (*Serbia and Montenegro* v. *Belgium*) (Preliminary Objections) [2004] ICJ Rep 279.

Land and Maritime Boundary between Cameroon and Nigeria (*Cameroon* v. *Nigeria: Equatorial Guinea intervening*) (Judgment) [2002] ICJ Rep 303.

Sovereignty over Pulau Ligitan and Pulau Sipadan (*Indonesia/Malaysia*) (Judgment) [2002] ICJ Rep 625.

Maritime Delimitation and Territorial Questions between Qatar and Bahrain (*Qatar v. Bahrain*) (Merits) [2001] ICJ Rep 40.

Case Concerning the Gabčíkovo-Nagymaros Project (*Hungary/Slovakia*) (Judgment) [1997] ICJ Rep 7.

Territorial Dispute (*Libyan Arab Jamahiriya/Chad*) (Judgment) [1994] ICJ Rep 6.

Maritime Delimitation in the Area between Greenland and Jan Mayen (*Denmark* v. *Norway*) (Judgment) [1993] ICJ Rep 38.

Land, Island and Maritime Frontier Dispute (*El Salvador/Honduras: Nicaragua intervening*) (Judgment) [1992] ICJ Rep 351.

Case Concerning Military and Paramilitary Activities in and against Nicaragua (*Nicaragua* v. *United States of America*) (Judgment) [1986] ICJ Rep 132.

Frontier Dispute (*Burkina Faso/Republic of Mali*) (Judgment) [1986] ICJ Rep 554.

Continental Shelf (*Libyan Arab Jamahiriya/Malta*) (Judgment) [1985] ICJ Rep 13.

Delimitation of the Maritime Boundary in the Gulf of Maine Area (*Canada/United States*) (Judgment) [1984] ICJ Rep 246.

Continental Shelf (*Tunisia/Libyan Arab Jamahiriya*) (Judgment) [1982] ICJ Rep 18.

Aegean Sea Continental Shelf (*Greece* v. *Turkey*) (Jurisdiction) [1978] ICJ Rep 3.

Fisheries Jurisdiction (*United Kingdom of Great Britain and Northern Ireland* v. *Iceland*) (Merits) [1974] ICJ Rep 3.

Fisheries Jurisdiction (*Federal Republic of Germany* v. *Iceland*) (Merits) [1974] ICJ Rep 175.

Fisheries Jurisdiction (*Federal Republic of Germany* v. *Iceland*) (Jurisdiction) [1973] ICJ Rep 4.

Fisheries Jurisdiction (*United Kingdom of Great Britain and Northern Ireland* v. *Iceland*) (Jurisdiction) [1973] ICJ Rep 3.

Legal Consequences for States of the Continued Presence of South Africa in Namibia (South West Africa) notwithstanding Security Council Resolution 276 (1970) (Advisory Opinion) [1971] ICJ Rep 16.

North Sea Continental Shelf (*Federal Republic of Germany/Netherlands*) (*Federal Republic of Germany/Denmark*) (Judgment) [1969] ICJ Rep 3.

Temple of Preah Vihear (*Cambodia* v. *Thailand*) (Merits) [1962] ICJ Rep 6.

Right of Passage over Indian Territory (*Portugal* v. *India*) (Merits) [1960] ICJ Rep 6.

Sovereignty over Certain Frontier Land (*Belgium/Netherlands*) (Judgment) [1959] ICJ Rep 209.

Anglo-Norwegian Fisheries (*United Kingdom* v. *Norway*) (Judgment) [1951] ICJ Rep 116.

Asylum (*Colombia* v. *Peru*) (Judgment) [1950] ICJ Rep 266.
Corfu Channel (*United Kingdom of Great Britain and Northern Ireland* v. *Albania*) (Merits) [1949] ICJ Rep 4.

PERMANENT COURT OF INTERNATIONAL JUSTICE

Case of the Free Zones of Upper Savoy and the District of Gex (*Switzerland* v. *France*) (Judgment) (1929) PCIJ Series A No 22.
Nationality Decrees Issued in Tunis and Morocco (French Zone) (*Great Britain* v. *France*) (Advisory Opinion) (1923) PCIJ Series C No 2: Speeches made and documents read before the court.

INTERNATIONAL TRIBUNAL FOR THE LAW OF THE SEA

Request for an Advisory Opinion Submitted by the Sub-Regional Fisheries Commission (Advisory Opinion) [2015] ITLOS, 54 ILM 890.
Delimitation of the Maritime Boundary between Bangladesh and Myanmar in the Bay of Bengal (*Bangladesh/Myanmar*) (Judgment) [2012] ITLOS, 51 ILM 844.
MOX Plant (*Ireland* v. *United Kingdom*) (Provisional Measures) [2001] ITLOS, 41 ILM 405.
Southern Bluefin Tuna Cases Nos 3 and 4 (*New Zealand* v. *Japan*; *Australia* v. *Japan*) (Provisional Measures) [1999] ITLOS, 38 ILM 1624.

ARBITRAL TRIBUNALS

South China Sea (*Philippines* v. *China*) (Merits) (2016) XXXIII RIAA 153.
South China Sea (*Philippines* v. *China*) (Award on Jurisdiction and Admissibility) (2015) XXXIII RIAA 1.
Chagos Marine Protected Area (*Mauritius* v. *United Kingdom*) (2015) XXXI RIAA 359.
Bay of Bengal Maritime Boundary (*Bangladesh* v. *India*) (2014) 167 ILR 1.
The Indus Waters Kishenganga Arbitration (*Pakistan* v. *India*) (2013) 150 ILR 311.
Award in the Arbitration Regarding the Delimitation of the Maritime Boundary between Guyana and Suriname (*Guyana* v. *Suriname*) (2007) XXX RIAA 1.
Delimitation of the Exclusive Economic Zone and the Continental Shelf (*Barbados* v. *Trinidad and Tobago*) (2006) XXVII RIAA 147.
Award in the Arbitration Regarding the Iron Rhine ('Ijzeren Rijn') Railway (*Kingdom of Belgium/Kingdom of the Netherlands*) (2005) XXVII RIAA 35.
Second Stage of the Proceedings between Eritrea and Yemen (Maritime Delimitation) (*Eritrea/Yemen*) (1999) XXII RIAA 335.

Delimitation of the Maritime Boundary between Guinea and Guinea-Bissau (*Guinea/Guinea-Bissau*) (1985) XIX RIAA 149.
Anglo-French Continental Shelf (*United Kingdom/France*) (1977) XVIII RIAA 3.
Trail Smelter Arbitration (*United States/Canada*) (1941) III RIAA 1905.
Island of Palmas Case (*Netherlands/USA*) (1928) II RIAA 829.
Bremen v. *Prussia* (29 June 1925) German Staatsgerichtshof, Annual Digest of Public International Law Cases, 1925–1926, case no 266.
Grisbådarna Arbitration (*Norway* v. *Sweden*) (1909) XI RIAA 155. Unofficial English Translation available at: https://pcacases.com/web/sendAttach/508 accessed 22 December 2020.

WTO APPELLATE BODY

WTO, Panel Report, EC – Tariff Classification of Certain Information Technology Products (21 September 2010) WT/DS375/R, WT/DS376/R, WT/DS377/R.
WTO, Panel Report, China – Measures Affecting the Protection and Enforcement of Intellectual Property Rights (20 March 2009) WT/DS362/R.
WTO, Appellate Body Report, EC – Customs Classification of Frozen Boneless Chicken Cuts (27 September 2005) WT/DS269/AB/R, WT/DS286/AB/R.
WTO, Appellate Body Report, US – Measures Affecting the Cross-border Supply of Gambling and Betting Services (20 April 2005) WT/DS285/AB/R.
WTO, Appellate Body Report, Japan – Taxes on Alcoholic Beverages (1 November 1996) WT/DS8/AB/R, WT/DS10/AB/R, WT/DS11/AB/R.

EUROPEAN COURT OF JUSTICE

A *Racke GmbH & Co* v. *Hauptzollamt Mainz*, European Court of Justice: Racke C-162/96 [1998] European Court Reports I-3655.

NATIONAL COURTS

The State of New Mexico v. *The State of Texas* (United States Supreme Court 1927) United States Reports, CCLXXV.

Table of Treaties and Legislation

MULTILATERAL TREATIES

(in chronological order by date of adoption)

Agreement to Prevent Unregulated High Seas Fisheries in the Central Arctic Ocean (adopted 3 October 2018, entered into force 25 June 2021) available at: www.dfo-mpo.gc.ca/international/agreement-accord-eng.htm accessed 22 December 2020.

Framework Arrangement between Greenland/Denmark, Iceland and Norway on the Conservation and Management of Capelin (adopted 21 June 2018), Norwegian Government paper Meld St 15 (2018–2019), 43–44.

The Paris Agreement (adopted 12 December 2015, entered into force 4 November 2016) UN Doc FCCC/CP/2015/L.9/Rev/1.

Kyoto Protocol to the United Nations Framework Convention on Climate Change (adopted 11 December 1997, entered into force 16 February 2005) 2303 UNTS 148.

Agreement for the Implementation of the Provisions of the United Nations Convention on the Law of the Sea of 10 December 1982 Relating to the Conservation and Management of Straddling Fish Stocks and Highly Migratory Fish Stocks (adopted 4 August 1995, entered into force 11 December 2001) 2167 UNTS 3.

Agreement Relating to the Implementation of Part XI of the United Nations Convention on the Law of the Sea of 10 December 1982 (adopted 28 July 1994, entered into force 28 July 1996) 1836 UNTS 3.

Convention for the Protection of the Marine Environment of the North-East Atlantic (adopted 22 September 1992, entered into force 25 March 1998) 2354 UNTS 67.

United Nations Framework Convention on Climate Change (adopted 9 May 1992, entered into force 21 March 1994) 1771 UNTS 107.

Convention on the Protection of the Black Sea against Pollution (adopted 21 April 1992, entered into force 15 January 1994) 1764 UNTS 3.

Convention on the Protection of the Marine Environment of the Baltic Sea (adopted 9 April 1992, entered into force 17 January 2000) 2099 UNTS 195.

Vienna Convention on the Law of Treaties between States and International Organizations or between International Organizations (adopted 21 March 1986, not yet in force) 25 ILM 543.

United Nations Convention on the Law of the Sea (adopted 10 December 1982, entered into force 16 November 1994) 1833 UNTS 3.

Convention on the Conservation of Antarctic Marine Living Resources (adopted 20 May 1980, entered into force 7 April 1982) 1329 UNTS 47.

Convention for the Protection of the Mediterranean Sea against Pollution (adopted 16 February 1976, entered into force 12 February 1978) 1102 UNTS 27.

Vienna Convention on the Law of Treaties (adopted on 23 May 1969, entered into force 27 January 1980) 1155 UNTS 331.

Convention on the Continental Shelf (adopted 29 April 1958, entered into force 10 June 1964) 499 UNTS 311.

Convention on Fishing and Conservation of the Living Resources of the High Seas (adopted 29 April 1958, entered into force 20 March 1966) 559 UNTS 285.

Convention on the Territorial Sea and the Contiguous Zone (adopted 29 April 1958, entered into force 10 September 1964) 516 UNTS 205.

Convention on the High Seas (adopted 29 April 1958, entered into force 30 September 1962) 450 UNTS 11.

Optional Protocol of Signature Concerning the Compulsory Settlement of Disputes (adopted 29 April 1958, entered into force 30 September 1962) 450 UNTS 169.

Montevideo Convention on the Rights and Duties of States (adopted 26 December 1933, entered into force 26 December 1934) 165 League of Nations Treaty Series 19.

General Act (Pacific Settlement of International Disputes) (adopted on 26 September 1928, entered into force 16 August 1929) 93 League of Nations Treaty Series 343.

BILATERAL TREATIES

(in chronological order by date of conclusion)

Treaty between the Federated States of Micronesia and the Republic of the Marshall Islands Concerning Maritime Boundaries and Cooperation on Related Matters (adopted 5 July 2006, entered into force 24 July 2015) in Colson D and Smith R (eds), *International Maritime Boundaries VI* (American Society of International Law, Martinus Nijhoff, 2011) 4348.

Exchange of Notes Constituting an Agreement to Amend the 1973 Canada – Denmark Continental Shelf Agreement (5 and 20 April 2004) Canada Treaty Series 2009/27.

Treaty between Romania and Ukraine on the Romanian-Ukrainian State Border Regime, Collaboration and Mutual Assistance on Border Matters (adopted 17 June 2003, entered into force 27 May 2004) 2277 UNTS 3.

Agreement between the Government of the Kingdom of Denmark along with the Local Government of Greenland on the One Hand, and the Government of the Republic of Iceland on the Other Hand on the Delimitation of the Continental Shelf and the Fishery Zone in the Area between Greenland and Iceland (adopted 11 November 1997, entered into force 27 May 1998) 2074 UNTS 58.

Agreement between Norway and Denmark Concerning the Delimitation of the Continental Shelf in the Area between Jan Meyen and Greenland and Concerning the Boundary between the Fishery Zones in the Area (adopted 18 December 1995, entered into force 18 December 1995) 1903 UNTS 171.

Agreement between the Government of the United Kingdom of Great Britain and Northern Ireland and the Government of the Kingdom of Belgium Relating to the Delimitation of the Continental Shelf between the Two Countries (adopted 29 May 1991, entered into force 14 May 1993) UK Treaty Series No 20 (1994).

Agreement between the Government of the French Republic and the Government of the Kingdom of Belgium on the Delimitation of the Continental Shelf (adopted 8 October 1990, entered into force 7 April 1993) 32 ILM 1068.

Agreement between France and Belgium Relating to the Delimitation of the Territorial Sea (adopted 8 October 1990, entered into force 7 April 1993) 1728 UNTS 273.

Agreement between Denmark (on behalf of Greenland), Iceland and Norway on the Stock of Capelin in the Waters between Greenland, Iceland and Jan Mayen (adopted 12 June 1989, entered into force 1 July 1989) 1548 UNTS 165.

Agreement between Poland and Sweden Concerning the Delimitation of the Continental Shelf and Fishing Zones (adopted 10 February 1989, entered into force 30 June 1989) 1590 UNTS 361.

Agreement between the Socialist Republic of the Union of Burma and the Republic of India on the Delimitation of the Maritime Boundary in the Andaman Sea, in the Coco Channel and in the Bay of Bengal (adopted 23 December 1986, entered into force 14 September 1987) 27 ILM 1144.

Convention between the Government of the French Republic (Wallis and Futuna) and the Government of the Kingdom of Tonga on the Delimitation of Economic Zones (adopted 11 January 1980, entered into force 11 January 1980) 1183 UNTS 343.

Treaty between Australia and the Independent State of Papua New Guinea Concerning Sovereignty and Maritime Boundaries in the Area between the Two Countries, including the Area known as Torres Strait, and Related Matters (adopted 18 December 1978, entered into force 15 February 1985) 1429 UNTS 207.

Agreement between the Government of the Republic of Turkey and the Government of the Union of Soviet Socialist Republics Concerning the Delimitation of the Continental Shelf (adopted 23 June 1978, entered into force 15 May 1981) 1247 UNTS 141.

Agreement between the Government of the Republic of Turkey and the Government of the Union of Soviet Socialist Republics Concerning the Delimitation of the Continental Shelf between the Republic of Turkey and the Union of Soviet Socialist Republics in the Black Sea (adopted 23 June 1978, entered into force 15 May 1981) 1247 UNTS 141.

Agreement between Canada and Denmark Relating to the Delimitation of the Continental Shelf between Greenland and Canada (adopted 17 December 1973, entered into force 13 March 1974) 950 UNTS 147.

Treaty to Resolve Pending Boundary Differences and Maintain the Rio Grande and Colorado River as the International Boundary between the United Mexican States and the United States of America (adopted 23 November 1970, entered into force 18 April 1972) 11873 UNTS 56.

Agreement between the Kingdom of Saudi Arabia and the State of Kuwait on the Partition of the Neutral Zone (adopted 7 July 1965, entered into force 25 July 1966) 4 ILM 1134.

Convention between the United States of America and Mexico, with Exchange of Notes (adopted 29 August 1963, entered into force 14 January 1964) (1963) 2 (5) ILM 874.

Agreement between the Royal Norwegian Government and the Government of the Union of Soviet Socialist Republics Concerning the Sea Frontier between Norway and the USSR in the Varangerfjord (adopted 15 February 1957, entered into force 24 April 1957) 312 UNTS 289.

Treaty of Peace, Friendship, Limits and Settlement between the United States of America and the Mexican Republic (adopted 2 February 1848, entered into force 30 May 1848) available at: www.loc.gov/law/help/us-treaties/bevans/b-mx-ust000009-0791.pdf accessed 17 January 2021.

Great Britain/Russia: Limits of their Respective Possessions on the North-West Coast of America and the Navigation of the Pacific Ocean (adopted 16 February 1825) 75 Consolidated Treaty Series 95.

LAW OF THE SEA BULLETIN

DOALOS, 'Observations by the Federated States of Micronesia in Connection with the Official Deposit of its Lists of Geographical Points of Coordinates, Accompanied by Illustrative Maps, for Maritime Baselines and Maritime Zones in Accordance with the 1982 United Nations Convention on the Law of the Sea' (15 January 2020) LOS Bulletin 102, 26.

DOALOS, 'Note verbale from the Permanent Mission of Egypt to the United Nations Addressed to the Division for Ocean Affairs and the Law of the Sea, Office of Legal Affairs of the United Nations' (31 December 2019) LOS Bulletin 102, 22.

DOALOS, 'Note verbale from the Permanent Mission of Myanmar to the United Nations addressed to the Secretary-General of the United Nations' (15 February 2019) LOS Bulletin 99, 41.

DOALOS, 'Nicaragua: Presidential Decree No. 17-2018, Decree of Reform to Decree No. 33 2013, "Baselines of the Maritime Spaces of the Republic of Nicaragua in the Caribbean Sea"' (10 October 2018) LOS Bulletin 99, 36.

DOALOS, 'Council of Minister's Decision No (5) 2009 in Respect of the Application of the Straight Baselines System to a Part of the Coast of the United Arab Emirates' LOS Bulletin 69, 78.

DOALOS, 'Maldives: Maritime Zones of Maldives Act No 6/96' LOS Bulletin 41, 16.

1

Law of the Sea and the Changing Marine Environment

1.1 INTERNATIONAL LAW OF THE SEA: A HISTORICAL OVERVIEW

The international law of the sea is among the oldest branches of public international law.[1] It originally consisted of customary law, shaped by State practice, and governed mainly the rights of States in two distinct maritime zones: the territorial sea and the high seas.[2] Efforts to codify the law of the sea commenced in 1930 with the League of Nations Conference for the Codification of International Law, in the Hague, and these efforts went on for half a century.[3] The 1930 Hague Conference did not result in the conclusion of a treaty, but the First United Nations Conference on the Law of the Sea, which was held in Geneva from 24 February to 27 April 1958, led to the adoption of four treaties and an optional protocol: the Convention on the Territorial Sea and the Contiguous Zone[4]; the Convention on the High Seas[5]; the Convention on Fishing and Conservation of the Living Resources of the High Seas[6]; the Convention on the Continental Shelf[7] (together referred to as the 1958 Geneva Conventions); and the Optional Protocol of Signature concerning the Compulsory Settlement of Disputes.[8]

The First Geneva Conference did not set a limit for fishing rights and it left unresolved an issue of great importance – the breadth of the territorial sea.[9]

1 Tullio Treves, 'Historical Developments of the Law of the Sea' in Donald R Rothwell, Alex Oude Elferink, Karen N Scott and Tim Stephens (eds) *The Oxford Handbook of the Law of the Sea* (Oxford University Press, 2015) 1.

2 Ibid., 7.

3 Ibid., 2.

4 Convention on the Territorial Sea and the Contiguous Zone (adopted 29 April 1958, entered into force 10 September 1964) 516 UNTS 205.

5 Convention on the High Seas (adopted 29 April 1958, entered into force 30 September 1962) 450 UNTS 11.

6 Convention on Fishing and Conservation of the Living Resources of the High Seas (adopted 29 April 1958, entered into force 20 March 1966) 559 UNTS 285.

7 Convention on the Continental Shelf (adopted 29 April 1958, entered into force 10 June 1964) 499 UNTS 311.

8 Optional Protocol of Signature Concerning the Compulsory Settlement of Disputes (adopted 29 April 1958, entered into force 30 September 1962) 450 UNTS 169.

9 Tullio Treves (n 1) 13–14.

A Second Conference on the Law of the Sea was convened in Geneva from 16 March to 26 April 1960 to address the outstanding issues but was unsuccessful.[10] The Third United Nations Conference on the Law of the Sea convened in New York in 1973 and it lasted nine years, culminating in the adoption of UNCLOS, a single instrument that has been described as the constitution for the oceans.

UNCLOS is the most important source governing the law of the sea and possibly even the most significant treaty ever concluded. Its predecessors, adopted in Geneva in 1958, all remain in force but have been superseded by UNCLOS for those States that have also ratified UNCLOS, in their relations with other Parties to UNCLOS.[11] The 1958 Geneva Conventions reflected customary international law to a large extent, at the time of their adoption, and many provisions were transferred directly into UNCLOS.[12] Yet, in addition to codifying well-established rules of customary international law, UNCLOS also signified progressive development of the law.[13]

At the time of writing, 168 States are Parties to UNCLOS.[14] Non-Parties are bound by customary international law, which is largely compatible with UNCLOS.[15] UNCLOS is a very comprehensive instrument, governing most uses of the world's oceans, but it may be amended if new challenges emerge. Supplementary agreements can be adopted under the Convention and rules can be further developed through State practice and jurisprudence. Amendments to the Convention are possible under articles 312–316, but the acceptance of a large majority of States Parties is required before they can enter into force. To date no amendments have been made under this procedure. However, two implementing agreements have been concluded and both have entered into force: the 1994 Part XI Implementing Agreement[16] and the 1995 Fish Stocks Agreement (hereinafter FSA).[17] Furthermore, the adoption of a third implementing agreement under UNCLOS is currently under consideration and is set to govern the conservation and sustainable use of marine biological diversity of areas beyond national jurisdiction (hereinafter BBNJ Draft Agreement).[18]

10 Ibid., 14.

11 UNCLOS article 311(1).

12 Tullio Treves (n 1) 16; Robin Churchill, 'The 1982 United Nations Convention on the Law of the Sea' in *The Oxford Handbook of the Law of the Sea* (n 1) 24, 30.

13 Robin Churchill (n 12) 30; James Harrison, *Making the Law of the Sea: A Study in the Development of International Law* (Cambridge University Press, 2011) 53.

14 DOALOS, 'Chronological Lists of Ratifications of, Accessions and Successions to the Convention and the Related Agreements' (UN, 2020) available at: www.un.org/Depts/los/reference_files/chronological_lists_of_ratifications.htm accessed 27 November 2020.

15 Robin Churchill (n 12) 37.

16 Agreement relating to the Implementation of Part XI of the United Nations Convention on the Law of the Sea of 10 December 1982 (adopted 28 July 1994, entered into force 28 July 1996) 1836 UNTS 3.

17 Agreement for the Implementation of the Provisions of the United Nations Convention on the Law of the Sea of 10 December 1982 relating to the Conservation and Management of Straddling Fish Stocks and Highly Migratory Fish Stocks (adopted 4 August 1995, entered into force 11 December 2001) 2167 UNTS 3.

18 See UNGA Res 72/249, 'International Legally Binding Instrument under the United Nations Convention on the Law of the Sea on the Conservation and Sustainable Use of Marine Biological

UNCLOS is meant to regulate all the different uses of the oceans. It does not contain detailed provisions on every aspect of ocean governance but 'sets out the legal framework within which detailed norms to regulate the various uses of the sea may be developed and applied'.[19] The international law of the sea has further evolved through case law and customary international law since the entry into force of UNCLOS. This has been necessary to interpret some of the less explicit provisions, such as those concerning maritime delimitation.[20] The law governing maritime delimitation has developed significantly through the years[21] but new challenges are now arising, particularly in relation to the changing marine environment. Some of those challenges will be addressed by the binding instrument currently under consideration by the intergovernmental conference convened under the auspices of the UN,[22] while others may call for new approaches and altered interpretation of existing rules.

UNCLOS has been described by a former United Nations Secretary-General (hereinafter UNSG) as 'possibly the most significant legal instrument in [the twentieth] century'.[23] The Convention's importance cannot be overstated and, as this book will demonstrate, it has the capacity to stand the test of time. Indeed, UNCLOS is a living instrument capable of addressing new challenges, such as those arising from climate change.

1.2 DELINEATION AND DELIMITATION OF MARITIME ENTITLEMENTS

Maritime entitlements are the rights that coastal States possess in the water columns, seabed and subsoil extending from their land territory. Coastal States have different rights and obligations within different maritime zones and UNCLOS entails rules governing the internal waters, archipelagic waters, territorial sea, contiguous zone, exclusive economic zone and continental shelf. Customary international law also provides for the right to an exclusive fisheries zone, which can replace the exclusive economic zone. The nature of maritime entitlements differs between maritime zones and so does their seaward extension from coastlines. Coastal features must

Diversity of Areas Beyond National Jurisdiction' (19 January 2018). It remains to be seen if and when this third implementing agreement will be adopted.

19 Robin Churchill (n 12) 30.

20 See particularly UNCLOS articles 74 and 83.

21 See, for example, *Bay of Bengal Maritime Boundary Arbitration (Bangladesh* v. *India)* (2014) 167 ILR 1, para 339; *Delimitation of the Maritime Boundary between Bangladesh and Myanmar in the Bay of Bengal (Bangladesh/Myanmar)* (Judgment) [2012] ITLOS, 51 ILM 844, paras 183 and 184; *Delimitation of the Exclusive Economic Zone and the Continental Shelf (Barbados* v. *Trinidad and Tobago)* (2006) XXVII RIAA 147, para 223.

22 UNGA Res 72/249 (n 18) article 1.

23 DOALOS, 'The United Nations Convention on the Law of the Sea (A Historical Perspective)' (UN, originally prepared in 1998) available at: www.un.org/Depts/los/convention_agreements/convention_historical_perspective.htm#-Key%20provisions accessed 7 January 2021, referring to the Statement of UNSG Javier Pérez de Cuéllar upon signing UNCLOS in 1982.

satisfy certain conditions to generate, and continuously support, claims to maritime zones; and maritime entitlements are only generated by naturally formed land.[24] The naturally formed land must be above water at high tide and sustain human habitation or economic life to justify a claim to an exclusive economic zone and continental shelf,[25] and above water at high tide, or above water at low tide and within range of an island or the mainland, to justify a claim to a territorial sea.[26]

Maritime entitlements are measured from each State's baselines. Unless otherwise specified, baselines follow the low-water line along relevant coastlines, as marked on large-scale charts officially recognized by coastal States.[27] States also have the option of drawing straight baselines 'where the coastline is deeply indented and cut into, or if there is a fringe of islands along the coast in its immediate vicinity'.[28] They may also draw straight closing lines to close off bays and river mouths.[29] Furthermore, States can draw archipelagic baselines where the requirements of UNCLOS article 47 are satisfied.[30]

The breadth of maritime zones is measured from baselines.[31] Internal waters are any water that falls between land and baselines[32]; the territorial sea may extend seawards up to 12 nm from baselines[33]; the contiguous zone up to 24 nm from baselines[34]; the outer limits of the exclusive economic zone up to 200 nm from baselines[35]; and the continental shelf may extend up to 200 nm from baselines, or further if the natural prolongation of the land territory justifies such a claim.[36]

Coastal States clarify the extent of their maritime entitlements through a process known as maritime delineation whereby they unilaterally lay down inner maritime limits (baselines) and outer limits. These are only opposable to other States insofar as they coincide with the governing international law.[37] Where neighbouring States have overlapping maritime entitlements, they must agree on bilateral boundaries delimiting their overlapping entitlements[38] or settle their disputes by other peaceful means.[39] Thus, baselines and outer maritime limits are established through

24 See UNCLOS articles 13(1), 60(8) and 121(1); *South China Sea (Philippines* v. *China)* (Merits) (2016) XXXIII RIAA 153, para 508.
25 UNCLOS article 121.
26 UNCLOS articles 13 and 121.
27 UNCLOS article 5.
28 UNCLOS article 7.
29 UNCLOS articles 9 and 10.
30 UNCLOS article 47.
31 UNCLOS articles 3, 8(1), 33(2), 48, 57 and 76(1).
32 UNCLOS article 8(1).
33 UNCLOS article 3.
34 UNCLOS article 33(2).
35 UNCLOS article 57.
36 UNCLOS article 76.
37 *Anglo-Norwegian Fisheries (United Kingdom* v. *Norway)* (Judgment) [1951] ICJ Rep 116, 132.
38 UNCLOS articles 15, 74(1), 83(1).
39 See UNCLOS part XV.

unilateral delineation while areas that are subject to overlapping claims are delimited through bilateral agreements or adjudication.

1.3 CHANGES TO THE MARINE ENVIRONMENT

The coastline is constantly changing. The low-water line fluctuates on a daily basis and the difference between high and low tide can be as much as 35 feet. These changes have been well understood for decades,[40] if not centuries. These ordinary fluctuations were anticipated by the ILC when discussing what later became the 1958 Geneva Conventions.[41] However, more permanent changes are now resulting from sea level rise, coastal erosion, melting ice and extreme weather events. In comparison to the previously anticipated changes, climate-related changes significantly impact the average position of the low-water line. Furthermore, marine ecosystems are increasingly threatened by other climate-related changes, particularly ocean acidification and ocean warming.

The Intergovernmental Panel on Climate Change (hereinafter IPCC) is the 'primary international scientific body compiling policy-relevant research on climate change'.[42] It provides clear scientific evidence on climate change and potential impacts.[43] The IPCC published its First Assessment Report in 1990 and addressed the potential effects of sea level rise.[44] That same year, Caron and Soons explained that changes to the low-water line (an inevitable consequence of sea level rise) would have an effect on the enforceability of unilaterally declared baselines.[45]

The IPCC has published numerous reports elaborating on the various effects of global warming. Global mean sea levels rose by 3.6 millimetres per year from 2006 to 2015, more than they ever did in the preceding century,[46] and the rise is still accelerating.[47] Sea levels are expected to rise, on average, by 0.26 to 0.77 metres

40 William Reisman and Gayl Westerman, *Straight Baselines in International Maritime Boundary Delimitation* (Macmillan Press, 1992) 4.

41 ILC, 'Report of the International Law Commission on the Work of Its Eighth Session' (4 July 1956) UN Doc A/CN.4/104, 267.

42 Timothy Meyer, 'Institutions and Expertise: The Role of Science in Climate Change Lawmaking' in Cinnamon Carlarne, Kevin Gray and Richard Tarasofsky (eds) *The Oxford Handbook of International Climate Change Law* (Oxford University Press, 2016) 442.

43 IPCC, 'Organization' available at: www.ipcc.ch/organization/organization.shtml accessed 13 January 2021. See further discussion about the IPCC in Section 3.3.2.2.

44 John Houghton, G Jenkins and James Ephraums (eds), *Climate Change: The IPCC Scientific Assessment* (Cambridge University Press, 1990) chapter 9.

45 See David Caron, 'When Law Makes Climate Change Worse: Rethinking the Law of Baselines in Light of a Rising Sea Level' (1990) 17 (4) Ecology Law Quarterly 634; Alfred Soons, 'The Effects of a Rising Sea Level on Maritime Limits and Boundaries' (1990) 37 (2) Netherlands International Law Review 216.

46 IPCC, '2019: Summary for Policymakers' in Hans-Otto Pörtner, Debra Roberts, Valérie Masson-Delmotte, Panmao Zhai, Melinda Tignor, Elvira Poloczanska, Katja Mintenbeck, Andrés Alegría, Maike Nicolai, Andrew Okem, Jan Petzold, Bard Rama and Nora Weyer (eds) *IPCC Special Report on the Ocean and Cryosphere in a Changing Climate* (World Meteorological Organization, 2019) para A.3.1.

47 Ibid., para A.3.2.

worldwide by 2100, if global warming is kept within 1.5°C, and by an additional 0.1 metre if global warming increases by 2°C from pre-industrialized levels.[48] The instability and melting of ice sheets in Greenland and Antarctica may result in a further rise of several metres and the trigger for that eventuality seems to lie in global warming of 1.5–2°C.[49] Ocean warming and acidification are increasing as oceans take up over 90 per cent of all excess heat and 20–30 per cent of anthropogenic CO_2 emissions from the 1980s.[50] These developments are threatening marine ecosystems and their habitats,[51] leading to loss of biodiversity and relocation of certain species.[52] Corals are particularly vulnerable[53] and fish stocks are expected to migrate and decline.[54]

The IPCC also predicts an increase in extreme waves, and frequent 'extreme sea level events and coastal hazards'.[55] Furthermore, erosion and flooding are expected to increase significantly over the course of this century, which will impact all low-lying coasts unless major adaptation measures are taken.[56] A small change in sea level can significantly increase the intensity and frequency of floods.[57] Some areas will experience significant deviations from the average predictions (up to 30 per cent), making sea level rise more severe in those parts of the world.[58] In sum, the IPCC explains that sea level rise is causing permanent submergence of land; intense floods; aggressive coastal erosion; loss of ecosystems; salinization of soils and freshwater; and impeded drainage. All communities are at risk, including those on continents and at high latitude.[59]

These changes will affect the living conditions of at least 300 million people by 2050.[60] They will also affect marine ecosystems, islands, rocks, shoals, reefs and the maritime entitlements they generate. The consequences will be particularly severe

48 IPCC, '2018: Summary for Policymakers' in Valérie Masson-Delmotte, Panmao Zhai, Hans-Otto Pörtner, Debra Roberts, James Skea, Priyadarshi Shukla, Anna Pirani, Wilfran Moufouma-Okia, Clotilde Péan, Roz Pidcock, Sarah Connors, JB Robin Matthews, Yang Chen, X Zhou, Melissa Gomis, Elisabeth Lonnoy, Tom Maycock, Melinda Tignor and Tim Waterfield (eds) *Global Warming of 1.5°C. An IPCC Special Report on the Impacts of Global Warming of 1.5°C above Pre-Industrial Levels and Related Global Greenhouse Gas Emission Pathways, in the Context of Strengthening the Global Response to the Threat of Climate Change, Sustainable Development, and Efforts to Eradicate Poverty* (World Meteorological Organization, 2018) para B.2.1.

49 Ibid., para B.2.2.

50 IPCC, '2019: Summary for Policymakers' (n 46) paras A.2 and A.2.5.

51 Ibid., paras A.5 and A.5.2.

52 Ibid., para A.6.3.

53 Ibid., para A.6.4.

54 Ibid., para B.8.

55 Ibid., para A.3 and B.3.

56 Michael Oppenheimer and Bruce Glavovic (coordination lead authors), '2019: Sea Level Rise and Implications for Low-Lying Islands, Coasts and Communities' in *IPCC Special Report on the Ocean and Cryosphere in a Changing Climate* (n 46) 324.

57 Ibid., 357.

58 IPCC, '2019: Summary for Policymakers' (n 46) para A 3.4.

59 Michael Oppenheimer and Bruce Glavovic (n 56) 328.

60 Scott Kulp and Benjamin Strauss, 'New Elevation Data Triple Estimates of Global Vulnerability to Sea-Level Rise and Coastal Flooding' (2019) 10 Nature Communications 1, 3.

for low-lying island States, such as Tuvalu, Kiribati, Micronesia, the Marshall Islands and the Maldives, which may become uninhabitable in the foreseeable future. Uninhabitable States may lose not only the maritime entitlements generated by habitable islands but also their statehood[61] and, thereby, all maritime entitlements.[62] To date, no island State has become uninhabitable as a result of climate change, but individual islands have. For example, the residents of the Indian island Loachara and Papua New Guinea's Cateret Island were evacuated in 2006 and 2007.[63] Submerging island States seem to have begun exploring their options for evacuation, in preparation for further loss of territory. To this end, the Tuvalu government approached officials from Australia and New Zealand in 2001 in the hopes of relocating the entire population if and when the island State becomes uninhabitable.[64] These efforts have not proved successful and relocation is now seen as a last resort for the Tuvaluans who hope to keep their land above water with sea walls, dredging, reclaimed land and even floating islands.[65]

These human-induced changes are unprecedented in the planet's history and they are possibly bringing about a new geological epoch.[66] The last (and formally still the current)[67] geological epoch is called the Holocene and it began approximately 11,700 years ago.[68] Scientific studies suggest that a new geological epoch

61 Rosemary Rayfuse, 'Chapter 6: Climate Change and the Law of the Sea' in Rosemary Rayfuse and Shirley Scott (eds) *International Law in the Era of Climate Change* (Edward Elgar Publishing, 2012) 147, 152. See also Emily Crawford and Rosemary Rayfuse, 'Chapter 10: Climate Change and Statehood' in Rosemary Rayfuse and Shirley Scott (eds) *International Law in the Era of Climate Change* (Edward Elgar Publishing, 2012) 243, 249.

62 Uninhabitable rocks, shoals and reefs can generate an entitlement to a territorial sea and contiguous zone but only a State can hold sovereignty over such features and the derived maritime entitlements.

63 See Geoffrey Lean, 'Disappearing World: Global Warming Claims Tropical Island' (*The Independent*, 2006) available at: www.independent.co.uk/environment/climate-change/disappearing-world-global-warming-claims-tropical-island-5331748.html accessed 13 January 2021; Richard Shears, 'The World's First Climate Change Refugees to Leave Island Due to Rising Sea Levels' (Daily Mail, 2007) available at: www.dailymail.co.uk/news/article-503228/The-worlds-climate-change-refugees-leave-island-rising-sea-levels.html accessed 13 January 2021.

64 Rosemary Rayfuse, 'International Law and Disappearing States: Maritime Zones and the Criteria for Statehood' (2011) 41 (6) Environmental Policy and Law 281, 285, referring to 'New Immigration Category for Pacific Migrants' (Ministry of Pacific Islands Affairs 2002).

65 Eleanor Roy, '"One Day We'll Disappear": Tuvalu's Sinking Islands' (The Guardian, 2019) available at: www.theguardian.com/global-development/2019/may/16/one-day-disappear-tuvalu-sinking-islands-rising-seas-climate-change accessed 20 April 2021.

66 See Jan Zalasiewicz, Mark Williams, Will Steffen and Paul J Crutzen, 'The New World of the Anthropocene' (2010) 44 (7) Environmental Science and Technology 2228.

67 Mike Walker, Sigfus Johnsen, Sune Olander Rasmussen, Trevor Popp, Jørgen-Peder Steffensen, Phil Gibbard, Wim Hoek, John Lowe, John Andrews, Svante Björck, Les Cwynar, Konrad Hughen, Peter Kershaw, Bernd Kromer, Thomas Litt, David Lowe, Takeshi Nakagawa, Rewi Newnham and Jakob Schwander, 'Formal Definition and Dating of the GSSP (Global Stratotype Section and Point) for the Base of the Holocene Using the Greenland NGRIP Ice Core, and Selected Auxiliary Records' (2009) 24 Journal of Quaternary Science 3, 3–4.

68 Ibid., 12.

might be emerging due to the fact that 'humans have replaced nature as the dominant environmental force on Earth'.[69]

A working group was established in August 2016 at the 35th International Geological Congress with the mandate of delivering a ratified conclusion on whether and when this new geological epoch formally began.[70] The new epoch is called the Anthropocene and the name refers to the 'growing impacts of human activities on Earth and atmosphere'.[71] The Anthropocene is characterized by profound alterations of several important geological conditions and processes affecting, for example, coastal erosion, sediment and the chemical composition of the oceans and subsoil.[72] While the Holocene was 'characterized by relative environmental stability [...] [t]he Anthropocene, on the contrary, is seen as characterized by uncertainty and, possibly, a considerable degree of instability'.[73]

Ongoing changes will have widespread legal, economic and political consequences. The international community will have to prepare for a global crisis with legal re-engineering as fundamental assumptions of international law are challenged. Environmental changes may affect international law on a grand scale altering, for example, the definition of a refugee, the law on State responsibility as it relates to diffuse action, requirements for statehood and ocean governance. Maritime limits and maritime boundaries provide a clear example of legal institutions that will be affected by the environmental crisis because they derive their existence from coastal geography. Yet, they only represent one aspect of a much larger challenge.

1.4 RELEVANCE OF ENVIRONMENTAL CHANGES FOR MARITIME LIMITS, MARITIME DELIMITATION AND SETTLED MARITIME BOUNDARIES

Changes to coastal geography can be relevant for maritime limits, maritime delimitation and settled maritime boundaries because maritime entitlements, upon which limits and maritime boundaries are based, are generated by the coastal front. Maritime entitlements are derived from land territory and they exist 'solely by virtue of the coastal State's sovereignty over the land'.[74] The ICJ has further explained that

69 William Ruddiman, Erle Ellis, Jed Kaplan and Dorian Fuller, 'Defining the Epoch We Live in' (2015) 348 (6230) Science 38.

70 Heidi Bostica and Meghan Howey, 'To Address the Anthropocene, Engage the Liberal Arts' (2017) 18 Anthropocene 105.

71 Anne Chin, Lindsey Gillson, Steven Quiring, Donald Nelson, Mark Taylor, Veerle Vanacker and Daniel Lovegrove, 'An Evolving Anthropocene for Science and Society' (2016) 3 Anthropocene 1.

72 Working Group on the Anthropocene, 'What Is the "Anthropocene"? – Current Definition and Status' (2019) available at: https://quaternary.stratigraphy.org/working-groups/anthropocene/ accessed 13 January 2021.

73 Davor Vidas, 'Sea-Level Rise and International Law: At the Convergence of Two Epochs' (2014) 4 Climate law 70, 80 referring to Jan Zalasiewicz, Paul Crutzen and Will Steffen, 'The Anthropocene' in Felix M Gradstein et al. (eds) *The Geologic Time Scale 2012, volume 2* (Elsevier, 2012) 1033–1040.

74 *Aegean Sea Continental Shelf (Greece* v. *Turkey)* (Jurisdiction) [1978] ICJ Rep 3, para 86.

it is the coastal front that creates maritime entitlements and constitutes a juridical link between a 'State's territorial sovereignty and its rights to certain adjacent maritime expanses'.[75]

Unilateral limits to maritime entitlements generally fluctuate with changing coastal geography because they follow the basis for title. Normal baselines are ambulatory as they correlate to the actual low-water line along coastlines.[76] In principle, all baselines and derived maritime limits fluctuate in accordance with changing coastlines, with the exception of permanently described continental shelf limits.[77] However, a clear distinction must be made between maritime limits and international boundaries between opposite or adjacent States. While unilateral maritime limits fluctuate in accordance with legal requirements, bilateral boundaries generally remain stable, at fixed coordinates, notwithstanding subsequent changes to the coastal front.[78] This discrepancy can break the juridical link between the coastal fronts and derived maritime entitlements in instances where States exercise jurisdiction over maritime areas, to which they have no entitlement under the applicable law.

The law of the sea is based on the fundamental assumption that 'the oceans will continue to provide a predictable and benign environment which allows clear jurisdictional boundaries to be drawn from'.[79] UNCLOS was concluded at a time when there was still limited understanding of the potential effects of anthropogenic global warming[80] and the Convention has no explicit rules relating to maritime entitlements in a changing environment, except for article 7(2). It has been widely acknowledged that changes to coastal geography have an effect on maritime limits that are based on the normal baseline.[81] However, the impacts of climate change on

75 *Continental Shelf (Libyan Arab Jamahiriya/Malta)* (Judgment) [1985] ICJ Rep 13, para 49.

76 ILA Baselines Committee, 'Conference Report Sofia 2012' (ILA 2012) 25.

77 ILA Committee on International Law and Sea Level Rise, 'Sydney Conference' (ILA 2018) 11–12. Note, however, that straight baselines established under UNCLOS Art 7(2) remain stable until changed by the coastal State.

78 Important exceptions are discussed in Chapter 5.

79 Tim Stephens, 'Warming Waters and Souring Seas: Climate Change and Ocean Acidification' in *The Oxford Handbook of the Law of the Sea* (n 1) 777, 778.

80 Alan Boyle, 'Law of the Sea Perspectives on Climate Change' in David Freestone (ed) *The 1982 Law of the Sea Convention At 30: Successes, Challenges and New Agendas* (Martinus Nijhoff, 2013) 157.

81 See, for example, Alfred Soons (n 45) 216; Lewis Alexander, 'Baseline Delimitations and Maritime Boundaries' (1983) 23 Virginia Journal of International Law 503, 535; David Freestone and John Pethick, 'Sea Level Rise and Maritime Boundaries: International Implications of Impacts and Responses' in Gerald Blake (ed) *Maritime Boundaries: World Boundaries, volume 5* (Routledge, 1994) 73, 76; Jenny Stoutenburg, 'Implementing a New Regime of Stable Maritime Zones to Ensure the (Economic) Survival of Small Island States Threatened by Sea-Level Rise' (2016) 26 The International Journal of Marine and Coastal Law 263, 267; Alain Khadem, 'Protecting Maritime Zones from the Effects of Sea Level Rise' (1998) 5 (3) IBRU Boundary and Security Bulletin 76, 77–78; Clive Schofield, 'Rising Waters, Shrinking States: The Potential Impacts of Sea Level Rise on Claims to Maritime Jurisdiction' (2011) 53 German Yearbook of International Law 189, 190; Moritaka Hayashi, 'Sea Level Rise and the Law of the Sea: Future Options' in Davor Vidas and Peter Schei (eds) *The World Ocean in Globalisation* (Martinus Nijhoff, 2011) 187, 188–190.

maritime entitlements extend much further. Coastal instability can influence the delimitation of bilateral boundaries because the status of individual coastal features is essential to the delimitation process. Furthermore, fundamental changes to coastal geography can impact the interpretation and enforceability of established maritime boundaries.

Climate change is also gravely affecting the ecosystems of the marine environment. This has prompted the codification of the BBNJ Draft Agreement, which aims to ensure sustainable development, and long-term conservation of 'marine biological diversity of areas beyond national jurisdiction'.[82] This particular instrument is beyond the scope of this book, which focuses on the demarcation of maritime entitlements under national jurisdiction. However, the marine environment is currently under tremendous pressure, both within and beyond national jurisdiction. In fact, States have various obligations relating to conservation and sustainable use of the living resources under their jurisdiction, in addition to general obligations to protect the marine environment and vulnerable ecosystems in all parts of the oceans.[83] These obligations are not extraneous to the study of maritime boundaries and, as Chapter 4 will demonstrate, they can influence the delimitation process.

Climate change has brought on a surge of new challenges for ocean governance and the legal consequences are uncertain. The ILA has formed two committees to address the legal uncertainty resulting from changing coastlines: the Committee on Baselines under the International Law of the Sea (hereinafter ILA Baselines Committee) and the Committee on International Law and Sea Level Rise (hereinafter ILA Committee on Sea Level Rise). Furthermore, the ILC has begun exploring these issues and legal reform has been proposed to prevent the destabilizing effects that climate change will otherwise have on baselines and maritime limits. It is abundantly clear that climate change is affecting the law of the sea. However, it remains to be seen whether laws will be changed to address these many challenges or whether new approaches and enhanced cooperation under existing legal frameworks will suffice.

82 Intergovernmental Conference on the BBNJ Agreement, 'Revised Draft Text of an Agreement Under the United Nations Convention on the Law of the Sea on the Conservation and Sustainable Use of Marine Biological Diversity of Areas Beyond National Jurisdiction' (23 March–3 April 2020) UN Doc A/CONF.232/2020/3, preamble and article 2.

83 See, for example, UNCLOS articles 192 and 194.

2

Unilaterally Declared Maritime Limits

2.1 INTRODUCTION

Coastal States are entitled to a territorial sea, contiguous zone, exclusive economic or fisheries zone and continental shelf under UNCLOS and customary international law. States enjoy an array of rights within these maritime zones. For example, the right to explore, exploit, conserve and manage offshore hydrocarbons, minerals and living resources of the sea. A majority of all the maritime resources with potential for economic exploitation is within 200 nm from the coast.[1] However, technological advances make it increasingly viable to exploit resources further offshore and it serves States' interests to extend their claims as far seawards as possible. Consequently, claims to maritime zones have come to encompass an area approximately the size of the world's land territory.[2]

Maritime limits are established on the basis of coastal geography because maritime entitlements are generated by naturally formed land territory.[3] More specifically, it is the coastal front that establishes the juridical link between sovereign territory and maritime entitlements.[4] Coastal features must satisfy certain conditions to generate, and continuously support, claims to maritime zones. They only generate entitlements to exclusive economic zones or continental shelves if they qualify as islands, that is, are above water at high tide and sustain human habitation or economic life.[5] Coastal features that do not meet these requirements can still generate territorial sea entitlements, that is, if they are above water at high tide and qualify as rocks,[6] or above water at low tide and less than 12 nm from the nearest

[1] See Gemma Andreone, 'The Exclusive Economic Zone' in Donald R Rothwell, Alex Oude Elferink, Karen N Scott and Tim Stephens (eds) *The Oxford Handbook of the Law of the Sea* (Oxford University Press, 2015) 159, 159.

[2] Clive Schofield, 'Parting the Waves: Claims to Maritime Jurisdiction and the Division of Ocean Space' (2012) 1 Penn State Journal of Law and International Affairs 40, 57.

[3] See UNCLOS articles 13(1), 60(80) and 121(1) and *South China Sea (Philippines* v. *China)* (Merits) (2016) XXXIII RIAA 153, para 508.

[4] *Continental Shelf (Libyan Arab Jamahiriya/Malta)* (Judgment) [1985] ICJ Rep 13, para 49.

[5] See UNCLOS article 121.

[6] UNCLOS article 121(3).

island or mainland.[7] Low-tide elevations that are situated beyond the breadth of the territorial sea from a mainland or an island generate no maritime entitlements.[8] Furthermore, States cannot claim sovereignty over low-tide elevations or submerged land territory.[9] This means that maritime limits are dependent upon the presence of, and proximity to, the coastal front. Climate-related changes are tearing at the foundations of such claims and, consequently, their enforceability.

The present chapter builds on the theory of ambulatory baselines. It explains how changing circumstances affect the extent of maritime entitlements under UNCLOS; how normal, straight and archipelagic baselines are affected; how outer maritime limits fluctuate; and how States can acquire permanent continental shelf limits. Practical examples are analysed to determine whether the charted or actual low-water line represents the legal baseline; whether States have an obligation to adjust maritime limits or whether this happens automatically; and to what extent States can rely on unlawful limits. After a thorough examination of the effects of natural changes to the coastal front, man-made changes are discussed, including the limits between permissible artificial conservation, legitimate harbour works and unlawful extension of the coastline. Finally, proposals to stabilize baselines will be examined, and the feasibility of permanently fixing all maritime limits evaluated.

2.2 MARITIME DELINEATION

All coastal States are entitled to maritime zones. 'The sovereignty of a coastal State extends, beyond its land territory and internal waters and, in the case of an archipelagic State, its archipelagic waters, to an adjacent belt of sea, described as the territorial sea.'[10] Coastal States have an entitlement to a territorial sea without any proclamation to that end,[11] the possession of a territorial sea may even be compulsory.[12] Coastal States inherently have a continental shelf. That entitlement exists ipso facto ab initio as an extension of the land territory.[13] However, States must claim other maritime zones (the contiguous zone, exclusive economic zone or exclusive fisheries zone) to activate such entitlements under UNCLOS or customary international law.[14]

7 UNCLOS article 13.
8 UNCLOS article 13(2).
9 *Philippines* v. *China* (n 3) para 309.
10 UNCLOS article 2(1).
11 John Noyes, 'The Territorial Sea and Contiguous Zone' in *The Oxford Handbook of the Law of the Sea* (n 1) 91, 94.
12 Ibid., referring to the dissenting opinion of Judge McNair in *Anglo-Norwegian Fisheries (United Kingdom* v. *Norway)* (Judgment) [1951] ICJ Rep 116, 160.
13 UNCLOS article 77; see also *North Sea Continental Shelf (Federal Republic of Germany/Netherlands) (Federal Republic of Germany/Denmark)* (Judgment) [1969] ICJ Rep 3, para 19; *Delimitation of the Maritime Boundary between Bangladesh and Myanmar in the Bay of Bengal (Bangladesh/Myanmar)* (Judgment) [2012] ITLOS, 51 ILM 844, para 409.
14 See John Noyes (n 11) 109 and Gemma Andreone (n 1) 162–163.

Limits to maritime zones are unilaterally defined through maritime delineation. Baselines mark the inner limits and outer limits are generally measured from baselines.[15] States can resort to different types of baselines and outer limits in certain localities. Normal baselines follow the low-water line along relevant coastlines[16] and such baselines are applicable by default, unless otherwise specified.[17] Furthermore, States may construct straight or archipelagic baselines and closing lines in certain circumstances, depending on the coastal geography of the area.[18] Straight or archipelagic baselines and closing lines must be clearly defined by the coastal State. Charts or lists of geographical coordinates must be given due publicity and copies must be deposited with the UNSG in accordance with UNCLOS article 16. Outer maritime limits are normally at a fixed distance from baselines and these must also be given due publicity as per UNCLOS article 16. However, the geomorphology of the continental margin can justify the use of different outer continental shelf limits. These extend beyond 200 nm from baselines and are permanently established on the basis of recommendations from the Commission on the Limits of the Continental Shelf (hereinafter CLCS).[19]

Rules governing the delineation of baselines and outer maritime limits are detailed in the following sections.

2.2.1 *Baselines*

Normal baselines are the most common method for determining baselines in international practice.[20] However, States may also employ closing lines, straight or archipelagic baselines, and it is the presence of certain geographical factors that determines whether the use of a particular type of baseline is permitted. States are free to use a combination of methods when establishing their baselines, whichever method suits different conditions of their coastlines.[21]

2.2.1.1 Normal Baselines

The Council of the League of Nations established a Committee of Experts for the Progressive Codification of International Law in 1924. It was tasked with the preparation of an agenda for topics in international law that could, subsequently, be codified.[22] One of those topics was the regime of territorial waters and in 1926 a sub-committee published

15 UNCLOS articles 3, 33(2), 57 and 76(1).

16 UNCLOS article 5.

17 Robert Beckman and Clive Schofield, 'Moving Beyond Disputes Over Island Sovereignty: ICJ Decision Sets Stage for Maritime Boundary Delimitation in the Singapore Strait' (2009) 40 (10) Ocean Development and International Law 1, 5.

18 See UNCLOS articles 7, 9, 10 and 47.

19 See UNCLOS article 76(4) and (8).

20 Clive Schofield (n 2) 55.

21 UNCLOS article 14.

22 Lewis Alexander (n 83), 'Baseline Delimitations and Maritime Boundaries' (1983) 23 Virginia Journal of International Law 505.

draft articles on the subject.[23] Among other things, the sub-committee found that 'the general practice of states, all projects of codification, and the prevailing doctrine agree in considering that the baseline should be the low-water mark along the coast'.[24] This was agreed upon at the League of Nations Conference for the Codification of International Law, convened in Hague in 1930. No convention was adopted at that time but rules relating to the normal baseline were codified in the 1958 Convention on the Territorial Sea and the Contiguous Zone[25] and in UNCLOS.[26]

The ILC proposed in its 1956 report to the United Nations General Assembly (hereinafter UNGA) that 'the breadth of the territorial sea [should be] measured from the low-water line along the coast, as marked on large-scale charts officially recognized by the coastal State', except where straight baselines or closing lines were justified.[27] Thus, baselines would normally follow the low-water mark but they could be substituted with straight baselines where all necessary requirements were satisfied.

UNCLOS article 5 provides that the normal baseline is 'the low-water line along the coast as marked on large-scale charts officially recognized by the coastal State'.[28] The low-water line fluctuates twice a day, depending on the relative position of the Earth, sun and the moon and the location and extent of these tides can vary from one foot to over 35 feet in areas like the Bay of Fundy, on the East coast of Canada.[29] The ILC acknowledged, in its 1956 commentary, that the reference to a low-water mark 'may have different meanings' and that 'there is no uniform standard by which States in practice determine this line'.[30] The Commission further noted that 'the omission of detailed provisions' governing the identification of the low-water mark was 'hardly likely to induce Governments to shift the low-water lines on their charts unreasonably'.[31] General practice now demonstrates that States use the average low-water line along the coast to establish their normal baselines.[32]

Commentators agree that climate-related changes to the coastal and marine environment were not anticipated when UNCLOS was negotiated and not provided for in the

23 Committee of Experts for the Progressive Codification of International Law, 'Report of the Subcommittee on Territorial Waters, League of Nations' Legal Questions 10, reprinted in (1926) 20 American Journal of International Law 62.

24 Ibid., 79.

25 Convention on the Territorial Sea and the Contiguous Zone article 3.

26 UNCLOS article 5.

27 ILC, 'Report of the International Law Commission on the Work of Its Eighth Session' (4 July 1956) UN Doc A/CN.4/104 257.

28 UNCLOS article 5.

29 William Reisman and Gayl Westerman, *Straight Baselines in International Maritime Boundary Delimitation* (Macmillan Press, 1992) 4.

30 UN Doc A/CN.4/104 (n 27) 267.

31 Ibid.

32 Ashley Roach and Robert Smith, 'Straight Baselines: The Need for a Universally Applied Norm' (2000) 31 Ocean Development and International Law 47, 50. See further discussion on the mean low-water mark in Section 2.3.1.

text.[33] Still, relevant actors were not oblivious to the possibility of future changes. For example, when negotiating the 1958 Geneva Conventions, the delegation of the United Kingdom explicitly referred to the potential impact of coastline change on bilateral continental shelf boundaries.[34] However, the *travaux préparatoires* demonstrates that neither the ILC nor State representatives addressed the implications for unilateral maritime limits until the Third Law of the Sea Conference. Even then, this was only in the context of inherently unstable coastlines and not classified a major concern.[35]

2.2.1.2 Straight and Archipelagic Baselines

States may draw closing lines along the mouths of rivers[36] and bays.[37] Furthermore, base points may be placed on ports[38] and low-tide elevations[39] to draw interconnected straight baselines. Straight baselines may be drawn along the general direction of the coast along coastlines that are very irregular, that is, 'deeply indented and cut into, or if there is a fringe of islands along the coast in its immediate vicinity'.[40]

States that qualify as archipelagic States can draw 'straight archipelagic baselines joining the outermost points of the outermost islands and drying reefs of the archipelago, provided that within such baselines are included the main islands and an area in which the ratio of the water to the area of the land, including atolls, is between 1 to 1 and 9 to 1'.[41] Straight and archipelagic baselines are constructed by reference to base points and not the low-water line along the coast.

The method of drawing straight baselines was meant as an alternative to the system of normal baselines. According to the ICJ's decision in the *Anglo-Norwegian Fisheries*

33 See David Caron, 'Climate Change, Sea Level Rise and the Coming Uncertainty in Oceanic Boundaries: A Proposal to Avoid Conflict' in Seoung-Yong Hong and Jon Van Dyke (eds) *Maritime Boundary Disputes, Settlement Processes and the Law of the Sea* (Martinus Nijhoff, 2008) 1, 5; Rosemary Rayfuse, 'W(h)ither Tuvalu? International Law and Disappearing States' (2009) 9 University of New South Wales Faculty of Law Research Series 1, 5; Moritaka Hayashi, 'Sea Level Rise and the Law of the Sea: Future Options' in Davor Vidas and Peter Schei (eds) *The World Ocean in Globalisation* (Martinus Nijhoff, 2011) 81; Clive Schofield, 'Rising Waters, Shrinking States: The Potential Impacts of Sea Level Rise on Claims to Maritime Jurisdiction' (2011) 53 German Yearbook of International Law 222; Tim Stephens, 'Warming Waters and Souring Seas: Climate Change and Ocean Acidification' in *The Oxford Handbook of the Law of the Sea* (n 1) 787.

34 The delegation of the United Kingdom noted that such boundaries 'should remain constant regardless of any subsequent changes in the coastline'. United Nations Conference on the Law of the Sea, 'Summary Records of the 31st to 35th Meetings of the Fourth Committee' (24 February to 27 April 1958) UN Doc A/CONF.13/C.4/SR.31–35, 93.

35 Jose Jesus, 'Rocks, New-Born Islands, Sea Level Rise and Maritime Space' in Jochen Frowein, Klaus Scharioth, Ingo Winkelmann and Rüdiger Wolfrum (eds) *Verhandeln für den Frieden – Negotiating for Peace: Liber Amicorum Tono Eitel* (Springer 2003) 579, 601.

36 UNCLOS article 9.

37 UNCLOS article 10.

38 UNCLOS article 11.

39 UNCLOS article 13.

40 UNCLOS article 7(1).

41 UNCLOS article 47(1).

case, the low-water mark would not have to be followed as a rule where the coast was deeply indented or cut into or characterized by insular features, like those along the Norwegian Skjaergaard.[42] The Court explained that straight baselines should not be considered to be exceptions to normal baselines because such an approach would necessitate too many derogations from the general rule. Instead, the method of drawing straight baselines should be viewed as a rule in its own right. According to the ICJ, straight baselines can 'depart from the physical line of the coast' but only 'within reasonable limits'.[43] Where the strict conditions of UNCLOS article 7 are not satisfied, States must rely on normal baselines – they are applicable unless and until a State establishes a system of straight baselines.[44] According to the ICJ, straight baselines may only be drawn in exceptional cases and should be applied restrictively.[45]

2.2.1.3 Straight Baselines at Highly Unstable Coastlines

UNCLOS article 7(2) provides that '[w]here because of the presence of a delta and other natural conditions the coastline is highly unstable', States may draw straight baselines. These remain stable 'notwithstanding subsequent regression of the low-water line'.[46] This is a subsequent addition to the original rule concerning straight baselines. The right to draw straight baselines along highly unstable coastlines was not addressed in the *Anglo-Norwegian Fisheries Case* or codified in the 1958 Geneva Conventions. In fact, the rule enshrined in UNCLOS article 7(2) was first introduced in 1975 as part of paragraph 1.[47] Bangladesh has maintained that UNCLOS article 7(2) was meant to deal specifically with the Bengal Delta.[48] Indeed, the provision was originally proposed by Bangladesh[49] but as highlighted by India, in *Bangladesh* v. *India*, 'article 7(2) is phrased in general terms and it makes no reference to the Bengal Delta'.[50]

It is not entirely clear whether an irregular coastline is always a prerequisite for straight baselines or whether coastal instability can suffice. Roach, Smith and Brown assume that UNCLOS article 7(2) applies in tandem with paragraph 1.[51] That means that an unstable coastline must also be highly indented and cut into or fringed with

42 *Anglo-Norwegian Fisheries* (n 12) 129.
43 Ibid.
44 ILC, 'Summary Record of the 335th meeting' (27 April 1956) UN Doc A/CN.4/SR.335, 9.
45 *Maritime Delimitation and Territorial Questions between Qatar and Bahrain (Qatar* v. *Bahrain)* (Merits) [2001] ICJ Rep 40, para 212.
46 See UNCLOS article 7(2).
47 Revised Consolidated Text on Baselines 'C.2/Blue Paper No 4, 9 April 1975' UN Doc A/Conf.62/C.2/WP.1 in Renate Platzöder (ed) *Third United Nations Conference on the Law of the Sea: Documents, volume 4* (Oceana Publications, 1983) 126.
48 See *Bay of Bengal Maritime Boundary Arbitration (Bangladesh* v. *India)* (2014) 167 ILR 1, para 237 referring to hearing transcript, 117, para 16.
49 Robin Churchill and Alan Lowe, *The Law of the Sea*, 3rd edition (Juris Publishing, 1999) 37.
50 *Bangladesh* v. *India* (n 48) para 245.
51 See Edward Brown, *The International Law of the Sea, volume 1* (Dartmouth, 1994) 27; Ashley Roach and Robert Smith, *Excessive Maritime Claims*, 3rd edition (Martinus Nijhoff, 2012) 67.

islands to justify the use of straight baselines. In contrast, the ILA Baselines Committee assumes that '[t]hese criteria are not cumulative and any one of these three geographic circumstances will be sufficient for the coastal State to become entitled to use the straight baseline method'.[52] According to the ILA Baselines Committee, UNCLOS article 7(2) was meant to be an addition, permitting the use of straight baselines in localities where they might not otherwise be justified.[53]

There is very limited jurisprudence to help clarify this issue. The ICJ has only once confirmed the legitimacy of straight baselines, in the *Anglo-Norwegian Fisheries* case, which did not deal with the use of straight baselines along unstable coastlines.[54] Examples from State practice also fail to give an unequivocal answer to whether UNCLOS article 7(2) must be read in conjunction with paragraph 1 because the juridical basis for straight baseline segments is usually left unstated. Yet, there is at least one example of a State establishing straight baselines along a river delta where the conditions of UNCLOS article 7(1) are not met: Egypt has drawn straight baselines along the Mediterranean coast and the river Nile, assumedly on the basis of UNCLOS article 7(2).[55] However, the United States has challenged those baselines on the grounds that they do not also satisfy the requirements of paragraph 1.[56]

The ICJ, in *Qatar* v. *Bahrain*, referred to two primary conditions for drawing straight baselines. Namely, that the coastline should be deeply indented and cut into or have a fringe of islands along the coast in the immediate vicinity.[57] This suggests that coastal instability does not suffice to permit the use of straight baselines. If that is the case, then UNCLOS article 7(2) simply provides stability for those instances where irregular coastlines are also highly unstable. At any rate, UNCLOS article 7(3) is tied to the first two paragraphs and provides that straight baselines may not depart to any appreciable extent from the general direction of the coast and that sea area within the baselines must be sufficiently linked to the land domain to be subject to the regime of internal waters. This applies to all straight baselines, whether drawn along coastlines that are deeply indented and cut into, fringed with islands and/or highly unstable.

2.2.2 *Outer Maritime Limits*

Outer maritime limits are generally determined by reference to distance from baselines. However, the continental shelf extends to the outer edge of the continental margin and is limited to 200 nm from baselines only if the continental margin does not exceed that distance.[58] Where the continental margin extends beyond the 200 nm limit, the State delineates its outer limits

[52] ILA Baselines Committee, 'Conference Report Washington 2014' (ILA, 2014) para 25.
[53] Ibid.
[54] See Robin Churchill and Alan Lowe (n 49) 38.
[55] Ibid.
[56] Ashley Roach and Robert Smith (n 51) 85 and 89.
[57] *Qatar* v. *Bahrain* (n 45) para 212.
[58] UNCLOS article 76(1). See also *Libyan Arab Jamahiriya/Malta* (n 4) para 34.

in accordance with paragraphs 4 to 6 of UNCLOS article 76.[59] This calls for scientific evaluations of the thickness of sedimentary rocks, the foot of the continental slope or the greatest change in gradient; and distinguishing between submarine ridges and submarine elevations.

The CLCS assists States in finding the outer edge of the continental margin beyond 200 nm from baselines. First, the coastal State submits information on the limits of its continental shelf to the CLCS and, after reviewing the necessary data, the CLCS makes recommendations concerning the establishment of the outer limits of the continental shelf. Finally, States can establish their outer limits on the basis of these recommendations and such limits are final and binding.[60] Coastal States shall also deposit charts and relevant information, including geodetic data, to permanently describe the outer limits of their continental shelf with the UNSG, who gives due publicity to the new, stable limits.[61] This process is unique for the continental shelf.

'The rights of the coastal State over the continental shelf do not depend on occupation, effective or notional, or on any express proclamation.'[62] Thus, States have an entitlement to a continental shelf regardless of whether they have established outer limits delineating their entitlements.[63] Still, the limits are only permanent if established in accordance with UNCLOS article 76(9).

2.3 THEORY OF AMBULATORY BASELINES

It is a firmly established principle of the law of the sea that 'maritime territory is an essential appurtenance of land territory'.[64] This reflects the 'land dominates the sea' principle, which provides that maritime entitlements extend from sovereign territory by means of the coast. Marston has explained how maritime zones reflect coastlines like shadows reflect the objects that create them.[65] In other words, maritime limits follow fluctuating coastlines, and they cease to exist when the coastal features generating them disappear under the waves. Maritime entitlements cannot persist without land territory because '[t]he juridical link between the State's territorial sovereignty and its rights to certain adjacent maritime expanses is established by means of its coast'.[66] States cannot claim sovereignty over low-tide elevations or submerged coastal features[67] and, consequently, such features cannot generate

59 UNCLOS article 76(2).
60 UNCLOS article 76(8).
61 UNCLOS article 76(9).
62 UNCLOS article 77(3); see also *North Sea Continental Shelf* (n 13) para 19; *Bangladesh/Myanmar* (n 13) para 409.
63 *Bangladesh/Myanmar* (n 13) para 409.
64 *Grisbådarna Arbitration (Norway v Sweden)* (1909) XI RIAA 155. Unofficial English Translation available here: https://pcacases.com/web/sendAttach/508 (accessed 22 December 2020) 1, 4.
65 Geoffrey Marston, 'The Stability of Land and Sea Boundary Delimitations' in Gerald Blake (ed) *Maritime Boundaries: World Boundaries*, volume 5 (Routledge, 1994) 144, 154.
66 *Libyan Arab Jamahiriya/Malta* (n 4) para 49.
67 *Qatar* v. *Bahrain* (n 45) paras 205–206; *Philippines* v. *China* (n 3) para 309.

maritime entitlements.[68] Likewise, complete inundation of a rock, shoal, reef or an island, must result in loss of derived maritime entitlements.

The theory of ambulatory baselines provides that the normal baseline follows the low-water line. Furthermore, when base points are submerged, straight and archipelagic baselines drawn from those base points have to be recalibrated and new baselines established 'on the basis of still valid exposed baselines points'.[69] Outer limits of maritime zones are also ambulatory as a consequence of the baselines being ambulatory because outer maritime limits generally follow baselines. Maritime zones will not grow larger as baselines recede, their width will continuously have to meet relevant conditions of UNCLOS. Instead, the inner and outer limits of maritime zones will shift in accordance with changes to coastal geography. Sea level rise and submergence of coastal features will cause a landward shift,[70] and maritime entitlements will expand further seawards with coastal accretion and the creation of new islands.[71]

UNCLOS is silent on the matter of fluctuation or stability of maritime limits, with the exception of UNCLOS articles 7(2), 76(8) and 76(9). From those provisions a general rule has been derived. The theory of ambulatory baselines provides that 'baselines and boundaries generated from them are "ambulatory" ... that is, the baselines – and therefore the boundaries – adjust themselves to a changing coastline'.[72] UNCLOS article 7(2) provides that '[w]here because of the presence of a delta and other natural conditions the coastline is highly unstable, the appropriate points may be selected along the furthest seaward extent of the low-water line and, notwithstanding subsequent regression of the low-water line, the straight baselines shall remain effective until changed by the coastal State in accordance with this Convention'. Similarly, States shall establish 'final and binding' outer limits to the continental shelf beyond 200 nm, as per UNCLOS article 76(8), and they are permanently described in accordance with UNCLOS article 76(9). This stability is subject to stringent requirements, which leaves non-conforming limits ambulatory.

The theory of ambulatory baselines is also rooted in the assumption that baselines must satisfy the conditions of UNCLOS provisions concerning the establishment of baselines on an ongoing basis since baselines that no longer meet the requirements of UNCLOS provisions become unlawful. Furthermore, the theory has been

[68] Low-tide elevations can only be used for the purpose of delineating the territorial sea if they are located within the territorial sea and for drawing straight baselines if lighthouses or similar installations that are permanently above sea level have been built on them. However, when outside the territorial sea, low-tide elevations generate no entitlements on their own. See UNCLOS articles 7(4) and 13; *Qatar* v. *Bahrain* (n 45) paras 201, 207.

[69] David Caron (n 33) 9.

[70] See Rosemary Rayfuse, 'International Law and Disappearing States: Maritime Zones and the Criteria for Statehood' (2011) 41 (6) Environmental Policy and Law 282.

[71] See, for example, William Hirst and David Robertson, 'Geographic Information Systems, Charts and UNCLOS – Can They Live Together?' (2004) 136 Maritime Studies 1.

[72] David Caron (n 33) 2.

supported by the view that baselines should be ambulatory like the phenomenon they are based upon: the low-water line. As previously stated, most scholars accept the ambulatory baselines thesis and agree that changes to coastal geography have an impact on maritime entitlements and zonal limits.

There is one notable exception. Purcell argues that baselines do not fluctuate with changing coastlines because States only need to retain territorial sovereignty to maintain established maritime entitlements. She submits that generally 'no other conditions must be satisfied' and that the rules governing spatial extent of maritime entitlements are a separate issue.[73] She seems to view the rules on maritime limits as constitutive and not requiring ongoing adherence. This interpretation is difficult to reconcile with the fact that UNCLOS specifically affords stability to two select instances (not to the more general types of maritime limits) and with UNCLOS article 7(3) stating that any sea on the landward side of baselines 'must be sufficiently closely linked to the land domain to be subject to the regime of internal waters'. Purcell also suggests that the principle of stability, generally applied to bilateral boundaries, extends also to unilateral maritime limits.[74]

The ILC added the topic 'sea-level rise in relation to international law' to its long-term programme of work in December 2018[75] and established an open-ended study group.[76] The Commission is currently mapping legal questions resulting from sea-level rise and the co-chairs of the study group have published one paper on the topic, at the time of writing (hereinafter First Issues Paper).[77] This preliminary paper does not explicitly endorse or reject the theory of ambulatory baselines. The First Issues Paper notes that UNCLOS has been 'interpreted as prescribing an ambulatory character for baselines and the outer limits of the maritime zones measured therefrom', excluding continental shelf limits and straight baselines at highly unstable deltaic coastlines.[78] However, it also explains that sea level rise did not necessitate special consideration at the time of conclusion of the Convention and that a level of flexibility was envisioned in instances of instability.[79] The First Issues Paper differentiates between maritime limits that have been given due publicity and those that have not and confirms that changing coastal geography can impact the effect given to islands in delineating maritime limits and delimiting maritime boundaries.[80]

73 Kate Purcell, *Geographical Change and the Law of the Sea* (Oxford University Press, 2019) 12–13.

74 Ibid., 146.

75 UNGA Res 73/265, 'Report of the International Law Commission on the work of its seventieth session' (22 December 2018), para 9.

76 GAOR, 'Report of the ILC on the Work of Its Seventy-First Session' (29 April–7 June and 8 July–9 August 2019) UN Doc A/74/10, para 265.

77 ILC, 'Sea-Level Rise in Relation to International Law: First Issues Paper' (27 April–5 June and 6 July–7 August 2020) UN Doc A/CN.4/740, see particularly para 51.

78 Ibid., para 104(a).

79 Ibid., para 104(b).

80 Ibid., para 143.

The following sections explain the legal impacts of the ambulatory baselines theory for baselines; straight baselines at highly unstable coastlines; outer maritime limits; and permanently described continental shelf limits.

2.3.1 *Ambulatory Baselines*

The ILA Baselines Committee concluded that 'the normal baseline is ambulatory, moving seaward to reflect changes to the coast caused by accretion, land rise, and the construction of humanmade structures ... and also landward to reflect changes caused by erosion and sea level rise'.[81] This assumedly also applies to archipelagic baselines and straight baselines established under UNCLOS article 7(1) because such baselines are not afforded stability, temporal or permanent, in cases of coastal recession or other changes. Geographical changes to the coastline, such as coastal erosion, submergence of islands, rocks, shoals, reefs and low-tide elevations, coastal accretion, sedimentation and seismic activity, will affect the capacity to generate normal baselines, archipelagic baselines and straight baselines. Islands that were permanently above high tide when baselines were first established may become partially or completely submerged. This can lead to the reclassification from an island to a rock, a low-tide elevation (which instead of generating all maritime zones could only be used to delineate the territorial sea or for the construction of straight baselines in limited cases),[82] or a fully submerged feature that no longer supports a claim to maritime entitlements.[83] The consequences of ambulatory baselines will be most severe where islands or other coastal features are submerged. Baselines along the mainland coast will recede landward with coastal erosion and sea level rise. However, baselines will disappear where they have been drawn around coastal features that lose the ability to generate baselines.

The gradient of the coast is an important factor when predicting how much of an impact sea level rise will have on baselines.

> Where the coastline is relatively steep the impact of sea-level rise will be limited in terms of shifting the location of baselines (and thus the maritime jurisdictional limits derived from them) horizontally. Conversely, where the coastline is gently shelving, even relatively slight changes in sea level vertically can result in significant

81 ILA Baselines Committee, 'Conference Report Sofia 2012' (ILA 2012) 31.

82 UNCLOS article 13 provides that the territorial sea may be measured from baselines on low-tide elevations only if they are situated wholly or partly at a distance not exceeding the breadth of the territorial sea from the mainland or an island. Furthermore, UNCLOS article 7(4) provides that straight baselines may extend to low-tide elevations only if lighthouses or similar installations which are permanently above sea level have been built on them or where the drawing of baselines to and from such elevations has received general international recognition.

83 Clive Schofield, 'Shifting Limits?: Sea Level Rise and Options to Secure Maritime Jurisdictional Claims' (2009) 4 Carbon and Climate Law Review 405, 409–410.

> shifts in the location of the low-water line horizontally and this, in turn, can have significant impacts on the spatial extent of national maritime claims.[84]

Consequently, States with large low-lying coasts are particularly vulnerable to baseline shifts. Furthermore, States may lose their archipelagic status as sea levels rise because the ratio between land and water within legitimate baselines may cease to satisfy the requirements of UNCLOS article 47. However, accretion and the formation of new islands through volcanic eruptions may also lead to expanding maritime claims and man-made changes may affect existing baselines, as described in Section 2.4.5.

Caron noted that baselines will shift either automatically in accordance with physical changes to coastlines or through mandatory adjustments enacted by coastal States. The outer limits of all maritime zones measured from baselines will also shift either automatically or following adjustments enacted by coastal States.[85] There is an important difference between these two theories because one imposes an obligation on States to actively change their limits to allow for fluctuations and the other leaves no such discretionary power.

Coastal States have an obligation to display all maritime limits on charts or lists of coordinates.[86] Even though there is no explicit obligation to submit such data regarding the normal baseline to the UNSG, UNCLOS article 5 clearly assumes that normal baselines are displayed on officially recognized charts. There must, therefore, exist an obligation to reflect changes to ambulatory limits on relevant charts if the provisions apply on a continuing basis. That would mean that coastal States have an obligation to display lawful maritime limits on charts or lists of coordinates at all times and fluctuations of maritime limits are reflected in such data. This does not mean that inaction leads to stable limits because, as discussed in later sections, unlawful limits may be challenged[87] and courts may resort to the actual low-water line when the charted line proves inaccurate.[88] According to this, there is an obligation to adjust maritime limits *and* the potential for automatic adjustment if the obligation is not satisfied.

State practice indicates that UNCLOS article 5 is generally understood as referring to 'the mean low-water line along the coast'.[89] The mean low-water line may be established through different methods but States have long used the datum best suited to advance their maritime claims.[90] Today, many States rely on the lowest astronomical tide for this purpose and, in such cases, the baseline reflects a part of

84 Clive Schofield and Robin Warner, *Climate Change and the Oceans Gauging the Legal and Policy Currents in the Asia Pacific and Beyond* (Edward Elgar Publishing, 2012) 136.
85 David Caron (n 33) 9.
86 See Section 2.4.2.1.
87 See Section 2.4.1.
88 See Section 2.4.2.2.
89 Ashley Roach and Robert Smith (n 32) 50.
90 William Reisman and Gayl Westerman (n 29) 10.

the coast that rarely sees the light of day. Therefore, the low-water line used for establishing normal baselines is not representative of some average position of the coastline, but rather a low position of the coastal State's choosing, for example, the lowest astronomical tide.[91] Any change in the low-water line along a State's coastline can affect normal baselines. However, the mean low-water mark can change frequently without affecting a mean low-water line that has been established over a long period of time.[92] Therefore, the normal baseline may not change unless the mean low-water line is affected and gradual sea level rise or coastal erosion will have such effect.

The location of baselines is determined by reference to the low-water datum but the high-water datum is crucial for the classification of coastal features. The arbitral tribunal in *Philippines* v. *China* confirmed that, for the purposes of determining the status of coastal features, States could use any high-water datum 'that reasonably corresponds to the ordinary meaning of the term "high tide" in Articles 13 and 121'.[93] The tribunal found 'nothing in the Convention, and no rule of customary international law, that would mandate that the status of low-tide elevations and high-tide features/islands be determined against any particular high-water datum'.[94] However, the ordinary meaning would commonly refer to average high tide over a nineteen-year period or average height of spring tides.[95] Furthermore, this would generally be the same datum as that used for nautical charts.[96] This indicates that coastal States are afforded some discretion in choosing the datum most suitable to advance their maritime claims. Thus, States can have an impact on how much and how often maritime limits fluctuate. In addition to using the lowest possible low-water datum for their baselines, States can use the lowest possible high-water datum to categorize low-lying features as rocks or islands (rather than low-tide elevations) and the longest possible time span to decelerate changes.

Straight baselines, archipelagic baselines and closing lines do not have the same direct correlation to the low-water line as normal baselines. Subsequent changes to coastlines will not affect the entitlement to draw closing lines at historic bays since such bays may be enclosed regardless of whether they meet the geographical requirements of UNCLOS article 10.[97] Moreover, the mean low-water line can undergo substantial changes without affecting the furthest seaward extensions, namely, the base points for closing lines, archipelagic and straight baselines. If

91 Clive Schofield, 'Departures from the Coast: Trends in the Application of Territorial Sea Baselines under the Law of the Sea Convention' (2012) 27 (4) The International Journal of Marine and Coastal Law 723, 724.

92 William Reisman and Gayl Westerman (n 29) 6.

93 *Philippines* v. *China* (n 3) para 311.

94 Ibid.

95 Ibid., para 310, referring to International Hydrographic Organization, *Hydrographic Dictionary*, 5th edition (IHO, 1994) 144.

96 Ibid., para 311.

97 See Coalter Lathrop, 'Baselines' in *The Oxford Handbook of the Law of the Sea* (n 1) 69, 84.

base points are on elevated peaks they may withstand coastal erosion and sea level rise, effectively making coastlines more heavily indented but without shifting the location of straight baselines or closing lines. Yet, this only applies where the coastal features still meet the geographic requirements to be used for the purpose of drawing baselines. Base points can only be used for delineating maritime entitlements as long as they are valid, that is, located on coastal features that satisfy all relevant requirements of UNCLOS. Base points can never be based on submerged features or low-tide elevations beyond territorial waters.[98] Furthermore, if islands or rocks, within the meaning of UNCLOS article 121, are submerged, their maritime entitlements may disappear completely,[99] that includes not only the outer limits but baselines as well.

2.3.2 *Provisional Stability of Straight Baselines at Highly Unstable Coastlines*

UNCLOS article 7(2) forms an exception to the general rule that all baselines become unenforceable when they cease to satisfy the requirements essential for their establishment. Straight baselines on highly unstable coastlines can remain effective when coastlines recede, even though they no longer correlate to the low-water line.[100] Yet, this stability is conditional.

Straight baselines drawn in accordance with UNCLOS article 7(2) 'shall remain effective until changed by the coastal State in accordance with this Convention'. This terminology suggests that States, relying on straight baselines along highly unstable coastlines, may be under an obligation to adjust such baselines when coastlines change. As explained by Soons, 'it was not the intention of this provision to grant the coastal State a discretionary power in this respect. If that were the case the reference in the provision to subsequent change by the coastal State would not have been necessary'.[101] Likewise, Churchill and Lowe have asserted that 'article 7(2) does, of course, require a State eventually to change its baselines'.[102] Indeed, it seems unlikely that States would ever update straight baselines, following the regression of the low-water line, unless they were under an obligation to do so.

UNCLOS article 7(3) necessitates close physical proximity between straight baselines and the relevant coastal front. The fact that, under UNCLOS article 7(2), straight baselines may 'remain effective until changed by the coastal State' does not make them exempt from UNCLOS article 7(3). Consequently, it must be assumed that the obligation to adjust straight baselines along highly unstable coastlines arises when coastal geography undergoes significant changes and impacts

98 See, for example, *Aegean Sea Continental Shelf (Greece* v. *Turkey)* (Jurisdiction) [1978] ICJ Rep 3, para 86; *Qatar* v. *Bahrain* (n 45) para 209; *Philippines* v. *China* (n 3) para 309.
99 UN Doc A/CN.4/740 (n 77) para 172.
100 'Conference Report Sofia 2012' (n 81) 8.
101 Alfred Soons (n 45) 220.
102 Robin Churchill and Alan Lowe (n 49) 38.

the correlation between baselines and relevant coastal geography. This does not change the fact that straight baselines can remain effective, notwithstanding changes to the low-water line and submergence of base points, as long as the general direction of the coast remains unaltered and internal waters, on the landward side of the straight baselines, are sufficiently close to the land domain.

UNCLOS article 7(2) applies to coastlines that are unstable due to deltas and other natural conditions. The second half of that sentence might be interpreted so as to include instability resulting from sea level rise and other natural changes. Such an approach has been promoted as a method for stabilizing otherwise ambulatory maritime limits.[103] Brown has noted that the precise scope of UNCLOS article 7(2) is unclear because the provision does not settle '[w]hat degree of change over what period of time would be considered to constitute a high degree of instability'.[104] Yet, the interpretation advanced by Brown is, arguably, too broad because UNCLOS article 7(2) was meant to be a narrow exception, designed to deal with the exceptional circumstances at the Bengal delta[105] and not large-scale changes to coastal geography, such as the complete submergence of islands. The ILC has considered the possibility of applying UNCLOS article 7(2) to unstable coastlines affected by sea level rise and concluded that this exception only applies to deltaic coastlines.[106]

2.3.3 *Ambulatory Outer Maritime Limits*

UNCLOS does not specify whether outer limits of maritime zones are ambulatory. Yet, outer maritime limits are generally measured from baselines and, if baselines are ambulatory, the same must apply to zonal limits measured therefrom (which excludes the permanently described continental shelf).[107] Outer limits of maritime zones can only fluctuate in accordance with the baselines from which they are measured. Therefore, outer limits will not recede with subsequent regression of the low-water line if measured from straight baselines established under UNCLOS article 7(2) – not until such baselines are adjusted by the coastal State.

Islands and rocks generate a territorial sea but if they completely disappear beneath the ocean's surface the entitlement is lost.[108] A low-tide elevation may be used as the baseline for measuring the breadth of the territorial sea if it is situated wholly or partly at a distance not exceeding the breadth of the territorial sea from the

103 Moritaka Hayashi (n 33) 79.
104 'Conference Report Washington 2014' (n 52) referring to Edward Brown (n 51) 27.
105 See *Bangladesh* v. *India* (n 48) para 237 referring to hearing transcript, 117, paras 1 and 16; Kate Purcell, 'Maritime Jurisdiction in a Changing Climate' in Michael B Gerrard and Katrina Fischer Kuh (eds) *The Law of Adaptation to Climate Change: U.S. and International Aspects* (The American Bar Association, 2012) 729, 740.
106 UN Doc A/CN.4/740 (n 77) para 79.
107 See, for example, David Caron (n 33) 9; Alfred Soons (n 45) 216–218; Rosemary Rayfuse (n 33) 3; and Louis Sohn and John Noyes, *Cases and Materials on the Law of the Sea* (Transnational, 2004) 235.
108 Alfred Soons (n 45) 216–217.

mainland or an island. However, a low-tide elevation cannot generate entitlement to a territorial sea if it is wholly situated at a distance exceeding the breadth of the territorial sea from the mainland or an island. Consequently, the territorial sea should not be measured from a low-tide elevation if the mainland or a neighbouring island has receded so that the distance between it and the low-tide elevation has increased to more than 12 nm or if the low-tide elevation has been completely inundated.[109] This means that the territorial sea will have to be recalibrated under such circumstances in order to comply with UNCLOS.

Islands that become uninhabitable or incapable of sustaining economic life because of inundation will no longer generate an exclusive economic zone or a continental shelf.[110] Indeed, the ILC has explained that the reduction of an island to a rock will have the most dire consequences for States, as areas once subject to the regimes of the exclusive economic zone and continental shelf become high seas or international seabed area.[111] This does not necessarily result in the loss of baselines but does significantly affect outer limits insofar as the outer limits to the exclusive economic zone and continental shelf may be lost. However, if islands become completely submerged they lose all entitlements, also to a territorial sea.[112]

It should be noted that outer limits of maritime zones are often drawn by application of the 'envelope of arcs' method whereby only the outermost points of the baseline contribute to the construction of the outer limits.[113] Consequently, physical changes to the low-water line may affect baselines but not, or only partially, affect the outer limits measured from those baselines. For example, normal baselines will always change to reflect fluctuations in the low-water line. However, if the base points stretching furthest seawards remain above water they can still be relied upon to generate maritime zones and the outer limits will continually be measured from those base points.

2.3.4 *Stability of Outer Continental Shelf Limits*

UNCLOS article 76(8) provides that coastal States shall submit to the CLCS information regarding the limits to their continental shelf, if it extends beyond 200 nm from baselines. In turn, the CLCS makes recommendations relating to the establishment of the outer continental shelf limits and 'limits of the shelf established by a coastal State on the basis of these recommendations shall be final and binding'.[114] Furthermore, coastal States shall, according to UNCLOS article

109 UNCLOS article 13.

110 UNCLOS article 121(3).

111 UN Doc A/CN.4/740 (n 77) paras 179–180.

112 Alfred Soons (n 45) 216–217.

113 Christopher Carleton and Clive Schofield, 'Developments in the Technical Determination of Maritime Space: Charts, Datums, Baselines, Maritime Zones and Limits' (2001) 3 (3) International Boundaries Research Unit Maritime Briefing 1, 62.

114 UNCLOS article 76(8).

76(9), deposit with the UNSG 'charts and relevant information, including geodetic data' to permanently describe these limits and the UNSG gives 'due publicity thereto'.

The outer limits of the continental shelf were not described as final and binding under the 1958 Convention on the Continental Shelf. On the contrary, article 1 provided that the outer limits of the continental shelf should extend seawards to a depth of 200 metres or to greater depths, as far as exploitation of resources was possible. As noted by Schofield, this suggests that the outer limits of the continental shelf were ambulatory before the entry into force of UNCLOS, because advances in technology that allowed exploitation of resources at greater depths could justify moving the outer limits of the continental shelf seawards.[115] Consequently, the final and binding nature of the outer limits of the continental shelf is a relatively new addition to the law of the sea.

In principle, the same rule applies to the continental shelf as to other maritime zones. 'A coastal State's entitlement to the continental shelf exists by the sole fact that the basis of entitlement, namely, sovereignty over the land territory, is present.'[116] Therefore, changes to coastal geography have an impact on the entitlement to a continental shelf; inundated former islands cease to generate continental shelf entitlements once they become rocks that cannot sustain human habitation or economic life of their own; low-tide elevations; or completely submerged features. Likewise, newly formed islands can generate entitlements to continental shelves like other land territory and, consequently, justify an extension of maritime limits. Nonetheless, despite changes to baselines, continental shelf limits remain final, binding and permanent once they have been established under UNCLOS articles 76(8) and 76(9).

The stability afforded to the outer limits of the continental shelf constitutes an exception to the general principle that outer limits of maritime zones fluctuate in accordance with baselines.[117] However, it should be highlighted that the stability of outer continental shelf limits has no impact on baselines. They remain ambulatory, which means that continental shelf zones grow larger as coastlines recede, potentially larger than permissible under UNCLOS article 76(5),[118] which may make them unenforceable against third States.

The fact that the continental shelf is subject to a different regime from that of other maritime zones can be explained by reference to important differences between the rights in question and the manner in which they are determined. The continental shelf comprises the natural prolongation of land territory and

[115] Clive Schofield (n 2) 44.

[116] *Bangladesh/Myanmar* (n 13) para 409.

[117] David Caron (n 33) 9.

[118] UNCLOS Article 76(5) provides that the outer continental shelf limits 'either shall not exceed 350 nm from the baselines from which the breadth of the territorial sea is measured or shall not exceed 100 nm from the 2,500 metre isobath, which is a line connecting the depth of 2,500 metres'.

affords sovereign rights to explore and exploit the resources of the continental margin, not the water column.[119] As explained by the ICJ in the *North Sea Continental Shelf* cases:

> What confers the ipso jure title which international law attributes to the coastal State in respect of its Continental shelf, is the fact, that submarine areas concerned may be deemed to be actually part of the territory over which the coastal State already has dominion, in the sense that, although covered with water, they are a prolongation or continuation of that territory, an extension of it under the sea.[120]

This continuation of land territory is much less susceptible to change than the low-water line, from which maritime limits are generally measured. Outer limits of the continental shelf beyond 200 nm are dependent upon the stable continental margin and are primarily concerned with immobile resources. In contrast, the fish stocks of the water column migrate and can be heavily affected by changing environmental circumstances. It seems reasonable to have ambulatory limits demarcate the rights to ambulatory resources and fixed limits around the more territorial, inherent rights of submarine areas. This may justify the discrepancy between the stable limits of the continental shelf and the fluctuating limits of other maritime zones. The argument is less persuasive when it comes to continental shelf limits that are measured from fluctuating baselines. However, such limits are ambulatory if UNCLOS article 76(9) is read in conjunction with article 76(8).

The procedure described in UNCLOS article 76(8), of submitting data to the CLCS and establishing final and binding continental shelf limits, is only available to States with a natural prolongation extending beyond 200 nm from baselines. However, UNCLOS article 76(9), allowing States to permanently describe their outer continental shelf limits, does not explicitly distinguish between States with a natural prolongation of more or less than 200 nm. If the two provisions are read together, they seem to indicate that continental shelf limits may only be permanently described, under UNCLOS article 76(9), once the limits have become final and binding on the basis of CLCS recommendations. If so, then the permanence is only available for continental shelf limits that extend beyond 200 nm from baselines and only after the CLCS has issued its recommendations. Yet, if UNCLOS article 76(9) is taken alone, it suggests that all outer limits of the continental shelf may be permanently described because, unlike article 76(8), it is not expressly limited to continental shelf limits extending beyond 200 nm from baselines.[121]

119 UNCLOS article 77(4).

120 *North Sea Continental Shelf* (n 13) para 43.

121 See Alex Oude Elferink, 'Article 76 of the LOSC on the Definition of the Continental Shelf: Questions Concerning Its Interpretation from a Legal Perspective' (2006) 21 (3) The International Journal of Marine and Coastal Law 269, 282.

If UNCLOS article 76(9) applies to all outer continental shelf limits, States may be able to permanently describe their continental shelf limits at 200 nm from baselines, without any involvement of the CLCS, and such limits would not be affected by subsequent changes of the baseline. The First Issues Paper suggests that the ILC's study group on sea level rise might endorse this interpretation.[122] However, UNCLOS article 84 obligates States to deposit copies of charts, describing boundaries and limits to the continental shelf, with the UNSG and this provision makes no mention of permanently describing the limits. It may be argued that this obligation, which is synonymous with that concerning the exclusive economic zone,[123] applies to continental shelf limits in general, while UNCLOS article 76(9) deals specifically with continental shelf limits beyond 200 nm. Otherwise, UNCLOS article 84 seems redundant. For this reason, and because UNCLOS article 76 should be read in a combined effort, the ILA Committee on the Outer Continental Shelf took the view that UNCLOS article 76(9) applies only to continental shelf limits beyond 200 nm.[124]

The stability afforded to outer limits of the continental shelf is logical if it only applies to outer limits that are measured from the natural prolongation of the continental margin (and not baselines) because, compared to baselines, the continental margin is much less susceptible to change. Yet, continental shelf limits beyond 200 nm are also anchored to changing baselines if the outer limits reach the 350 nm limits[125] and such limits are final and binding once established on the basis of recommendations from the CLCS.[126] The main rationale behind the stability afforded to continental shelf limits applies equally to all continental shelf limits, at and beyond 200 nm from baselines: the regime of the continental shelf affords sovereign rights to explore and exploit the resources of the seabed and subsoil[127] and the investments made in relation to these resources require permanence and stability.[128] As noted by Soons, this supports the view that all continental shelf limits might be permanently described.[129]

States cannot establish final and binding continental shelf limits without the recommendations of the CLCS.[130] Therefore, there is a matter of urgency in acquiring CLCS recommendations, particularly where islands are at risk of

122 UN Doc A/CN.4/740 (n 77) paras 73–75.
123 See UNCLOS article 75.
124 ILA Committee on the Outer Continental Shelf 'Conference Report Toronto 2006' (ILA, 2006) 16.
125 UNCLOS article 76(5).
126 UNCLOS article 76(8).
127 UNCLOS article 77(4).
128 See *Bangladesh* v. *India* (n 48) para 218.
129 See Alfred Soons (n 45) 217.
130 UNCLOS article 76(8), see also *Maritime Delimitation in the Indian Ocean (Somalia* v. *Kenya)* (Preliminary Objections) [2017] ICJ Rep 1, para 66 and *Questions of the Delimitation of the Continental Shelf Between Nicaragua and Colombia Beyond 200 Nautical Miles from the Nicaraguan Coast (Nicaragua* v. *Colombia)* (Preliminary Objections) [2016] ICJ Rep 1, paras 107–108.

submergence. Article 4 of UNCLOS Annex II provides that States that wish to establish their continental shelf limits on the basis of CLCS recommendations must submit relevant data to the Commission 'as soon as possible but in any case, within 10 years of the entry into force of this Convention for that State'. The earliest deadline for submitting relevant data to the CLCS was, therefore, 16 November 2004, ten years after the entry into force of UNCLOS for the first member States. However, this process proved more arduous than originally expected (particularly difficult for some developing States)[131] and the deadline was pushed back to 13 May 2009 – ten years after the adoption of the Scientific and Technical Guidelines of the CLCS.[132] This meant that the earliest date would be 13 May 2009 and that, for those States that became bound by UNCLOS after 13 May 1999, the deadline would be ten years after the entry into force of the Convention for that State.[133] Due to these complications, States Parties also concluded that preliminary submissions would suffice to halt the ten-year deadline for submissions.[134]

Article 4 of UNCLOS Annex II is not clear in regard to whether there are any consequences for non-compliance with the ten-year deadline. Oude Elferink has argued that States might either be barred from submitting their data to the CLCS after their deadline expires or that the CLCS would not be obligated to consider any submissions after that time.[135] However, this view is not widely held and, according to Judge Heiðar, 'there is no sanction for failure to make a submission within [the ten-year] period'.[136]

At the time of writing, eighty-eight submissions have been made to the CLCS regarding the location of continental shelves beyond 200 nm and thirty-five recommendations have been issued.[137] The CLCS is expected to need a couple of decades to go through all the submissions lodged with it so far.[138] Thus, it remains to be seen

131 See *Somalia* v. *Kenya* (n 130) para 17.

132 CLCS, 'Scientific and Technical Guidelines of the Commission on the Limits of the Continental Shelf' (New York, 3–14 May 1999) UN Doc CLCS/11.

133 UNCLOS: Meeting of States Parties 'Decision Regarding the Date of Commencement of the Ten-Year Period for Making Submissions to the Commission on the Limits of the Continental Shelf Set Out in Article 4 of Annex II to the United Nations Convention on the Law of the Sea' (29 May 2001) UN Doc SPLOS/72.

134 See UNCLOS: Meeting of States Parties 'Decision Regarding the Workload of the Commission on the Limits of the Continental Shelf and the Ability of States, Particularly Developing States, to Fulfil the Requirements of Article 4 of Annex II to the Convention, as well as the Decision Contained in SPLOS/72, paragraph (a)' (20 June 2008) UN Doc SPLOS/183.

135 Alex Oude Elferink (n 121) 279.

136 Tómas Heiðar, 'Legal Aspects of Continental Shelf Limits', in Myron Nordquist, John Norton Moore and Tómas Heiðar (eds) *Legal and Scientific Aspects of Continental Shelf Limits* (Martinus Nijhoff, 2004) 19, 30.

137 DOALOS 'Submissions, through the Secretary-General of the United Nations, to the Commission on the Limits of the Continental Shelf, pursuant to article 76, paragraph 8, of the United Nations Convention on the Law of the Sea of 10 December 1982' (UN, 2021) available at: www.un.org/Depts/los/clcs_new/commission_submissions.htm accessed 16 January 2021.

138 Alex Oude Elferink, 'The Continental Shelf in the Polar Regions: Cold War or Black-Letter Law?' (2009) 40 Netherlands Yearbook of International Law 121, 133.

whether all the States that have made submissions to the CLCS will actually acquire stable outer limits to continental shelves extending more than 200 nm from baselines. In the meantime, some islands that currently generate an entitlement to a continental shelf may be reduced to rocks, incapable of sustaining human habitation or economic life; low-tide elevations; or even be completely submerged.

It should also be noted that some States do not have sufficient resources to collect the necessary data. This is a prerequisite for making submissions to the CLCS in order to establish permanent continental shelf limits.[139] Furthermore, it seems that non-Parties may be precluded from submitting their data to the CLCS and establishing final and binding limits on that basis. This is not explicitly dealt with in UNCLOS but according to Judge Heiðar, non-Parties have no such right under UNCLOS or customary international law.[140] One of the arguments supporting this conclusion is that UNCLOS article 82, concerning revenue sharing and contributions to the Authority, only applies to member States. If these obligations, relating to the outer continental shelf beyond 200 nm, are only carried by member States then it makes sense that they are also the only ones that can acquire final and binding limits to their continental shelf beyond 200 nm.

The ICJ has explained that States Parties to UNCLOS are obligated to submit relevant data to the CLCS. However, 'the making of a recommendation, following examination of that information, is a prerogative of the CLCS'.[141] Non-member States certainly have no obligation to make submissions to the CLCS but this does not preclude the possibility of them submitting their data to the CLCS. Still, they would always be at the Commission's mercy and probably be placed at the end of a long line. Consequently, not all States will be able to acquire final and binding outer continental shelf limits; the much-desired stability cannot be guaranteed, even for those States that have a continental margin extending beyond 200 nm from baselines.

2.4 AMBULATORY LIMITS IN PRACTICE

In theory, maritime limits generally fluctuate with changing coastal geography. The foregoing pages set out the theoretical basis for this assertion and this section deals with the practical implications.

States arguably have an obligation to bring their maritime limits in conformity with the applicable law. At least, maritime limits may be unenforceable if inconsistent with UNCLOS or corresponding customary international law. As explained by the arbitral tribunal in *Philippines* v. *China*, '[a]ccession to the Convention reflects a commitment to bring incompatible claims into alignment with its provisions, and

139 Ibid., 139.
140 Tómas Heiðar (n 136) 31.
141 *Questions of the Delimitation of the Continental Shelf Between Nicaragua and Colombia Beyond 200 Nautical Miles from the Nicaraguan Coast* (n 130) para 107.

its continued operation necessarily calls for compromise by those States with prior claims in excess of the Convention's limits'.[142]

The fluctuation of maritime limits has implications, not only for the coastal States whose maritime zones are directly affected but also for third States. This applies even to landlocked States, because fluctuations of outer maritime limits affect the extent of areas beyond national jurisdiction, which are subject to the principles of freedom and common heritage of mankind. Maritime limits can fluctuate within otherwise stable, bilateral boundaries and the regression of outer maritime limits can make maritime boundaries redundant. This may occur when maritime entitlements no longer extend as far seawards as the boundary and the strip of sea or seabed surrounding the boundary has turned into high seas or international seabed area.[143] Bilateral boundaries might also remain in force between relevant States without interfering with the rights of third States.[144] If so, they would represent lines that neither State could extend its claim beyond – even if significant recession on one side of the boundary might otherwise justify such an extension. Furthermore, fundamental changes to maritime limits can justify termination or revision of maritime boundaries, as explained in Chapter 5.

Although most commentators assume that baselines will fluctuate in accordance with geographical changes, they do not all agree whether the theory of ambulatory baselines entails an obligation to adjust baselines to changed circumstances, so as to conform to UNCLOS provisions on a continuing basis; or an automatic shift, led by the fluctuating low-water line. Caron has suggested that baselines may automatically shift in accordance with changing coastlines, that they adjust themselves.[145] Hayashi assumes an obligation to adjust baselines and outer limits of maritime zones to geographic changes,[146] but Alexander refers to the possibility that affected States might challenge official baselines.[147] These assertions may all be correct because, as mentioned in Section 2.3.1, States have an obligation to adjust their limits but, if they fail to do so, their limits may be otherwise adjusted, following a challenge by another State. As subsequent sections demonstrate, States can challenge excessive or unlawful maritime limits and such challenges can affect their validity. Baselines can also shift in accordance with changing coastlines when courts and tribunals reject outdated charts and, instead, rely on the actual low-water line. Finally, States have

142 *Philippines* v. *China* (n 3) para 262.

143 See more about such potential changes in Julia Lisztwan, 'Stability of Maritime Boundary Agreements' (2012) 37 Yale Journal of International Law 153, 176–177.

144 Maritime limits are only opposable to third States if compatible with relevant UNCLOS provisions or accepted through acquiescences. See *Philippines* v. *China* (n 3) para 261; *Chagos Marine Protected Area (Mauritius* v. *United Kingdom)* (2015) XXXI RIAA 359, para 451. Bilateral boundaries cannot prevent third States from exercising their rights under UNCLOS to the high seas and the international seabed area.

145 David Caron (n 33) 2.

146 Moritaka Hayashi (n 33) 78.

147 Lewis Alexander (n 22) 535.

an obligation to portray certain maritime limits, and continued reliance upon such limits entails an obligation of adjustment.

The following sections will delve deeper into these issues. They explore, in practical terms, legal possibilities of challenging excessive or unlawful maritime limits; the identification of lawful baselines; the process of adjusting baselines and maritime limits; the opposability of permanent continental shelf limits; and the impact of man-made changes.

2.4.1 *Challenges and Judicial Review*

Maritime limits cannot be opposable to other States unless they are consistent with international law.[148] 'Although it is true that the act of delimitation [of baselines and outer limits] is necessarily a unilateral act, because only the coastal State is competent to undertake it, the validity of the delimitation with regard to other States depends upon international law.'[149] Therefore, States can challenge baselines and maritime limits on the grounds that they are inconsistent with the applicable international law[150] and UNCLOS States Parties are bound to settle their disputes.[151] The United States seem to have a policy of challenging excessive limits but other States have also lodged protests, particularly where they are interested in the location of limits, for example, due to fishing.[152] Challenges can incite revision of maritime limits but they can also escalate into judicial disputes. The following examples consider decisions of courts and tribunals concerning the lawfulness of challenged maritime limits.

Disputes concerning the validity of established maritime limits are subject to mandatory dispute settlement under UNCLOS article 287(1) if they are concerned with the interpretation or application of UNCLOS provisions.[153] This was confirmed in *Philippines* v. *China* where the Philippines challenged Chinese maritime limits.[154] The tribunal found that it had jurisdiction to determine the lawfulness of China's 'nine dash line' and the capacity of specific features to generate maritime entitlements.[155] The tribunal's decision in *Philippines* v. *China* is particularly noteworthy in this context because China had activated all of the optional exceptions available under UNCLOS article 298, excluding maritime boundary delimitations (among other things) from compulsory settlement. In this context, the

[148] *Anglo-Norwegian Fisheries* (n 12) 132 (addressing the unilateral act of declaring straight baselines: the same issues apply with respect to normal baselines).

[149] Ibid., 132.

[150] See, for example, *Fisheries Jurisdiction (Federal Republic of Germany* v. *Iceland)* (Merits) [1974] ICJ Rep 175, para 59 and *Qatar* v. *Bahrain* (n 45) para 212.

[151] See UNCLOS articles 279 and 280.

[152] Kate Purcell (n 73) 31.

[153] See, for example, *Qatar* v. *Bahrain* (n 45) para 212.

[154] *South China Sea (Philippines* v. *China)* (Award on Jurisdiction and Admissibility) (2015) XXXIII RIAA 1, para 157.

[155] *Philippines* v. *China* (n 3) paras 278 and 692.

tribunal confirmed the difference between maritime delineation and delimitation.[156] It confirmed its jurisdiction and explained that the Philippines had not requested delimitation of overlapping entitlements but rather, a finding of no overlapping entitlements.[157] Thus, the case involved maritime limits and the existence of maritime entitlements, which does not necessarily involve maritime delimitation.[158] However, the tribunal also noted that it would not have jurisdiction to determine whether specific features fell within national jurisdiction of either State in areas where there were overlapping entitlements.[159]

The *Philippines* v. *China* award confirms that courts and tribunals have jurisdiction to determine the lawfulness of baselines and maritime limits for UNCLOS States Parties, even when all the optional exceptions of UNCLOS article 298 have been invoked. Nonetheless, a prerequisite for judicial review is a challenge from an interested State. Therefore, States' reactions to excessive or unlawful maritime limits are crucial.[160] After all, there are no other mechanisms for surveillance or enforcement of UNCLOS provisions concerning baselines and maritime limits. States can continuously rely upon unchallenged limits, even if they are inconsistent with international law, and other States may be seen as acquiescing to maritime limits if they raise no objections to their use.[161] Consequently, States may be later estopped from challenging such limits if all the requirements of estoppel are satisfied.[162] As explained by the ICJ in *Gulf of Maine*, 'acquiescence is equivalent to tacit recognition manifested by unilateral conduct which the other party may interpret as consent'.[163]

Churchill and Lowe have clearly articulated the effect that acquiescence may have on maritime limits:

> Where a baseline is clearly contrary to international law, it will not be valid, certainly in respect of States which have objected to it, though a State which has accepted the baseline (for example in a boundary treaty) might be stopped from later denying its validity. In border-line cases—for example, where there is doubt as to whether a State's straight baseline system conforms to all the criteria laid down in customary and conventional law—the attitude of other States in acquiescing in or objecting to the baseline is likely to prove crucial in determining its validity.[164]

156 *Philippines* v. *China* (Award on Jurisdiction and Admissibility) (n 154) para 156.
157 Ibid., para 402.
158 *Philippines* v. *China* (n 3) para 204.
159 See Ibid., para 393 and *Philippines* v. *China* (Award on Jurisdiction and Admissibility) (n 154) para 402.
160 Ashley Roach and Robert Smith (n 32) 65.
161 Julia Lisztwan (n 143) 165.
162 For a general discussion on estoppel, see *Chagos Marine Protected Area* (n 144) paras 436–438.
163 *Delimitation of the Maritime Boundary in the Gulf of Maine Area (Canada/United States)* (Judgment) [1984] ICJ Rep 246, para 130.
164 Robin Churchill and Alan Lowe, *The Law of the Sea*, 2nd revised edition (Manchester University Press, 1988) 46–47.

The ICJ's decision in the *Black Sea* case suggests that challenges should generally be raised shortly after submission of data to the UNSG, or earlier, to avoid acquiescence. In this case the Court refused to accept a base point on the seaward end of Sulina dyke[165] but the decision had no effect on the validity of Romania's baselines, which gave that same base point full effect. This was partly due to the fact that Romania had submitted its data, designating a base point on Sulina dyke, to the UNSG, in accordance with UNCLOS article 16(2), and Ukraine had raised no objections.[166] This suggests that acquiescence upon due publicity in accordance with UNCLOS article 16(2) can cement the lawfulness of maritime limits.

Excessive maritime limits, which are inconsistent with the applicable law from their inception, should not be confused with maritime limits that are lawfully established but become inconsistent with international law due to subsequent environmental changes. States can acquiesce to excessive maritime limits and, thus, become estopped from later challenges. However, there is no acquiescence to lawful maritime limits because States have no reason to object to such limits. Indeed, States must have the opportunity to challenge maritime limits once they become inconsistent with the applicable law; when grounds for a challenge arise.

States generally have a legal interest in making sure that maritime limits of other States satisfy the requirements of UNCLOS. Even if they have no overlapping claims to maritime zones, they may have legitimate interests relating to claims encroaching upon the high seas or the international seabed area as these detract from the common rights of the international community.[167] The ILA Baselines Committee has referred to 'a total of 82 protests or other forms of objection' to straight baselines. These challenges were submitted by twenty-one States and the EU and lodged against thirty-nine States, covering almost 50 per cent of all straight baseline claims.[168] The United States has been very active in objecting to the unlawful use of baselines worldwide, not only in areas where it has overlapping entitlements. This has instigated discussions on the use of straight baselines, particularly in the Asia-Pacific region.[169] The official views of the United States on the law of baselines have been published and other efforts have been made to persuade States to adjust their baselines to international law.[170]

Requirements for the use of straight baselines are strict. When the ICJ first confirmed the legitimacy of the straight baselines system, in the *Anglo-Norwegian Fisheries* case in 1951, it clearly stipulated that this method was only permissible 'where the coast of the mainland does not constitute, as it does in practically all other

165 *Maritime Delimitation in the Black Sea (Romania* v. *Ukraine)* (Judgment) [2009] ICJ Rep 61, para 217.
166 Ibid., 107.
167 See, for example, *Chagos Marine Protected Area* (n 144) para 153; *Anglo-Norwegian Fisheries* (n 12) 125.
168 ILA Baselines Committee, 'Johannesburg Conference' (ILA, 2016) 17, para 65.
169 Ashley Roach and Robert Smith (n 32) 48.
170 Ibid.

countries [apart from Norway], a clear dividing line between land and sea'.[171] In more recent cases, the Court has confirmed that straight baselines should only be employed on the rare occasions where all necessary requirements are satisfied[172] and that the method of drawing straight baselines 'must be applied restrictively'.[173] Straight baselines should, according to Roach and Smith, not only 'be used sparingly' but also 'drawn conservatively' because their purpose is to simplify and rationalize delineation of maritime entitlements extending from irregular coasts.[174]

Several States have made straight baselines claims that clearly contradict these stipulations. For example, a vast majority of States in the Asia-Pacific region have excessive limits and they have been contested vigorously.[175] If successfully challenged, such baselines are invalid vis-à-vis other States, as demonstrated by the *Philippines* v. *China* case.[176] Furthermore, when constructing maritime boundaries, courts and tribunals can disregard baselines that do not meet relevant requirements of UNCLOS and select more appropriate base points in their stead.[177]

The ICJ has refrained from expounding the validity of baselines, where it has had the opportunity. The *Tunisia/Libyan Arab Jamahiriya* case concerned the validity of straight baselines established by Tunisia.[178] In this case, the ICJ ruled on the method of delimitation but did not rule on the validity or enforceability of Libya's straight baselines.[179] In *Libyan Arab Jamahiriya/Malta* the ICJ was faced with questions concerning the validity of base points along straight baselines when it delimited the continental shelf between the two States. Malta had proposed a line measured from the low-water line of Libya but straight baselines along the Maltese coastline. The Court did not declare the straight baselines invalid as such but rejected the use of an uninhabited island off the coast of Malta as a base point for delimitation, even though this island had been used as a base point for the purpose of drawing Malta's straight baselines.[180] The Court explained that 'the baselines, as determined by coastal States, are not per se identical with the points chosen on a coast to make it possible to calculate the area of continental shelf appertaining to that State'.[181] Therefore, the rejection, by courts and tribunals, of base points for the purpose of boundary delimitation does not necessarily signify the invalidity of related baselines or derived maritime limits. Indeed, baselines may be lawful even if they are not an appropriate basis for boundary delimitation.

171 *Anglo-Norwegian Fisheries* (n 12) 127.

172 See, for example, *Qatar* v. *Bahrain* (n 45) para 212.

173 Ibid.

174 Ashley Roach and Robert Smith (n 32) 49; William Reisman and Gayl Westerman (n 29) xv.

175 Ashley Roach and Robert Smith (n 32) 66.

176 See, for example, *Philippines* v. *China* (n 3) paras 278 and 1203 B.(2).

177 See, for example, *Maritime Delimitation in the Black Sea* (n 165) para 137; *Bangladesh* v. *India* (n 48) para 264. Further discussion in Section 3.4.1.

178 *Continental Shelf (Tunisia/Libyan Arab Jamahiriya)* (Judgment) [1982] ICJ Rep 18.

179 Ibid., para 104.

180 *Libyan Arab Jamahiriya/Malta* (n 4) para 64.

181 Ibid.

The Court elaborated on this in the *Black Sea* case, where it stated that the identification of base points for the purpose of drawing baselines, on the one hand, and for delimiting boundaries, on the other, were two different things.[182] This difference lies, essentially, in that the drawing of baselines is a unilateral act (although it always has an international aspect)[183] while the delimitation of boundaries involves two or more States. In such cases, 'the Court should not base itself solely on the choice of base points made by one of those Parties'.[184]

The International Tribunal for the Law of the Sea (hereinafter ITLOS or the Tribunal) also explained, in the *Bangladesh/Myanmar* case, that maritime boundaries could be delimited in 'the absence of established outer limits' and despite a '[l]ack of agreement on baselines'.[185] Furthermore, in *Bangladesh* v. *India*, the parties separated the issues of baselines and delimitation as they agreed not to rely on the straight baselines used for their unilateral limits when proposing base points for the boundary delimitation.[186] The Tribunal condoned this decision as it noted that while reliance upon low-tide elevations might be feasible for the purpose of maritime delineation, it might not be appropriate to rely on the same base points when delimiting a maritime boundary.[187] This arguably supports the assertion that the fixing of a bilateral boundary does not stabilize the maritime limits therein. Baselines and outer maritime limits continue to fluctuate even after a maritime boundary has been agreed upon because the legitimacy of those unilateral limits continuously depends on the applicable international law.

The arbitral award in *Eritrea/Yemen* had an impact on the baselines as the tribunal asserted that a reef that is not above water at low-tide cannot be used as a base point for the purpose of UNCLOS article 6.[188] The reef in question, Negileh Rock, failed to meet the requirements of UNCLOS article 7(4) and could, therefore, not be used to establish straight baselines.[189] This effectively meant that Eritrea's claim to straight baselines could no longer extend to Negileh Rock and, consequently, had to be adjusted to conform to relevant UNCLOS provisions. Finally, in *Qatar* v. *Bahrain* the ICJ concluded that the straight baselines established by Qatar were not justified and that certain low-tide elevations should be disregarded when delimiting maritime zones between the two States.[190]

These examples demonstrate that baselines are not necessarily unlawful if specific points on the baselines are inappropriate for the delimitation of bilateral boundaries.

182 *Maritime Delimitation in the Black Sea* (n 165) para 137.
183 See *Anglo-Norwegian Fisheries* (n 12) 132.
184 *Maritime Delimitation in the Black Sea* (n 165) para 137.
185 *Bangladesh/Myanmar* (n 13) para 370.
186 *Bangladesh* v. *India* (n 48) para 250.
187 Ibid., para 260.
188 *Second stage of the proceedings between Eritrea and Yemen (Maritime Delimitation) (Eritrea/Yemen)* (1999) XXII RIAA 335, para 143.
189 Ibid., para 146.
190 *Qatar* v. *Bahrain* (n 45) para 215.

However, courts and tribunals can render existing limits unopposable by stating that coastal features are incapable of generating maritime entitlements or that officially recognized charts do not accurately reflect the low-water mark. Furthermore, States can acquiesce to maritime limits of questionable lawfulness; baselines may acquire validity once registered with the UNSG, as evidenced by the *Black Sea* case, particularly if no objections are raised. Yet, maritime limits may generally be challenged following the occurrence of circumstances that make them inconsistent with the applicable law.

2.4.2 *Identifying the Legal Baseline and Derived Limits*

States can challenge baselines and derived limits of coastal States, as explained in the foregoing section. Courts and tribunals can confirm the invalidity of baselines in contentious cases and States can ignore unopposable limits.[191] But how do courts and tribunals determine the location of the legal baseline? States are obligated to display straight and archipelagic baselines, and outer maritime limits, on charts and to give them due publicity.[192] However, these charts are not always determinative for the legally valid baseline or derived maritime limits because charted limits may be ignored where they are inconsistent with actual circumstances.[193]

States generally have an obligation to display maritime limits and they must update relevant charts or lists of coordinates to reflect coastline changes.[194] They, consequently, have some discretion as to how and when their maritime limits are updated. However, Courts and tribunals seem to revert to the actual low-water mark if charted lines are inconsistent with international law and in such cases, maritime limits fluctuate without adjustment by the coastal State. In other words, the charted line takes precedence, but the actual low-water line (which fluctuates automatically) can be decisive if maritime limits are not accurately displayed.

2.4.2.1 Obligation to Display Maritime Limits

Territorial sea boundaries, straight baselines, closing lines around river mouths, bays and roadsteads and limits derived therefrom, must be displayed on charts of adequate scales for determining their position. These may be substituted by lists of geographical coordinates that specify the geodetic datum.[195] These charts or lists of geographical coordinates shall be given due publicity and coastal States must also

191 This is supported by practice of several States defying China's Nine-Dash Line in the South China Sea. See, for example, Joe Cochrane, 'Indonesia, Long on Sidelines, Starts to Confront China's Territorial Claims' (New York Times, 2017) available at: www.nytimes.com/2017/09/10/world/asia/indonesia-south-china-sea-military-buildup.html accessed 16 January 2021.

192 This is explained in Section 2.4.2.1.

193 See Section 2.4.2.2.

194 See Section 2.3.1.

195 UNCLOS article 16(1).

deposit copies of each chart or list with the UNSG.[196] Synonymous provisions can be found in regard to the scale of charts and due publication of archipelagic baselines;[197] boundaries and outer limits of the exclusive economic zone;[198] and the continental shelf.[199] Finally, as explained in Section 2.3.4, the outer limits of the continental shelf shall be permanently described by submission of relevant data to the UNSG[200] and this permanence seems to be afforded only to outer limits beyond 200 nm. This conclusion is based on the assumption that UNCLOS article 76(9) is an exception from the general rule enshrined in UNCLOS article 84 and it reflects the majority view of the ILA Baselines Committee.[201]

UNCLOS does not explicitly require the publication of normal baselines. UNCLOS article 16 explicitly refers to UNCLOS articles dealing with straight baselines, roadsteads, closing lines of bays and rivers and delimitation of the territorial sea, but not to normal baselines. Neither are States obligated to display the outer limits of the territorial sea on official charts. UNCLOS article 5, governing the delineation of normal baselines, assumes that such baselines are portrayed on 'large-scale charts officially recognised by the coastal State' and the reference to charts of a scale or scales adequate for ascertaining their position might be a more precise description of the same type of chart as referred to in UNCLOS article 5. If so, then the only difference between the charts needed for normal baselines and other limits is that the latter must be given due publicity with copies submitted to the UNSG.

UNCLOS article 5 states that '[e]xcept where otherwise provided in this Convention, the normal baseline for measuring the breadth of the territorial sea is the low-water line along the coast as marked on large-scale charts officially recognized by the coastal State'. As noted by the ILA Baselines Committee, two readings of the provision are available[202] and these are addressed in the following section. The large-scale charts that States rely on for determining their low-water line are not necessarily their own. They can officially recognize charts that are published by foreign hydrographic services, for example, the UK Hydrographic Office Admiralty Charts or the United States Defence Mapping Agency/National Geospatial-Intelligence Agency Digital Nautical Charts.

Many States fail to submit relevant data to the UNSG. Some States adopt legislation concerning their limits but according to the UN Division for Ocean Affairs and the Law of the Sea (hereinafter DOALOS), such acts do not suffice to satisfy obligations arising under UNCLOS articles 16(2), 47(9), 75(2), 76(9) and 84(2). 'The mere existence or adoption of legislation or the conclusion of a maritime

196 UNCLOS article 16(2).
197 UNCLOS articles 47(8) and 47(9).
198 UNCLOS article 75.
199 UNCLOS article 84.
200 UNCLOS article 76(9).
201 'Conference Report Toronto 2006' (n 124) 16.
202 'Conference Report Sofia 2012' (n 81) 3.

boundary delimitation treaty registered with the Secretariat, even if they contain charts or lists of coordinates, cannot be interpreted as an act of deposit with the Secretary-General under the Convention.'[203] In *Nicaragua* v. *Colombia*, the ICJ referred to Nicaragua's failure to notify the UNSG of the location of base points, in accordance with UNCLOS article 16(2) and found that, for that reason, the relevant area would have to be 'determined only on an approximate basis'.[204] Therefore, it may be concluded that failure to deposit charts and coordinates with the UNSG affects the right to rely upon certain maritime limits.

DOALOS notifies all States of the location of maritime limits, in accordance with the charts and geographical coordinates deposited with the UNSG.[205] This publicity is important for opposability of the limits because it makes them readily available to interested parties.[206] Furthermore, charted lines may even be constitutive of the legal limits, which would make uncharted limits unenforceable. However, failure to properly display maritime limits on charts does not mean that States have no opposable limits. States are not required to actively claim normal baselines or publicize them in any way; they exist by default.[207] Failure to deposit required data with the UNSG thus calls for reliance upon the normal baseline, as established by reference to the actual low-water line displayed on officially recognized charts. This begs another question: does the actual low-water line take precedence over the charted line, or vice versa?

The following section examines how the legal baseline is determined and how the relevant line has been identified in contentious cases.

2.4.2.2 Charted or Actual Low-Water Line

Baselines should correspond to the low-water lines along coastlines. There is only one exception to that rule and it relates to the provisional stability afforded by UNCLOS article 7(2). That provision 'distinguishes between the actual low-water line and the representational version of that low-water line'.[208] It provides that the 'representational version' remains effective until changed by the coastal State.[209] Straight baselines, archipelagic baselines and outer maritime limits are also displayed on charts and these charted lines form the legal limits. However, normal baselines are not subject to the same charting requirements and they can be identified by reference to UNCLOS article 5, without reliance upon the charted line.

203 DOALOS 'Deposit of Charts and/or Lists of Geographical Coordinates and DOALOS Geographic Information System (GIS)' (UN, 2016) available at: www.un.org/depts/los/doalos_activities/about_doalos.htm#GIS accessed 16 January 2021.

204 *Territorial and Maritime Dispute (Nicaragua* v. *Colombia)* (Judgment) [2012] ICJ Rep 624, para 159.

205 DOALOS (n 203).

206 'Conference Report Sofia 2012' (n 81) 8–9.

207 Robert Beckman and Clive Schofield (n 17) 5.

208 'Conference Report Sofia 2012' (n 81) 8.

209 Ibid.

UNCLOS article 5 can be read in two distinct ways. It provides that the normal baseline is either the documented low-water line on officially recognized charts (making charts the legal documents that determine the position of the legal baseline) or the actual low-water line along relevant coasts, as displayed on officially recognized charts.[210] In *Eritrea/Yemen*, the arbitral tribunal used the low-water line depicted on officially recognized charts to identify the median line boundary.[211] Similarly, the ILC seemed to assume, in its 1956 commentary on the draft article on normal baselines, that the low-water mark, as displayed on large-scale charts, would be determinative for the legal normal baseline. This is deduced from the fact that, while acknowledging the autonomy States have in determining the low-water mark for normal baselines, the Commission indicated that charted lines should be reasonably representative of actual low-water lines.[212] An unreasonable shift of a charted line would carry no weight unless the chart constituted the legal baseline and, therefore, the ILC's remarks suggest that the charted line may be determinative. However, the ILC seems to have assumed that States would not abuse the discretion given to them in charting their own baselines and that, arguably, supports the conclusion that outdated limits must be adjusted.

Kapoor and Kerr are of the view that 'once the normal baseline has been established and cartographically depicted on large scale charts, it remains in place until such time as it is redrafted, irrespective of whether or not the actual low-water line has physically moved'.[213] '[N]ormal baselines change every time a new edition of a large scale nautical chart is published', according to Elema and Dorst from the Hydrographic Service of the Royal Netherlands Navy.[214] Similarly, Carleton and Schofield assert that physical changes to the coastline have no bearing on the location of the legal baseline until the chart is updated.[215] This appears to be a minority view in scholarly writing.[216] Nonetheless, it is hereby submitted that the charted line is the first point of reference for determining the legally valid baseline. However, when charted lines become inconsistent with international law and coastal States neglect their obligation to adjust maritime limits, the charted line may become unenforceable, which justifies resort to the actual low-water line. Consequently, the second point of reference has to be the actual low-water line, which becomes determinative of the

210 'Conference Report Sofia 2012' (n 81) 3.

211 *Eritrea/Yemen* (n 188) para 40.

212 UN Doc A/CN.4/104 (n 27) 267.

213 'Conference Report Sofia 2012' (n 81) 23 referring to D Kapoor and Adam Kerr, *A Guide to Maritime Boundary Delimitation* (Carswell, 1986) 31.

214 Leendert Dorst and Ina Elema, 'The Effects of Changing Baselines on the Limits of the Netherlands in the North Sea' (Conference Paper for ABLOS, 2008) available at: www.researchgate.net/publication/265167053 accessed 16 January 2021.

215 Christopher Carleton and Clive Schofield, 'Developments in the Technical Determination of Maritime Space: Charts, Datums, Baselines, Maritime Zones and Limits' (2001) 3 (3) International Boundaries Research Unit Maritime Briefing 24–25.

216 'Conference Report Sofia 2012' (n 81) 24.

legal normal baseline if the charted line departs from the low-water mark to an appreciable extent. As noted by Oude Elferink, a coastal State may in principle be 'entitled to rely on the low-water line as depicted on its nautical charts but this may not be the case if an area is not regularly surveyed and the relevant nautical chart is outdated'.[217]

A majority of the scholarship maintains that charts are not constitutive for the location of the normal baseline.[218] According to O'Connell, '[t]here is no doubt that changes in the shoreline, however and how quickly effected, result in changes in the baseline from which the territorial sea is measured'.[219] Similarly, Reed asserts that '[i]t is the actual low-water line and not the charted line that is to be used as the baseline under the Convention'.[220] According to these authors, all changes to the low-water line affect the legal normal baseline regardless of whether 'large-scale charts officially recognised by the coastal State' have been updated, as per UNCLOS article 5. Indeed, technical experts assembled by the UN have explained that '[t]he low-water line along the coast is a fact irrespective of its representation on charts'.[221] This view is endorsed by the case law but the proposals discussed later, in Section 2.5, support the interpretation that charted limits should take priority because that gives States more discretion in adjusting to sea level rise.[222]

Fitzmaurice explained in 1956 that '[a] straight baseline system had to be specially established, and unless and until that had been done, a country was deemed to operate the low-water-mark system'.[223] The same logic arguably applies to all outdated maritime limits – unless legitimately established, States may be 'deemed to operate the low-water mark system'. If such limits are challenged, and officially recognized charts have become inconsistent with reality, resort to the *actual* low-water line is arguably justified. National legislation relating to baselines and maritime limits sometimes refers to the use of particular charts as evidence for ascertaining the location of baselines and other maritime limits.[224] However, when challenged, courts and tribunals have sought further evidence to determine the actual location of the coast.[225]

217 Ibid., 22, footnote 145.

218 Ibid., 22.

219 Daniel O'Connell, *The International Law of the Sea, volume* 2 (Clarendon Press, 1984) 682.

220 'Conference Report Sofia 2012' (n 81) 23 referring to Michael Reed, *Shore and Sea Boundaries, volume* 3 (United States Government Printing Office, 2000) 182–185.

221 'Conference Report Sofia 2012' (n 81) 23 referring to UN Office of Ocean Affairs and Law of the Sea, *Baselines: An Examination of Relevant Provisions of the United Nations Convention on the Law of the Sea* (UN, 1989).

222 See, for example, UN Doc A/CN.4/740 (n 77) para 91.

223 UN Doc A/CN.4/SR.335 (n 44) 9.

224 'Conference Report Sofia 2012' (n 81) 17: 'These provisions appear in the legislation of the following states: Barbados, Brunei, Grenada, Namibia, New Zealand, Saint Kitts and Nevis, Saint Lucia, Samoa, Seychelles, Solomon Islands, Sri Lanka, Tuvalu, and United Kingdom.'

225 See, for example, *Award in the arbitration regarding the delimitation of the maritime boundary between Guyana and Suriname (Guyana* v. *Suriname)* (2007) XXX RIAA 1, para 396; *Territorial and Maritime Dispute (Nicaragua* v. *Colombia)* (n 204) para 38.

The tribunal dealt with the legitimacy of charts at unstable coasts in *Bangladesh* v. *India*. The parties 'presented opposing views on the accuracy of the maps and charts produced, due in particular to the rapid erosion of the coastline'.[226] The tribunal used the most recent large-scale charts to take changing circumstances into account[227] and various materials were used for determining the relevant coastal geography. The tribunal did not consider published baselines, instead, resort was had to official nautical charts that the parties provided.[228] The tribunal made use of particular software to determine the actual low-water line in uncharted areas[229] and computation of the relevant area also relied on the information and data from the CLCS.[230] Thus, the tribunal resorted to the actual low-water line, instead of published limits.

The accuracy of official charts was also disputed in *Guyana* v. *Suriname*. The coastlines between Guyana and Suriname are largely made up of unstable mud banks, causing fluctuations of the relevant coastline.[231] The boundary proposed by Suriname relied on a base point located on Vissers Bank, according to the officially recognized Netherlands Hydrographic Office Chart 2218. However, Guyana based its claims on several different charts[232] and challenged base point S14 on the basis that it did not reflect the actual low-water line.[233] Guyana argued that the Dutch Chart 2218 had been produced in co-operation with Suriname after the commencement of the arbitration.[234] Furthermore, it asserted that another chart prepared by Dutch authorities disproved the legitimacy of Suriname's base point S14 at Vissers Bank.[235] The tribunal admitted further evidence from both States to help it determine whether base point S14 reflected the actual low-water line but ultimately accepted the base point, as it was not evidenced that the Dutch depiction of the low-water line on chart 2218 was inaccurate.[236] The tribunal did not discuss its evaluation of the charts presented to it in any detail and seemed to reject Guyana's challenge simply because it was not convinced that the disputed chart was inaccurate. This may suggest a presumption in favour of the accuracy of officially recognized charts.

The ICJ did not rely on officially recognized charts in *Nicaragua* v. *Colombia*. Instead, it asked both States to produce new data to help the Court identify the actual location of the low-water line, particularly to identify any naturally formed high-tide elevations at Quitasueño.[237] Colombia presented two reports that were published in

226 *Bangladesh* v. *India* (n 48) para 224.
227 Ibid., para 224.
228 Ibid., Appendix, para 30.
229 Ibid.
230 Ibid., Appendix, para 31.
231 *Guyana* v. *Suriname* (n 225) para 133.
232 Ibid., para 240.
233 Ibid., para 242; Reply of Guyana, vol I, 1 April 2006, para 3.19.
234 *Guyana* v. *Suriname* (n 225) para 395 referring to Reply of Guyana, vol I, 1 April 2006, paras 1.10, 3.19; Transcript, 170–172; Suriname Rejoinder, Annex SR43.
235 *Guyana* v. *Suriname* (n 225) para 395 referring to Reply of Guyana, vol I, 1 April 2006, para 3.19.
236 Ibid., para 396.
237 *Territorial and Maritime Dispute (Nicaragua* v. *Colombia)* (n 204) para 35.

2008 by the Colombian Navy.[238] Nicaragua opposed their use, partly because they were prepared specifically for the proceedings.[239] Nicaragua relied on various charts, surveys and other material spanning several decades,[240] and a contemporaneous chart prepared by the UK Hydrographic Office.[241] The Court explained that:

> It does not consider that surveys conducted many years (in some cases many decades) before the present proceedings are relevant in resolving that issue. Nor does the Court consider that the charts on which Nicaragua relies have much probative value with regard to that issue. Those charts were prepared in order to show dangers to shipping at Quitasueño, not to distinguish between those features which were just above, and those which were just below, water at high tide.[242]

The Court went on to confirm that the relevant evidence would have to be 'the contemporary evidence' and that the most important contemporary evidence was the report 'based upon actual observations of conditions at Quitasueño and scientific evaluation of those conditions'.[243] The Court emphasized the importance of having sufficient evidence to determine the status of coastal features[244] and before making its final decision, it reviewed charts, reports, tidal models, photographic evidence and further information submitted by the parties,[245] clearly going beyond officially recognized charts and data submitted to the UNSG.

It may be concluded that even though the charted line is a starting point for determining the location of the normal baseline and derived maritime limits, courts and tribunals can seek further clarifications to accurately determine the location of the actual low-water line, particularly if any doubt is cast on the accuracy of charted lines. Furthermore, if straight and archipelagic baselines are not duly published in accordance with UNCLOS, courts and tribunals may, instead, rely on the low-water line. Therefore, the primacy afforded to the charted line depends on its consistency with the applicable law.

2.4.3 *Opposability of Permanently Described Continental Shelf Limits*

Continental shelf limits beyond 200 nm are final and binding if established on the basis of CLCS recommendations, as per UNCLOS article 76(8). Moreover, continental shelf limits are permanently fixed when relevant data is submitted to the UNSG in accordance with UNCLOS article 76(9). On one reading these two paragraphs suggest the same thing: that subject to the requirements of each

238 Ibid., para 29.
239 Ibid., para 30.
240 Ibid., para 28.
241 Ibid., para 31.
242 Ibid., para 35.
243 Ibid., para 36.
244 Ibid.
245 *Territorial and Maritime Dispute (Nicaragua v. Colombia)* (n 204) para 38.

paragraph, continental shelf limits become opposable to other States notwithstanding subsequent changes to the underlying maritime entitlements. However, there is an arguable case that the two references to finality and permanence have different legal implications. As explained in Section 2.3.4, UNCLOS articles 76(8) and 76(9) may have to be read together and such reading provides that continental shelf limits cannot be permanently fixed unless they first become final and binding. This begs the question whether States can acquire final and binding continental shelf limits without submitting the relevant data to the UNSG.

Oude Elferink maintains that the outer limits of the continental shelf become final and binding at the time when a coastal State deposits relevant data with the UNSG, permanently describing the outer limits of its continental shelf.[246] According to Oude Elferink, '[t]his deposit signifies the completion of the process of establishment of the outer limits of the outer continental shelf by the coastal state under article 76'.[247] If so, then the phrase 'final and binding', in UNCLOS article 76(8), has limited independent significance as no finality is achieved until the limits are permanently described, as per UNCLOS article 76(9). This, arguably, supports the view that paragraphs 8 and 9 must be read together: the outer continental shelf limits do become final and binding but only when the procedural requirements of paragraph 9 are satisfied.

As an objective technical body, the CLCS serves an important role in confirming the location of the outer limits beyond 200 nm before they can be permanently opposable. ITLOS has confirmed that the significance of the outer continental shelf limits being final and binding is that it enhances 'opposability with regard to other States'.[248] ITLOS also noted, in *Bangladesh/Myanmar*, that the continental shelf limits beyond 200 nm are opposable to third States, despite being based on unilateral acts, as long as they are compliant with UNCLOS article 76 and the recommendations of the CLCS.[249]

Permanent outer continental shelf limits are not only opposable to other States but, arguably, also binding upon the coastal State. In *Questions of the Delimitation of the Continental Shelf Between Nicaragua and Colombia Beyond 200 Nautical Miles from the Nicaraguan Coast*, Nicaragua argued that CLCS recommendations were 'not binding on the submitting State'.[250] Furthermore, Nicaragua asserted that States could make new or revised submissions if they disagreed with the recommendations of the CLCS.[251] The ICJ did not confirm this but, explained that '[w]hen the CLCS addresses its recommendations on questions concerning the outer limits of its continental shelf to coastal States, those States establish, on that basis, limits which,

246 Alex Oude Elferink (n 121) 282.

247 Ibid.

248 *Bangladesh/Myanmar* (n 13) para 407.

249 Ibid.

250 *Questions of the Delimitation of the Continental Shelf Between Nicaragua and Colombia Beyond 200 Nautical Miles from the Nicaraguan Coast* (n 130) para 102.

251 Ibid.

pursuant to paragraph 8 of Article 76 of UNCLOS, are "final and binding" upon the States parties to that instrument'.[252] This suggests that States are bound by the recommendations of the CLCS insofar as they can only establish final and binding outer continental shelf limits on that basis and that the resulting limits are binding for the submitting State.

The ILA Baselines Committee has echoed this interpretation, stating that coastal States cannot change final and binding continental shelf limits unless they are successfully challenged by other States.[253] Consequently, coastal States may not be allowed to make revisions to their continental shelf limits, once they have been established in accordance with UNCLOS articles 76(8) and 76(9).

2.4.3.1 Challenges to Unlawful Continental Shelf Limits

Judicial review of outer continental shelf limits has a somewhat elaborate relationship with the CLCS. Therefore, this section begins with an analysis of the fine line between delineation and delimitation of outer continental shelf limits beyond 200 nm from baselines. Article 9 of UNCLOS Annex II provides that '[t]he actions of the Commission shall not prejudice matters relating to delimitation of boundaries between States with opposite or adjacent coasts'. Indeed, ITLOS confirmed, in *Bangladesh/Myanmar*, that it has the competence to delimit overlapping continental shelf entitlements in the absence of recommendations of the CLCS and that this does not constitute 'an encroachment on the functions of the Commission'.[254] Yet, in a subsequent case, *Nicaragua* v. *Colombia*, the ICJ found that it could not delimit a boundary concerning the outer continental shelf beyond 200 nm because it had not been sufficiently established that Nicaragua's continental margin extended far enough beyond the 200 nm limit to overlap with Colombia's continental shelf.[255]

In 2017, *Questions of the Delimitation of the Continental Shelf between Nicaragua and Colombia beyond 200 Nautical Miles from the Nicaraguan Coast* were again put before the ICJ. This time, the Court explained that it had refused to delimit the continental shelf beyond 200 nm (in its earlier decision of 2012) because at that time, Nicaragua had not yet submitted the necessary information to the CLCS.[256] This shortcoming had been remedied at the time of the second proceedings and, consequently, Nicaragua's request for delimitation was admissible.[257]

In this recent decision, the ICJ confirmed that 'since the delimitation of the continental shelf beyond 200 nautical miles can be undertaken independently of a recommendation from the CLCS, the latter is not a prerequisite that needs to be

[252] Ibid., para 108.

[253] 'Conference Report Toronto 2006' (n 124) 18.

[254] *Bangladesh/Myanmar* (n 13) para 393. See also *Somalia* v. *Kenya* (n 130) para 67.

[255] *Territorial and Maritime Dispute (Nicaragua* v. *Colombia)* (n 204) para 129.

[256] *Questions of the Delimitation of the Continental Shelf Between Nicaragua and Colombia Beyond 200 Nautical Miles from the Nicaraguan Coast* (n 130) paras 82 and 84.

[257] Ibid., para 115.

satisfied by a State party to UNCLOS before it can ask the Court to settle a dispute with another State over such a delimitation'.[258] Therefore, courts and tribunals have the competence to delimit overlapping entitlements to continental shelves beyond 200 nm and they can exercise such jurisdiction before the CLCS issues its recommendations. However, it is not the role of courts and tribunals to delineate outer continental shelf limits. The procedures for delimitation and delineation are distinct and the latter is the prerogative of the CLCS.[259] Nonetheless, continental shelf limits may be challenged before courts and tribunals, after they are established on the basis of CLCS recommendations.

One might assume that outer continental shelf limits were inviolable once they become final and binding, as per UNCLOS article 76(8), or once permanently described, in accordance with UNCLOS article 76(9). However, this does not seem to be the case. The ILA Baselines Committee has submitted that outer continental shelf limits are not permanently fixed and opposable to other States immediately after the relevant data is deposited with the UNSG. This is to give States the time to challenge the limits. They only become permanently fixed if no protests are raised and some time has passed.[260]

As explained in Section 2.4.1, failure to object to maritime limits may translate into acquiescence and this applies equally to continental shelf limits at and beyond 200 nm from baselines. Consequently, continental shelf limits beyond 200 nm can become opposable to other States, even if they do not conform to the recommendations of the CLCS, but only if other States with legitimate interests have failed to object to such limits. All States have an interest in the size of the international seabed area as it is the common heritage of mankind. Therefore, continental shelf limits that are inconsistent with UNCLOS or customary international law can be challenged by any State, as long as it has not acquiesced to the limits. As with other maritime limits, their opposability to other States depends on whether they conform to international law and also on the reactions of other States.[261]

States can challenge outer continental shelf limits after they have been permanently described if the limits are not in conformity with the recommendations of the CLCS or if the CLCS has gone beyond its competence in issuing recommendations.[262] This confirms that outer limits of the continental shelf, which are inconsistent with the CLCS's recommendations, may be challenged by other States.[263] Furthermore, since

258 Ibid., para 114.

259 Ibid., para 112.

260 'Conference Report Toronto 2006' (n 124) 18 referring to Ted McDorman, 'The Role of the Commission on the Limits of the Continental Shelf: A Technical Body in a Political World' (2002) 17 International Journal of Marine and Coastal Law 301, 317.

261 See Ashley Roach and Robert Smith (n 32) 65.

262 ILA Committee on the Outer Continental Shelf 'Berlin Conference (2004)' (ILA, 2004) 24, see particularly footnote 116.

263 Suzette Suarez, 'The Outer Limits of the Continental Shelf: Legal Aspects of their Establishment' (2009) 199 Beiträge zum ausländischen öffentlichen Recht und Völkerrecht 239, 243.

the CLCS does not have authority to decide whether established limits conform to its recommendations, other States can challenge limits on those grounds.[264] 'If the outer limits of the continental shelf have not been established in accordance with the substantive and procedural requirements of article 76 this issue may be raised by other States Parties under Part XV of the Convention.'[265]

States can undoubtedly challenge continental shelf limits before courts and tribunals. Moreover, States seem to be able to influence the CLCS recommendation process. Article 5(a) of the Rules of Procedure of the CLCS, Annex I, provides that:

> where a land or maritime dispute exists, the Commission shall not consider and qualify a submission made by any of the States concerned in the dispute. However, the Commission may consider one or more submissions in the areas under dispute with prior consent given by all States that are parties to such a dispute.

Consequently, the CLCS does not consider a submission or issue recommendations when there is an ongoing boundary dispute and one or more relevant States withholds its consent. According to the ICJ: 'A State will thus be unable to establish the outer limits of its continental shelf if it has a dispute with one or more other States and they have not consented to the consideration of its submission by the CLCS.'[266] Yet, as explained by Oude Elferink, 'the procedure for establishing the outer limits of the continental shelf under [UNCLOS] does not envisage a role for third states in the consideration of the submission of the coastal state by the Commission'.[267] Even so, the CLCS has refrained from considering submissions when there is a potential for dispute and the necessary consent has not been given.[268] Moreover, it seems to have considered note verbales from China and the Republic of Korea when determining the procedure concerning Japan's submission to the CLCS relating to a contentious area surrounding Okinotorishima.[269] Alternatively, the CLCS has also taken a narrow approach, for example, refusing to take into account a letter from the United States relating to the Brazilian submission, on the grounds that there was no dispute between the two States.[270]

States that are not Parties to UNCLOS do not seem to be barred from submitting their objections to the CLCS and they can challenge continental shelf limits on the same grounds as Parties to UNCLOS. However, they may not have the same incentive to do so because permanently fixed outer continental shelf limits may

264 Alex Oude Elferink (n 121) 281.

265 'Conference Report Toronto 2006' (n 124) 16.

266 *Somalia* v. *Kenya* (n 130) para 69.

267 Alex Oude Elferink (n 138) 149.

268 See, for example, Twenty-sixth session of the CLCS 'Statement by the Chairperson of the Commission on the Limits of the Continental Shelf on the Progress of Work in the Commission' (27 September 2010) UN Doc CLCS/68, para 30–31; *Somalia* v. *Kenya* (n 130) paras 20 and 69.

269 See CLCS, 'Twenty-Fourth session' (1 October 2009) UN Doc CLCS/64, para 26.

270 CLCS 'Statement by the Chairman of the CLCS on the Progress of the Work in the Commission' (Fourteenth session, 30 August–3 September 2004) UN Doc CLCS/42, para 17.

not be opposable to non-Parties to UNCLOS who have not accepted the authority of the CLCS or the procedures embedded in UNCLOS articles 76(8) and 76(9).

The status of customary international law, relating to UNCLOS article 76, is not completely clear.[271] The ICJ confirmed, in *Nicaragua* v. *Colombia*, that paragraph 1 reflects customary international law but in that case, it did not find it necessary to determine whether the same applies to other provisions of UNCLOS article 76.[272] Both States agreed that the definition of the continental shelf and rules governing delimitation of the continental shelf reflect customary international law and that the entitlement to a continental shelf exists ipso facto ab initio. However, they disagreed on which rules govern entitlements to a continental shelf beyond 200 nm from baselines.[273] Nicaragua maintained that paragraphs 1 to 7 of UNCLOS article 76 reflect customary international law,[274] while Colombia accepted only the customary status of paragraph 1 and raised doubts concerning such status of paragraphs 4 to 9.[275]

The United States, which is not party to UNCLOS, submits that paragraphs 1–7 of UNCLOS article 76 reflect customary international law.[276] The procedural requirements of paragraphs 8, 9 and 10 do probably not possess the status of customary international law since they are not of a 'fundamentally norm-creating character' as is necessary for a rule of customary international law.[277] Treaty obligations do not create obligations for third States without their express consent.[278] Therefore, limits established on the basis of CLCS recommendations may only be opposable to States that have ratified UNCLOS. This suggests that even when permanently fixed continental shelf limits have become opposable to States Parties to UNCLOS, they may not be opposable to non-Parties unless and until they are opposable on the basis of acquiescence. When it comes to exploitation of the international seabed area, the international community is represented by the International Seabed Authority, which does not have competence to determine the extent of the international seabed area.[279] Instead, its approximate extent must be ascertained from lawful continental shelf limits.

271 Alex Oude Elferink (n 138) 132. See also Robin Churchill 'The 1982 United Nations Convention on the Law of the Sea' in Donald R Rothwell, Alex Oude Elferink, Karen N Scott and Tim Stephens (eds) The Oxford Handbook of the Law of the Sea (Oxford University Press, 2015 37–38: Although many UNCLOS provisions are reflective of custom, the rules relating to the CLCS may not be.

272 *Territorial and Maritime Dispute (Nicaragua* v. *Colombia)* (n 204) para 118.

273 Ibid., paras 114–115.

274 Ibid., para 116.

275 Ibid., para 117.

276 See US Interagency Group on the Law of the Sea and Ocean Policy 'Policy Governing the Continental Shelf of the United States of America' (17 November 1987) reproduced in Ashley Roach and Robert Smith (n 51) 188.

277 See *North Sea Continental Shelf* (n 13) para 72.

278 See VCLT articles 35 and 36.

279 Alex Oude Elferink, 'The Continental Shelf beyond 200 Nautical Miles: The Relationship between the CLCS and Third Party Dispute Settlement', in Alex Oude Elferink and Donald Rothwell (eds) *Oceans Management in the 21st Century: Institutional Frameworks and Responses* (Martinus Nijhoff, 2004) 107, 118 referring to L Dolliver and M Nelson, 'Claims to the Continental Shelf beyond the 200-Mile Limit' in

2.4.3.2 Revision of Continental Shelf Limits

UNCLOS articles 76(8) and 76(9) make no references to subsequent adjustments of the stable continental shelf limits. Section 2.4.3 explained that coastal States are barred from revising final and binding continental shelf limits on their own accord. Still, the CLCS can request a re-submission where it disagrees with the submissions brought before it[280] and States will have to make revised submissions and establish new continental shelf limits when their limits are successfully challenged.

The CLCS has accepted new data relating to areas it already issued recommendations on but only after advising the submitting State to provide further data and before the limits were permanently described. The Russian Federation submitted a 'partial revised submission' regarding the Sea of Okhotsk, on 28 February 2013, after having made a partial submission in respect of the Sea of Okhotsk and other areas on 20 December 2001. All neighbouring States in the Arctic Ocean reacted to the first submission[281] and the CLCS advised the Russian Federation to make another submission and base it on the recommendations from 2002.[282] The CLCS, thus, issued two recommendations, first on 27 June 2002[283] and again on 11 March 2014.[284] This allowed Russia to revise its submission to the CLCS. However, the revision occurred before the limits were final and binding or permanently described. Therefore, this does not indicate that States can make revised submissions on their own accord, after the issuance of recommendations, or that the CLCS would accept new submissions relating to permanently fixed outer continental shelf limits.

States may wish to revise permanently described continental shelf limits due to new data relating to the continental margin or changes in coastal geography, geology or geomorphology, for example, if a new volcanic island appears. However, this may not be possible once the limits have become permanently stable, that is, if the limits are not only binding upon other States but also on the coastal State that establishes them.[285] Unilateral declarations create obligations for the declaring State and their binding nature is rooted in the principle of good faith and other States' reliance upon the unilateral act.[286] The extent to which a unilateral act creates legal obligations also

Volkmar Götz, Peter Selmer and Rudiger Wolfrum (eds) *Liber Amicorum Günther Janicke – Zum 85 Geburtstag* (1998) 573, 575.

280 Alex Oude Elferink (n 138) 130; UNCLOS Annex II, article 8.

281 Ibid., 146.

282 Ibid., 151, referring to GAOR, 'Fifty-seventh Session' (8 October 2002) UN Doc A/57/57/Add.1, para 41.

283 CLCS 'Statement by the Chairman of the Commission on the Limits of the Continental Shelf on the Progress of Work in the Commission' (Eleventh session, 24–28 June 2002) UN Doc CLCS/34, para 33.

284 CLCS 'Progress of Work in the Commission on the Limits of the Continental Shelf' (Thirty-fourth session, 27 January–14 March 2014) UN Doc CLCS/83, para 40.

285 See 'Conference Report Toronto 2006' (n 124) 18.

286 General Assembly Official Records (hereinafter GAOR), 'Report of the International Law Commission Fifty-eighth Session' (1 May–9 June and 3 July–11 August 2006) UN Doc A/61/10, 370.

depends on the intention of the declaring State[287] and when the scope of an obligation is unclear, unilateral acts are interpreted restrictively.[288] Coastal States surely intend to accept lasting legal obligations when establishing final and binding outer continental shelf limits and other States may rely on the permanence of such an undertaking. However, unilateral declarations may be revoked when there has been a fundamental change of circumstances, satisfying the conditions of Vienna Convention on the law of treaties (hereinafter VCLT)[289] article 62.[290] Permanently described continental shelf limits may, consequently, be subject to revocation when the essential basis for delineation is affected by a fundamental change of circumstances.[291]

'No obligation may result for other States from the unilateral declaration of a State.' Still, other States can incur obligations relating to such declarations if they clearly accept the declaration.[292] UNCLOS member States accept the binding nature of continental shelf limits established in accordance with UNCLOS article 76(8) and (9), by virtue of their accession to UNCLOS. They are consequently bound by such unilateral acts, at least to the extent that they are consistent with relevant law. Nonetheless, as explained in Chapter 5, a fundamental change of circumstances may justify termination or revision of agreements relating to maritime limits and maritime boundaries under rebus sic stantibus or VCLT article 62. Similarly, outer continental shelf limits might be challenged on the basis of fundamental changes because VCLT article 62 can apply mutatis mutandis to unilateral declarations establishing final and binding continental shelf limits.[293] According to this, revision of permanently described continental shelf limits might be initiated by the coastal State or other interested States, by reference to a fundamental change of circumstances.

2.4.4 *Man-Made Changes to Coastal Geography*

The prospect of sea level rise and coastal erosion has led many States to artificially conserve their coastlines and reinforce vulnerable coastal features such as rocks, shoals and low-tide elevations. The purpose may be to prevent submergence of land

[287] See *Frontier Dispute (Burkina Faso/Republic of Mali)* (Judgment) [1986] ICJ Rep 554, 573, para 39; *Case concerning Military and Paramilitary Activities in and against Nicaragua (Nicaragua v. United States of America)* (Judgment) [1986] ICJ Rep 132, para 261.

[288] UN Doc A/61/10 (n 286) 377.

[289] Vienna Convention on the law of treaties (adopted on 23 May 1969, entered into force 27 January 1980) 1155 UNTS 331.

[290] Ibid., 381, referring to *Fisheries Jurisdiction (Federal Republic of Germany v. Iceland)* (Jurisdiction) [1973] ICJ Rep 4, 63, para 36, and *Case Concerning the Gabčíkovo-Nagymaros Project (Hungary/Slovakia)* (Judgment) [1997] ICJ Rep 7, 64, para 104.

[291] See Chapter 5 for a detailed discussion on this principle.

[292] UN Doc A/61/10 (n 286) 379.

[293] ILC, 'Ninth Report on Unilateral Acts of States' (6 April 2006) UN Doc A/CN.4/569 and Add.1, para 115.

territory, fluctuations of maritime limits or the extension of land and maritime entitlements further out to sea. UNCLOS has several provisions relating to the capacity of man-made structures in generating maritime entitlements. These are discussed in the following sections to determine whether, and to what extent, human efforts can generate and maintain maritime entitlements.

2.4.4.1 Permanent Harbour Works

Baselines are only established along the coastline of naturally formed land. This does not include artificial islands, installations or structures such as oil drilling rigs, navigational towers and off-shore docking and oil pumping facilities. Man-made structures do not generate maritime entitlements and, therefore, they are generally not used to establish baselines.[294] However, 'the outermost permanent harbour works which form an integral part of the harbour system are regarded as forming part of the coast' and, consequently, baselines can be drawn to and from permanent harbour works.[295]

Jetties, moles, quays, coastal terminals, wharves, breakwaters and sea walls may be considered as permanent harbour works.[296] The same does not apply to off-shore installations or artificial islands.[297] Roadsteads normally used for the loading, unloading and anchoring of ships, and which would otherwise be situated wholly or partly beyond the outer limits of the territorial sea, are included within the territorial sea,[298] but baselines are not drawn from roadsteads because they do not generate maritime zones in the sea around them.[299]

Ports form part of the coast.[300] Therefore, baselines are drawn to and from ports when delimiting the territorial sea and other maritime boundaries.[301] New harbour works affect the location of normal baselines, as they can move 'seaward to reflect changes to the coast caused by . . . human-made structures associated with harbour systems, coastal protection and land reclamation projects'.[302] Similarly, States can update straight or archipelagic baselines to reflect such changes. However, it remains unclear whether States can choose to disregard harbour works for the purpose of drawing their baselines or establishing bilateral boundaries. Article 8 of the Convention on the Territorial Sea

294 UNCLOS articles 11, 60(8), 147(2) and 259.
295 UNCLOS article 11.
296 *Baselines: An Examination of Relevant Provisions of the United Nations Convention on the Law of the Sea* (n 221) 56.
297 UNCLOS article 11.
298 UNCLOS article 12.
299 Ashley Roach and Robert Smith (n 32) 53.
300 UNCLOS article 11.
301 International Hydrographic Organization, International Oceanographic Commission, International Association of Geodesy and ABLOS, *A Manual on Technical Aspects of the United Nations Convention on the Law of the Sea – 1982: Special Publication No 51*, 4th edition (International Hydrographic Bureau, 2006) Appendix 1–6.
302 'Conference Report Sofia 2012' (n 81) 31. See also Lewis Alexander (n 22) 535, referring to human-made structures.

and Contiguous Zone states that harbour works 'shall be regarded as forming part of the coast' and Norway proposed to change the wording to 'may be regarded' because 'shall' seemed to obligate States to adjust their maritime limits to account for ports, whereas 'may' would indicate that it was a choice.[303] Members of the ILC were of the view that 'may' and 'shall' meant the same thing[304] and that the Norwegian proposal would detract from the clarity of the provision.[305] 'States had long regarded harbour works such as jetties as part of their land territory and that practice should be universally recognized as unchallengeable.'[306]

The Norwegian proposal was rejected by 54 votes to 6, with 10 abstentions. Article 8 (with the term 'shall') was eventually adopted by 70 votes to none, with 1 abstention.[307] A compromise seems to have been reached at the Third Law of the Sea Conference because UNCLOS article 11 provides that permanent harbour works 'are' to be regarded as part of the territory. Consequently, no choice is explicitly indicated but the Advisory Board on the Law of the Sea (hereinafter ABLOS) Manual on Technical Aspects of UNCLOS employs the term 'may', stating that harbour works 'may be used as part of the baseline for the purpose of delimiting the territorial sea and other maritime zones'.[308] This interpretation suggests that the impact of harbour works is in fact discretionary.

2.4.4.2 Artificial Conservation of the Coastline

Many coastal States have responded to coastal erosion and sea level rise with structures that reinforce the coastline.[309] These may serve to protect the low-water line and important base points. According to Soons '[a]rtificial conservation of the coastline, including that of islands, is fully permitted under public international law: this is proved by abundant State practice'.[310] However, artificial conservation of naturally formed land must not be confused with artificial structures that extend beyond naturally formed land because artificial structures do not generate maritime entitlements in their own right,[311] except in the case of permanent harbour works. The Palm Islands on the coast of Dubai are an example of such artificial features, which explains why they cannot contribute to the maritime entitlements of the United Arab Emirates.[312]

303 UNCLOS, Official Records, Volume III 'Summary Records of Meetings and Annexes' (24 February 27 April 1958) UN Doc: A/CONF.13/39, 141.
304 Ibid., 142.
305 Ibid., 141.
306 UN Doc: A/CONF.13/39 (n 303) 142.
307 Ibid., 142.
308 International Hydrographic Organization et al (n 301).
309 See Alfred Soons (n 45) 222.
310 Ibid., 216–218, 222.
311 See UNCLOS article 60(8).
312 See DOALOS, 'Council of Minister's Decision No (5) 2009 in respect of the Application of the Straight Baselines System to a Part of the Coast of the United Arab Emirates' LOS Bulletin 69, 78.

The ILC asserted, in 1956, that '[p]ermanent structures erected on the coast and jutting out to sea (such as jetties and coast protective works) are assimilated to harbour works'.[313] Similarly, the ILA Baselines Committee has concluded that structures for protecting the coast can contribute to the drawing of the baseline whether they lie along the coastline or abut out to sea.[314] There is no requirement that the coast protective works form, in any way, part of the permanent harbour works.[315] McDougal and Burke have noted that '[t]here would seem to be no substantial objection to assimilating "coast protective works" to harbor installations even when they are isolated structures if, as is usually the case, they are not extensive'.[316] Carleton has referred to coast protective works of the Netherlands as contributing to the normal baseline even though they cover approximately 17 per cent of the coastline.[317] Those coast protective works fall behind the normal baseline and do not extend the maritime entitlements of the Netherlands further seawards. Therefore, the Dutch protective works might be 'assimilated to harbour works' and regarded as being 'not extensive'.[318]

Measures to artificially conserve the coastline have been employed worldwide. States use various structures to stabilize their coasts, such as sea walls, groynes, wave reduction structures, offshore breakwaters and landfill. For instance, the islet Kolbeinsey was predicted to be submerged by 2020 and the Icelandic Government attempted to reinforce the feature in 1989 by building a helicopter platform on top of it. The platform was also eroded and collapsed by 2006 but traces of the island still remain.[319] Iceland updated its baselines in 2017 but did not abandon a base point on Kolbeinsey.[320] Iceland's exclusive economic zone has long been measured from the islet, but in the maritime delimitation agreement between Iceland and Denmark (Greenland) in 1997 Kolbeinsey was given 30 per cent effect.[321]

313 'Conference Report Sofia 2012' (n 81) 27 referring to GAOR, 'Report of the International Law Commission Covering the Work of Its Eight Session' (23 April–4 July) UN Doc A/3159, 253, 266 and 270.

314 'Conference Report Sofia 2012' (n 81) 27 referring to Victor Prescott and Clive Schofield, *The Maritime Political Boundaries of the World*, 2nd edition (Martinus Nijhoff, 2005) 101, 135 and Christopher Carleton, 'Problems Relating to Man-made Basepoints under UNCLOS' presented at *Current Problematic Issues in the Law of the Sea* (Dublin, 3–4 June 2010) 13.

315 'Conference Report Sofia 2012' (n 81) 27–28.

316 Ibid., 27 referring to Myres Mcdougal and William Burke, *The Public Order of the Oceans* (Yale University Press, 1962) 422–423.

317 'Conference Report Sofia 2012' (n 81) 27, footnote 185, referring to Christopher Carleton (n 314) 13.

318 Ibid., 27 referring to Myres Mcdougal and William Burke (n 316) 422–423.

319 Atli Ísleifsson, 'Kolbeinsey nú tuttugu metrar frá vestur- og að austurodda" (Vísir, 2021) available at: www.visir.is/g/20212102115d/kol-beins-ey-nu-tuttugu-metrar-fra-vestur-og-ad-austur-odda?fbclid=IwAR2ZHicSbiB5CVoeoL9K9ihsDFqC3SSLuTRSZQdUMYjOtVoor-GNhc3xDIQ accessed 27 April 2021.

320 Law no 58, 14 June 2017, amending Law no 41/1979 on Iceland's Territorial Sea, Exclusive Economic Zone and Continental Shelf.

321 Agreement between the Government of the Kingdom of Denmark along with the Local Government of Greenland on the one hand, and the Government of the Republic of Iceland on the other hand on

The Japanese Government has gone to great lengths to preserve Japan's maritime entitlements extending from Okinotorishima, an uninhabited atoll, which, according to China and South Korea, cannot generate entitlements to an exclusive economic zone or a continental shelf. Japan has built walls of cement, steel blocks and titanium mesh around the coral reefs and in 1988 a platform was constructed housing researchers for a weather monitoring station,[322] presumably to meet the requirement of sustaining economic life. However, UNCLOS article 60(8) clearly states that artificial islands, installations and structures do not possess the status of islands and that their presence does not affect the delimitation of the territorial sea, the exclusive economic zone or the continental shelf. Furthermore, according to UNCLOS article 121(1) the definition of an island is 'a naturally formed area of land, surrounded by water, which is above water at high tide'.

In response to China's persistent objections to the classification of Okinotorishima as an island and to deal with the continuing erosion, the Japanese Government has begun growing corals to add to the reef.[323] The method used entails the transportation of adult corals from Okinotorishima to a laboratory, 680 miles away, where coral eggs are fertilized and the resulting larvae and juvenile corals are returned to repopulate the Okinotori reef.[324] The capacity of the coral reefs to turn Okinotorishima into an island, within the meaning of UNCLOS article 121, will depend on whether they are considered to be naturally formed. According to Oude Elferink, accretion to artificial islands does not qualify them as islands,[325] likewise, accretion to the artificial extension of this reef will hardly turn it into an island within the meaning of UNCLOS article 121. It does not suffice that islands are made up of natural elements; they must also be formed through natural processes.[326] Furthermore, as explained by the tribunal in *Philippines* v. *China*, 'the inclusion of the term "naturally formed" in the definition of both a low-tide elevation and an island indicates that the status of a feature is to be evaluated on the basis of its natural condition'.[327] The addition inserted through human intervention, that is, the man-made coral reefs, is not part of Okinotorishima in its 'natural condition'. The corals are created through artificial processes and as artificial structures they cannot be qualified as islands.[328]

the Delimitation of the Continental Shelf and the Fishery Zone in the Area between Greenland and Iceland (adopted 11 November 1997, entered into force 27 May 1998) 2074 UNTS 58.

322 Yuriko Nagano, 'Growing Coral to Keep a Sea Claim Above Water' (The New York Times, 2014) available at: www.nytimes.com/2014/11/19/business/energy-environment/growing-coral-to-keep-a-sea-claim-above-water.html?_r=0 accessed 17 January 2021.

323 Ibid.

324 Ibid.

325 Alex Oude Elferink, 'Artificial Islands, Installations and Structures' in *Max Planck Encyclopedia of Public International Law, volume 1* (2012) 662.

326 UNCLOS article 121(1).

327 *Philippines* v. *China* (n 3) para 305.

328 UNCLOS article 60(8).

The growing of coral reefs on or around Okinotorishima might be regarded as artificial conservation of the naturally formed land that was already there, that is, coast protective works around the disputed features. Soons maintains that such measures are permitted under international law and that natural features, preserved through artificial means, can be valid base points.[329] He further explains that islands can be conserved through artificial means even if exclusively for that purpose because UNCLOS article 60(8) refers to 'newly constructed artificial islands'. The important difference is whether States are preserving pre-existing rights or trying to generate new entitlements.[330] This means that the coral reefs at the Okinotorishima can serve to protect the maritime entitlements generated by the natural features as they were when the artificial conservation commenced but they cannot justify a reclassification of coastal features. In other words, artificial conservation cannot turn rocks, low-tide elevations, or fully submerged features into islands, in the legal sense.

The ILC has, so far, given no definitive answer to whether naturally formed features can lose their status due to artificial conservation. However, the co-chairs highlight several different perspectives in their First Issues Paper, citing the earlier examples from Soons, Oude Elferink and others.[331] It notes that, according to Van Dyke, Okinotorishima is an artificial island but formerly a reef. However, according to Song, Kolbeinsey and similar islets must not necessarily be considered artificial due to artificial reinforcement measures.[332]

2.4.4.3 Artificial Extension of the Coastline

A clear distinction should be drawn between artificial conservation of natural coastlines and artificial extension of the coastline. Furthermore, a distinction should be drawn between the artificial extension of baselines through land reclamation and the re-categorization of a coastal feature as a rock or an island. Whereas the artificial conservation of natural features is fully permissible, the seaward extension of baselines is only possible through the construction of permanent harbour works and cannot change the classification of coastal features.

The arbitral tribunal in the *Philippines* v. *China* arbitration explicitly addressed the impact of artificially extended coastal features. It found that, 'as a matter of law, human modification cannot change the seabed into a low-tide elevation or a low-tide

329 Alfred Soons (n 45) 222.

330 Soons A, 'An Ocean under Stress: Climate Change and the Law of the Sea': Addendum to 'Climate Change: Options and Duties under International Law' (2018) 145 Mededellingen van de Koninklijke Nederlandse Verenigling voor International Recht, 71, 108.

331 UN Doc A/CN.4/740 (n 77) para 215.

332 UN Doc A/CN.4/740 (n 77) para 215, referring to Jon Van Dyke, 'Legal Issues Related to Sovereignty over Dokdo and Its Maritime Boundary' (2007) 38 Ocean Development and International Law, 157–224; Yann-huei Song, 'Okinotorishima: A "rock" or an "island"? Recent Maritime Boundary Controversy between Japan and Taiwan/China' in Seoung-Yong Hong and Jon Van Dyke (eds) *Maritime Boundary Disputes, Settlement Processes, and the Law of the Sea* (Martinus Nijhoff, 2009) 145, 165.

elevation into an island'.[333] The tribunal confirmed that 'low-tide elevations do not form part of the land territory of a State in the legal sense'[334] and that a 'low-tide elevation will remain a low-tide elevation under the Convention, regardless of the scale of the island or installation built atop it'.[335] This seems conclusive as far as the re-categorization of coastal features is concerned. Yet, it does not settle the question whether baselines can be drawn along artificial coastlines of mainland that has been extended seawards through land reclamation.

UNCLOS articles 13(1) and 121(1) make clear that low-tide elevations and islands are composed of naturally formed land. The Convention holds no definition of what constitutes a coast, in the context of UNCLOS articles 5, 7 and 47, but article 60(8) provides that artificial islands, installations and structures generate no maritime entitlements. The only exception from this general rule can be found in UNCLOS article 11, which states that 'the outermost permanent harbour works which form an integral part of the harbour system are regarded as forming part of the coast'. This is why man-made structures that form part of harbour systems affect the drawing of baselines.[336] It can be deduced, from this exception, that the coast is otherwise made up of naturally formed land. Indeed, the same argument applies to mainland coastlines and individual coastal features: States should not be allowed to unilaterally and arbitrarily increase their entitlements. Otherwise, as noted by the Danish representative to the General-Assembly in 1982, insignificant coastal features 'looked upon in the past as mere obstacles to navigation, would miraculously become the golden keys to vast maritime zones. That would indeed be an unwarranted and unacceptable consequence of the new law of the sea'.[337]

The ILA Baselines Committee has concluded that the coast, as referred to in UNCLOS article 5, includes 'any coast protective work which extends above the chart datum, and any human-induced extension of the natural coast'.[338] This is a broad interpretation of the article that could result in the unwarranted extension of maritime entitlements referred to above. The Baselines Committee supports this finding by reference to very limited State practice.[339] Indeed, the applicable law can be clarified or amended through subsequent State practice.[340] However, such practice must satisfy strict requirements to justify a deviation from the ordinary meaning of the provision, as established by reference to its context and objective. It

333 *Philippines* v. *China* (n 3) para 305.

334 Ibid., para 309.

335 Ibid., para 305.

336 'Conference Report Sofia 2012' (n 81) 31. See also Lewis Alexander (n 22) 535 referring to human-made structures.

337 Third United Nations Conference on the Law of the Sea, '171st Plenary Meeting' (16 April 1982) UN Doc A/CONF.62/SR.171, 106, para 8.

338 'Conference Report Sofia 2012' (n 81) 28.

339 Ibid.

340 See, for example, Robin Churchill, 'The Impact of State Practice on the Jurisdictional Framework Contained in the LOS Convention' in Alex Oude Elferink (ed) *Stability and Change in the Law of the Sea: The Role of the Los Convention* (Martinus Nijhoff, 2005) 91, 93.

would have to be consistent and uniform and either establish a subsequent agreement between UNCLOS States Parties or be accompanied by *opinio juris* to support the development of a superseding rule of customary international law.[341] These conditions do not seem to be met in regard to interpretation of the word 'coast' in UNCLOS article 5.

The Baselines Committee refers to examples from the Netherlands, the United Arab Emirates, Singapore and Japan to support the conclusion that baselines can be extended through artificial means.[342] Indeed, the Netherlands and Singapore have drawn baselines around reclaimed land.[343] This has been the consistent practice of the Dutch authorities and Malaysia seems to accept that Singapore's baselines could be affected by land reclamation.[344] However, the world and palm islands in Dubai do not affect the legal baseline of the United Arab Emirates.[345] Furthermore, Japanese efforts to extend maritime entitlements through artificial extension of the coastline have been criticized.[346] These examples are too dispersed to affect the interpretation of UNCLOS article 5. Nonetheless, artificial extension of the baseline might be justified on the basis of UNCLOS article 11.

UNCLOS article 11 gives no clear definition of 'permanent harbour works' and land reclamation projects can always extend the baseline if they qualify as such. This is why, for example, Rotterdam harbour justifies an extension of the Dutch baselines.[347] A proposal has been put forth to extend Schiphol airport out to sea[348] and such a construction might be assimilated to permanent harbour works. Airports and other extensions of the coastline may, therefore, extend the baseline seawards but only if the construction in question qualifies as permanent harbour works as per UNCLOS article 11.

For the above-mentioned reasons it is concluded that the status of coastal features cannot be changed through artificial means and that baselines can only be drawn along the naturally formed coast. Human-induced extension of the coastline should not be considered to be naturally formed coast, for the purposes of UNCLOS articles 5, 7 and 47, unless it qualifies as coast protective works or permanent harbour works. State practice that suggests otherwise is not yet sufficiently widespread or uniform to support a different conclusion.

341 See VCLT article 31(3)(b) and *Asylum (Colombia* v. *Peru)* (Judgment) [1950] ICJ Rep 266, 277; *Right of Passage over Indian Territory (Portugal* v. *India)* (Merits) [1960] ICJ Rep 6, 40.

342 'Conference Report Sofia 2012' (n 81) referring to Christopher Carleton (n 314) 19–22.

343 Ibid., referring to Christopher Carleton (n 314) 21–22.

344 'Conference Report Sofia 2012' (n 81) 28.

345 Ibid., referring to Christopher Carleton (n 314) 23–26.

346 'Growing Coral to Keep a Sea Claim Above Water' (n 322).

347 See 'Conference Report Sofia 2012' (n 81) 28 referring to Maritime zones gewijzigd door aanleg Maasvlakte 2 (Dutch Ministry of Defence, press release of 22 December 2009).

348 J Pieters, 'Schiphol Expansion Would Move Miles Into North Sea in New Proposal' (NL Times, 12 March 2018) available at: https://nltimes.nl/2018/03/12/schiphol-expansion-move-miles-north-sea-new-proposal accessed 16 January 2021.

2.5 PROPOSALS TO STABILIZE MARITIME LIMITS

Recession of maritime limits can have adverse effects for coastal States as they lose control over resources previously under their jurisdiction. This can affect low-lying coastal States and their inhabitants and in extreme cases may lead to loss of statehood.[349] To address these problems, leading academics have put forth proposals to stabilize baselines and/or outer maritime limits for the purpose of promoting stability in the distribution of maritime entitlements and reducing the risk of international conflicts and wasted resources.[350] Furthermore, the ILA Committee on Sea Level Rise has proposed that once maritime limits have been lawfully established, States should not be obligated to adjust them to reflect sea level change.[351]

These proposals would make it possible for States to fix the location of baselines and/or all outer limits of maritime zones, notwithstanding subsequent changes to relevant coastlines.[352] Next sections consider the feasibility of departing from the theory of ambulatory baselines; the possibility of stabilizing either baselines or outer maritime limits; available methods; and the extent to which existing rules can be altered.

2.5.1 *Feasibility of Freezing Maritime Limits*

The ILC's First Issues Paper on sea level rise has outlined the various ways in which sea level rise may impact States and their maritime entitlements. Coastal States can lose sovereignty and rights to regulate navigation where territorial seas become subject to the regimes of the exclusive economic zone and continental shelf. The First Issues Paper indicates that continental shelf entitlements extending from an island can be lost if the island is fully submerged, even if the outer limits had previously been permanently described.[353] If the continental shelf becomes part of the international seabed area, the coastal State loses sovereign rights over valuable offshore resources. Those changes can affect the continuation of agreements with private actors and other States concerning exploitation of those resources. According to the ILC's preliminary findings, the most severe loss, for coastal States, would result from the loss of exclusive economic zone entitlements, that is, when such zones are turned into high seas. Many States are dependent upon revenue generated

349 Rosemary Rayfuse, 'Chapter 6: Climate Change and the Law of the Sea' in Rosemary Rayfuse and Shirley Scott (eds) *International Law in the Era of Climate Change* (Edward Elgar Publishing, 2012) 152. See also Emily Crawford and Rosemary Rayfuse, 'Chapter 10: Climate Change and Statehood' in Rosemary Rayfuse and Shirley Scott (eds) *International Law in the Era of Climate Change* (Edward Elgar Publishing, 2012) 249.

350 See, for example, David Caron (n 33) 12, 14; Jonathan Lusthaus, 'Shifting Sands: Sea Level Rise, Maritime Boundaries and Inter-state Conflict' (2010) 30 (2) Politics 113, 117; Alfred Soons (n 45) 225; Rosemary Rayfuse (n 70) 283.

351 ILA, 'Conference Resolution Sydney' (2018) ILA Res 5/2018.

352 ILA Committee on International Law and Sea Level Rise 'Minutes of the Lopud Intersessional Meeting' (ILA, 2017) 14.

353 UN Doc A/CN.4/740 (n 77) para 190(c).

by living resources of the exclusive economic zone and this change could threaten the continuation of fisheries agreements because States could lose the capacity to administer the resources. Finally, the adjustment of maritime limits could be expensive.[354] For all these reasons, the ILC's First Issues Paper concludes that 'the best option would be the preservation of maritime entitlements'.[355]

The purpose of freezing maritime limits would be to prevent the consequences outlined earlier. The new rules should provide stability, certainty and predictability in the regime of maritime entitlements and prevent or reduce inequitable consequences for vulnerable coastal States. In particular, they would reduce the inequitable difference resulting from the economic capacity to artificially conserve coastlines.

The proposed changes would adversely affect the rights of third States. The First Issues Paper explains that third States stand to benefit from ambulatory maritime limits.[356] Indeed, coastline retreat increases the size of the high seas, under the theory of ambulatory baselines.[357] A new rule of stable limits would prevent other States from enjoying their rights in these areas and that gives them the incentive to impede the development of new rules. Lisztwan notes that '[i]f coastal States were to claim the increased ocean area, they would be further advantaged in comparison to land-locked and geographically disadvantaged States'.[358] Coastal States would be entitled to all new ocean area and the international community, which has shared interests in areas beyond national jurisdiction, would gain nothing.[359] Furthermore, the proposed changes would arguably create a form of historic waters where States would have historic rights based on 'sovereignty over maritime areas derived from historical circumstances'.[360] However, historic title is only relevant for the delimitation of territorial waters and demarcation of historic bays[361] and the Convention's prohibition on reservations indicates that other forms of historic rights should not prevail over UNCLOS.[362]

Caron has suggested that the freezing of maritime limits might be an equitable solution. No State would gain a larger area of the Earth's surface than agreed upon when UNCLOS was adopted in 1982.[363] Yet, the ratio between land and water would clearly be affected and coastal States would gain larger maritime expanses than permissible under existing rules. Caron has also argued that ambulatory limits threaten international peace and stability because States may frequently challenge

354 Ibid., para 190.
355 Ibid.
356 Ibid., para 190(c).
357 Julia Lisztwan (n 143) 170.
358 Ibid., 170.
359 Areas beyond national jurisdiction are receiving increased attention with the codification of the new BBNJ agreement. Several States may be interested in making these emerging areas subject to that regime.
360 See *Philippines* v. *China* (n 3) para 226.
361 Ibid., paras 225–226.
362 Ibid., paras 245 and 254.
363 David Caron (n 45) 640–641. See also David Caron (n 33) 16.

each other's maritime claims.[364] However, a new rule of stable maritime limits might also be highly contentious as opposing States might continue to rely on contrary rules concerning the breadth of maritime zones and firmly established principles of the law of the sea.[365] States might object to the exercise of coastal State jurisdiction where no land supports such claims and they might wish to exercise their own rights in new strips of high seas and the international seabed area.

It will be difficult to change existing rules. It has been argued that rules, allowing States to rely on the outer limits of their maritime zones as established before the occurrence of a landward shift of baselines could develop into customary international law or be codified in a treaty or implementation agreement within the framework of UNCLOS.[366] However, a new rule of customary international law would have to take precedence over currently applicable UNCLOS provisions, customary international law, general principles and judicial precedents. It might take time to reach consensus on the exact content of the rule; uniform State practice; and *opinio juris*. This process might cause uncertainty and might induce a surge of new challenges to excessive or outdated maritime limits, causing a similar disruption to international peace and stability as the gradual adjustment of ambulatory maritime limits. An amendment to UNCLOS or a new international treaty fixing maritime limits might reduce the risk of legal uncertainty inevitable with the development of new customary law. However, formal amendments seem like a distant possibility. The best option might be to change the interpretation of UNCLOS through subsequent State practice.[367]

The proposed freezing of maritime limits may not be the most feasible way to secure maritime entitlements. All maritime entitlements can be preserved through artificial conservation and such measures seem to be the only method available, under existing international law, for stabilizing otherwise fluctuating unilateral maritime limits.[368] Artificial conservation of the coastline has the benefit of being consistent with international law but the disadvantage of being very expensive.[369] As noted by Caron, artificial conservation may lead to economic inefficiency and waste and it may be of greater benefit for the global community if resources are invested in climate change mitigation and adaptation activities rather than the preservation of maritime limits.[370] Indeed, fluctuation of maritime entitlements is not the gravest threat of sea level rise. Issues such as salt-water intrusion can affect water and food security in low-lying

364 David Caron (n 33) 13.
365 Particularly, the land dominates the sea principle.
366 Alfred Soons (n 45) 224–225.
367 These options are further explored in Section 2.5.3.
368 'Conference Report Sofia 2012' (n 81) 422.
369 Alfred Soons (n 45) 222.
370 See David Caron (n 45) 639–640.

island States and coastal erosion and flooding is threatening homes and infrastructure.[371] Moreover, the very survival of States is at risk.[372]

Artificial conservation also creates a disparity between States that do have the economic capacity to defend their limits and those that do not. This affords an inequitable advantage to richer States as they will be able to reinforce their maritime limits while developing States may not have the means to do the same. Consequently, the negative impacts of baseline recession will, in all likelihood, be heaviest for States that bear little responsibility for climate-related coastline changes. This is an unfortunate result of the existing law and, surely, the strongest argument in favour of a new rule stabilizing zonal limits. Inequitable consequences of a similar nature were discussed at the third United Nations Conference on the Law of the Sea, in relation to UNCLOS article 7(4), which permits the drawing of straight baselines to and from low-tide elevations if lighthouses or similar installations are built on them. A number of States argued that this might discriminate against those with insufficient means to build such structures and, consequently, the second half of the provision (referring to instances of general recognition) was adopted.[373] This shows a willingness to minimize any discrepancy between States that have the financial capacity to further their maritime claims and those that do not.

Recourse to artificial conservation of the coastline will surely increase in coming years and decades, regardless of the stability or fluctuations of baselines, because it may prove necessary to protect coastal habitations from inundation. Sea defences and shoreline protection are important tools to prevent or delay displacement of the large portion of the world's population that lives on territory that is currently at risk of inundation.[374] Consequently, a rule stabilizing maritime limits would only to a limited extent reduce the need for costly sea defences.

Stable maritime limits do not address the more severe implications of sea level rise. Climate-related changes are threatening the existence of small island States and other low-lying States and the freezing of maritime limits is no solution to problems such as seawater intrusion into fresh water supplies, storms and hurricanes, deterioration of fish stocks and loss of habitable territory. It may seem inequitable that States that are heavily dependent on oceanic resources must lose maritime entitlements while faced with other catastrophic consequences of climate change. However, the freezing of maritime limits would only address a small portion of the problems associated with sea level rise and coastal erosion and it would only be a temporary solution. Vulnerable States are in need of a holistic approach that may entail, for example, coastline defences,

371 UN Office of Legal Affairs, 'Information and Examples of State Practice on "Sea-level rise in relation to international law" A Submission by the Republic of Maldives' (31 December 2019) available at: https://legal.un.org/ilc/sessions/72/pdfs/english/slr_maldives.pdf accessed 17 January 2021.

372 GAOR, 'Summary Record of the 20th Meeting' (28 November 2017) UN Doc A/C.6/72/SR.20, Para 64.

373 Myron Nordquist, Satya Nandan og Shabtai Rosenne, *United Nations Convention on the Law of the Sea 1982, volume 2, A Commentary* (Brill Nijhoff, 1982) 102.

374 Anil Ananthaswamy, 'Going, going . . . ' (2009) 202 (2715) New Scientist 26, 30–31.

development assistance from the World Bank and humanitarian aid. The prospect of fluctuating maritime limits is not the biggest threat to low-lying coastal States or the only inequity resulting from climate change. This issue extends far beyond the scope of the law of the sea and revision of UNCLOS is not the most obvious or useful remedy.

The idea of stabilizing baselines and zonal limits is ill suited to deal with the eventuality of complete inundation or uninhabitability of island States. Rayfuse has noted that only States are entitled to maritime zones[375] and to qualify as a State there is a prerequisite of land territory and a permanent population inhabiting that territory.[376] Submerging island States may become uninhabitable and eventually completely submerged, which may lead to them losing their statehood and, consequently, all entitlements to maritime zones.[377] Submerging States might merge with other States and thereby retain maritime entitlements despite the loss of habitable territory. Frozen limits would enable such States to keep all original entitlements. However, the loss of statehood will inevitably affect maritime limits and maritime boundaries because only States can have maritime entitlements.[378] Consequently, the freezing of maritime limits would create a discrepancy between States that can maintain all their maritime entitlements despite severe inundation and States that will cease to exist and, consequently, lose all entitlements.

The methods for freezing maritime limits would involve either giving the charted line priority over the actual low-water line (regardless of any inconsistency) or permanently fixing declared maritime limits. The first option would go against the developing jurisprudence discussed in Section 2.4.2.2. Furthermore, it might cause uncertainty to have different charts and coordinates in circulation, showing both the actual low-water line, for navigational safety, and the legal baseline. The second option would essentially freeze all unilaterally declared limits, ideally by reference to data submitted to the UNSG. However, this might permanently establish excessive limits, as there is no surveillance of the legitimacy of such limits and it would not extend to normal baselines, which are not subject to the obligation that requires States to submit information to the UNSG.

2.5.2 *Freezing of Baselines or Outer Maritime Limits*

Proposals to stabilize maritime limits involve the freezing of existing baselines or established outer limits.[379] The freezing of baselines essentially stabilizes all maritime limits. In contrast, baselines remain ambulatory if only the outer limits are frozen. The ILA Committee on Sea Level Rise has expressed a preference for

375 Ibid., 284.

376 Montevideo Convention on the Rights and Duties of States (adopted 26 December 1933, entered into force 26 December 1934) 165 League of Nations Treaty Series 19, article 1.

377 Rosemary Rayfuse (n 70) 284.

378 Ibid.

379 ILA Committee on International Law and Sea Level Rise 'Johannesburg Conference' (ILA, 2016), 14.

freezing the outer limits of maritime zones instead of baselines,[380] although possibly not by consensus.

Both options have some merit but neither is without fault. UNCLOS provisions concerning the breadth of maritime zones would have to be changed if only the outer limits of maritime zones were permanently fixed. Otherwise coastal regression and sea level rise would result in larger zones than permitted under UNCLOS.[381] However, the freezing of baselines could result in large expanses of internal waters, which would not be closely linked to the land domain as required under UNCLOS Article 7(3).

The freezing of baselines might be the more practically feasible option. It involves less significant legal reform as it affects fewer and more ambiguous rules. UNCLOS would have to be interpreted in such a way as not to impose an obligation to update maritime limits once they become inconsistent with the requirements for baselines. This is not an explicit obligation but an implication derived from UNCLOS article 7(2). UNCLOS article 7(3) clearly states that internal waters must be 'sufficiently closely linked to the land domain' but this involves a subjective evaluation. This option could be achieved through subsequent State practice and revised interpretation of several UNCLOS provisions because it mostly relates to implied, as opposed to express, obligations.

On the other hand, the freezing of outer maritime limits would have an impact on explicit requirements, such as those concerning the maximum breadth of maritime zones. Baselines would continuously meet the conditions of UNCLOS, internal waters would be closely linked to land, as per UNCLOS article 7(3), and the normal baseline could be identified by reference to officially recognized charts. However, the correlation between baselines and outer limits would be broken and there would be a clear violation of UNCLOS articles 3, 33(2), 57 and 76(1) as maritime zones grew larger than expressly permitted. This would call for more extensive changes to the applicable law; an arduous process as further explained in the following sections.

2.5.3 *Changing the Applicable Law to Stabilize Maritime Limits*

The ILC's preliminary findings in relation to the theory of ambulatory baselines indicate an acceptance of the theory and some scepticism as to its feasibility due to the widespread desire for stability. According to the First Issues Paper, the question of fluctuations or stability of maritime entitlements cannot be resolved by permanently establishing all maritime limits on the basis of UNCLOS articles 7 and 76(9). However, the paper also notes that preservation of maritime limits is not expressly prohibited under the Convention. Support is indicated for stabilizing all maritime entitlements by reinforcing coastlines and not updating established maritime limits. However, the co-chairs of the study group submit that there is not (yet)

380 Ibid., 15.
381 Moritaka Hayashi (n 33) 33.

enough evidence for the conclusion that this is permissible under customary international law.[382]

UNCLOS will not be easily changed or superseded but three possible methods have been identified. First, UNCLOS could be amended either directly or through an implementing agreement. Second, subsequent State practice can have an impact on UNCLOS and give rise to a new rule of customary international law superseding the Convention. Third, subsequent practice can 'be used as an element in interpreting the Convention'.[383]

2.5.3.1 Amending UNCLOS

The constitution of the oceans is not easily amended. It is 'a package comprising certain elements that constitute a single and indivisible entity'.[384] No reservations or exceptions are allowed unless expressly permitted under the Convention.[385] After all, the principal objective of UNCLOS was the establishment of an integrated legal order governing all uses of the oceans.[386] Amendments to the Convention are subject to UNCLOS articles 312–316. UNCLOS article 314 deals specifically with amendments to provisions relating exclusively to activities in the Area and calls for the approval of organs of the International Seabed Authority.

If a State party wishes to alter the integrated legal order of UNCLOS, it must propose specific amendments to the UNSG. An amendment conference is only convened if at least half of the States Parties reply favourably to a request for a conference to address the proposed amendments.[387] A large majority is required before an amendment can enter into force (unless otherwise agreed at the conference). States Parties must make every effort to reach a consensus relating to potential amendments and there shall be no voting until all efforts at consensus have been exhausted.[388] A simplified amendment procedure does not require a conference and is only available if no State Party objects to the amendment or the simplified procedure within twelve months after it is communicated to them by the UNSG. The amendment is considered to be adopted after twelve months if no State Party has objected to the proposed amendment or to the proposal for its adoption by the simplified procedure. It is otherwise considered to be rejected.[389]

382 UN Doc A/CN.4/740 (n 77) para 104.
383 Robin Churchill (n 340) 91, 93.
384 Third United Nations Conference on the Law of the Sea, 'Note by the President on the Final Clauses' UN Doc FC/1 (23 July 1979) reproduced in Renate Platzöder (ed) *Third United Nations Conference on the Law of the Sea: Documents, volume 12* (Oceana Publications, 1987) 349.
385 UNCLOS article 309.
386 'Note by the President on the Final Clauses' (n 384) 349.
387 UNCLOS article 312(1).
388 UNCLOS article 312(2).
389 UNCLOS article 313.

If a proposal to stabilize maritime limits and change UNCLOS to that effect is put forward and at least one State Party objects to the use of the simplified procedure, an amendment conference must be convened and that would require the support of eighty-four States parties.[390] Even if a majority of States Parties agreed that maritime limits should be frozen, they might be reluctant to reopen a convention that took nine years to negotiate and another twelve to enter into force. Indeed, to this day, no amendments have been ratified and the international community has favoured the adoption of implementing agreements to change UNCLOS.[391]

Two implementing agreements[392] have been concluded to supplement, and in some ways amend, UNCLOS.[393] This approach might be used to stabilize baselines or outer maritime limits and might be more feasible than formally amending UNCLOS. However, it must be considered a distant possibility. The process of adopting the two earlier implementing agreements was prolonged and arduous. Furthermore, the ongoing discussions concerning a third implementing agreement on marine biodiversity of areas beyond national jurisdiction clearly demonstrate how time-consuming this option can be.[394]

2.5.3.2 Subsequent Practice as Evidence for a New Rule of Customary International Law

UNCLOS reflects the customary international law on maritime limits and takes precedence over rules that may have been applicable before accession to the Convention.[395] However, treaty obligations can be superseded by subsequent customary international law. Indeed, customary law is never written in stone and it can, theoretically, change to reflect the proposals discussed earlier.

Subsequent State practice can be indicative of an emerging rule of customary international law. It must, however, be accompanied by the necessary *opinio juris*. State practice that has, thus far, contradicted UNCLOS provisions concerning maritime limits cannot form a basis for a general rule of customary international law for two reasons. It has not been sufficiently widespread or uniform[396] and it has been challenged by several States. In fact, the ILA Baselines Committee has listed eighty-five protests to the straight baseline claims of thirty-nine States. This covers almost 50 per cent of all

390 That is, half the States parties to UNCLOS, as per UNCLOS article 312(1).

391 ILA Committee on International Law and Sea Level Rise, 'Working Session report Sydney 2018' (ILA, 2018) 11.

392 The 1994 Part XI Implementing Agreement and the FSA.

393 The 1994 Part XI Implementing Agreement does more than implement UNCLOS, it actually changes it. See Alan Boyle, 'Further Development of the Law of the Sea Convention: Mechanisms for Change' (2005) 54 International and Comparative Law Quarterly 563, 569.

394 For information on the BBNJ Agreement process, see www.un.org/bbnj/ (accessed 4 December 2020).

395 *Philippines* v. *China* (n 3) para 262.

396 State practice must be uniform, see, for example, *Colombia* v. *Peru* (n 341) 277; *Portugal* v. *India* (n 341) 40.

claims to straight baselines.[397] There is an important difference between maritime limits that are excessive from their inception and those that gradually become inconsistent with legal requirements due to geographic changes. It is possible that State practice and *opinio juris* differ in these respects and that States are more willing to tolerate outdated maritime limits. Indeed, there is evidence of State practice contradicting the theory of ambulatory baselines[398] and several low-lying island States have declared that maritime entitlements must be stabilized and preserved against sea level rise.[399] Still, this might be seen as an expression *de lege ferenda* rather than *opinio juris*. Also, important naval powers such as the United States, the United Kingdom and the Netherlands, recently expressed the view that baselines are ambulatory.[400] An emerging rule of customary international law is dependent upon uniform state practice[401] and this requirement will not be met while important actors maintain the position that baselines are ambulatory.

The jurisprudence of the ICJ reflects two possible approaches to the identification of *opinio juris*. General practice can itself be indicative of the belief that such practice is lawful. Alternatively, positive evidence is needed to demonstrate the recognition of *opinio juris*.[402] There is not, at present, general practice reflecting the belief that maritime limits are stable irrespective of changing coastlines. However, an UNGA resolution might serve to progressively develop the applicable customary international law and synchronize State practice to this end.[403] This would be dependent on broad political support and even if supporters of ambulatory limits were persuaded to change their positions, the threshold for superseding UNCLOS is exceptionally high.

When two sources of law are in conflict the more recent rule can take precedence (*lex posterior derogat legi priori*). On those grounds, custom can modify a treaty. While this is true in a general sense, UNCLOS seems to enjoy a distinct level of primacy over inconsistent sources of law. UNCLOS article 311 explicitly limits the extent to which States can derogate from the Convention's provisions through bilateral or multilateral agreements and strictly prohibits modification of the basic principles. The primacy afforded to UNCLOS over incompatible agreements surely extends to emerging rules of customary international law.[404] Churchill has also

397 ILA Baselines Committee, 'ILA Straight Baselines Study-Protests' (ILA, 2016) 1.

398 Robin Churchill (n 340) 108.

399 Pacific Islands Forum members, 'Submission to the ILC: Submission of the Pacific Islands Forum, forwarded through letter of 30 December 2019 of the Permanent Representative of Tuvalu to the United Nations' (ILC, 2019) available at: https://legal.un.org/ilc/guide/8_9.shtml#govcoms accessed 17 January 2021, 2.

400 UN Doc A/CN.4/740 (n 77) para 88.

401 See, for example, *Colombia* v. *Peru* (n 341) 277; *Portugal* v. *India* (n 341) 40.

402 Ian Brownlie, *Principles of Public International Law* (Clarendon Press, 1998) 7–11.

403 UNGA resolutions have been relied on to identify *opinio juris*, see, for example, *Nicaragua* v. *United States of America* (n 287) para 188.

404 Robin Churchill (n 340) 99.

expressed doubts as to whether UNCLOS can be modified by subsequent custom, given the special procedure governing formal changes to the Convention.[405]

The ICJ's decision in the *Libyan Arab Jamahiriya/Malta* continental shelf case has been cited as an example of subsequent practice superseding treaty obligations.[406] Here the Court confirmed that the entitlement to an exclusive economic zone had become part of customary international law,[407] even though this was contrary to the existing rules codified in the 1958 Convention on the High Seas. Furthermore, the Court relied on UNCLOS, instead of the 1958 Convention on the Continental Shelf, to identify the 'modern law' concerning delimitation of the continental shelf, although UNCLOS had not yet entered into force.[408] This was a landmark decision and it clearly demonstrates how State practice and the conclusion of treaties can further the development of customary international law. However, it is not a definitive precedence of subsequent practice overriding treaty obligations because neither the 1958 Convention on the High Seas nor the 1958 Convention on the Continental Shelf were applicable in this case.[409] Moreover, UNCLOS had been codified and agreed upon. It consequently provided a clear basis for identifying the developing customary international law, which, in the view of both parties, governed the dispute.[410] Furthermore, the 1958 Conventions had no provisions comparable to articles 309–311 of UNCLOS so they were not afforded the same primacy. At any rate, the Court did not have to decide on the hierarchy between customary international law and inconsistent treaty obligations. It had simply to identify the applicable custom, and in doing so, it looked to the more recent (albeit not directly applicable) international treaty.

Courts and tribunals will be presented with a difficult task if they must decide between UNCLOS and inconsistent customary international law allowing States to freeze maritime limits. The *lex posterior derogat legi priori* principle would suggest that the customary international law should take precedence but the Convention's special status might eclipse that principle. At any rate, this unprecedented situation will not arise unless and until new rules of customary international law emerge from State practice and *opinio juris*. Proposals to coordinate such practice (without first changing UNCLOS) do, in effect, encourage States to violate the Convention and non-compliance of a significant number of UNCLOS member States 'undermines the integrity and legitimacy of [UNCLOS]'.[411] Therefore, efforts to change UNCLOS through subsequent customary international law risk undermining the

405 Ibid 97.
406 See, for example, ibid., 96, referring to the development of the exclusive economic zone.
407 *Libyan Arab Jamahiriya/Malta* (n 4) para 34.
408 Ibid., para 33.
409 Malta was party to the Convention on the Continental Shelf, but Libya was not, see ibid., para 26.
410 Ibid.
411 Robin Churchill, 'The Persisting Problem of Non-compliance with the Law of the Sea Convention: Disorder in the Oceans' (2012) 27 (4) The International Journal of Marine and Coastal Law 813, 815.

integrity and legitimacy of UNCLOS, and may result in subordinate rules that are inapplicable in cases of conflict.

2.5.3.3 Subsequent Practice Affecting the Interpretation of UNCLOS

Even if widespread practice of UNCLOS member States will not create a customary rule superseding UNCLOS, it may potentially modify the interpretation that renders maritime limits ambulatory. VCLT article 31(3) provides that when interpreting a treaty, '[a]ny subsequent agreement between the parties regarding the interpretation of the treaty or the application of its provisions' and '[a]ny subsequent practice in the application of the treaty which establishes the agreement of the parties regarding its interpretation' 'shall be taken into account, together with the context'.[412]

The ILC has classified subsequent agreements and subsequent practice under VCLT article 31(3) as 'authentic means of interpretation'. A subsequent agreement represents 'an authentic interpretation by the parties which must be read into the treaty for purposes of its interpretation'.[413] The 1994 Implementing Agreement is an example of such an agreement.[414] Subsequent practice, on the other hand, 'constitutes objective evidence of the understanding of the parties as to the meaning of the treaty'[415] and does not require opinio juris. A subsequent agreement is an agreement in which the parties elaborate on the interpretation or application of certain treaty provisions. However, subsequent practice under VCLT article 31(3)(b) 'consists of conduct in the application of a treaty, after its conclusion, which establishes the agreement of the parties regarding the interpretation of the treaty'.[416] Subsequent practice can also be relevant as supplementary means of interpretation under VCLT 32 if interpretation under article 31 leaves the provision ambiguous or obscure, or results in a manifestly absurd or unreasonable outcome.[417] The rules embodied in VCLT articles 31(3) and 32 reflect customary international law[418] and are, therefore, relevant for the interpretation of UNCLOS, regardless of the direct applicability of the VCLT.

The UNGA adopted the ILC's Draft conclusions on subsequent agreements and subsequent practice in relation to the interpretation of treaties in December 2018.[419] The UNGA Resolution confirms that subsequent measures can contribute to the clarification of a treaty. 'This may result in narrowing, widening, or otherwise

412 VCLT Article 31(3)(a) and (b).

413 GAOR, 'Report of the International Law Commission on the Work of the Second Part of Its Seventeenth Session' (3–28 January 1966) UN Doc A/6309/Rev.1, 221, para 14.

414 Alan Boyle (n 393) 570.

415 UN Doc A/6309/Rev.1 (n 413) para 15.

416 UNGA Res 73/202, 'Subsequent agreements and subsequent practice in relation to the interpretation of treaties' (20 December 2018), Conclusion 4.

417 GAOR, 'Report of the International Law Commission' (Sixty-eighth session, 2 May-10 June and 4 July–12 August 2016) UN Doc A/71/10, 125–126.

418 Ibid., Conclusion 2.

419 UNGA Res 73/202 (n 416).

determining the range of possible interpretations, including any scope for the exercise of discretion which the treaty accords to the parties.'[420] However, subsequent agreements and subsequent practice are only meant to interpret treaties, and it is important to note that subsequent practice is generally understood to be unable to amend or modify a treaty.[421] The ICJ has endorsed this view, finding that VCLT article 31(3)(b) cannot be used to give priority to State practice over treaty provisions or the absence of specific provisions.[422] After all, treaty interpretation is primarily based on the text of the treaty.[423] Still, according to Dörr, subsequent practice establishing an agreement on the interpretation of a treaty may 'override the original understanding of the text of the treaty, which prior to the subsequent developments may have appeared perfectly clear'. Such an understanding would have to be arrived at by consensus.[424]

Subsequent practice under VCLT article 31(3)(b) can take various forms. It relates to the conduct of States Parties in applying the treaty and includes, for example, official acts, statements and voting at the international level, national legislation and even inaction.[425] Moreover, subsequent agreements and subsequent practice under VCLT article 31(3) can take the form of binding treaties and soft law instruments, such as memoranda of understanding.[426]

An UNGA resolution, stating that baselines and/or outer maritime limits should be stable, notwithstanding subsequent changes to relevant coastlines, could constitute subsequent practice and be relevant for interpreting UNCLOS, as per VCLT article 31(3)(b). Similarly, an implementing agreement could direct UNCLOS States Parties to an interpretation of UNCLOS that stabilizes maritime limits. However, these methods could only be used to interpret UNCLOS, not to change it.[427] The fact that the ILC has categorized subsequent agreements and subsequent practice as 'authentic means of interpretation' does not 'imply that these means necessarily possess a conclusive, or legally binding, effect'.[428] They should only be taken into account in the 'single combined operation' that is treaty interpretation.[429] This is why the ILC would not say that interpretation in accordance with a subsequent agreement necessarily nullifies other means of interpretation.[430]

420 UNGA Res 73/202 (n 416), Conclusion 7(1).

421 Ibid., Conclusion 7(3).

422 *Land, Island and Maritime Frontier Dispute (El Salvador/Honduras: Nicaragua intervening)* (Judgment) [1992] ICJ Rep 351, para 380.

423 See, for example, *Territorial Dispute (Libyan Arab Jamahiriya/Chad)* (Judgment) [1994] ICJ Rep 6, para 41; *Legality of the Use of Force (Serbia and Montenegro* v. *Belgium)* (Preliminary Objections) [2004] ICJ Rep 279, para 100.

424 Oliver Dörr, 'Article 31. General Rule of Interpretation' in Oliver Dörr and Kirsten Schmalenbach (eds) *Vienna Convention on the Law of Treaties: A Commentary* (Springer, 2012) 521, 523.

425 UN Doc A/71/10 (n 417) 163–164.

426 Ibid., 164.

427 See ibid., 165.

428 Ibid., 133.

429 Ibid.

430 Ibid., 134.

The clarity and precision of subsequent agreements and subsequent practice have an impact on their relevance.[431] VCLT article 31(3) does not provide an exhaustive list and among other relevant aspects is the timing of a subsequent agreement or practice establishing an agreement.[432] The ICJ and arbitral tribunals have afforded more weight to subsequent practice that relates specifically to the interpretation of a treaty[433] and an UNGA resolution, clearly aimed at coordinating subsequent practice of UNCLOS member States, might well meet such requirements.

The ICJ considered the effect of subsequent practice on treaty interpretation in the *Whaling in the Antarctic* case. Australia argued that resolutions of the International Whaling Commission should affect the interpretation of Article VIII of the International Convention for the Regulation of Whaling under paragraphs (a) and (b) of VCLT article 31(3).[434] The article in question provides that lethal methods may be permissible in the conduct of scientific research but Australia and New Zealand maintained that aforementioned resolutions had limited its scope to instances were no non-lethal methods were available.[435] The Court rejected this contention and found that resolutions of the International Whaling Commission could not be afforded such legal significance for two reasons. First, because they had been 'adopted without the support of all States Parties to the Convention and, in particular, without the concurrence of Japan'.[436] Second, because the resolutions and guidelines that had been adopted by consensus did not prohibit the use of lethal methods when other options were available. They merely urged States to consider whether research objectives could be met with the use of non-lethal methods.[437] This decision indicates that soft-law instruments can shape treaty obligations but it also highlights the importance of unanimity in subsequent practice.

The ILC has confirmed the significance of the number of States involved in subsequent practice under VCLT article 31(3)(b). This may differ from one instance to another and '[s]ilence on the part of one or more parties can constitute acceptance of the subsequent practice when the circumstances call for some reaction'.[438] According to Sinclair, the weight given to subsequent practice 'depends on the extent to which it is concordant, common and consistent'.[439] Aust goes even further, explaining that the practice in question must be expressly or tacitly accepted by all States Parties to be relevant under VCLT article 31(3)(b).[440] Indeed, the decision of

431 Ibid., 122.
432 Ibid., 188.
433 Ibid., 189.
434 *Whaling in the Antarctic (Australia* v. *Japan: New Zealand intervening)* (Merits) [2014] ICJ Rep 226, para 79.
435 Ibid., paras 80–81.
436 Ibid., para 83.
437 Ibid.
438 Ibid., 122.
439 Ian Sinclair, *The Vienna Convention on the Law of Treaties*, 2nd edition (Manchester University Press, 1984) 137.
440 Anthony Aust, *Modern Treaty Law and Practice*, 2nd edition (Cambridge University Press, 2000) 194.

the ICJ in the *Whaling in the Antarctic* case suggests that an UNGA resolution might have to be approved by consensus in order to alter UNCLOS provisions.

The World Trade Organization (hereinafter WTO) Appellate Body has elaborated further on the number of States necessarily involved in subsequent practice and the evidence required for such practice. The Appellate Body has confirmed that '(i) there must be a common, consistent, discernible pattern of acts or pronouncements; and (ii) those acts or pronouncements must imply agreement on the interpretation of the relevant provision'.[441] Furthermore,

> in international law, the essence of subsequent practice in interpreting a treaty has been recognized as a 'concordant, common and consistent' sequence of acts or pronouncements which is sufficient to establish a discernible pattern implying the agreement of the parties regarding its interpretation. An isolated act is generally not sufficient to establish subsequent practice; it is a sequence of acts establishing the agreement of the parties that is relevant.[442]

The WTO Appellate Body has confirmed that a common and concordant practice necessitates more than a few examples from Member States.[443] For example, in *China – Measures Affecting the Protection and Enforcement of Intellectual Property Rights*, the Appellate Body concluded that policies of two Member States, coupled with a draft Directive and free trade agreements were insufficient.[444] Furthermore, in *EC – Chicken Cuts*, the WTO Appellate Body noted that, although it was not necessary that 'each and every party must have engaged in a particular practice for it to qualify as a "common" and "concordant" practice', it would be difficult to establish such a pattern based on the acts or statements of very few parties.[445] The Appellate Body also concluded that a lack of protest should not be regarded, on its own, as support of State practice.[446]

In view of the above, it may be asserted that subsequent practice concerning maritime limits would have to be very compelling to affect the interpretation of UNCLOS. Furthermore, sufficient evidence would have to be provided by the party invoking VCLT article 31(3). Negative votes would surely reduce the interpretative weight given to an UNGA resolution as establishing an agreement between the parties concerning the interpretation of UNCLOS. However, even without a large

441 WTO, *Appellate Body Report, US – Measures Affecting the Cross-border Supply of Gambling and Betting Services* (20 April 2005) WT/DS285/AB/R, para 192.

442 WTO, *Appellate Body Report, Japan – Taxes on Alcoholic Beverages* (1 November 1996) WT/DS8/AB/R, WT/DS10/AB/R, WT/DS11/AB/R, 97.

443 WTO, *Panel Report, EC – Tariff Classification of Certain Information Technology Products* (21 September 2010) WT/DS375/R, WT/DS376/R, WT/DS377/R, para 7.565.

444 WTO, *Panel Report, China – Measures Affecting the Protection and Enforcement of Intellectual Property Rights* (20 March 2009) WT/DS362/R, paras 7.580 and 7.581.

445 WTO, *Appellate Body Report, EC – Customs Classification of Frozen Boneless Chicken Cuts* (27 September 2005) WT/DS269/AB/R, WT/DS286/AB/R, para 259.

446 Ibid., para 272.

majority, an UNGA resolution might be relevant under VCLT article 32[447] and, consequently, qualify as supplementary means of interpretation.

2.5.3.4 Current State Practice

Maritime limits are often challenged as being inconsistent with international law. Several examples were given in Section 2.4.1, which was concerned with the criteria laid down by courts and tribunals regarding the establishment of maritime limits. This section, however, focuses on State practice that may be relevant for proposed changes to the law.

There are many recent examples of States challenging maritime limits on the basis of them not being generated by appropriate territory. For example, China has challenged maritime limits extending from Japan's Okinotorishima[448] and Mexico challenged the French exclusive economic zone limits extending from Clipperton Island.[449] Myanmar challenged an adjustment of maritime limits enacted by Bangladesh as not conforming to the ITLOS decision[450] and Egypt has challenged the allegedly excessive maritime limits of Palestine.[451] There are also recent examples of States updating their maritime limits, due to objections. For example, Australia has updated its charts and coordinates at least five times,[452] and Indonesia has updated its archipelagic baselines.[453] One of the changes made to the Indonesian baselines was a division of one long baseline into three segments to satisfy requirements of UNCLOS article 47(2). This caused a minimal landward shift of the baseline, reducing the extent of archipelagic waters.[454] Nicaragua has also modified its limits at least once following challenges from Colombia, Costa Rica and the United

447 UN Doc A/71/10 (n 417) 164.

448 See, for example, Note verbale, Permanent Mission of the People's Republic of China to the United Nations, notification regarding Japan's submission on the continental shelf beyond 200 nm to the Commission on the Limits of the Continental Shelf, No. CML/2/2009, available at www.un.org/depts/los/clcs_new/submissions_files/jpn08/chn_6feb09_e.pdf accessed 9 January 2021.

449 Yann-huei Song, 'The Application of Article 121 of the Law of the Sea Convention to the Selected Geographical Features Situated in the Pacific Ocean' (2010) 9 Chinese Journal of International Law, 663, 667–668.

450 DOALOS, 'Note verbale from the Permanent Mission of Myanmar to the United Nations addressed to the Secretary-General of the United Nations' (15 February 2019) LOS Bulletin 99, 41.

451 DOALOS, 'Note verbale from the Permanent Mission of Egypt to the United Nations addressed to the Division for Ocean Affairs and the Law of the Sea, Office of Legal Affairs of the United Nations' (31 December 2019) LOS Bulletin 102, 22.

452 Australian Government (Geoscience Australia), 'Australian Maritime Boundaries (AMB)', available at: www.ga.gov.au/webtemp/image_cache/GA7675.pdf accessed 16 January 2021, Section 2.5.

453 See Act no 6/1996 on Indonesian Waters.

454 Ashley Roach, 'Archipelagic States Practice: Update on Article 47 in Committee's final first report Archipelagic States Practice' (ILA Baselines Committee, 2017) para 78, referring to Clive Schofield and Andi Arsana 'Closing the Loop: Indonesia's Revised Archipelagic Baselines System' (2009) 1 (2) Australian Journal of Maritime and Ocean Affairs 57, 61–62.

States[455] and the United Kingdom abandoned its claim to an exclusive economic zone and continental shelf around Rockall in response to significant protests by Ireland.[456] These examples demonstrate that many States take interest in whether or not maritime limits conform to international law and some States update their limits accordingly. However, there is also recent State practice demonstrating the view that there is no obligation to adjust maritime limits to changes caused by sea level rise.[457]

In 2019, the ILC requested information of State practice relevant to the impact of sea level rise on maritime limits and boundaries. Several States responded and gave a clear indication of what they believe the effects of sea level rise on maritime entitlements are, or ought to be. These can be divided into two groups. The first one consists of States that reflect the understanding that baselines fluctuate. The United Kingdom belongs to this group as it has ambulatory baselines.[458] The Netherlands also has ambulatory baselines and relies on coastal defences to safeguard its maritime entitlements.[459] Syria and Qatar also seem to view baselines as ambulatory and are emphasizing physical reinforcement of their coasts as a response to sea level rise.[460]

Romania also has ambulatory baselines[461] and indicates that some modifications to coordinates of the maritime boundary may be necessary.[462] The United States confirms its understanding that baselines are generally ambulatory under UNCLOS and the corresponding customary international law. Moreover, the United States have a baseline committee that addresses shifts in the coastline of 500 metres or more, and it enacts changes to the baselines, closing lines and outer maritime limits, where relevant.[463] According to the United States, bilateral boundaries are unaffected by sea level rise, and it endorses efforts to stabilize maritime limits through coastal reinforcement and the adoption of boundary treaties.[464] Finally, Singapore remarks that it defends its coastlines with protective works, such as sea

455 DOALOS, 'Nicaragua: Presidential Decree No. 17–2018, Decree of Reform to Decree No. 33 2013, "Baselines of the Maritime Spaces of the Republic of Nicaragua in the Caribbean Sea"' (10 October 2018) LOS Bulletin 99, 2019, 36.

456 Clive Schofield and David Freestone, 'Options to Protect Coastlines and Secure Maritime Jurisdictional Claims in the Face of Global Sea Level Rise' in Michael Gerrard and Gregory Wannier (eds) *Threatened Island Nations: Legal Implications of Rising Seas and a Changing Climate* (Cambridge University Press, 2013) 141, 147.

457 See, for example, DOALOS, 'Observations by the Federated States of Micronesia in connection with the official deposit of its lists of geographical points of coordinates, accompanied by illustrative maps, for maritime baselines and maritime zones in accordance with the 1982 United Nations Convention on the Law of the Sea' (dated 15 January 2020) LOS Bulletin 102, 26.

458 See UK Territorial Sea (Baselines) Order 2014, available at: www.legislation.gov.uk/uksi/2014/1353/contents/made accessed 8 January 2021.

459 UN Doc A/CN.4/740 (n 77) para 88.

460 Ibid., para 87.

461 Law no 17/1990 concerning the Legal Regime of the Internal Waters, the Territorial Sea and the Contiguous Zone of Romania Article 2(3).

462 UN Doc A/CN.4/740 (n 77) para 88.

463 Ibid.

464 Ibid., para 97.

walls and dykes, and that it has concluded boundary agreements to fix its maritime boundaries.[465] One of those agreements states that '[t]here shall be no alteration to the territorial waters boundary'.[466]

The second group of States consists of those opposing the theory of ambulatory baselines. The Maldives is among those States, and one with particular interest in this issue as it is a low-lying archipelago. It asserts that 'once a State has determined the extent of its maritime entitlements in accordance with UNCLOS and deposited the appropriate charts and/or geographic coordinates with the UN Secretary-General, as the Maldives has done, these entitlements are fixed and will not be altered by any subsequent physical changes to a States' geography as a result of sea-level rise'.[467] Still, the Maldives is also reinforcing the coast because it is committed to preserving not only its maritime entitlements but also its territory.[468]

It is also relevant to note that the Maldives considers all bilateral boundaries to be permanently stable and not subject to termination due to sea level rise.[469] The archipelagic status of the Maldives is confirmed in the State's constitution.[470] The coordinates of archipelagic base points are firmly established in domestic legislation[471] and duly published in accordance with UNCLOS article 47.[472] Micronesia also notes that it is particularly vulnerable to the effects of sea level rise and submits the understanding that is not obligated to update its maritime limits once duly published.[473]

The Pacific Island Forum jointly submitted to the ILC information about their State practice and special considerations. The Forum notes that climate change has particularly severe consequences for low-lying island States and their maritime entitlements, although these States bear little responsibility for climate change. It further explains that this is an inequitable outcome, that preservation of maritime entitlements is essential for these States, and goes on to list arguments in support of an interpretation making duly published limits and bilateral boundaries stable.[474] The Forum notes increased efforts, in the region, towards establishing final continental shelf limits beyond 200 nm; concluding boundary agreements; and a recent shift from reliance upon charts, in maritime boundary agreements, to the specification of geographic coordinates.[475]

465 Ibid., para 87.

466 Agreement between the Government of Malaysia and the Government of the Republic of Singapore to Delimit Precisely the Territorial Waters Boundary in Accordance with the Straits Settlements and Johore Territorial Waters Agreement 1927, article 2.

467 UN Doc A/CN.4/740 (n 77) para 84.

468 Ibid.

469 Ibid., para 122.

470 Constitution of the Republic of Maldives 2008. Section 3 (Annex II).

471 Law Number 6/96 (Maritime Zones Act of the Maldives) Ibid., Annex III and Schedule 1.

472 See DOALOS, 'Maldives: Maritime Zones of Maldives Act No 6/96' LOS Bulletin 41, 16.

473 UN Doc A/CN.4/740 (n 77) para 85.

474 Ibid., para 86.

475 Ibid.

This information submitted to the ILC demonstrates that several important naval States adhere to the ambulatory baselines theory while particularly vulnerable States object to it. Some strong arguments are presented, particularly supporting the interpretation that bilateral boundaries are stable and not subject to termination due to a fundamental change of circumstances. However, arguments against the theory of ambulatory baselines are primarily vested in principles of stability and equity and the proposition that vulnerable States have a better chance of changing the law than protecting their coastlines through artificial means. Still, the ILC has detected strong support from other States in favour of ensuring the right to maintain stable baselines and outer maritime limits.[476] Thus, many States seem willing to change the relevant international law, if necessary. However, as demonstrated in earlier sections, the conditions for change are strict and according to the ILC, more State practice is needed to enable an assessment of the *opinio juris*.[477]

2.5.4 *Extent to Which Existing Rules Can Be Altered through Subsequent Practice*

UNCLOS can be altered through articles 312–316 or an implementing agreement. There are no limits to the extent of such changes, except for those contained in UNCLOS article 311(2), (3) and (6). Likewise, there are no restrictions on the extent to which a subsequent rule of customary international law may modify a treaty, although, as previously explained, such rules may not be able to override the constitution of the oceans. However, there are limits on the extent to which treaties can be altered by subsequent practice because such practice can only affect the interpretation of existing provisions, not rewrite them.

The draft convention on the law of treaties originally contained an article that would have expressly permitted the modification of a treaty through subsequent practice. It was highly contentious[478] and ultimately rejected with 53 votes to 15 and 26 abstentions.[479] Commentators have argued that the decision not to explicitly recognize modification through subsequent practice does not exclude the possibility.[480] However, this finds limited support in international jurisprudence, according to the ILC.[481] As previously mentioned: 'The possibility of amending or

476 Ibid., para 89.

477 Ibid., para 104(i).

478 See United Nations Conference on the Law of Treaties 'First Session' (26 March–24 May 1968) UN Doc A/CONF.39/11, 207–215.

479 UN Doc A/71/10 (n 417) 175.

480 Ibid., 175, referring to, for example, Ian Sinclair (n 439) 138; Richard Gardiner, *Treaty Interpretation*, 2nd edition (Oxford University Press, 2015) 275–280; Anthony Aust (n 440) 213; Mark Villiger, Commentary on the 1969 Vienna Convention on the Law of Treaties (Martinus Nijhoff, 2009) 432, para 23; Oliver Dörr (n 424) 555, para 76; Malcolm Shaw, *International Law*, 6th edition (Cambridge University Press, 2008), 934.

481 See UN Doc A/71/10 (n 417) 175.

modifying a treaty by subsequent practice of the parties has not been generally recognized.'[482]

The ICJ has never concluded that subsequent practice modified a treaty. Still, it has gone beyond the ordinary meaning of treaty provisions, opted for broad interpretations and done so by reference to subsequent practice of the parties.[483] Indeed, 'the dividing line between the interpretation and the amendment or modification of a treaty is in practice sometimes "difficult, if not impossible, to fix"'.[484] Nonetheless, it would jeopardize the stability of treaty relations if subsequent practice could modify treaties.[485] Therefore, this possibility must not be presumed.

VCLT article 31(3) can lead to a narrower or broader interpretation of UNCLOS provisions or support any other plausible reading of its provisions.[486] This range of possibilities then marks the extent to which a treaty can be modified by reference to subsequent agreements or subsequent practice. Vague or ambiguous treaty provisions can leave more room for interpretation and the same is true of provisions that afford discretion to the member States. The range of possible interpretations can be broad and, therefore, subsequent practice can lead to significant revisions. For example, the 1944 Convention on International Civil Aviation was, with reference to subsequent practice, interpreted so as to require prior permission for landing, although no such requirement is stipulated in the treaty.[487]

The UNCLOS provisions that would be affected by the proposed changes are in some cases flexible. For example, UNCLOS article 76(9) might apply to all outer continental shelf limits, including those at 200 nm from baselines, and UNCLOS article 7(2) might not entail an obligation but an option to adjust straight baselines on highly unstable coastlines, at the discretion of each coastal State. Likewise, it is open to interpretation whether UNCLOS articles 47, 75 and 84 entail an obligation to update charts or lists of coordinates when circumstances change. These provisions can certainly be clarified through subsequent practice of UNCLOS member States. However, the provisions concerning maximum breadth of maritime zones and

482 Ibid., 122.

483 See in particular *Legal Consequences for States of the Continued Presence of South Africa in Namibia (South West Africa) notwithstanding Security Council Resolution 276 (1970)* (Advisory Opinion) [1971] ICJ Rep 16, para 53.

484 UN Doc A/71/10 (n 417) 176, referring to Ian Sinclair (n 439) 138; Richard Gardiner (n 480) 275; Sean Murphy, 'The Relevance of Subsequent Agreement and Subsequent Practice for the Interpretation of Treaties' in Georg Nolte (ed) *Treaties and Subsequent Practice* (Oxford University Press, 2013) 82, 90; Bruno Simma, 'Miscellaneous Thoughts on Subsequent Agreements and Practice' in Georg Nolte (*op cit*) 46; Wolfram Karl, *Vertrag und spätere Praxis im Völkerrecht* (Springer, 1983) 42–43; Jean-Marc Sorel and Valérie Boré Eveno, '1969 Vienna Convention, Article 31: General Rule of Interpretation' in Olivier Corten and Pierre Klein (eds) The Vienna Conventions on the Law of Treaties: A Commentary (Oxford University Press, 2011) 804, 825, para 42; Oliver Dörr (n 424) 555, para 76.

485 Ibid., 180.

486 See UNGA Res 73/202 (n 416), Conclusion 7(1).

487 Sean Murphy (n 484) 85; Anthony Aust (n 440) 215.

requirements for baselines are crystal clear and so are the provisions guaranteeing other States rights to areas beyond those limits.

UNCLOS article 311(3) provides that while States can modify or suspend the operation of UNCLOS provisions through bilateral or multilateral agreements, such agreements may never affect the application of the basic principles embodied in the Convention or the rights or obligations of States not party to such arrangements. UNCLOS article 311(6) further explains the primacy of basic principles and prohibits any amendment or derogation from the common heritage of mankind principle. This prohibition is more general than that of article 311(3) insofar as it refers to any amendment and is not limited to bilateral or multilateral agreements. However, it is explicitly tied to the common heritage of mankind principle. Thus, paragraph 6 precludes any amendment to the common heritage of mankind principle through any means while paragraph 3 arguably precludes derogation from the land dominates the sea principle on the basis of bilateral or multilateral agreements. The latter does not preclude a modification of the land dominates the sea principle through an amendment of UNCLOS but it does suggest that changes to the application of any of the basic principles are a matter of great severity.

The freezing of maritime limits arguably affects the application of three basic principles of UNCLOS. Namely, the principles of the common heritage of mankind, freedom of the high seas and the land dominates the sea principle. The first two principles are codified in UNCLOS.[488] The freedom of the high seas applies in the water column beyond 200 nm of baselines[489] and the common heritage of mankind principle governs the use of resources in the seabed and subsoil beyond national jurisdiction.[490] If baselines or outer limits are frozen, these principles will govern a smaller portion of the world's oceans, seabed and subsoil, than currently prescribed by UNCLOS. This would arguably affect the principles' sphere of application without constituting a fundamental deviation from the principles. It might be assimilated to the modifications enacted by pre-existing implementing agreements, and consequently be admissible.

The land dominates the sea principle is reflected in several UNCLOS provisions. It is never explicitly mentioned but enshrined in Article 2(1) of the Convention which states that sovereignty of coastal States extends from land territory and internal waters to the adjacent belt of territorial sea. This is the fundamental norm for all maritime zone under national jurisdiction.[491] Indeed, all maritime entitlements are generated by the coastal front[492] or individual coastal features.[493] Inner limits of

488 See, for example, UNCLOS articles 87 and 136.

489 UNCLOS articles 86 and 87.

490 UNCLOS articles 1(1) and 136.

491 Vladimir Ibler, 'Jus Cogens and the Law of the Sea' in Marcelo Kohen (ed) *Promoting Justice, Human Rights and Conflict Resolution through International Law* (Brill, 2007) 747, 761–763.

492 See, for example, *Tunisia/Libyan Arab Jamahiriya* (n 178) para 73.

493 UNCLOS articles 7(4), 13 and 121.

these entitlements are dependent upon coastal geography[494] and so are the outer limits.[495] Maritime boundaries are also constructed by reference to coastal geography[496] and the ICJ has relied on this principle in numerous decisions.[497] The freezing of maritime limits through subsequent agreement, custom or practice, might be seen as a violation of this principle, and consequently inconsistent with UNCLOS article 311(3).

2.6 SUMMARY

This chapter has explained how baselines, and outer maritime limits derived therefrom, fluctuate in accordance with changes to coastal geography to continuously meet the requirements of UNCLOS. In theory, all maritime limits (with the exception of straight baselines along highly unstable coastlines and permanently stable continental shelf limits) fluctuate as a direct consequence of changes to the low-water mark along relevant coastlines or coastal features. However, maritime limits are generally identified by reference to officially recognized large-scale charts or information submitted to the UNSG. This assumes positive action by coastal States in updating maritime limits. States may in some instances delay the fluctuation of their maritime limits by relying on outdated charts or lists of coordinates and enforcing their rights accordingly. There is no automatic surveillance that ensures that maritime limits are immediately updated when coastal geography changes.

Unilateral maritime limits are only opposable to other States if they are consistent with international law. Consequently, non-conforming maritime limits may be challenged and disputes concerning the validity of maritime limits are subject to mandatory dispute settlement under UNCLOS. Officially recognized charts or submissions to the UNSG are usually the first point of reference for identifying the location of maritime limits. However, where these sources no longer reflect the low-water mark or still valid base points, courts and tribunals may instead refer to the actual low-water mark. Therefore, the charted line is constitutive of the legally valid baseline, but it is abandoned and substituted with the actual low-water line if inconsistent with international law.

Ambulatory maritime limits may cause friction in international relations. Changing coastal geography has already given rise to numerous challenges and these may lead to a growing number of international disputes. Entitlements can be preserved with coast protective works. This method of preserving maritime entitlements creates a discrepancy between States that have the resources to artificially conserve their coastlines and those that do not. Therefore, more economically viable

494 See UNLOS article 5, 7 and 47.

495 See UNCLOS articles 3, 33, 48, 57 and 76.

496 See Section 3.3.

497 See, for example, *North Sea Continental Shelf* (n 13) para 96; *Tunisia/Libyan Arab Jamahiriya* (n 178) para 73; *Maritime Delimitation in the Black Sea* (n 165) para 77.

methods have been proposed with the purpose of freezing all maritime limits and promoting peace, stability, certainty and predictability in ocean governance.

Existing rules can be altered to stabilize baselines and/or outer maritime limits. The freezing of baselines might be achieved with formal amendments to UNCLOS, development of overriding customary international law or through revised interpretation of UNCLOS, by reference to subsequent practice. The last option is arguably most feasible of the three. State practice is still divided on important points but States have been encouraged to derogate from generally accepted interpretation of UNCLOS. However, those efforts to prevent loss of maritime entitlements arguably threaten the stability of the legal order of the oceans and present a departure from its most fundamental principle.

The new geographical order is one of instability and laws regulating maritime claims should adapt to the instability of nature.[498] Existing international law can accommodate impending changes by obligating States to gradually change their maritime limits and the option of freezing certain limits with artificial constructions. This is disadvantageous for poorer States that are unable to protect their coastlines, but it strikes a balance between the desired stability for maritime limits and the increasing instability of nature. The alternative is to change or reinterpret existing rules to create judicial, instead of factual, stability around increasingly unstable coastlines. However, such measures only provide temporary solutions because the complete inundation of territory will eventually affect maritime entitlements.

While changing coastal geography makes previously acceptable baselines and base points unopposable, agreed or judicially decided maritime boundaries remain stable and enforceable. This is true even if they are constructed on the basis of baselines or base points that subsequently fluctuate. Baselines and outer maritime limits may fluctuate within the confines of a stable maritime boundary without having any effect on the location of the boundary. This means that changing coastlines bring about a discrepancy between maritime limits and maritime boundaries – while unilateral limits continue to reflect relevant coastal geography, the correlation between relevant coastlines and bilateral boundaries is lost when coastlines change. Maritime boundaries may become redundant when maritime limits recede so far back that the boundaries no longer delimit overlapping entitlements and they may potentially be terminated when fundamental changes affect the essential basis of the underlying agreements.[499] However, such eventualities may be averted if coastal instability is considered when boundaries are delimited, that is, if foreseeable fluctuations of maritime entitlements have an effect on maritime boundary delimitation.

498 See Davor Vidas, 'Sea-Level Rise and International Law: At the Convergence of Two Epochs' (2014) 4 Climate law 83.

499 See Section 5.4.

3

Maritime Delimitation and Coastal Instability

3.1 INTRODUCTION

States with overlapping maritime entitlements are obliged to delimit maritime boundaries.[1] Maritime boundaries must be effected by agreements, and, if States fail to agree, their maritime boundaries are settled through compulsory dispute settlement: arbitration, adjudication or conciliation.[2] Maritime delimitation differs from maritime delineation insofar as it produces bilateral boundaries, as opposed to unilateral limits. Agreed or adjudicated boundaries are of a permanent nature because they are safeguarded by the principles pacta sunt servanda (protecting the sanctity of treaty obligations) and res judicata (preventing the revision of adjudicated boundaries). Furthermore, UNCLOS article 296(1) provides that any decision rendered by a court or tribunal with jurisdiction under the compulsory dispute settlement regime of UNCLOS shall be final and complied with by all the parties to the dispute.

No method of maritime delimitation is obligatory in all circumstances. UNCLOS article 15, which deals with delimitation of the territorial sea, refers to a method of delimitation commonly known as the equidistance/special circumstances method. Failing an agreement to the contrary, the territorial sea is delimited on the basis of the equidistance method. However, an equidistance line may be abandoned or adjusted, by reference to special circumstances or historic title, to ensure an equitable solution.[3] UNCLOS articles 74 and 83, which govern the delimitation of the exclusive economic zone and the continental shelf, obligate States to achieve an equitable solution on the basis of international law but make no explicit reference to a delimitation method. The applicable international law requires consideration of all relevant circumstances and it is on the basis of those circumstances that a delimitation method is selected.[4]

[1] See UNCLOS articles 15, 74 and 83.

[2] See UNCLOS articles 15, 74, 83, 286 and 287(1). Note, however, that maritime boundary delimitation may be excluded from mandatory dispute settlement under UNCLOS article 298(1)(a)(i).

[3] *Delimitation of the Maritime Boundary between Bangladesh and Myanmar in the Bay of Bengal (Bangladesh/Myanmar)* (Judgment) [2012] ITLOS, 51 ILM 844, para 151; *Bay of Bengal Maritime Boundary Arbitration (Bangladesh v. India)* (2014) 167 ILR 1, para 272.

[4] *Continental Shelf (Tunisia/Libyan Arab Jamahiriya)* (Judgment) [1982] ICJ Rep 18, para 110.

Courts and tribunals have shown a preference for the equidistance/relevant circumstances method of delimitation. They generally start with a provisional equidistance line and subsequently adjust it by reference to relevant circumstances.[5] This method can lead to inequitable results and different methods may be justified.[6] The equidistance method does not have automatic priority over other methods of delimitation,[7] and it should never be applied mechanically[8] to the detriment of a proper consideration of all relevant circumstances.

Maritime entitlements are generated by the coastal front.[9] Therefore, coastal geography is fundamental to maritime boundary delimitation.[10] Maritime boundaries have been delimited by reference to changing coastlines.[11] However, courts and tribunals have also rejected the relevance of foreseeable changes to coastal geography,[12] partly to defuse potential threats to the stability of previously settled boundaries.[13] Such efforts are understandable but they do not justify derogation from existing rules governing maritime boundary delimitation and the delimitation of unsettled boundaries has no direct effect on previously settled boundaries. Moreover, the quest for peace and stability may be better served by constructing boundaries with due regard for imminent changes so that the boundaries can remain equitable and unchallenged as circumstances change. This would extend the correlation between maritime boundaries and lawful entitlements, and, thus, promote peaceful relations. After all, 'good fences make good neighbours'.[14]

This chapter explores the relevance of changing coastal geography for maritime delimitation and explains how coastal instability can affect the delimitation process.

3.2 MARITIME DELIMITATION

States must cooperate in delimiting overlapping maritime entitlements. They must negotiate in good faith 'with the genuine intention of achieving a positive

5 See, for example, *Bangladesh/Myanmar* (n 3) para 238.

6 See, for example, *Tunisia/Libyan Arab Jamahiriya* (n 4) paras 109, 110; Continental Shelf (Libyan Arab Jamahiriya/Malta) (Judgment) [1985] ICJ Rep 13, paras 60–64; *Territorial and Maritime Dispute between Nicaragua and Honduras in the Caribbean Sea (Nicaragua* v. *Honduras)* (Judgment) [2007] ICJ Rep 659, para 287.

7 *Nicaragua* v. *Honduras* (n 6) para 272.

8 *Territorial and Maritime Dispute (Nicaragua* v. *Colombia)* (Judgment) [2012] ICJ Rep 624, para 194.

9 See *Libyan Arab Jamahiriya/Malta* (n 6) 30, paras 27 and 61; *North Sea Continental Shelf (Federal Republic of Germany/Netherlands) (Federal Republic of Germany/Denmark)* (Judgment) [1969] ICJ Rep 3, para 96; *Tunisia/Libyan Arab Jamahiriya* (n 4) para 74; *Delimitation of the Maritime Boundary in the Gulf of Maine Area (Canada/United States)* (Judgment) [1984] ICJ Rep 246, (n 248) para 205.

10 See, for example, *Land and Maritime Boundary between Cameroon and Nigeria (Cameroon* v. *Nigeria: Equatorial Guinea intervening)* (Judgment) [2002] ICJ Rep 303, para 295.

11 See, for example, *Nicaragua* v. *Honduras* (n 6) para 277; Agreement between the Government of the French Republic and the Government of the Kingdom of Belgium on the delimitation of the continental shelf (adopted 8 October 1990, entered into force 7 April 1993) 32 ILM 1068, article 2.

12 See *Anglo-French Continental Shelf (United Kingdom/France)* (1977) XVIII RIAA 3; *Bangladesh* v. *India* (n 3) para 217.

13 Ibid., para 217.

14 Robert Frost, *The Mending Wall* (David Nutt, 1914).

result'.[15] Whenever an agreement cannot be reached recourse is had to the dispute settlement mechanisms provided for in UNCLOS Part XV, which can entail binding settlement by a court or tribunal.[16] States may exclude maritime boundary delimitation from compulsory dispute settlement. However, they are still obligated to subject such disputes to conciliation at the request of either party, if they fail to agree otherwise within a reasonable period of time.[17]

Different rules apply when delimiting maritime boundaries, depending on the maritime zone in question. The equidistance method is the default method for delimiting the territorial sea[18] but delimitation of the exclusive economic zone and the continental shelf need not necessarily be effected by the equidistance method.[19] Courts and tribunals often establish single-purpose boundaries delimiting all relevant maritime zones, insofar as they are coincident.[20] Thus, overlapping claims to maritime zones can be delimited with one line, which marks the seaward extent of all maritime zones that reach as far as the boundary. The ICJ has confirmed that where it is tasked with the delimitation of a single maritime boundary, 'the so-called equitable principles/relevant circumstances method may usefully be applied, as in these maritime zones this method is also suited to achieving an equitable result'.[21]

'[T]he concept of a single maritime boundary does not stem from multilateral treaty law but from State practice, and [...] it finds its explanation in the wish of States to establish one uninterrupted boundary line delimiting the various – partially coincident – zones of maritime jurisdiction appertaining to them.'[22] The construction of single-purpose boundaries has been generally accepted and widely practiced since first employed in the *Gulf of Maine* case in 1984.[23] However, the application of international law can have different results for different maritime zones, resulting in different boundaries.[24] For example, certain circumstances that are relevant for exclusive economic zone delimitation may be irrelevant for delimitation of the continental shelf, and vice versa. Therefore, maritime boundaries of different maritime zones can be conceptually different, even where the locations of the

15 *Gulf of Maine* (n 9) para 112(1).

16 Whatever forum is applicable under UNCLOS article 287(1).

17 See UNCLOS article 298(1)(a)(i). The provision further provides 'that any dispute that necessarily involves the concurrent consideration of any unsettled dispute concerning sovereignty or other rights over continental or insular land territory shall be excluded from such submission'.

18 Failing agreement to the contrary, special circumstances or historic title justifying derogation from equidistance, see UNCLOS article 15.

19 *Bangladesh* v. *India* (n 3) 104.

20 See, for example, *Maritime Delimitation and Territorial Questions between Qatar and Bahrain (Qatar* v. *Bahrain)* (Merits) [2001] ICJ Rep 40, paras 173–174; *Nicaragua* v. *Honduras* (n 6) 739–740.

21 ILC, 'Summary Record of the 3016th Meeting' (7 July 2009) UN Doc A/CN.4/3016, 122, para 24–25, referring to *Nicaragua* v. *Honduras* (n 6) para 271.

22 *Qatar* v. *Bahrain* (n 20) para 173.

23 See *Gulf of Maine* (n 9) 252.

24 Thomas Cottier, *Equitable Principles of Maritime Boundary Delimitation: The Quest for Distributive Justice in International Law* (Cambridge University Press, 2015) 218.

boundaries coincide.[25] Moreover, the equidistance method may be applicable for delimitation of the territorial sea while another method is required for delimitation of the exclusive economic zone and the continental shelf. Consequently, certain circumstances may call for different boundaries delimiting the territorial sea, the exclusive economic zone and the continental shelf, which means that single-purpose boundaries are not suitable in all cases.

The following sections explore the different rules governing maritime delimitation under UNCLOS.

3.2.1 *Delimitation of the Territorial Sea: The Equidistance Method*

Delimitation of the territorial sea is governed by UNCLOS article 15:

> Where the coasts of two States are opposite or adjacent to each other, neither of the two States is entitled, failing agreement between them to the contrary, to extend its territorial sea beyond the median line every point of which is equidistant from the nearest points on the baselines from which the breadth of the territorial seas of each of the two States is measured. The above provision does not apply, however, where it is necessary by reason of historic title or other special circumstances to delimit the territorial seas of the two States in a way which is at variance therewith.

UNCLOS article 15 codifies the customary equidistance/special circumstances rule.[26] The equidistance method is the only method explicitly referred to in UNCLOS, and the 1958 Conventions, and most maritime boundaries incorporate the equidistance method.[27]

The equidistance/special circumstances method essentially involves drawing a boundary midway between the coasts of two opposite or adjacent States. Base points are identified on each State's coastline and a boundary line is constructed at an equal distance from the nearest points along each State's coastline.[28] After a provisional boundary line is constructed on the basis of valid base points, special circumstances are examined to determine whether the equidistance line must be adjusted.[29] An equidistance line can be modified by reference to special circumstances or historic title, but these factors can also justify derogation from the

25 *Maritime Delimitation in the Area between Greenland and Jan Mayen (Denmark* v. *Norway)* (Judgment) [1993] ICJ Rep 38, 56–57.

26 *Qatar* v. *Bahrain* (n 20) para 176.

27 Approximately 89 per cent of maritime boundary agreements concluded between opposite coastal states are based on some form of equidistance and around 38 per cent of agreements between adjacent states. See Clive Schofield, 'Parting the Waves: Claims to Maritime Jurisdiction and the Division of Ocean Space' (2012) 1 Penn State Journal of Law and International Affairs 54, referencing Leonard Legault and Blair Hankey, 'Method, Oppositeness and Adjacency, and Proportionality in Maritime Boundary Delimitation' in Jonathan Charney and Lewis Alexander (eds) *International Maritime Boundaries, volume 1* (Martinus Nijhoff, 1993) 203.

28 *Qatar* v. *Bahrain* (n 20) para 177.

29 Ibid., para 176.

equidistance method altogether when delimiting the territorial sea. For example, the ICJ decided not to apply the equidistance method when delimiting the territorial sea in *Nicaragua* v. *Honduras* because of special circumstances.[30] The Court found that '[n]othing in the wording of article 15 suggests that [. . .] "special circumstances" may only be used as a corrective element to a line already drawn' and that jurisprudence did not contradict this interpretation.[31]

UNCLOS article 15 is identical to article 12(1) of the 1958 Convention on the Territorial Sea and the Contiguous Zone, and article 6 of the Convention on the Continental Shelf, except for minor editorial changes. The drafters of those earlier provisions assumed that some types of coasts might call for different methods.[32] Indeed, the arbitral tribunal in the *Anglo/French Continental Shelf* case asserted that the condition relating to special circumstances in article 6 of the Convention on the Continental Shelf was added because 'owing to particular geographical features or configurations, application of the equidistance principle might not infrequently result in an unreasonable or inequitable delimitation of the continental shelf'.[33] The tribunal went on to say that the safety valve of special circumstances should ensure an equitable solution.[34]

Where no territorial sea boundary has been delimited, neither State may extend its territorial sea beyond the median line. Thus, the median line represents a default boundary for the territorial sea, one which cannot be crossed by either party, unless, and until, so agreed. States may agree to divert from applicable law when delimiting their maritime boundaries,[35] and in so doing they may abandon the equidistance line. However, when delimited by courts and tribunals on the basis of UNCLOS article 15 or customary international law, the applicable method is always the equidistance method, and any variance from a strict equidistance line must be justified by reference to special circumstances or historic title.[36]

The equidistance method was deemed to be a suitable method for delimitation of the territorial sea in ordinary circumstances but other methods may be more suitable when delimiting larger maritime zones.[37] In fact, different rules apply for delimitation of the exclusive economic zone and the continental shelf.

30 *Nicaragua* v. *Honduras* (n 6) para 281.
31 Ibid., para 280.
32 Ibid., para 280, referring to ILC, 'Documents of the Fourth Session Including the Report of the Commission to the General Assembly' (6 June 1952) UN Doc A/CN.4/SER.A/1952/Add.l, 38, para 4.
33 *Anglo-French Continental Shelf* (n 12) para 70.
34 Ibid.
35 Bjarni Magnússon, 'Outer Continental Shelf Boundary Agreements', (2013) 62 (02) International and Comparative Law Quarterly 345, 350.
36 *Qatar* v. *Bahrain* (n 20) para 176.
37 *Gulf of Maine* (n 9) para 160.

3.2.2 Delimitation of the Exclusive Economic Zone and the Continental Shelf

UNCLOS article 74(1) governs the delimitation of exclusive economic zone boundaries and UNCLOS article 83(1) applies to the delimitation of continental shelf boundaries. Both provisions are identical, except that where the former refers to the exclusive economic zone, the latter refers to the continental shelf. Delimitation of the exclusive fisheries zone is not explicitly governed by UNCLOS but the ICJ has held that the customary law enshrined in UNCLOS article 74 also applies to delimitation of an exclusive fisheries zone.[38] The provisions provide the following:

> The delimitation of the [exclusive economic zone/continental shelf] between States with opposite or adjacent coasts shall be effected by agreement on the basis of international law, as referred to in Article 38 of the Statute of the International Court of Justice, in order to achieve an equitable solution.

These provisions are less explicit than UNCLOS article 15, which refers to the equidistance method. The reason is that State representatives were unable to agree on one applicable method of delimitation for the exclusive economic zone and continental shelf. One group of States wished to base the delimitation on equidistance while the other group advocated for an obligation to apply equitable principles.[39] Therefore, instead of making one method obligatory for all instances of exclusive economic zone and continental shelf boundary delimitation, UNCLOS articles 74(1) and 83(1) refer to the applicable law as it may evolve through State practice and judicial settlement. In light of this, it must be concluded that the interpretation of UNCLOS articles 74(1) and 83(1) may change over time.

Despite a degree of flexibility, these provisions carry three clear obligations. First, maritime boundaries delimiting exclusive economic zone and continental shelf boundaries must be effected by agreements between coastal States with overlapping maritime entitlements. Second, these agreements must be established on the basis of international law, as referred to in article 38 of the ICJ Statute. Third, this process must result in an equitable solution. The first requirement is fairly straightforward: States must agree on a boundary to delimit any overlapping entitlements. However, the requirement that the delimitation be effected by an agreement does not necessitate that States reach an agreement, only that negotiations are conducted in good faith.[40] The obligation to agree on a boundary is merely a preliminary obligation and if agreement cannot be reached, an equitable boundary must still be delimited on the basis of international law.[41] This can entail conciliation or judicial settlement.[42]

38 *Denmark* v. *Norway* (n 25) para 47.

39 Myron Nordquist (ed) *United Nations Convention on the Law of the Sea 1982 – A Commentary, volume 2* (Martinus Nijhoff, 1993) 801 and 954.

40 *Maritime Delimitation in the Indian Ocean (Somalia* v. *Kenya)* (Preliminary Objections) [2017] ICJ Rep 1, para 90 referring to *Cameroon* v. *Nigeria: Equatorial Guinea intervening* (n 10) para 244.

41 Jonathan Charney, 'Progress in International Maritime Boundary Delimitation Law' (1994) 88 (2) American Journal of International Law 227, 254.

42 See UNCLOS article 298(1)(a).

The second requirement calls for an analysis of the applicable international law, and the third requirement can only be explained by first examining the term 'equitable solution' and possible methods for achieving such solutions under the applicable international law. The following sections will address these issues by discussing, first, the applicable international law; second, equitable solutions in the context of maritime boundary delimitation; and, third, the application of these rules through different methods of delimitation.

3.2.2.1 Applicable International Law

Article 38 of the ICJ Statute lists the sources of international law, relevant for equitable maritime delimitation. These are (a) treaty obligations; (b) customary international law; (c) general principles of law; and (d) as subsidiary means for determination of the rules of law, judicial decisions and teachings of the most highly qualified publicists. Therefore, UNCLOS articles 74 and 83 require that equitable maritime boundaries conform to UNCLOS and other applicable treaties, rights of third States, customary international law, general principles, judicial decisions and scholarly works.[43] In fact, the relevant applicable law is primarily manifested in two sources of law: custom and jurisprudence.[44]

UNCLOS articles 74 and 83 do not make one method mandatory in all cases. Instead, the provisions incorporate those methods that may be applicable under international law under the developing jurisprudence and customary international law. Maritime boundary agreements are not the best source to identify the applicable customary law because State practice often contradicts relevant jurisprudence.[45] After all, States may agree to divert from customary international law when negotiating maritime boundaries[46] and State practice cannot make customary international law without *opinio juris*.[47] A better source to identify the applicable international law is the decisions of courts and tribunals.[48]

International law governing equitable maritime delimitation is largely judge made. As confirmed by the ICJ in *Nicaragua* v. *Colombia*, the customary international law relevant for delimitation of the continental shelf is 'reflected in the case

43 See Thomas Cottier (n 24) 223.

44 See, for example, *Bangladesh* v. *India* (n 3) para 339; *Bangladesh/Myanmar* (n 3) paras 183 and 184; *Delimitation of the Exclusive Economic Zone and the Continental Shelf (Barbados* v. *Trinidad and Tobago)* (2006) XXVII RIAA 147, para 223.

45 Maritime boundaries negotiated by States often refer to economic or environmental considerations and exploitation of fish stocks or minerals but courts and tribunals have generally not considered such circumstances to be relevant for maritime boundary delimitation. See Barbara Kwiatkowska, 'Economic and Environmental Considerations in Maritime Boundary Delimitations' in Jonathan Charney and Lewis Alexander (n 27) 75, 75–76.

46 See, for example, Bjarni Magnússon (n 35) 350; Jonathan Charney and Lewis Alexander (n 27) 11.

47 Thomas Cottier (n 24) 377.

48 The ICJ explained how extensive evidence of state practice could not suffice to support the emergence of customary international law in *Libyan Arab Jamahiriya/Malta* (n 6) 38, para 44.

law of this Court, the International Tribunal for the Law of the Sea (ITLOS) and international arbitral courts and tribunals'.[49] The case law arguably constitutes 'an *acquis judiciare* [. . .] and should be read into articles 74 and 83 of the Convention'.[50] The ICJ's 1969 decision in the *North Sea Continental Shelf* cases made a tremendous impact on the customary international law governing maritime delimitation. Relevant jurisprudence has continued to evolve, and the methods used to delimit boundaries on the basis of international law have crystallized in recent decisions, most notably the *Black Sea* case of 2009.

In the *North Sea Continental Shelf* cases, the ICJ declared that boundaries to overlapping entitlements should be effected by agreements on the basis of equitable principles.[51] This obligation was rooted in the 1945 Truman proclamation,[52] and the Court went on to say that the *opinio juris* in the field of maritime delimitation (as evidenced by the *travaux préparatoires* of the 1958 Geneva Conventions) was entirely dominated by these two notions:

> first, that no one single method of delimitation was likely to prove satisfactory in all circumstances, and that delimitation should, therefore, be carried out by agreement (or by reference to arbitration); and secondly, that it should be effected on equitable principles.[53]

An arbitral tribunal endorsed this view in 1977 when it referred to a general norm of international law, providing that equitable principles must be applied when delimiting continental shelves between neighbouring States (failing agreement).[54] In 1982, the ICJ stated that, although the explicit reference to equitable principles was omitted from the UNCLOS provisions, such an obligation existed under customary international law.[55] This was reaffirmed by a chamber of the ICJ in the *Gulf of Maine* case in 1984, which found that the customary international law in the field of maritime delimitation required application of 'equitable principles, or rather equitable criteria, without any indication as to the choice to be made among [them] or between the practical methods to implement them'.[56] Similarly, in 1993, the Court declared that the customary rule of maritime delimitation between opposite coastal States was bilateral delimitation based upon equitable principles.[57] States have endorsed this view by arguing that the customary international law governing maritime boundary

49 *Territorial and Maritime Dispute (Nicaragua* v. *Colombia)* (n 8) para 114.

50 *Bangladesh* v. *India* (n 3) para 339.

51 *North Sea Continental Shelf* (n 9) para 47.

52 See Harry Truman, '150 – Proclamation 2667 – Policy of the United States with Respect to the Natural Resources of the Subsoil and Sea Bed of the Continental Shelf' (28 September 1945).

53 *North Sea Continental Shelf* (n 9) para 55.

54 *Anglo-French Continental Shelf* (n 12) para 70.

55 See *Tunisia/Libyan Arab Jamahiriya* (n 4) para 70.

56 *Gulf of Maine* (n 9) para 123.

57 *Denmark* v. *Norway* (n 25) para 46.

delimitation requires the application of equitable principles,[58] taking account of all relevant circumstances.[59]

The equitable criteria that can be taken into account in the delimitation process are variable.[60] According to the ICJ's decision in the *Tunisia/Libyan Arab Jamahiriya* case, '[t]he equitableness of a principle must be assessed in the light of its usefulness for the purpose of arriving at an equitable result'.[61] Therefore, application of equitable principles necessarily implies consideration of the circumstances that are relevant for reaching an equitable solution, namely, the relevant circumstances.

The significance of equitable principles, as a basis for boundary delimitation, has diminished. Courts and tribunals have largely ignored references to equitable principles in recent years[62] and the last instance of a court or tribunal referring to equitable principles as part of the customary international law applicable for maritime boundary delimitation was the *Eritrea/Yemen* arbitration of 1999.[63] Still, it remains well established that boundaries must be delimited with due regard for the relevant circumstances of each particular case.[64] Relevant circumstances can be assimilated to the special circumstances referred to in UNCLOS article 15 and they are the circumstances that justify modification of a strict equidistance or median line.[65] Relevant (or special) circumstances are factors that require adjustment of provisional equidistance lines in order to ensure an equitable outcome.[66]

The importance of transparency and predictability in maritime boundary delimitation has recently increased.[67] This has caused a shift from the abstract notion of equitable principles to a clearly defined method of delimitation, often referred to as the equidistance/relevant circumstances method. However, applicable international law has not evolved in such a way as to make the equidistance/relevant circumstances method obligatory in all cases.[68] It certainly has become the preferred method for achieving an equitable solution on the basis of international law, but the applicable international law still entails an obligation to ensure an equitable solution with due regard for all relevant circumstances.

58 See, for example, *Libyan Arab Jamahiriya/Malta* (n 6) 31, para 29; *Bangladesh/Myanmar* (n 3) para 6.
59 *Nicaragua* v. *Honduras* (n 6) para 104; *Territorial and Maritime Dispute (Nicaragua* v. *Colombia)* (n 8) para 15.
60 *Gulf of Maine* (n 9) para 157.
61 *Tunisia/Libyan Arab Jamahiriya* (n 4) 59.
62 See, for example, *Bangladesh/Myanmar* (n 3) para 58; *Maritime Delimitation in the Black Sea (Romania* v. *Ukraine)* (Judgment) [2009] ICJ Rep 61, para 125.
63 *Second stage of the proceedings between Eritrea and Yemen (Maritime Delimitation) (Eritrea/Yemen)* (1999) XXII RIAA 335, para 130.
64 See, for example, *North Sea Continental Shelf* (n 9) para 85; *Gulf of Maine* (n 9) 77.
65 *Denmark* v. *Norway* (n 25) para 55. See also *Cameroon* v. *Nigeria: Equatorial Guinea intervening* (n 10) para 288.
66 *Maritime Delimitation in the Black Sea* (n 62) para 155.
67 Particularly since *Bangladesh* v. *India* (n 3) para 339.
68 *Bangladesh/Myanmar* (n 3) para 225; *Bangladesh* v. *India* (n 3) paras 338–339.

3.2.2.2 An Equitable Solution

An equitable solution is a solution based on equity. Equity is a legal concept, tracing back to early rule-based legal systems from all over the world, and it serves to provide justice where codified rules cannot.[69] Moreover, arguments raised under equity have developed into self-standing legal concepts and principles through the passing of time. These include the principles of proportionality, good faith, pacta sunt servanda, estoppel, acquiescence and the doctrine of abuse of rights.[70] 'For centuries, equity has served the purpose of facilitating legal adjustment and bringing laws in line with contemporary perceptions of justice and regulatory needs.'[71] Thus, it enables law to adapt to changed circumstances and respond to new challenges,[72] for example, the challenge of climate change. Cottier explains that equity co-exists with law; it supplements and develops static and rigid concepts of law and, thus, differs from ex aequo et bono decisions, based on exceptional powers.[73] Equity is further distinct from ex aequo et bono decisions insofar as it demands that a rule of law is applied to reach a just decision.[74]

The overarching objective of any delimitation process is the achievement of an equitable solution.[75] The concept of an equitable solution must be understood not in a vacuum but in relation to the applicable law.[76] Equity is not applied as a matter of abstract justice but it demands due regard for all relevant circumstances for the achievement of an equitable solution. Equity should provide consistency and some degree of predictability, but the particular circumstances of each case always shape the results.[77] The reference to equity in UNCLOS articles 74 and 83 does not refer to a specific method of delimitation but, rather, 'an aim that should be borne in mind in effecting the delimitation'.[78] Still, the law governing maritime boundary delimitation has evolved into a relatively clear process, as explained in the following section.

An equitable solution is not the same as an equal solution.[79] After all, maritime delimitation is not meant to rectify the inequalities of nature[80] or entail distributive justice.[81] Where there exists 'a geographical situation of quasi-equality as between a number of States', equity demands that 'the effects of an incidental special feature from which an unjustifiable difference of treatment could result'

69 Thomas Cottier (n 24) 8–9.
70 Ibid., 13–14, 20.
71 Ibid., 9.
72 Ibid.
73 See *Libyan Arab Jamahiriya/Malta* (n 6) 60, para 71.
74 *North Sea Continental Shelf* (n 9) para 88.
75 *Bangladesh* v. *India* (n 3) para 397.
76 *Fisheries Jurisdiction (United Kingdom of Great Britain and Northern Ireland* v. *Iceland)* (Merits) [1974] ICJ Rep 3, para 78.
77 *Libyan Arab Jamahiriya/Malta* (n 6) 39, para 45.
78 *Cameroon* v. *Nigeria: Equatorial Guinea intervening* (n 10) para 294.
79 *Maritime Delimitation in the Black Sea* (n 62) para 111.
80 *Libyan Arab Jamahiriya/Malta* (n 6) para 46.
81 *Bangladesh* v. *India* (n 3) para 397; *Libyan Arab Jamahiriya/Malta* (n 6) para 46.

are abated.[82] Therefore, equity should not remedy natural inequalities but an 'unjustifiable difference of treatment' should be avoided and the effects of such circumstances minimized.

Equity is often used to adjust provisional boundaries and reduce inequitable results. As such it seems to be used as a corrective element.[83] However, the obligation to achieve an equitable solution must be seen as a primary obligation of UNCLOS articles 74 and 83. Therefore, equity should guide the entire delimitation process at all its stages. This proposition finds some support in the jurisprudence. For example, in *Denmark* v. *Norway*, the ICJ used 'equity *a priori* to work towards a result, and *a posteriori* to check a result thus reached'.[84] Furthermore, in the *Tunisia/Libyan Arab Jamahiriya* case, the Court explained that the equidistance method should not be applied automatically before considering all relevant circumstances.[85] In *Nicaragua* v. *Honduras*, the ICJ chose a delimitation method specifically to avoid an inequitable solution.[86] Similarly, the Court considered, in *Nicaragua* v. *Colombia*, whether the construction of a provisional equidistance line was 'appropriate as a starting-point for the delimitation'[87] because the location of the San Andrés Archipelago had the effect of pushing the equidistance line close to the Nicaraguan mainland.[88]

Courts and tribunals often start with strict equidistance lines. Such provisional lines are adjusted, to achieve equitable solutions, at later stages of the delimitation process. However, they can also work towards equitable solutions from the beginning of the delimitation process by choosing base points by reference to relevant circumstances.[89] Courts and tribunals have declared that relevant circumstances are only considered at later stages of the delimitation process, that is, when provisional boundaries are adjusted.[90] Yet, they generally choose their own base points instead of relying on baselines unilaterally constructed by the disputing States. In choosing such base points, courts and tribunals must give some consideration to the feasibility of individual base points. For example, in *Bangladesh* v. *India*, the existence of some low-tide elevations was disputed[91] and the arbitral tribunal had to determine which base points to use for the provisional boundary line, before considering subsequent adjustments. The tribunal did not articulate a clear rule regarding the use of low-tide elevations as base points[92] but went on a site visit to evaluate the disputed features.[93]

82 *North Sea Continental Shelf* (n 9) para 91.
83 See Thomas Cottier (n 24) 378.
84 *Denmark* v. *Norway* (n 25) Separate Opinion of Judge Weeramantry, para 20.
85 *Tunisia/Libyan Arab Jamahiriya* (n 4) para 110.
86 *Nicaragua* v. *Honduras* (n 6) para 277.
87 *Territorial and Maritime Dispute (Nicaragua* v. *Colombia)* (n 8) para 195.
88 Ibid., paras 21 and 201.
89 See detailed discussion in Section 3.4.1.
90 See, for example, *Territorial and Maritime Dispute (Nicaragua* v. *Colombia)* (n 8) para 195.
91 *Bangladesh* v. *India* (n 3) para 196.
92 See ibid., paras 196 and 260–262.
93 *Bangladesh* v. *India* (n 3) para 22.

This demonstrates how important the unique circumstances of each case are, not just as a corrective element but for the entire process of equitable delimitation.

3.2.2.3 Achieving an Equitable Solution on the Basis of International Law

The ILC considered the matter of maritime boundary delimitation, as between adjacent States, from 1950 to 1956. In doing so, it did not find that any method of delimitation had priority over others or the status of customary international law.[94] The ILC considered several different methods of delimitation, for example, 'delimitation by agreement, by reference to arbitration, by drawing lines perpendicular to the coast, [and] by prolonging the dividing line of adjacent territorial waters'. The Commission referred the issue to the Committee of Hydrographic Experts before drafting the 1958 Conventions on the Territorial Sea and the Contiguous Zone, and on the Continental Shelf. The Committee of Experts promoted the method of equidistance in a report from 1953 and that was when equidistance first began taking precedence over other methods of delimitation.[95] The Committee of Experts concluded that territorial sea boundaries should be drawn in accordance with an established formula and that such a formula could be used also to delimit continental shelf boundaries. The most suitable formula was, in the Committee's view, the equidistance method, although it would not always lead to an equitable solution. In such cases a different method should be agreed upon.[96] Thus, equidistance was expected to produce an equitable solution in some but not all cases, and it was adopted on the basis of practical considerations rather than legal theory.[97]

The ICJ confirmed, in the 1969 *North Sea Continental Shelf* cases, that no customary rule required the application of equidistance or other particular method of delimitation.[98] Different methods could be employed, either in combination with the equidistance method or alone.[99] The Court found that the States involved were under an obligation to achieve an equitable solution, which in the specific case involved taking all circumstances into account and applying equitable principles. The equidistance method was said to be suitable in the case at hand, although other methods could also be employed.[100] The Court also declared that 'in certain geographical configurations, which are quite frequently met with,[101] the equidistance method, despite its known advantages, leads unquestionably to inequity'.[102] This landmark decision resulted in a 'shift away from equidistance as a preferred

94 *North Sea Continental Shelf* (n 9) para 50.
95 Ibid., para 50.
96 There are no official records of this discussion, see *North Sea Continental Shelf* (n 9) paras 51–52.
97 *North Sea Continental Shelf* (n 9) para 53.
98 Ibid., para 81.
99 Ibid., para 85.
100 Ibid., 47.
101 The Court was specifically referring to concave and convex coastlines.
102 Ibid., para 89.

method of delimitation'.[103] Thirteen years later, in the *Tunisia/Libyan Arab Jamahiriya* case, the ICJ placed unprecedented emphasis on the equitable nature of the resulting boundary[104] and held that equidistance was not 'a mandatory legal principle, or a method having some privileged status in relation to other methods'.[105] The Court noted that it was not obliged to apply equidistance, not even as a preliminary step.[106] The methods or principles used to delimit a maritime boundary were seen as subordinate to the predominant goal of achieving an equitable solution.[107] Similarly, in the 1985 *Libyan Arab Jamahiriya/Malta* case, the ICJ asserted that the equidistance method did not 'have the benefit of a presumption in its favour' and that it should not be applied unless it could be demonstrated that it would lead to an equitable result.[108] However, courts and tribunals have diverted from this extremely results-oriented approach in subsequent decisions as the pre-eminence of equidistance has grown.

In the *Jan Mayen* case in 1993, the ICJ drew a provisional equidistance line, before adjusting it by reference to special circumstances.[109] Similarly, the Court applied this two-step equidistance method in *Qatar* v. *Bahrain*, in 2001,[110] and in *Cameroon* v. *Nigeria: Equatorial Guinea intervening*, in 2002.[111] Furthermore, in *Barbados* v. *Trinidad and Tobago* in 2006, an arbitral tribunal held that it would normally be appropriate to start with the two-step equidistance approach and that the certainty it provided was highly desirable, even though no method could be considered to be compulsory.[112] A year later, the arbitral tribunal in the *Guyana* v. *Suriname* arbitration declared that international courts and tribunals had 'come to embrace a clear role for equidistance'.[113]

The ICJ developed the equidistance/relevant circumstances approach further in the *Black Sea* case of 2009. This was the first time it applied and clearly articulated the three-stage method.[114] First a provisional boundary line was drawn using geometrically objective standards,[115] then the Court assessed whether there were any 'factors calling for the adjustment or shifting of the provisional equidistance line in order to achieve an equitable result'.[116] Finally,

103 Clive Schofield (n 27) 49.
104 *Tunisia/Libyan Arab Jamahiriya* (n 4) para 70.
105 Ibid., para 110.
106 Ibid., para 110.
107 Ibid., para 70.
108 *Libyan Arab Jamahiriya/Malta* (n 6) para 63.
109 *Denmark* v. *Norway* (n 25) para 51.
110 *Qatar* v. *Bahrain* (n 20) para 230.
111 *Cameroon* v. *Nigeria: Equatorial Guinea intervening* (n 10) paras 288–290.
112 *Barbados* v. *Trinidad and Tobago* (n 44) paras 242 and 306.
113 *Award in the arbitration regarding the delimitation of the maritime boundary between* Guyana and Suriname *(*Guyana v. Suriname*)* (2007) XXX RIAA 1, para 335.
114 *Maritime Delimitation in the Black Sea* (n 62).
115 Ibid., para 116.
116 Ibid., para 120 referring to *Cameroon* v. *Nigeria: Equatorial Guinea intervening* (n 10) para 288.

the third stage entailed what the ICJ referred to as a 'disproportionality test', which involved evaluating whether the boundary line 'lead to an inequitable result by reason of any marked disproportion between the ratio of the respective coastal lengths and the ratio between the relevant maritime area of each State by reference to the delimitation line'.[117] Soon the ICJ followed this precedent in the *Nicaragua* v. Colombia case, in 2012,[118] as did ITLOS in the *Bangladesh/Myanmar* case, the same year,[119] and an arbitral tribunal constituted under UNCLOS Annex VII in the *Bangladesh/India* case, in 2014.[120]

While consistently applying some form of equidistance in recent decades, courts and tribunals have not held that an equitable solution under UNCLOS articles 74 and 83 can only be achieved on the basis of equidistance. In *Cameroon* v. *Nigeria: Equatorial Guinea intervening*, in 2002, the ICJ held that there was no presumption in favour of equidistance.[121] Rather, it should be demonstrated that the equidistance method would lead to an equitable result in the case at hand.[122] Similarly, the Court confirmed, in *Nicaragua* v. *Honduras*, in 2007, that 'the equidistance method does not automatically have priority over other methods of delimitation and, in particular circumstances, there may be factors which make the application of the equidistance method inappropriate'.[123] Even in the *Black Sea* case, the Court held that the equidistance/relevant circumstances method could be substituted by a different method where 'compelling reasons' made it 'unfeasible'.[124]

The search for consistency and predictability has definitely led to the advancement of the equidistance/relevant circumstances method. Indeed, it fits well with the obligation to ensure an equitable solution on the basis of all relevant circumstances, as it can generally ensure an equitable result.[125] However, the equidistance/relevant circumstances method must not be conflated with the applicable law under UNCLOS articles 74 and 83.[126] While equidistance is generally preferred, certain circumstances can justify resort to different methods.[127]

The following sections explore the prospects for achieving equitable solutions through the principal delimitation methods employed by courts and tribunals: the equidistance/relevant circumstances method and the angle-bisector method.

117 *Maritime Delimitation in the Black Sea* (n 62) paras 122, 214–215.
118 *Territorial and Maritime Dispute (Nicaragua* v. *Colombia)* (n 8) paras. 190–194.
119 *Bangladesh/Myanmar* (n 3) para 240.
120 *Bangladesh* v. *India* (n 3).
121 *Cameroon* v. *Nigeria: Equatorial Guinea intervening* (n 10) para 293 referring to *Libyan Arab Jamahiriya/Malta* (n 6) para 63.
122 *Cameroon* v. *Nigeria: Equatorial Guinea intervening* (n 10) para 294.
123 *Nicaragua* v. *Honduras* (n 6) para 272.
124 *Maritime Delimitation in the Black Sea* (n 62) para 116.
125 *Cameroon* v. *Nigeria: Equatorial Guinea intervening* (n 10) para 288.
126 UNCLOS articles 74 and 83 do not demand the use of equidistance, see, for example, *Bangladesh/Myanmar* (n 3) para 225; *Bangladesh* v. *India* (n 3) paras 338–339.
127 *Barbados* v. *Trinidad and Tobago* (n 44) para 306.

3.2.2.3.1 THE EQUIDISTANCE/RELEVANT CIRCUMSTANCES METHOD. The equidistance/relevant circumstances method is quite similar to the equidistance/special circumstances method codified in UNCLOS article 15.[128] They both require consideration for special or relevant circumstances and subsequent adjustment to the equidistance line where required for an equitable result.[129] Yet, the three-stage equidistance/relevant circumstances method is more elaborate than the traditional equidistance method.[130]

The traditional equidistance method, applicable to territorial sea delimitation, entails the construction of a strict equidistance line, which is abandoned or derogated from upon agreement or if special circumstances or historic title so require.[131] This involves first drawing a provisional equidistance line and subsequently considering whether that line must be adjusted to account for special circumstances.[132] In contrast, the strict equidistance line constructed under the equidistance/relevant circumstances method is 'nothing more than a first step and in no way prejudges the ultimate solution'.[133] This provisional equidistance line is subject to adjustments, as required by reference to relevant circumstances, and, finally, a disproportionality test.[134] Thus, both methods require consideration for special or relevant circumstances and adjustments to the provisional equidistance lines to ensure equitable solutions. The distinguishing factor is the disproportionality test, which is only an integral part of the three-step equidistance/relevant circumstances method.

When applying the equidistance/relevant circumstances method, relevant circumstances are not considered until the second stage of delimitation. This is, according to the ICJ, because the provisional equidistance line is 'plotted on strictly geometrical criteria on the basis of objective data'.[135] However, the provisional equidistance line is constructed by reference to relevant coastal geography, which calls for a decision on whether individual coastal features, or parts of the coastline, are relevant for this purpose. The second stage involves an assessment of factors that qualify as relevant circumstances requiring an adjustment of the provisional boundary.[136] At the third stage, the ratio between maritime areas and coastal length is measured.[137]

128 Ibid., para 305. See also *Cameroon* v. *Nigeria: Equatorial Guinea intervening* (n 10) para 288.
129 See, for example, *Bangladesh* v. *India* (n 3) para 272.
130 This distinction is reflected in, for example, *Nicaragua* v. *Honduras* (n 6) para 271. See also Robin Churchill 'The Greenland-Jan Mayen Case and Its Significance for the International Law of Maritime Boundary Delimitation' (1994) 9 The International Journal of Marine and Coastal Law 1, 18. Note, however, that this distinction is not always reflected in the jurisprudence; see, for example, *Bangladesh* v. *India* (n 3).
131 See, for example, *Nicaragua* v. *Honduras* (n 6) para 280.
132 *Qatar* v. *Bahrain* (n 20) para 167. See also *Bangladesh* v. *India* (n 3) para 246.
133 *Territorial and Maritime Dispute (Nicaragua* v. *Colombia)* (n 8) para 196.
134 See *Maritime Delimitation in the Black Sea* (n 62) paras 115–116 and 120–122.
135 Ibid., para 118.
136 *Maritime Delimitation in the Black Sea* (n 62) para 120.
137 Ibid., para 122.

Relevant circumstances can justify a significant shift in a provisional boundary. The adjusted boundary can depart far from the starting point and end up resembling an angle-bisector more than an equidistance or median line.[138] This suggests that the equitable nature of the end result is not necessarily dependent on a provisional equidistance line. Yet, the applicable international law seems to require that the delimitation process begin with a provisional equidistance line, which may be abandoned if circumstances of the case make it unfeasible. A presumption in favour of the equidistance/relevant circumstances method arguably influences the end result, even if the equidistance line is shifted or abandoned due to relevant circumstances. This is based on the fact that decisions are often shaped by their starting points.[139] Therefore, the decision to start with a provisional equidistance line can affect how far courts and tribunals are willing to go in adjusting the line for an equitable result.

When negotiating UNCLOS, State representatives aired opposing views on whether to emphasize equidistance in maritime delimitation provisions or relevant circumstances in the area concerned.[140] The equidistance/relevant circumstances method has the potential to reconcile both approaches, but only if relevant circumstances are given sufficient weight. Significant adjustments to the provisional equidistance line can result in a boundary that is quite remote from the original equidistance line and the anchoring to equidistance can come at the expense of adequate consideration for relevant circumstances. Relevant circumstances should be considered throughout the delimitation process and they should lead to the use of a different method when equidistance is inappropriate.

3.2.2.3.2 THE ANGLE-BISECTOR METHOD. The equidistance/relevant circumstances method is the preferred method of delimitation in ordinary circumstances.[141] It is generally applied by courts and tribunals unless relevant circumstances make it unfeasible.[142] Approximately 60 per cent of all maritime boundaries have relied on equidistance as a starting point[143] but the angle-bisector method is a viable alternative, which has been employed in a number of cases and boundary agreements.[144] In theory, this is not the only alternative to the equidistance

138 The final boundary established by the tribunal in *Bangladesh* v. *India* was closer to the angle-bisector line proposed by Bangladesh than a strict equidistance line. See *Bangladesh* v. *India* (n 3), Appendix, A3–A5.

139 Gretchen Chapman and Eric Johnson, 'The Limits of Anchoring' (1994) 7 Journal of Behavioural Decision Making 223.

140 Bernard Oxman 'The Third United Nations Conference on the Law of the Sea: The Ninth Session' (1980) 75 (2) American Journal of International Law 211, 237.

141 *Bangladesh/Myanmar* (n 3) para 238.

142 *Nicaragua* v. *Honduras* (n 6) para 272.

143 Thomas Cottier (n 24) 375.

144 See, for example, *Nicaragua* v. *Honduras* (n 6) para 286; *Tunisia/Libyan Arab Jamahiriya* (n 4); *Gulf of Maine* (n 9); *Delimitation of the maritime boundary between Guinea and Guinea-Bissau (Guinea/Guinea-Bissau)* (1985) XIX RIAA 149.

method, but it is the only one that has been applied by courts and tribunals, and, consequently, the only method that forms part of the applicable law under article 38(1)(d) of the ICJ Statute.

The angle-bisector method was one of the methods seriously considered by the ILC when drafting the 1958 Conventions on the Territorial Sea and the Contiguous Zone, and on the Continental Shelf.[145] It involves a linear approximation of both States' coastlines; straight lines are drawn along both coastlines to create an angle and this angle is bisected to create the boundary.[146]

The angle-bisector method traces back to, at least, 1909. It was applied in the first maritime boundary dispute settled before an international court or tribunal: the *Grisbådarna Arbitration*.[147] In delimiting the territorial sea between Norway and Sweden, the tribunal was asked to take relevant facts and principles into account.[148] The tribunal applied equitable principles with due consideration for relevant circumstances to reach an equitable solution and this led to the drawing of a line 'perpendicular to the general direction of the coast'.[149] The line was adjusted to go around the Grisbådarna bank, so the tribunal constructed an angle-bisector boundary except in a particular area between Grisbådarna and Skjöttegrunde where the circumstances called for a median line.[150]

In the *Nicaragua* v. *Honduras* case, the ICJ described this method 'as an approximation of the equidistance method'. It is a geometrical approach that can result in a simple and equitable solution by having due regard to special circumstances while aiming for an equal division of overlapping maritime entitlements.[151] The angle-bisector method uses an approximation based on 'macro-geography of a coastline as represented by a line drawn between two points on the coast' as opposed to specific base points relied upon when an equidistance line is drawn.[152] The angle-bisector does not correlate to coastal geography as closely as the equidistance method does. Therefore, the ICJ has explained that when applying the angle-bisector method 'care must be taken to avoid "completely refashioning nature"'.[153]

3.3 RELEVANT CIRCUMSTANCES: COASTAL GEOGRAPHY

Maritime entitlements are generated by the coastal front.[154] This is why maritime limits are measured from baselines along the coastline and maritime boundaries are

145 *North Sea Continental Shelf* (n 9) para 51.
146 *Gulf of Maine* (n 9) para 195.
147 Sang-Myon Rhee, 'Sea Boundary Delimitation between States Before World War II' (1982) 76 American Journal of International Law 555, 566; *Grisbådarna Arbitration* (n 64).
148 *Grisbådarna Arbitration* (n 64) 2.
149 Ibid., 6.
150 Ibid., 8.
151 *Nicaragua* v. *Honduras* (n 6) para 287.
152 Ibid., 674.
153 Ibid., 674, referring to *North Sea Continental Shelf* (n 9) para 91.
154 See, for example, *Tunisia/Libyan Arab Jamahiriya* (n 4) para 73.

constructed by reference to base points on the coast. Indeed, coastal geography is essential to the process of maritime delimitation. A strict equidistance line relies purely on coastal geography, and the relevant circumstances used to adjust provisional boundaries generally relate to coastal geography. There are some examples of adjustments based on non-geographic factors, for example, access to fisheries,[155] but such considerations are negligible in comparison to coastal geography. Indeed, the *travaux préparatoires* of UNCLOS, jurisprudence in the field and prominent scholars unanimously hold that coastal geography is of paramount concern to the legal process of maritime delimitation and crucial to an equitable outcome.[156] For example, the ICJ referenced the land dominates the sea principle in the *North Sea Continental Shelf* cases and based the boundary on the geographical configuration of relevant coastlines.[157] In the case of the land and maritime boundary between Cameroon and Nigeria from 2002, the ICJ confirmed that the maritime delimitation had to be based on the incontrovertible criteria of the coastal geography.[158] Also, in 2006, in the *Barbados* v. *Trinidad and Tobago* award, the arbitral tribunal found that, for the purposes of equity, certain criteria should be identified[159] and that, with very few exceptions, 'the quest for neutral criteria of a geographical character prevailed in the end over area-specific criteria such as geomorphological aspects or resource specific criteria such as the distribution of fish stocks'.[160]

The ICJ has referred to relevant circumstances as the factors that call for an adjustment of provisional boundary lines.[161] Their purpose is to verify that a provisional boundary line is not perceived as being inequitable.[162] In the *Black Sea* case, the Court held that relevant circumstances should not be considered until the second stage of delimitation.[163] Yet, geographical features are relevant at all stages of maritime delimitation, from the drawing of a provisional equidistance line to subsequent adjustments and disproportionality tests. In that sense, geographical circumstances dominate the delimitation process.[164] A distinction may be drawn

155 *Denmark* v. *Norway* (n 25) para 78, *Gulf of Maine* (n 9) para 237. See also Victor Prescott and Clive Schofield, *The Maritime Political Boundaries of the World*, 2nd edition (Martinus Nijhoff, 2005) 239–241.

156 See, for example, *Cameroon* v. *Nigeria: Equatorial Guinea intervening* (n 10) para 295; *Anglo-French Continental Shelf* (n 12) para 84; *North Sea Continental Shelf* (n 9) para 96; Massimo Lando, *Maritime Delimitation as a Judicial Process* (Cambridge University Press, 2019) 32; Davor Vidas, 'Sea-Level Rise and International Law: At the Convergence of Two Epochs' (2014) 4 Climate law 76; Prosper Weil, *The Law of Maritime Delimitation – Reflections* (Cambridge University Press, 1989) 217–218.

157 *North Sea Continental Shelf* (n 9) para 96.

158 *Cameroon* v. *Nigeria: Equatorial Guinea intervening* (n 10) para 295.

159 *Barbados* v. *Trinidad and Tobago* (n 44) para 232.

160 Ibid., para 228.

161 *Maritime Delimitation in the Black Sea* (n 62) para 155.

162 Ibid., para 155.

163 Ibid., para 118.

164 Ki Lee, *The Demise of Equitable Principles and the Rise of Relevant Circumstances in Maritime Boundary Delimitation*, submitted for the Degree of PhD School of Law (The University of Edinburgh, 2012) 14.

between 'relevant coasts' (the areas that generate maritime entitlements and are, consequently, relevant for delimitation)[165] and 'relevant circumstances' (the factors calling for adjustments of provisional boundary lines). The following discussion on relevant coastal geography may be understood as referring to geographical circumstances relevant for all stages of delimitation: the selection of delimitation methods, the plotting of provisional boundaries and their subsequent adjustments.

3.3.1 *Relevance of Coastal Instability*

Relevant coastal geography can be disseminated into several sub-categories. The configuration of relevant coastlines is paramount because provisional equidistance and angle-bisector boundaries are constructed by reference to base points or general directions of relevant coasts. Coastal concavity and potential cut-off effects can constitute relevant circumstances.[166] So too can relative coastal lengths,[167] the configuration of coastlines (adjacency or oppositeness),[168] the size of coastal features[169] and their distance from mainland.[170] However, courts and tribunals have been divided in their assessments of the relevance of coastal instability. An arbitral tribunal expressly rejected the relevance of climate-related changes to coastal geography in the *Bangladesh* v. *India* arbitration of 2014.[171] In contrast, the ICJ assessed the viability of base points and chose a delimitation method by reference to foreseeable changes to coastal geography in the 2007 *Nicaragua* v. *Honduras* case.[172] Furthermore, the tribunal in the *Philippines* v. *China* arbitration indicated, in 2016, that the capacity to qualify as an island, under UNCLOS article 121, should include an assessment of whether the coastal feature could sustain human habitation over an extended period of time.[173]

Judicial decisions are, as previously mentioned, the best source to identify the law applicable to maritime delimitation. Nonetheless, a majority of maritime boundaries is delimited through agreements and these reflect trends in State practice, which can develop into customary international law. Some boundary agreements have accounted for changing coastal geography and made provisions to ensure continuously equitable division of maritime entitlements. For example, the 1973 continental shelf boundary agreement between Canada and Denmark established a boundary by adjusting the provisional equidistance line by reference to foreseeable recession of

165 See *Maritime Delimitation in the Black Sea* (n 62) para 77.
166 See, for example, *Bangladesh/Myanmar* (n 3) and *Bangladesh* v. *India* (n 3).
167 See, for example, *Barbados* v. *Trinidad and Tobago* (n 44) para 239; *Maritime Delimitation in the Black Sea* (n 62) para 164; *Cameroon* v. *Nigeria: Equatorial Guinea intervening* (n 10) para 301; *Denmark* v. *Norway* (n 25) para 69: *Libyan Arab Jamahiriya/Malta* (n 6) para 50.
168 *Barbados* v. *Trinidad and Tobago* (n 44) para 233.
169 *Nicaragua* v. *Honduras* (n 6) para 202.
170 *Maritime Delimitation in the Black Sea* (n 62) para 149.
171 *Bangladesh* v. *India* (n 3) para 217.
172 *Nicaragua* v. *Honduras* (n 6) para 277.
173 *South China Sea (Philippines* v. *China)* (Merits) (2016) XXXIII RIAA 153, para 487.

the Greenland glacier.[174] Moreover, in a delimitation agreement between the Federated States of Micronesia and the Republic of the Marshall Islands, the States anticipate revision of their boundary to reflect changes in the location of islands.[175] Similarly, Belgium and the United Kingdom decided not to use a base point on Shipwash Sands in an agreement delimiting their continental shelves, although it had previously been relied upon by the United Kingdom, because a survey conducted during negotiations showed that it had been eroded.[176]

It is clear that foreseeable changes to coastal geography can affect the terms of boundary agreements and lead to mutual revision. However, this chapter is primarily concerned with the international law governing boundary delimitation, as evidenced by the jurisprudence. The following sections explore case law in more detail in order to determine whether changing coastal geography has any bearing on the delimitation of equitable maritime boundaries under UNCLOS articles 74 and 83 and the consonant customary international law.

3.3.1.1 Case Law Indicating Relevance of Coastal Instability

Courts and tribunals have considered ongoing geographic changes in several disputes relating to the division of maritime entitlements. For example, the ICJ took coastal instability into account when constructing a maritime boundary between Nicaragua and Honduras. In particular, it considered whether the solution would be equitable in the near future. The area to be delimited was undergoing rapid changes at the time of delimitation as the mouth of the River Coco was constantly changing. Cape Gracias a Dios (a protrusion into the Atlantic) was being projected towards the sea, along with huge amounts of alluvium and sediment, forming unstable islands. As a result, shoals and delta sediments were being re-deposited along the coastlines of Nicaragua and Honduras. This was all due to the river delta and 'a very active morpho-dynamism', which led to continuous changes to relevant coastlines.[177]

Both Nicaragua and Honduras argued that coastal instability should affect the delimitation process. However, they disagreed on what the consequences should be. Nicaragua argued that geographical changes and instability of the coastline should lead to application of the angle-bisector method, while Honduras favoured the equidistance principle with due consideration for the gradual movement of the

174 Barbara Kwiatkowska (n 45) 102.

175 Treaty between the Federated States of Micronesia and the Republic of the Marshall Islands Concerning Maritime Boundaries and Cooperation on Related Matters (adopted 12 July 2006), article 2(5) in David Colson and Robert Smith (eds) *International Maritime Boundaries VI* (American Society of International Law, Martinus Nijhoff, 2011) 4325, 4327.

176 David Anderson, 'Recent Boundary Agreements in the Southern North Sea' in (1992) 41 (2) International and Comparative Law Quarterly 414, 418, referring to the Agreement between the Government of the United Kingdom of Great Britain and Northern Ireland and the Government of the Kingdom of Belgium relating to the Delimitation of the Continental Shelf between the two Countries (adopted 29 May 1991, entered into force 14 May 1993) UK Treaty Series No 20 (1994).

177 *Nicaragua* v. *Honduras* (n 6) para 32.

mouth of the Coco River. The Court ultimately concluded that the instability of the river delta 'might render any equidistance line so constructed today arbitrary and unreasonable in the near future'.[178] Moreover, the Court asserted that '[a]ll deltas are by definition geographical accidents of an unstable nature and suffer changes in size and form in relatively short periods of time'.[179]

The changing conditions also had an impact on the ICJ's decision relating to sovereignty over islands and cays in *Nicaragua* v. *Honduras*. The Court held that it was 'not in a position to make a determinative finding on the maritime features in the area in dispute', particularly as regards Media Luna Cay (which was submerged at the time of delimitation) and Logwood Cay (which was above sea level according to Honduras but submerged in Nicaragua's view).[180] The instability of the river delta meant that large islands could join the riverbank on either side and smaller islands could disappear. These changing circumstances lead the Court to make 'no finding as to sovereign title over islands in the mouth of the River Coco'.[181] If a court or tribunal cannot confirm sovereignty over a feature because of its unstable nature, it should arguably also refrain from permanently ascribing sovereignty and sovereign rights in surrounding maritime areas on the basis of that unstable feature.

The tribunal in the *Philippines* v. *China* case assessed the capacity of coastal features to qualify as islands under UNCLOS article 121(3). This case was not concerned with delimitation of overlapping maritime entitlements but with the capacity of coastal features to generate maritime entitlements, which is a precondition to maritime delimitation. The tribunal took into account not only circumstances existing at the time of the award, but also those occurring over an extended time. It found that UNCLOS article 121(3) 'is concerned with whether, objectively, the feature is apt, able to, or lends itself to human habitation or economic life'.[182] According to the tribunal, this calls for an evaluation of the feature's ability to sustain human habitation 'over a continuous period of time' or commence and continue economic 'activity over a period of time in a way that remains viable on an ongoing basis'.[183] The tribunal did not address coastal instability or future changes in the context of sea level rise or coastal erosion. On the contrary, it was confronted with features that had already undergone substantial artificial modification to extend maritime entitlements. The tribunal considered the intrinsic, natural capacity of the coastal features[184] and found that historical evidence could be relevant for constituting evidence that a feature met the requirements of UNCLOS article 121(3). This decision demonstrates that courts and tribunals can look beyond coastal geography existing at the time of delimitation and assess relevant circumstances over a prolonged period. However, it also shows a willingness to ignore

178 Ibid., para 277.
179 Ibid., para 32.
180 Ibid., paras 143–144.
181 Ibid., para 145.
182 *South China Sea (Philippines* v. *China)* (Merits) (2016) XXXIII RIAA 153, para 483.
183 Ibid., para 487.
184 Ibid., paras 306 and 549.

potential impacts of human-induced changes, including '[w]ar, pollution, and environmental harm'.[185] That might, as suggested by Kaye, mean that coastal features should be assessed by reference to their natural state, prior to anthropogenic sea level rise.[186]

In the *Jan Mayen* case, the ICJ viewed foreseeable seasonal changes to coastlines and natural resources as potentially relevant circumstances. The Court decided to shift the provisional median line eastwards to take account of the seasonal migration of capelin.[187] The presence of ice was also deemed potentially relevant, being 'a considerable seasonal restriction of access to the waters'.[188] The ice did not prevent the exploitation of capelin, the only commercially exploitable fish resource in the area, because the capelin was expected to appear at times and in areas where there was no ice. Therefore, it did not lead to an adjustment of the provisional boundary line.[189] This case is important for deciphering the relevance of changing environmental circumstances and will be further analysed in Chapter 4. For the present purposes, it suffices to say that the *Jan Mayen* case confirmed the relevance of foreseeable environmental changes and demonstrated that fluctuating ice could be relevant to an equitable delimitation. This decision clearly indicates that courts and tribunals can base their decisions on foreseeable or ongoing changes.

3.3.1.2 Case Law Renouncing Relevance of Coastal Instability

In 1977, the tribunal in the *Anglo-French Continental Shelf* arbitration concluded that when looking at geographical circumstances it should only consider the physical circumstances as they were at that time of delimitation. Only the 'present-day coasts' and 'present-day seabed' were relevant for boundary delimitation.[190] Moreover, the ICJ declared in the *Black Sea* case in 2009 that it would 'use as base points those which the geography of the coast identifies as a physical reality at the time of the delimitation'.[191] Similarly, the tribunal constituted under UNCLOS Annex VII, in *Bangladesh* v. *India*, delimited the boundary on the basis of base points that were 'appropriate in reference to the time of the delimitation, i.e. the date of its Award'.[192] Indeed, courts and tribunals should not delimit a maritime boundary relying on previously used base points that have become inappropriate at the time of delimitation; the physical reality at the time of delimitation is the obvious starting point. However, it may be appropriate, considering the circumstances existing at the

185 Ibid., para 549.
186 Stuart Kaye, 'The Law of the Sea Convention and Sea Level Rise after the South China Sea Arbitration' (2017) 93 International Law Studies Series, US Naval War College, 423, 431.
187 *Denmark* v. *Norway* (n 25) para 76.
188 Ibid., para 78.
189 Ibid.
190 *Anglo-French Continental Shelf* (n 12) para 84.
191 *Maritime Delimitation in the Black Sea* (n 62) para 131.
192 *Bangladesh* v. *India* (n 3) para 212.

date of the award, to choose base points or delimitation methods that produce solutions that remain equitable notwithstanding ongoing coastal instability.

The tribunal specifically addressed the issue of foreseeable changes to coastal geography in *Bangladesh* v. *India*. Bangladesh argued that the instability of the coastline and the potential effect of climate change and sea level rise should be taken into account as constituting special or relevant circumstances. It further alleged that there was 'scientific evidence of extreme coastal instability in the Bengal Delta'[193] and that within a few years several low-tide elevations proposed as base points probably would be submerged.[194] The Bengal Delta had been eroding for two centuries at the time of delimitation.[195] This erosion was accelerating due to sea-level rise and major changes to the coastline were anticipated by 2100.[196] Bangladesh presented convincing arguments in relation to the foreseeable changes affecting relevant coastal features. It highlighted the unstable nature of the coastline of the Bengal Delta and argued that this instability should lead to the application of the angle-bisector method or an adjustment of a provisional equidistance line.[197] Yet the tribunal rejected Bangladesh's arguments. It concluded that 'future instability of the coastline' was irrelevant for the delimitation,[198] and adjusted its provisional equidistance line only by reference to the concavity in the area and the cut-off effect it would produce.[199]

The tribunal in *Bangladesh* v. *India* made a clear distinction between *future* and *present* circumstances of the coast. It rejected the relevance of 'future changes'[200] and focused on the feasibility of chosen base points for 'the present time'.[201] The tribunal went on to state that 'only the present geophysical conditions' were relevant for boundary delimitation.[202] That is, the 'physical reality at the time of delimitation'.[203] The tribunal quoted the following sentence from the *Black Sea* case when explaining what it meant by the 'physical reality at the time of the delimitation'. '[G]eographical reality covers not only the physical elements produced by geodynamics and the movements of the sea, but also any other material factors that are present'.[204]

The term 'material factors' could be interpreted broadly to encompass those relating to the nature of the physical reality, for example, the presence of a delta or ongoing coastal instability. Coastal instability could be seen as an inseparable part of the 'present-day coast' and 'present geophysical conditions' and, therefore,

193 Ibid., para 237.
194 Ibid., para 213.
195 Ibid., para 373. See also Bangladesh's Reply, paragraph 3.59.
196 *Bangladesh* v. *India* (n 3) para 376. See Bangladesh's Reply, paragraphs 4.116–4.117.
197 Ibid. 111.
198 Ibid., para 215.
199 Ibid., para 421.
200 Ibid., para 399, see also para 215.
201 Ibid., para 214.
202 Ibid., para 399.
203 Ibid., para 215.
204 *Maritime Delimitation in the Black Sea* (n 62) para 131.

relevant for selecting appropriate base points. In sum, coastal instability that exists at the time of delimitation could be relevant, even if courts and tribunals will not address *future* instability of the coastline. However, this interpretation is not supported by the *Bangladesh* v. *India* decision, which advanced a narrow interpretation of relevant coastal geography to reject the potential impact of climate change.

Future geographic changes should be distinguished from ongoing changes. The former category might include, inter alia, changes resulting from seismic and volcanic activity or extreme weather events. The second category would include ongoing changes to coastal geography such as those relating to deltas, sea level rise or coastal erosion. The latter are relatively predictable. One of the reasons why the tribunal would not take coastal instability into account in *Bangladesh* v. *India* was that it considered the impacts of climate-related changes to be uncertain and unpredictable.[205] However, the IPCC publishes reliable predictions concerning future changes to coastal geography, which can be evidenced in judicial proceedings.[206] Furthermore, even if the effects of climate change are not sufficiently foreseeable, certain geophysical conditions can be clearly established.

The presence of a delta is a good example of circumstances that can be taken into account in maritime delimitation, as forming part of the geographical conditions existing at the time of delimitation. The instability of a delta is a given; future changes are not only possible but quite certain and they can be evidenced, not only by predicting future events, but by reference to past and ongoing changes. This was evidenced in *Nicaragua* v. *Honduras*, where the area to be delimited was undergoing rapid changes[207] and the Court looked to past changes spanning the last century to determine the unstable nature of coastal features in the mouth of the river.[208] It noted that cays were 'extremely vulnerable to tropical storms and hurricanes which occur frequently in the Caribbean'[209] and that this instability was sufficiently evident to affect the delimitation.

The tribunal's decision to reject the relevance of coastal instability in *Bangladesh* v. *India* seems to have been rooted in a policy argument rather than a rule of law. The argument was that 'neither the prospect of climate change nor its possible effects can jeopardize the large number of settled maritime boundaries throughout the world'.[210] This is unconvincing because the relevance of coastal instability for boundary delimitation cannot, in itself, jeopardize existing maritime boundaries. They generally remain final and binding once agreed upon or settled through judicial means.[211] The delimitation of boundaries has no bearing on the validity of pre-existing international boundaries. Therefore, the main argument for rejecting

205 Ibid., para 399.
206 This is discussed further in Section 3.3.2.
207 *Nicaragua* v. *Honduras* (n 6) para 32.
208 Ibid., paras 144–145.
209 Ibid., para 28.
210 *Bangladesh* v. *India* (n 3) para 217.
211 See Chapter 5.

the relevance of coastal instability should be dismissed and difficulties in determining coastal instability can be overcome, as explained below, in Section 3.3.2.

The process of maritime delimitation involves many subjective evaluations. When applying the law, courts and tribunals must choose between different interpretations the one that leads to the most equitable solution.[212] Coastal instability may only be relevant on rare occasions and it is not submitted that general rules should be drawn from exceptional precedents. Nonetheless, coastal instability can arguably be considered to form part of relevant circumstances existing at the time of delimitation and in such cases, it should not be ignored.

3.3.2 *Evidence of Foreseeable Changes to Coastal Geography*

Having determined that coastal instability can be an inseparable part of the relevant coast and qualify as relevant circumstances in maritime delimitation, this section explains how coastal instability can be proven and relied upon by courts and tribunals in contentious cases.

The tribunal held, in *Bangladesh* v. *India*, that, '[n]atural evolution, uncertainty and lack of predictability as to the impact of climate change on the marine environment, particularly the coastal front of States, make all predictions concerning the amount of coastal erosion or accretion unpredictable'.[213] However, courts and tribunals must often deal with scientific evidence in environmental disputes[214] and in disputes concerning maritime boundaries.[215] Some reluctance to engage with complex scientific evidence can be detected but courts and tribunals are increasingly meeting the challenge.

In the *Gabčíkovo-Nagymaros* case, in 1997, both Hungary and Slovakia provided an abundance of scientific evidence demonstrating the environmental/ecological and seismic impacts stemming from the Nagymaros Project.[216] The ICJ did not engage with it as much as could have been expected.[217] Similarly, in *Bangladesh* v. *India*, the tribunal showed little regard for evidence demonstrating 'extreme coastal instability in the Bengal Delta'[218] and outright denied the relevance of foreseeable changes.[219] The tribunal also noted that these changes were too

212 *Tunisia/Libyan Arab Jamahiriya* (n 4) para 71.

213 *Bangladesh* v. *India* (n 3) para 399.

214 See, for example, *Pulp Mills on the River Uruguay (Argentina* v. *Uruguay)* (Judgment) [2010] ICJ Rep 14, para 165; Alan Boyle and James Harrison, 'Judicial Settlement of International Environmental Disputes: Current Problems' (2013) 4 (2) Journal of International Dispute Settlement 245, 266.

215 See, for example, *Bangladesh/Myanmar* (n 3) para 446: 'In view of uncontested scientific evidence regarding the unique nature of the Bay of Bengal and information submitted during the proceedings, the Tribunal is satisfied that there is a continuous and substantial layer of sedimentary rocks extending from Myanmar's coast to the area beyond 200 nm.'

216 *Case Concerning the Gabčíkovo-Nagymaros Project (Hungary/Slovakia)* (Judgment) [1997] ICJ Rep 7, 64, para 140.

217 See Alan Boyle and James Harrison (n 214) 268.

218 *Bangladesh* v. *India* (n 3) para 237.

219 Ibid., para 421.

unpredictable to shape the outcome of the case.[220] Nonetheless, they arguably did affect the tribunal's choice of base points.[221]

Courts and tribunals have successfully engaged with scientific evidence in several cases. For example, in *Whaling in the Antarctic*,[222] *Pulp Mills*[223] and *Nicaragua* v. *Colombia*.[224] A good example is the *Kishenganga* arbitration, where the tribunal relied on estimations concerning the 'potential changes' in the ecosystem of the Kishenganga river[225] and explicitly referred to the 'evolving science of predicting the environmental changes'.[226] Difficulties relating to the use of scientific evidence can be overcome and relevant facts should not be disregarded by reference to lack of such evidence. After all, courts and tribunals can gather further evidence on their own accord.

Courts and tribunals are generally not limited to the evidence provided by disputing parties. It is within their power, depending on the procedure of each case, to request further evidence[227] or to appoint their own independent experts.[228] They can even go on site visits *propriu motu*.[229] However, it seems most reasonable to expect judicial bodies to consider scientific evidence in their decisions if parties to a dispute have relied heavily on such material in their submissions.[230] Therefore, courts and tribunals can request further evidence if they wish to construct equitable boundaries by reference to changing circumstances. Moreover, States can encourage such an outcome by emphasizing the relevance of coastal instability in judicial proceedings and/or maritime boundary negotiations, and by presenting relevant scientific evidence.

States often disagree on which evidence is most reliable.[231] They may also disagree on how to interpret available evidence, such as maps and treaties,[232] and they often present incompatible evidence.[233] Nonetheless, the judicial bodies settling their disputes must decide the facts of each case before applying the relevant law. For

220 Ibid., para 399.
221 See Section 3.4.1.
222 *Whaling in the Antarctic (Australia* v. *Japan: New Zealand intervening)* (Merits) [2014] ICJ Rep 226, paras 134–136.
223 *Pulp Mills on the River Uruguay* (n 214) 72.
224 *Territorial and Maritime Dispute (Nicaragua* v. *Colombia)* (n 8) para 35.
225 *The Indus Waters Kishenganga Arbitration (Pakistan* v. *India)* (2013) 150 ILR 311, para 100.
226 Ibid., para 98.
227 See PCA Arbitration Rules 2012 article 27(3); Article 62 of the Rules of the ICJ; Article 77 of the Rules of ITLOS.
228 See *Philippines* v. *China* (n 182) para 15.
229 See article 66 of the Rules of the ICJ.
230 Alan Boyle and James Harrison (n 214) 268.
231 See, for example, *Pulp Mills on the River Uruguay* (n 214) 72.
232 See, for example, Jocelyn Bowden, 'The Texas-New Mexico Boundary Dispute along the Rio Grande' (1959) 63 The Southwestern Historical Quarterly 221, 225; *Frontier Dispute (Burkina Faso/Republic of Mali)* (Judgment) [1986] ICJ Rep 554, 573 *Maritime Delimitation in the Black Sea* (n 62) para 72.
233 See, for example, *Whaling in the Antarctic* (n 222) para 134; *Case Concerning the Gabčíkovo-Nagymaros Project* (n 216) para 140.

example, the ICJ engaged with scientific evidence in the *Pulp Mills* case where both Argentina and Uruguay presented 'a vast amount of factual and scientific material in support of their respective claims'.[234] The Court confirmed that it bore the responsibility of carefully considering all information submitted to it, however complex, before establishing the relevant facts of the case.[235]

The following sections provide an overview of the standard of proof, reliable scientific evidence and the most appropriate methods of presenting scientific evidence.

3.3.2.1 Standard of Proof

It is generally the party invoking a claim that bears the burden of proof.[236] Therefore, a State, arguing that coastal instability should affect maritime delimitation, will have to give evidence supporting its claim. States shall provide 'clear', 'convincing', 'conclusive' or 'sufficient' evidence to courts and tribunals[237] and there are several methods available for doing so. The scientific evidence presented in maritime boundary cases can be clear and incontrovertible.[238] However, the procurement of such evidence can be made more challenging by the presence of coastal instability.

The standard of proof may be lowered in environmental disputes. Judge Greenwood advocated for a standard of proof known as the balance of probabilities, in his Separate Opinion in the *Pulp Mills* case. His reasoning was that 'the nature of environmental disputes is such that the application of the higher standard of proof would have the effect of making it all but impossible for a State to discharge the burden of proof'.[239] The classification of maritime boundary disputes as environmental disputes might be subject to criticism but even if cases concerning the delimitation of boundaries at unstable or changing coastlines do not fall within that category, the same rationale applies. It can be very difficult to assess environmental changes with absolute certainty. Nonetheless, such changes can be paramount for the determination of maritime entitlements and thereby, for the outcome of any maritime delimitation. Both the ICJ and ITLOS seem to have used this standard of proof in contentious cases,[240] accepting claims without being able to 'conclusively assess the scientific evidence presented by the parties'.[241]

234 *Pulp Mills on the River Uruguay* (n 214) 71.
235 Ibid., 72–73.
236 See, for example, *Maritime Delimitation in the Black Sea* (n 62) para 68; *Pulp Mills on the River Uruguay* (n 214) para 162; *Application of the Convention on the Prevention and Punishment of the Crime of Genocide (Bosnia and Herzegovina* v. *Serbia and Montenegro)* (Judgment) [2007] ICJ Rep 75, para 204. See also article 27(1) of the PCA Arbitration Rules 2012.
237 *Pulp Mills on the River Uruguay* (n 214) paras 225, 228, 254, 259, 262, 264, 265.
238 Alan Boyle and James Harrison (n 214) 268.
239 *Pulp Mills on the River Uruguay* (n 214) Separate Opinion of Judge Greenwood, paras 25–26.
240 Alan Boyle and James Harrison (n 214) 267–268.
241 *Southern Bluefin Tuna Cases Nos 3 and 4 (New Zealand* v. *Japan; Australia* v. *Japan)* (Provisional Measures) [1999] ITLOS, 38 ILM 1624, para 80.

3.3.2.2 Reliable Scientific Evidence: The IPCC Reports

Independent scientific data is favoured over evidence produced by disputing parties. It is often the States, party to judicial proceedings, or their representatives who produce factual evidence presented to courts and tribunals.[242] The evidence can be unreliable or biased for that reason. Indeed, reports produced by independent experts or agencies should carry more weight. This question was addressed to Argentina and Uruguay in the *Pulp Mills* case. According to Argentina, the weight given to scientific evidence should depend, among other things, on the independence of the authors who should neither have any vested interests in the dispute, nor be employees of the government.[243] Similarly, the Uruguayan representatives stated that reports should not qualify as independent if prepared by experts retained for the proceedings. In contrast, expert testimony and assessments given by competent international organizations should be treated as independent evidence and consequently, afforded more weight.[244] The ICJ did not comment on this issue and it did consider all the evidence presented to it (including reports prepared by experts and consultants of either party) before making its decision.[245]

Evidence gathered by independent actors, experienced in processing such information, is given careful consideration.[246] Thus, scientific evidence presented in judicial proceedings should preferably originate from an independent source. In addition to meriting special attention, it can escape much of the criticism that one-sided evidence faces. For example, evidence produced by either party can favour that party's arguments in a biased manner and there can be an asymmetry between the parties in terms of their ability to produce such evidence due to lack of financial resources, access to expertise knowledge or access to relevant data.

The IPCC provides information on the potential impacts of climate-related changes on coastal geography. The IPCC was created by two Agencies: the United Nations Environment Programme and the World Meteorological Organization.[247] Its role is to 'assess on a comprehensive, objective, open and transparent basis the scientific, technical and socio-economic information relevant to understanding the

[242] See, for example, *The Indus Waters Kishenganga Arbitration* (n 225) para 14; *Pulp Mills on the River Uruguay* (n 214) para 165.

[243] *Pulp Mills on the River Uruguay* (n 214) para 166.

[244] Ibid.

[245] Ibid., para 168.

[246] *Case Concerning Armed Activities on the Territory of the Congo (Democratic republic of Congo v. Uganda)* (Judgment) [2005] ICJ Rep 168, para 61.

[247] Navraj Ghaleigh, 'Science and Climate Change Law – the Role of the IPCC in International Decision-making' in Cinnamon Carlarne, Kevin Gray and Richard Tarasofsky (eds) *The Oxford Handbook of International Climate Change Law* (Oxford University Press, 2016) 56, 59 referring to Philippe Sands and Jacqueline Peel, *Principles of International Environmental Law*, 3rd edition (Cambridge University Press, 2012) 70, 76.

scientific basis of risk of human-induced climate change'.[248] It compiles information relating to climate change and aims to convey it to policymakers and the general public.[249] The IPCC has 195 member States and it draws on expertise from all over the world when examining the most recent scientific data available for understanding the effects of climate change.[250] All member States have the opportunity to nominate authors and the authors must all sign a statement affirming that they have no conflict of interest, the point of which is to minimize the risk of bias.[251]

The IPCC is an epistemic institution, which means that it combines research from a network of leading experts.[252] The IPCC is the '*primus inter pares*' in predicting the effects of climate change,[253] 'singular in its expertise, independence, and legitimacy'.[254] Among the publications of the IPCC are the Assessment Reports, produced with regular intervals detailing the potential impacts of climate change, and the so-called Special Reports, assessing specific issues.[255] Courts and tribunals can rely on these reports because they contain practical scientific information, relevant to decision-makers.[256]

3.3.2.3 Methods of Conveying Expert Evidence

Evidence of coastal instability can be presented and interpreted in a number of ways. 'Scientific facts are rooted in methods of science [. . .] and not in methods of law'.[257] This makes the evaluation of scientific evidence particularly difficult for judges and arbitrators because even accessible data such as the IPCC reports can seem cryptic to an untrained eye. Experts can help decipher complex scientific data and apply it to the facts of a judicial dispute, enabling judges and arbitrators to use it accurately.

To this end, courts and tribunals can appoint experts or assessors to give evidence. Experts may sit with courts and tribunals when they settle disputes that involve scientific or technical matters under the auspices of UNCLOS. This may be requested by either party or decided *proprio motu* by the court or tribunal and the

248 IPCC, 'The Role of the IPCC and Key Elements of the IPCC Assessment process' (IPCC, 2010) available at: www.ipcc.ch/2010/02/04/the-role-of-the-ipcc-and-key-elements-of-the-ipcc-assessment-process/ accessed 16 January 2021.

249 IPCC, 'Organization' available at: www.ipcc.ch/organization/organization.shtml accessed 13 January 2021 Timothy Meyer, 'Institutions and Expertise: The Role of Science in Climate Change Lawmaking' in *The Oxford Handbook of International Climate Change Law* (n 247) 442.

250 IPCC, 'Organization' (n 249); Navraj Ghaleigh (n 247) 62.

251 Navraj Ghaleigh (n 247) 62.

252 Timothy Meyer (n 249) 443.

253 Navraj Ghaleigh (n 247) 61.

254 Ibid., 61 referring to Lee Kimball, 'Treaty Implementation: Scientific and Technical Advice Enters a New Stage' (1996) 28 Studies in Transnational Legal Policy 177, 196–197.

255 IPCC, 'Activities' available at: www.ipcc.ch/activities/activities.shtml accessed on 6 August 2017.

256 Timothy Meyer (n 249) 447.

257 Jean D'Aspremont and, Makane Mbengue, 'Strategies of Engagement with Scientific, Fact-Finding in International Adjudication (2014) 5 Journal of International Dispute Settlement 240, 246.

experts do not have the right to vote.[258] States can also call expert witnesses or even have experts act as counsel.[259] In particular, the Rules of Procedure of ITLOS provide that the Tribunal shall 'take all appropriate measures in order to establish the facts'.[260] It may 'at any time during the arbitral proceedings, require the Parties to produce documents, exhibits or other evidence'[261] and it can appoint independent experts to report on specific issues.[262]

Experts have assisted courts and tribunals in numerous cases. Often in environmental disputes[263] but also in disputes concerning maritime limits and boundaries, for example, *Bangladesh/Myanmar*,[264] *Philippines* v. *China*[265] and the *Barbados* v. *Trinidad and Tobago Boundary Delimitation*.[266] An expert sat with the tribunal in *Philippines* v. *China*[267] and the Philippines presented its own expert as a witness.[268]

According to Judges Al-Khasawneh and Simma of the ICJ:

> The adjudication of disputes in which the assessment of scientific questions by experts is indispensable [...] requires an interweaving of legal process with knowledge and expertise that can only be drawn from experts properly trained to evaluate the increasingly complex nature of the facts put before the Court.[269]

The judges held that, in the *Pulp Mills* case, the ICJ was 'not in a position adequately to assess and weigh complex scientific evidence of the type presented by the Parties' and that it could not do so without the assistance of experts.[270] In the words of the ICJ, 'the purpose of the expert opinion must be to assist the Court in giving judgment upon the issues submitted to it for decision'.[271] Therefore, expert opinions should be requested and awarded whenever they can help courts and tribunals decipher complicated evidence to reach just decisions.

258 UNCLOS article 289.

259 See articles 30(2) and 50 of the Statute of the ICJ; Articles 9, 21(2), 62(2) and 67(1) of the Rules of the ICJ; Article 15 of the Rules of ITLOS; UNCLOS article 289; Article 27 of the PCA Optional Rules for Arbitrating Disputes between Two States from 1992.

260 ITLOS Rules of Procedure article 22(2).

261 Ibid., article 22(4).

262 Ibid., article 24.

263 See, for example, *Trail Smelter Arbitration (United States/Canada)* (1941) III RIAA 1905 and *Award in the Arbitration regarding the Iron Rhine ("Ijzeren Rijn") Railway (Kingdom of Belgium/Kingdom of the Netherlands)* (2005) XXVII RIAA 35.

264 *Bangladesh/Myanmar* (n 3) para 446.

265 *Philippines* v. *China* (n 182) paras 58 and 64–65.

266 *Barbados* v. *Trinidad and Tobago* (n 44) 153.

267 See, for example, *Philippines* v. *China* (n 182) para 58.

268 Ibid., paras 64–65.

269 Joint Dissenting Opinion of Judges Al-Khasawneh and Simma in *Pulp Mills on the River Uruguay* (n 214) para 3 referring to Caroline Foster, *Science and the Precautionary Principle in International Courts: Expert Evidence, Burden of Proof and Finality* (Cambridge University Press, 2011) Chapter 2.

270 Joint Dissenting Opinion of Judges Al-Khasawneh and Simma in *Pulp Mills on the River Uruguay* (n 214) para 3.

271 Ibid., para 5.

Expert scientists have appeared as agents, counsel or representatives in a number of cases. For example the *Gabčíkovo-Nagymaros* case,[272] the *Barbados* v. *Trinidad and Tobago Boundary Delimitation*[273] and the *Pulp Mills* case.[274] Both Argentina and Uruguay used experts as counsel in the *Pulp Mills* case but the ICJ declared that it 'would have found it more useful had they been presented by the Parties as expert witnesses under Articles 57 and 64 of the Rules of Court, instead of being included as counsel in their respective delegations'.[275] The ICJ went on to say that, experts providing evidence in judicial proceedings should appear as experts or witnesses, rather than as counsel, so that the opposing party and the Court could question them.[276]

The ICJ can, in addition to admitting experts as witnesses, agents, counsel, representatives or judges, appoint assessors who differ from experts insofar as they can sit with the Court during judicial deliberations, albeit without a vote.[277] Furthermore, the Court can arrange for enquiries to be carried out[278] by, for example, having a specialist committee gathering scientific data on a particular question and reporting back to the arbitral tribunal. This was done in the *Trail Smelter* case where two technical consultants were given specific tasks.[279]

The rules governing ITLOS and the PCA 'Optional Rules for Arbitrating Disputes between Two States' make no mention of assessors or enquiries. However, States can allow for the use of assessors in arbitral proceedings where procedure is optional. Additionally, States have the right to request that at least two experts sit with any court or tribunal having jurisdiction over a dispute under UNCLOS Section 2 (if it involves scientific or technical matters) and the relevant court or tribunal may decide this *proprio motu*.[280] Furthermore, experts can sit as arbitrators in arbitral proceedings and, thereby, take part in deliberations with other arbitrators and vote, unlike assessors.[281] This method was used, for example, in the *Kishenganga Arbitration* where a specialist in hydrology, Professor Howard Weather, acted as an arbitrator.[282]

One or more of these methods should be used in maritime boundary delimitation proceedings when courts and tribunals have to consider complex scientific data concerning changes to coastal geography and/or environmental circumstances, as discussed in Chapter 4.

272 See *Case Concerning the Gabčíkovo-Nagymaros Project* (n 216) 9–10.
273 *Barbados* v. *Trinidad and Tobago* (n 44) 153.
274 *Pulp Mills on the River Uruguay* (n 214) 22–24.
275 Ibid., para 167.
276 Ibid.
277 Article 30(2) of the Statute of the ICJ and articles 9 and 21(2) of the Rules of the ICJ.
278 Article 67(1) of the Rules of the ICJ. This was done, for example, in *Corfu Channel (United Kingdom of Great Britain and Northern Ireland* v. *Albania)* (Merits) [1949] ICJ Rep 4, 151.
279 *Trail Smelter Arbitration* (n 263) 1934.
280 UNCLOS article 289.
281 Article 9(1) of the Rules of the ICJ.
282 *The Indus Waters Kishenganga Arbitration* (n 225).

3.4 ACHIEVING AN EQUITABLE SOLUTION WITH DUE REGARD FOR COASTAL INSTABILITY

Maritime boundaries delimit maritime entitlements. Maritime entitlements change when islands become inhabitable, when they submerge and when baselines recede. These changes may not only affect maritime limits within bilateral boundaries but also the enforceability of various agreements relating to boundaries, for example, concerning exploitation of resources or environmental protection. It is reasonable to think that States may want to consider ongoing and imminent changes when establishing permanent boundaries. Even if courts and tribunals reject the relevance of such changes under the applicable law, States can always incorporate them into the negotiating process.

Several measures are available for delimiting maritime boundaries with due consideration for coastal instability. Four viable options have been identified and these are explained in subsequent sections.

3.4.1 *Selection of Base Points*

An equidistance line is constructed on the basis of selected base points. These are located on relevant coastlines and coastal features. Therefore, courts and tribunals are required to determine which parts of the relevant coastlines are to form the basis of an equidistance line and, consequently, which base points to use.[283] In this respect, they cannot rely solely on the base points proposed by the disputing parties.[284] When constructing an equidistance line, courts and tribunals must assess the status of coastal features to determine whether they are islands, rocks, shoals, reefs, low-tide elevations or submerged features, and thus, which maritime zones they can generate, if any.[285] Subsequently, courts and tribunals must choose 'the most appropriate points on the coasts of the two States concerned'.[286] Arguably, the most appropriate base points for an equitable boundary are those that will continue to generate maritime entitlements in the near future.

Base points used for unilateral delineation are not always suitable for the delimitation of maritime boundaries. For example, in *Bangladesh* v. *India*, the tribunal held that, although low-tide elevations could be appropriate base points for measuring the breadth of the territorial sea, under UNCLOS article 13, they might not be appropriate for delimitation of a bilateral boundary.[287] The reason may be that, while unilateral limits can change to reflect changing circumstances, bilateral

[283] See, for example, *Territorial and Maritime Dispute (Nicaragua* v. *Colombia)* (n 8) para 200; *Cameroon* v. *Nigeria: Equatorial Guinea intervening* (n 10) para 290.

[284] *Maritime Delimitation in the Black Sea* (n 62) para 137.

[285] See, for example, *Philippines* v. *China* (n 182) and *Territorial and Maritime Dispute (Nicaragua* v. *Colombia)* (n 8) para 145.

[286] *Maritime Delimitation in the Black Sea* (n 62) para 117.

[287] *Bangladesh* v. *India* (n 3) para 260.

boundaries generally cannot. Their permanence should be borne in mind when base points are chosen.

The selection of base points should take account of all relevant circumstances throughout the delimitation process. When drawing a provisional equidistance line, courts and tribunals should look to ongoing and foreseeable changes to relevant coasts and refrain from using base points that will soon become unfeasible. This is different from the adjustment of a provisional equidistance line by reference to relevant circumstances, which happens at the second stage, after a provisional boundary has been established on the basis of appropriate base points. The second stage could lead courts and tribunals to abandon or reduce the weight of unstable base points. Thus, under the equidistance/relevant circumstances method, coastal instability can affect the drawing of a boundary at two stages.

The selection of base points is a very delicate matter because '[t]he slightest irregularity in a coastline is automatically magnified by the equidistance line as regards the consequences for the delimitation'.[288] The effect of any irregularity is exaggerated when it is further from the coastline, and, therefore, the unreasonableness of a boundary that is based on an irregularity of the coastline increases in correlation with the extent of the irregularity and the distance from the coastline to the boundary.[289] Furthermore, 'any variation or error in situating [base points at a close proximity] would become disproportionately magnified in the resulting equidistance line'.[290] Therefore, a choice between two possible base points can drastically affect the resulting equidistance boundary. This is why base points must be selected with great care.

According to ITLOS 'neither case law nor State practice indicates that there is a general rule concerning the effect to be given to islands in maritime delimitation. It depends on the particular circumstances of each case'.[291] Courts and tribunals have chosen not to establish base points on coastal features by reference to their size and distance from the mainland. For example, in the *Black Sea* case, the ICJ decided that no base points would be located on Serpents' Island (a feature of 0.17 square km, 20 nm from Ukraine's coastline) because doing so 'would amount to grafting an extraneous element onto Ukraine's coastline; the consequence would be a judicial refashioning of geography, which neither the law nor practice of maritime delimitation authorizes'.[292] Similarly, in the *Nicaragua* v. *Colombia* case, the Court decided not to place any base points on the high tide elevation Quitasueño, a tiny Colombian feature 38 nm from the nearest Colombian island, because its effect on an equidistance line would be to 'push that line significantly closer to Nicaragua'.[293]

288 *North Sea Continental Shelf* (n 9) para 89.
289 Ibid.
290 *Nicaragua* v. *Honduras* (n 6) para 277.
291 *Bangladesh/Myanmar* (n 3) para 147.
292 *Maritime Delimitation in the Black Sea* (n 62) para 149.
293 *Territorial and Maritime Dispute (Nicaragua* v. *Colombia)* (n 8) para 202.

In *Gulf of Maine*, the ICJ held that base points should not be placed on 'tiny islands, uninhabited rocks or low-tide elevations', as to do so can distort the equidistance line.[294] Similarly, in *Nicaragua* v. *Honduras*, the ICJ confirmed that it is appropriate to disregard very small coastal features, when selecting base points, if they otherwise 'distort the relevant geography'.[295] This same rationale can be applied when constructing boundaries at unstable coastlines. Thus, insignificant coastal features can be disregarded for the purpose of selecting base points if they otherwise distort the relevant geography in the near future, for example, where they are about to be submerged.

In *Bangladesh* v. *India*, the tribunal found that low-tide elevations were not a suitable basis for base points.[296] 'If alternative base points situated on the coastline of the parties are available, they should be preferred to base points located on low-tide elevations.'[297] The tribunal went on a site visit to ascertain the nature of proposed features[298] and it found no low-tide elevation that it deemed suitable for base points.[299] The visibility of a base point on South Talpaty/New Moore Island could not be denied and yet, the feature 'could in no way be considered as situated on the coastline, much less a "protuberant coastal point"'.[300] Indeed, the feature has now been submerged as a result of sea level rise.[301] The reasoning put forth by the arbitral tribunal in *Bangladesh* v. *India* supports the conclusion that reliable base points should be preferred to those on submerging low-tide elevations, or even rocks.

3.4.2 *Adjustment of a Provisional Boundary*

The selection of base points and construction of a provisional equidistance line is 'nothing more than a first step and in no way prejudges the ultimate solution which must be designed to achieve an equitable result'.[302] The second step under the equidistance/relevant circumstances method is the adjustment of the provisional boundary by reference to relevant circumstances. Courts and tribunals must consider any factors justifying a modification of that line, before they reach an equitable solution.[303]

Jurisprudence has evidenced that courts and tribunals may decide to give specific coastal features limited or no effect. That is, less than 'their full potential entitlement

294 *Gulf of Maine* (n 9) para 201.
295 *Nicaragua* v. *Honduras* (n 6) para 202.
296 *Bangladesh* v. *India* (n 3) para 261.
297 Ibid., para 262.
298 Ibid., para 22.
299 Ibid., paras 360–362.
300 Ibid., para 263, referring to *Maritime Delimitation in the Black Sea* (n 62) para 117.
301 ILC, 'Sea-Level Rise in Relation to International Law: First Issues Paper' (27 April–5 June and 6 July–7 August 2020) UN Doc A/CN.4/740, para 195.
302 *Territorial and Maritime Dispute (Nicaragua* v. *Colombia)* (n 8) para 196.
303 *Cameroon* v. *Nigeria: Equatorial Guinea intervening* (n 10) para 288.

to maritime zones'.[304] For example, two delimitation lines may be drawn, one giving a feature full effect and another one ignoring the feature. 'The delimitation line actually adopted is then drawn between the first two lines, either in such a way as to divide equally the area between them, or as bisector of the angle which they make with each other, or possibly by treating the island as displaced toward the mainland by half its actual distance therefrom.'[305] Thus, foreseeable changes to coastal geography can affect the construction of an equidistance line first, when choosing viable base points, and, second, when adjusting the provisional boundary line and determining the relative weight given to each feature. Moreover, other boundary lines can also be adjusted by reference to relevant circumstances. Therefore, an angle-bisector line may be adjusted in the same manner as a provisional equidistance line.[306]

The size of islands has played a role in maritime boundary delimitation as small islands have been given less than full effect. This was done, for example, in the *Anglo-French Continental Shelf* case (in respect of the Isles of Scilly),[307] the *Tunisia/Libyan Arab Jamahiriya* case (in respect of the Kerkennah Islands)[308] and the *Gulf of Maine* case (in respect of Seal Island).[309] All of these islands were given half effect.[310] Similarly, coastal instability can amount to relevant circumstances, and such circumstances can lead to the adjustment of provisional boundary lines, giving coastal features partial or no effect on the grounds that they cannot maintain the ability to sustain maritime entitlements.

The ICJ had to decide, in *Qatar* v. *Bahrain*, whether the tiny, uninhabited and unstable island of Qit'at Jaradah met the requirements to constitute an island under UNCLOS article 121.[311] The parties disputed its status as an island or a low-tide elevation. Bahrain submitted that the upper part of the feature's surface had been removed in 1986 and that it had, thereafter, 'recovered its island status by natural accretion'.[312] Qatar, however, argued that Qit'at Jaradah had never been portrayed as an island on nautical charts, but rather, as a low-tide elevation, even though Bahrain had sought to alter its nature in 1985–1986.[313] Furthermore, Qatar submitted that even if it had, at times been elevated above high tide, the instability of the feature should result in the legal classification of a shoal.[314] The physical status of Qit'at Jaradah had changed significantly in the decades leading up to the case but scientific

304 See *Maritime Delimitation in the Black Sea* (n 62) para 185; *Libyan Arab Jamahiriya/Malta* (n 6) 48, para 64; *Qatar* v. *Bahrain* (n 20) para 219; *Nicaragua* v. *Honduras* (n 6) paras 302 *et seq*.

305 *Tunisia/Libyan Arab Jamahiriya* (n 4) para 129.

306 See *Nicaragua* v. *Honduras* (n 6) para 294.

307 *Anglo-French Continental Shelf* (n 12) para 251.

308 *Tunisia/Libyan Arab Jamahiriya* (n 4) para 129.

309 *Gulf of Maine* (n 9) para 222.

310 Robin Churchill (n 130) 25.

311 *Qatar* v. Bahrain (n 20) para 191.

312 Ibid., para 192.

313 Ibid., para 193.

314 Ibid.

experts supported the Court's conclusion that it was, at the time of delimitation, above water at high tide and could, therefore, qualify as an island, at the time of delimitation.[315]

Judge Vereshchetin commented on the instability of the feature and upheld Qatar's claim that because of its constantly changing physical condition it should not be considered an island.[316] In fact, the Court decided, after having determined that the feature was an island under UNCLOS article 121, to give it no effect, noting that 'a disproportionate effect would be given to an insignificant maritime feature' if the boundary line would be measured from Qit'at Jaradah.[317] Furthermore, the Court drew two provisional boundary lines, one with a base point on Fasht al Azm (regarding it as part of another island) and another line without a base point on Fasht al Azm (regarding it as a separate low-tide elevation). The feature in question was a small island and less than 20 per cent of the island was permanently above water. In light of this feature's limited significance, the Court decided to let the boundary line pass between the two provisional lines, giving it limited effect.[318]

It seems very likely that coastal instability had an effect on the Court's decision. Still, the justification explicitly only referred to the features' 'insignificance' and small size.[319] The features should arguably have been disregarded for the purpose of plotting the provisional equidistance line but the reason why they were given any effect was that coastal features under Bahraini sovereignty would fall on the Qatari side of the boundary if Qit'at Jaradah and Fasht al Azm were completely ignored. Therefore, the boundary line was adjusted to pass between the features and make sure that they fell on the 'right' side of the boundary.[320] This decision demonstrates that the adjustment of a provisional boundary line does not necessarily require geometric calculations from coastal features that have been assigned a specific weight. Instead, an equitable solution can be arrived at in an ad hoc manner.

Submerging features have been given partial or no effect in maritime boundary agreements. This was done, for example, in the boundary agreements between Belgium/France and Belgium/the United Kingdom[321] and the agreement between Iceland and Denmark (Greenland).[322] The British low-tide elevation Long Sand Head was given only about one-third effect in the agreement between Belgium and

315 Ibid., paras 194–195.

316 Declaration of Judge Vereshchetin in *Qatar* v. *Bahrain* (n 20) 184.

317 *Qatar* v. *Bahrain* (n 20) para 219.

318 Ibid., para 218.

319 Ibid., para 219.

320 *Qatar* v. *Bahrain* (n 20) paras 218–220.

321 Agreement between the Government of the United Kingdom of Great Britain and Northern Ireland and the Government of the Kingdom of Belgium relating to the Delimitation of the Continental Shelf between the two Countries (n 176).

322 Agreement between the Government of the Kingdom of Denmark along with the Local Government of Greenland on the one hand, and the Government of the Republic of Iceland on the other hand on the Delimitation of the Continental Shelf and the Fishery Zone in the Area between Greenland and Iceland (adopted 11 November 1997, entered into force 27 May 1998) 2074 UNTS 58.

the United Kingdom relating to the delimitation of the continental shelf between the two countries.[323] Similarly, Kolbeinsey, an islet that was expected to be submerged by 2020, was given only about one-third effect in the agreement between Iceland and Denmark (Greenland) in 1997.[324] Furthermore, the boundary line delimiting the continental shelf between Belgium and France was arrived at by drawing a line with consideration for the low-tide elevations in front of the French and Belgian coasts and another line following the low-water line of the coasts.[325] Thus, the low-tide elevations of both France and Belgium were given roughly half effect.

3.4.3 *The Angle-Bisector Method as a Response to Coastal Instability*

The equidistance/relevant circumstances method is the preferred method of delimitation. It is considered to be an objective method, reflecting the basis for title and prima facie leading to an equitable solution.[326] However, the equidistance method is not the only method that is centred on the root of maritime entitlements, that is, coastal geography. So too is the angle-bisector method. The equidistance/relevant circumstances method has been described as having an intrinsic value due to its scientific character.[327] Nonetheless, both methods are 'based upon geometric techniques'.[328] The tribunal in *Bangladesh* v. *India* gave the following reasons for preferring the equidistance method over the angle-bisector method:

> the advantage of the equidistance/relevant circumstances method lies in the fact that it clearly separates the steps to be taken and is, thus, more transparent. The identification of a provisional equidistance line is based on geometrically objective criteria, while at the same time account is taken of the geography of the area through the selection of appropriate base points. By contrast, depicting the relevant coasts as straight lines under the angle-bisector method involves subjective considerations.[329]

Accordingly, the equidistance method has been preferred on the grounds of a perceived predictability and objectivity. However, 'it is the virtue – though it may also be the weakness – of the equidistance method to take full account of almost all variations in the relevant coastlines'.[330] These considerations for all

323 Agreement between the Government of the United Kingdom of Great Britain and Northern Ireland and the Government of the Kingdom of Belgium relating to the Delimitation of the Continental Shelf between the two Countries (n 176).

324 Agreement between the Government of the Kingdom of Denmark along with the Local Government of Greenland on the one hand, and the Government of the Republic of Iceland on the other hand on the Delimitation of the Continental Shelf and the Fishery Zone in the Area between Greenland and Iceland (n 322).

325 Agreement between the Government of the French Republic and the Government of the Kingdom of Belgium on the delimitation of the continental shelf (n 595) article 2.

326 Prosper Weil (n 156) 282.

327 *Guinea/Guinea-Bissau* (n 118) para 102.

328 *Bangladesh* v. *India* (n 3) para 343.

329 Ibid., para 343.

330 *Tunisia/Libyan Arab Jamahiriya* (n 4) para 126.

relevant circumstances may well be seen as a weakness insofar as they involve various subjective considerations and, consequently, make the equidistance/relevant circumstances method less objective than it may appear at first glance. The second stage of the equidistance/relevant circumstances method involves arbitrary adjustments by reference to numerous different circumstances and the disproportionality test arguably has unpredictable consequences.[331]

Olorundami explains that 'it is unnecessary to proceed with the three-stage methodology simply for the sake of standardization, if clarity and objectivity will be sacrificed thereby'.[332] The equidistance approach should arguably be abandoned when another method is more suitable. Indeed, equidistance is not obligatory as a preliminary step,[333] relevant circumstances can render it wholly unsuitable,[334] and the obligation to reach an equitable solution may require the use of a different method, even for the delimitation of a territorial sea boundary.[335]

UNCLOS makes one reference to unstable coastlines and that is in article 7(2). It prescribes the use of straight baselines at coastlines that are highly unstable due to the presence of a delta or other natural conditions. Thus, UNCLOS expressly indicates that where coastal instability is present, it may be appropriate to determine a State's maritime entitlements on the basis of an approximation of the coastline, which is precisely the effect of the angle-bisector method. The angle-bisector method is based upon the '[g]eneral direction of the coast, minimizing the effects of irregularities, reducing them to their truer proportions'.[336] Furthermore, 'one of the practical advantages of the bisector method is that a minor deviation in the exact position of endpoints, which are at a reasonable distance from the shared point, will have only a relatively minor influence on the course of the entire coastal front line'.[337] Therefore, the angle-bisector approach is particularly suitable for unstable coastlines.

Angle-bisector boundaries do not correlate precisely to the coastline. Thus, minor changes will usually be of little, if any, significance for the equitableness of the solution. In fact, future changes to the coastline would not affect the equitable nature of an angle-bisector boundary line unless they were significant enough to alter the linear approximation of relevant coastlines. The submergence of small or incidental coastal features might have no effect as such features would generally not

331 Malcolm Evans, 'Maritime Boundary Delimitation: Where Do We Go from Here?' in David Freestone, Richard Barnes and David Ong (eds), *The Law of the Sea: Progress and Prospects* (Oxford University Press, 2006) 137, 153.

332 Fayokemi Olorundami, 'Objectivity versus Subjectivity in the Context of the ICJ's Three-Stage Methodology of Maritime Boundary Delimitation' (2017) 32 The International Journal of Marine and Coastal Law 36, 53, referring to *Territorial and Maritime Dispute (Nicaragua* v. *Colombia)* (n 8) Declaration of Judge Xue, para 9.

333 See, for example, *Libyan Arab Jamahiriya/Malta* (n 6) para 63.

334 *Libyan Arab Jamahiriya/Malta* (n 6) 44, para 56.

335 *Nicaragua* v. *Honduras* (n 6) para 281.

336 *North Sea Continental Shelf* (n 9) para 98.

337 *Nicaragua* v. *Honduras* (n 6) para 294.

impact the location of an angle-bisector line. Consequently, the angle-bisector method seems optimal for achieving long-lasting and equitable solutions where coastal geography is expected to undergo moderate changes.

The ICJ was faced with particular difficulties in relation to the selection of viable base points in the *Nicaragua* v. *Honduras* case because of extreme coastal instability.[338] The Court ultimately constructed an angle-bisector boundary[339] because the circumstances of the case made it 'impossible for the Court to identify base points and construct a provisional equidistance line for the single maritime boundary delimiting maritime areas off the Parties' mainland coasts'.[340] In their arguments, both Nicaragua and Honduras referred to changing circumstances as relevant for the delimitation process. Nicaragua argued for use of the angle-bisector method because of the instability of the river delta, while Honduras relied on the principle of *uti possidetis juris* and on a tacit agreement between the parties allegedly constituting a traditional boundary. However, Honduras also asked the Court to take the changing geographical characteristics of the mouth of the River Coco into account when determining the location of this boundary.[341] It did 'not deny that geometrical methods of delimitation, such as perpendiculars and bisectors, are methods that may produce equitable delimitations in some circumstances'.[342]

Nicaragua maintained that it would be 'technically impossible to draw an equidistance line because it would have to be entirely drawn on the basis of the two outermost points of the mouth of the river, which are extremely unstable and continuously change position'.[343] The instability of these two base points should not matter if the relevant coastal geography was only that existing at the date of the award, but the Court clearly looked beyond a snapshot of the existing circumstances. That is why the identification of viable base points was impossible. The Court concluded that the 'continued accretion at the Cape might render any equidistance line so constructed today arbitrary and unreasonable in the near future'.[344] It consequently established an angle-bisector boundary.[345]

The parties also disagreed on the method best suited for the purpose of achieving an equitable maritime boundary in *Bangladesh* v. *India*. India argued for the application of the equidistance/relevant circumstances method and maintained that no adjustment of the equidistance line was warranted by relevant circumstances. Bangladesh, however, argued that the instability due to coastal erosion at the Bengal Delta called for an angle-bisector boundary line or, in the alternative, an

338 Ibid., para 28.
339 Further discussion in Section 3.4.2.
340 *Nicaragua* v. *Honduras* (n 6) para 280.
341 Ibid., para 18.
342 Ibid., para 274.
343 Ibid., para 102.
344 Ibid., para 277.
345 Ibid., para 294.

adjustment of a provisional equidistance line.[346] According to Bangladesh, 'instability of the coastline is a major factor weighing against the use of the provisional equidistance/relevant circumstances method'. This was particularly relevant 'in view of the potential effect of climate change and sea level rise in the Bay of Bengal' because within a few years of the delimitation, many of the low-tide elevations proposed as base points by Bangladesh would be submerged.[347]

The tribunal rejected Bangladesh's arguments relating to coastal instability and opted for the equidistance/relevant circumstances method instead of an angle-bisector. The tribunal did not reject the idea that the angle-bisector method could be permissible. Nonetheless, it submitted that the equidistance/relevant circumstances method should be preferred over the angle-bisector method unless particular factors made the former inappropriate.[348] It held that the delimitation process should aim for transparency and predictability,[349] and asserted that the angle-bisector method involved 'subjective considerations'.[350] However, as previously explained, the equidistance/relevant circumstances method is also immersed in subjective considerations. The perceived transparency and predictability come from the preliminary first step but are lost at the two subsequent stages. Indeed, there are numerous ways of adjusting provisional equidistance lines by reference to relevant circumstances.

It is interesting to note that the final boundary established between Bangladesh and India was very similar to the one proposed by Bangladesh.[351] Assuming that the end result was equitable, and considering the similarities between the end result and the boundary proposed by Bangladesh, one might conclude that application of the angle-bisector method would also have produced an equally equitable boundary, which is the 'paramount objective' of boundary delimitation.[352] If the equidistance/relevant circumstances method would lead to a solution almost identical to that of another method, such as the angle-bisector method, then the equidistance/relevant circumstances could well be preferential as the most predominant method in the field of delimitation. However, the legal reasoning underpinning judicial decisions is of great importance for subsequent cases and for the development of the law. An equitable solution may have been achieved in *Bangladesh* v. *India* (allegedly) without consideration for changing circumstances. However, this may not be possible in all cases and, therefore, the relevance of changing circumstances should not be categorically rejected.

346 *Bangladesh* v. *India* (n 3) paras 208 and 210.
347 Ibid., para 213.
348 Ibid., paras 344–345.
349 Ibid., para 339.
350 Ibid., para 343.
351 Marcin Kaldunski, 'A Commentary on Maritime Boundary Arbitration between Bangladesh and India Concerning the Bay of Bengal' (2015) 28 (4) Leiden Journal of International Law 799, 845.
352 *Bangladesh* v. *India* (n 3) para 339.

3.4.4 *Fluctuating Boundaries*

Coastal instability can be accounted for by selecting base points that are viable by reference to changing circumstances; adjusting provisional baselines; or using the angle-bisector method. These methods do not ensure that a maritime boundary continues to reflect relevant maritime entitlements in the wake of significant or unforeseeable geographical changes. However, fluctuating boundaries can do just that. In *Bangladesh* v. *India*, Bangladesh submitted that 'it would be against equity and common sense to draw a permanent boundary line using base points on an unstable coast'.[353] Perhaps the problem is not the unstable coastline but, rather, the demand that the boundary be stable. Indeed, Caron explained that baselines are ambulatory and boundaries that are measured from baselines may also be ambulatory.[354] 'If the baseline moves, the boundary moves. If a baseline point such as an exposed rock disappears, the boundary generated by that point also disappears.'[355]

The following sections will demonstrate that UNCLOS article 15 establishes an ambulatory equidistance boundary that fluctuates until and unless otherwise agreed; that maritime boundaries can fluctuate on the basis of bilateral agreements; that courts and tribunals can produce fluctuating maritime boundaries; and that even land boundaries can fluctuate.

3.4.4.1 Fluctuating Boundaries to the Territorial Sea

UNCLOS article 15 establishes a provisional, fluctuating boundary. The article sets a bilateral limit to the territorial sea and explains what governs this bilateral relationship in the absence of a delimitation agreement.[356] The equidistance line arguably functions as a boundary that neither State can cross until a more definitive boundary is settled, unless States can demonstrate that they have a lawful claim to an area beyond the equidistance or median line on the grounds of special circumstances or historic title. Such a claim might represent the provisional boundary if well founded, particularly if no objections were made. These types of provisional boundaries assumedly fluctuate in accordance with ambulatory baselines to continuously reflect relevant coastlines, unless and until otherwise agreed.

Article 12(1) of the 1958 Convention on the Territorial Sea and the Contiguous Zone and article 6 of the Convention on the Continental Shelf mirror UNCLOS article 15.

353 Ibid., 112. See Bangladesh's Memorial, paragraph 6.83.

354 David Caron, 'Climate Change, Sea Level Rise and the Coming Uncertainty in Oceanic Boundaries: A Proposal to Avoid Conflict' in Seoung-Yong Hong and Jon Van Dyke (eds) *Maritime Boundary Disputes, Settlement Processes and the Law of the Sea* (Martinus Nijhoff, 2008) 2.

355 ILA Baselines Committee, 'Conference Report Sofia 2012' (ILA 2012) 22 referring to David Caron (n 45) 634.

356 *Maritime Delimitation in the Caribbean Sea and the Pacific Ocean (Costa Rica* v. *Nicaragua) and Land Boundary in the Northern Part of Isla Portillos (Costa Rica* v. *Nicaragua)* (Judgment) [2018] ICJ Rep 139, para 92.

Therefore, Article 6 of the 1958 Convention on the Continental Shelf arguably establishes a provisional equidistance boundary to the continental shelf. This is of course the predecessor of UNCLOS article 83(1) and might be relevant for informing the content of that provision. However, since UNCLOS articles 74 and 83 make no reference to the equidistance method, it is less clear whether undelimited, overlapping claims to an exclusive economic zone and continental shelf are subject to provisional boundaries.[357]

The 2007 maritime boundary arbitration between Guyana and Suriname dealt with the legal effects of a provisional equidistance boundary established under UNCLOS article 15. The tribunal was tasked with the delimitation of territorial sea entitlements extending from a highly unstable coastline. The adjacent States had previously agreed on a fixed location for a territorial sea boundary reaching 3 nm seawards but no location was agreed upon when both States extended their territorial sea limits to 12 nm in 1977 and 1978.[358] The tribunal found that a 3 nm territorial sea boundary had been established by reference to the N10°E line.[359] No explicit arrangement was concluded beyond that point.[360] According to Guyana, both States relied on the 'historical equidistance line' along the N34°E azimuth, beyond the established 3 nm limit.[361] However, the equidistance line had shifted because relevant coasts were made up of mud banks 'constantly subjected to erosion and accretion'.[362]

Suriname sought to rely on the settled practice of the States in relation to the 10° line, allegedly amounting to a 'perfected instrument'. However, the tribunal found that no legal obligations had been created beyond the 3 nm limit.[363] The provisional arrangement concerning delimitation beyond 3 nm had not resulted in a permanent boundary. The tribunal concluded that the territorial sea boundary should follow the N10°E line from relevant coasts seawards to 3 nm and, thereafter, intersect the equidistance line as it was at the time of delimitation[364] – not the 'historical equidistance line'. That meant that the boundary had shifted in accordance with the relevant coastal geography. This case demonstrates that the location of a lawful equidistance line, satisfying the conditions of UNCLOS article 15, can fluctuate from the time when a provisional arrangement is established until a permanent boundary is delimited through adjudication or agreement. However, it also indicates that, in other circumstances, the practice of States could amount to a 'perfected instrument', creating a stable boundary that would be unaffected by changing baselines.

357 See Soons A, 'The Effects of Sea Level Rise on Baselines and Outer Limits of Maritime Zones' in Tómas Heiðar (ed) *New Knowledge and Changing Circumstances in the Law of the Sea* (Brill Nijhoff, 2020) 358, 367.

358 *Guyana* v. *Suriname* (n 113) para 310.

359 Ibid., para 306.

360 Ibid., para 310.

361 Ibid., para 288.

362 Ibid., para 133.

363 Ibid., para 312, referencing *Sovereignty over Certain Frontier Land (Belgium/Netherlands)* (Judgment) [1959] ICJ Rep 209, 229.

364 *Guyana* v. *Suriname* (n 113) para 325.

3.4.4.2 Agreements Establishing Fluctuating Maritime Boundaries

Equidistance boundaries arguably fluctuate unless and until otherwise agreed. A majority of the world's overlapping maritime zones remain undelimited,[365] and all those potential or provisional boundaries presumably fluctuate. In fact, a decision not to delimit maritime boundaries or rely on the default equidistance line may represent a conscious decision to employ a fluctuating boundary. Furthermore, States can explicitly agree to establish fluctuating boundaries, delimiting the territorial sea and other maritime zones. This method may produce equitable boundaries and guarantee continuing adherence to the land dominates the sea principle.

States have established international boundaries by reference to naturally fluctuating phenomena.[366] For example, by referencing the thalweg of a river or watersheds, instead of fixed locations,[367] or equidistance or median lines. These States have, according to Soons, 'deliberately opted for a (potentially) fluctuating boundary line'.[368] The lack of maritime delimitation can even mean that the States have tacitly established a fluctuating, equidistant boundary. This seems to be how the United States have delimited overlapping, exclusive economic zone entitlements with Haiti and in the Pacific. According to Ásgeirsdóttir, these are delimited by de facto equidistance boundaries.[369] Moreover, fluctuating boundaries can result from explicit treaty provisions or omission of geographic coordinates in boundary treaties. This is true not only of maritime boundaries but also of boundaries demarcating land territory.[370] The natural phenomena can undergo unforeseeable changes due to floods, earthquakes, and other environmental occurrences, which can affect the interpretation and application of dependent boundary treaties.[371]

The omission of geographic coordinates leaves room for debate concerning whether the parties intended to establish a fixed or fluctuating boundary. For example, the 1825 Treaty concerning the border of Alaska and, arguably, the maritime boundary in the Beaufort Sea,[372] refers to the 'frozen ocean',[373] a natural limit that is undoubtedly

[365] Davor Vidas (n 156) 76; Clive Schofield (n 27) 48.

[366] See David Freestone and John Pethick , 'Sea Level Rise and Maritime Boundaries: International Implications of Impacts and Responses' in Gerald Blake (ed) *Maritime Boundaries: World Boundaries, volume* 5 (Routledge, 1994) 78.

[367] Julia Lisztwan , 'Stability of Maritime Boundary Agreements' (2012) 37 Yale Journal of International Law 190.

[368] Alfred Soons, 'The Effects of a Rising Sea Level on Maritime Limits and Boundaries' (1990) 37 (2) Netherlands International Law Review 227.

[369] Áslaug Ásgeirsdóttir, 'Settling of the Maritime Boundaries of the United States: Cost of Settlement and the Benefits of Legal Certainty' (2016) 73 Marine Policy, 187, 188.

[370] For example, the 1799 border between Suriname and Berbice (a former colony where Guyana is now) ran along the west bank of the Corentyne River. See *Guyana* v. *Suriname* (n 113) para 137.

[371] See ILC, 'Fifth Report on the Law of Treaties by Sir Humphrey Waldock, Special Rapporteur' (15 November 1965–18 January 1966) UN Doc A/CN.4/183 and Add.1–4, 44.

[372] Canada and the United States have different positions on this matter. See Michael Byers, *International Law and the Arctic* (Cambridge University Press, 2013) 59.

[373] Great Britain/Russia: Limits of their Respective Possessions on the North-West Coast of America and the Navigation of the Pacific Ocean (adopted 16 February 1825) 75 Consolidated Treaty Series 95.

receding with global warming. Neither the United States nor Canada currently argues that the boundary should be measured from the ice-edge and it might not be practically feasible for either State to do so. It is still a plausible interpretation, which would result in a fluctuating boundary. Moreover, the maritime boundary agreement between France and Tonga establishes an exclusive economic zone boundary by reference to the equidistance line, without fixing any coordinates.[374] Wallis and Futuna consist of volcanic islands and fringing reefs[375] and Tonga is made up of islands of coral or limestone on a volcanic base.[376] The islands are very small, there is geological activity in the area and earthquakes are frequently felt, particularly in Futuna.[377] If these coastlines change, for example, due to sea level rise or volcanic activity, France and Tonga could argue that the equidistance boundary should fluctuate.

Other examples of potentially fluctuating maritime boundaries include the equidistance boundary between the Solomon Islands and Vanuatu. This agreement from 2016 establishes fixed coordinates but explicitly provides that the parties will monitor the location of the median line, using specific software, and adjust the boundary if new surveys indicate significant changes in the location of base points.[378] Similarly, the Agreement between Canada and Denmark relating to the Delimitation of the Continental Shelf between Greenland and Canada from 1973 provides that the boundary can be adjusted in accordance with more accurate information from new surveys.[379] Such an adjustment was made in 2004 through an exchange of notes.[380] Another example is the delimitation agreement between France and New Zealand (on behalf of the Cook Islands), which stipulates that if changes are detected in the locations of designated base points, and if the changes are 'sufficiently significant to require adjustments of the maritime boundary, the Parties agree that an adjustment will be carried out on the basis of the same principles as those used in determining the maritime boundary'[381] This seems to be a good solution, as it provides general stability (in geographic terms) but ensures that maritime boundaries can change to reflect fundamental changes to relevant coasts.

Purcell maintains that a reference to an equidistant line warrants no assumption in favour of a fluctuating boundary.[382] According to her, the principle of

374 Convention between the Government of the French Republic (Wallis and Futuna) and the Government of the Kingdom of Tonga on the delimitation of economic zones (adopted 11 January 1980, entered into force 11 January 1980) 1183 UNTS 343.

375 Rober McColl (ed) *Encyclopedia of World Geography, volume 1* (Facts on File, Inc, 2005) 978.

376 Ibid., 907.

377 Ibid., 907 and 978.

378 Treaty between the Solomon Islands and the Republic of Vanuatu concerning their Maritime Boundaries of 7 October 2016, UNTS articles 5 and 6.

379 Agreement between Canada and Denmark relating to the Delimitation of the Continental Shelf between Greenland and Canada (adopted 17 December 1973) 950 UNTS 147, article 4.

380 Exchange of Notes Constituting an Agreement to Amend the 1973 Canada – Denmark Continental Shelf Agreement (5 and 20 April, 2004) Canada Treaty Series 2009/27.

381 UN Doc A/CN.4/740 (n 301) para 135.

382 Kate Purcell, *Geographical Change and the Law of the Sea* (Oxford University Press, 2019) 151.

stability should support the opposite conclusion. Still, she also explains that the establishment of fluctuating boundaries would not necessarily be inconsistent with the principle of stability because such boundaries could promote the stability of the legal order.[383] Indeed, geographic stability is no precondition of legal stability.

3.4.4.3 Fluctuating Boundaries Resulting from Judicial Decisions

Courts and tribunals consistently establish geographically stable maritime boundaries. However, since geographic stability is not always attainable, the ICJ left fluctuating segments in two recently established maritime boundaries, in *Nicaragua* v. *Honduras* and *Costa Rica* v. *Nicaragua*.

The coastal accretion at the river delta made it very difficult for the ICJ to identify suitable base points in *Nicaragua* v. *Honduras*.[384] This was particularly problematic at the first segment of the boundary, from the land boundary terminus and seaward. Therefore, the first 3 nm of the boundary were not fixed at geographic coordinates and the purpose was to allow for adjustments to the land boundary terminus, the fluctuating Coco River.[385] Nicaragua and Honduras both proposed, in their written submissions, that due to the changing nature of the coastline the 'starting-point for the boundary line between them should be located some distance from the mainland coast, but disagreed on exactly where'.[386] During the oral proceedings, Nicaragua advocated for a fluctuating boundary, which would connect the geographically fixed maritime boundary by a straight line to the land boundary terminus, 'wherever it [might] be located on any given day'.[387] However, Honduras urged that a diplomatic solution be found for the first 3 nm of the boundary.[388] The Court ultimately concluded that the Parties should 'negotiate in good faith with a view to agreeing on the course of the delimitation line of that portion of the territorial sea located between the endpoint of the land boundary [...] and the starting-point of the single maritime boundary determined by the Court'.[389] Thus, the first segment was left to fluctuate unless and until otherwise agreed by the parties.

The solution presented by Nicaragua in the oral proceedings went even further. It would have involved a permanent decision to establish a fluctuating boundary. The Court favoured the approach originally advanced in written proceedings by both parties, that is, to fix no boundary for the first segment.[390] In so doing, the Court relied on judicial precedents confirming that maritime delimitation might 'begin at

383 Ibid., 148.
384 *Nicaragua* v. *Honduras* (n 6) paras 277 and 280.
385 Ibid., paras 311 and 320.
386 Ibid., para 307.
387 Ibid., para 309.
388 Ibid.
389 Ibid., para 321(4).
390 Ibid., para 311.

some distance out at sea', particularly where there was 'an uncertain land boundary terminus'.[391]

The ICJ recently took the next step and explicitly established a fluctuating maritime boundary. In *Costa Rica* v. *Nicaragua*, the Court constructed a 'mobile line' connecting a point on solid land to the median line 2 nm offshore. This was due to the 'high instability and narrowness of the sandspit near the mouth of the San Juan River which constitutes a barrier between the Caribbean Sea and a sizeable territory appertaining to Nicaragua'.[392] The Court found it more appropriate to create a fluctuating boundary-segment connecting the delimitation line to a fixed point on solid land rather than placing base points on the unstable sandspit. To this end, a court-appointed expert identified the point on solid land (on the Costa Rican side), which was closest to the mouth of the San Juan River. The Court explained where this point would be '[f]or the present' while also noting that there might 'be geomorphological changes over time'.[393]

The *Costa Rica* v. *Nicaragua* decision demonstrates a clear effort to create a stable legal outcome while also acknowledging the fact that geographic stability is sometimes unattainable. The Court used salient base points on land because of 'a relatively higher stability than points placed on sandy features'[394] but it also established a 'mobile line' for the most unstable segment and even indicated that the point anchoring this segment might be changed in the future.

3.4.4.4 Fluctuating Boundaries on Land

Even land boundaries can fluctuate if established by reference to fluctuating phenomena. This has been the case in respect of the boundary between the United States and Mexico where it follows the Rio Grande. This dispute spans more than a century and can be traced back to a time when war existed between the United States and Mexico. This war came to an end when the two States concluded an agreement in 1848,[395] establishing a territorial boundary. The boundary began in the ocean of the Gulf of Mexico, in front of the mouth of the Rio Grande and ran up the middle of the river.[396] Each State appointed representatives to survey and fix the location of the boundary in 1850 but this resulted in a boundary that departed some thirty miles from the river as shown on the original map.[397] Another treaty was

391 Ibid., para 311 referencing *Delimitation of the maritime boundary between Guinea and Guinea-Bissau (Guinea/Guinea-Bissau)* (1985) XIX RIAA 149.

392 *Costa Rica* v. *Nicaragua* (n 356) para 104.

393 Ibid.

394 Ibid., para 100.

395 Treaty of Peace, Friendship, Limits and Settlement between the United States of America and the Mexican Republic (adopted 2 February 1848, entered into force 30 May 1848) available at: www.loc.gov/law/help/us-treaties/bevans/b-mx-ust000009-0791.pdf acccessed 17 January 2021.

396 Jocelyn Bowden (814) 225 referring to House Executive Documents, 30th Congress, 1st Session (Serial No 521), Document no 69, 13–14.

397 Jocelyn Bowden (814) 226.

concluded in 1853 to move the boundary[398] and the United States bought the land that had been allotted to Mexico, allegedly by mistake.[399] These acts established the international boundary along the Rio Grande but did not explain whether the boundary should be final and invariable. The lack of indication that the boundary should be stable meant that it was ambulatory under the doctrine of accretion and avulsion.[400]

The course of the river changed drastically over time and both States claimed sovereignty over land territory that was on the opposite side of the border. The United States Supreme Court found in its decision of 12 December 1927[401] that the international boundary was a fixed line following the channel of the Rio Grande, but since the river was ambulatory the Court said that the channel of the river should be where it was at the time of the conclusion of the 1850 treaty. This decision was contradictory since the boundary could clearly not be both a fixed line *and* the channel of the river as long as the river remained ambulatory.[402] Hence, it did not end the feud between the United States and Mexico, but in 1963 the two States made a new treaty establishing their boundary.[403] Again, the boundary would follow the thalweg of the Rio Grande but this time a concrete river channel was built to prevent floods and further fluctuations.[404] Still, in 1970, another agreement was needed to further modify the international boundary because part of the States' territory had, again, ended up on the wrong side of the Rio Grande. This time, the boundary remained in place but the position of the river was modified and hundreds of acres of the disputed territory transferred across the river.[405]

The dispute concerning the Rio Grande shows that international boundaries can fluctuate to reflect environmental changes. However, it also demonstrates the shortcomings of this proposed method for maritime boundary delimitation. The fluctuating boundary between the United States and Mexico was a source of friction for over a century, it called for the operation of an International Boundary and Water Commission and still, the end result was a fixed boundary.

Courts and tribunals have emphasized the importance of transparency, certainty, stability and predictability when delimiting maritime boundaries.[406] Fluctuating boundaries may not meet these requirements but perfect stability cannot be achieved when relying on the coastline as an essential basis because it is inherently

398 Gadsen Treaty (United States and Mexico) (adopted on 30 December 1853).

399 Jocelyn Bowden (814) 227–228.

400 Ibid., 229.

401 The State of New Mexico v. The State of Texas (United States Supreme Court 1927) United States Reports, CCLXXV, 279.

402 Ibid., 236–237.

403 Convention between the United States of America and Mexico, with Exchange of Notes (adopted 29 August 1963, entered into force 14 January 1964) (1963) 2 (5) ILM 874.

404 See ibid., articles 1–3.

405 Treaty to resolve pending boundary differences and maintain the Rio Grande and Colorado River as the international boundary between the United Mexican States and the United States of America (adopted 23 November 1970, entered into force 18 April 1972) 11873 UNTS 56, article 1.

406 See, for example, *Barbados* v. *Trinidad and Tobago* (n 44) para 244.

unstable.[407] Fluctuating boundaries may be the only viable option capable of incorporating consideration for increasing changes to relevant coastal geography. States can leave undelimited territorial sea entitlements to fluctuate with the equidistance line, they can establish fluctuating boundaries through bilateral agreements, and they can confer such competence upon courts and tribunals. Moreover, courts and tribunals may resort to fluctuating boundary segments when coastal instability prevents the drawing of geographically stable boundaries.

3.5 SUMMARY

UNCLOS articles 74 and 83 require that equitable solutions are achieved on the basis of international law. This entails an obligation to consider all relevant circumstances and those primarily relate to coastal geography. The tribunal in *Bangladesh v. India* expressed its concerns that settled maritime boundaries would be jeopardized if climate-related changes were allowed to influence the delimitation process. However, a significant portion of the world's overlapping maritime boundaries have yet to be delimited and the maritime boundary agreements that have been concluded are often partial or incomplete in character, only dealing with part of the disputed area or not all maritime zones.[408] Furthermore, two wrongs do not make a right; the fact that previously settled maritime boundaries showed no consideration for relevant changes does not justify continued disregard for such changes. At any rate, the delimitation of new boundaries has no effect on the validity of previously settled boundaries.

The environmental changes described in Chapter 1 are bound to affect maritime entitlements, upon which maritime boundary delimitation is based. Maritime limits fluctuate on an ongoing basis, as discussed in Chapter 2, and it seems logical to consider this fact when establishing permanent and equitable maritime boundaries. Coastlines are changing worldwide, that is not a fact open to interpretation or an idea that can simple be ignored. The international community values stability, certainty and predictability but changing conditions raise the question whether geographic stability should be prioritized over legal stability.

UNCLOS articles 74 and 83 provide flexibility in the law governing maritime delimitation. Courts and tribunals are not obligated to employ the equidistance/relevant circumstances method in all cases and it can be unfeasible in certain situations, particularly where few reliable base points can be identified. Significant adjustments to the provisional equidistance line can defeat the purpose of transparency and predictability and the fact that this method is always anchored to equidistance inevitably shapes the end result. For these reasons, different methods must be

[407] Louis Sohn and John Noyes, *Cases and Materials on the Law of the Sea* (Transnational, 2004) 235, referring to Robert Hodgson and Robert Smith, 'The Informal Single Negotiating Text (Committee II): A Geographical Perspective' (1976) 3 Ocean Development and International Law 225, 234.

[408] Clive Schofield (n 27) 48.

permissible in the pursuit of equitable solutions. Furthermore, this chapter has demonstrated that coastal instability and foreseeable changes, such as the imminent inundation of islands or ongoing changes to sand and mud banks, can affect the judicial process that is maritime delimitation. These changes can affect the selection of base points; adjustment of provisional boundaries; and choice of delimitation methods, justifying use of the angle-bisector method or fluctuating boundaries, instead of fixed boundaries based on equidistance.

Judicial decisions can rely on foreseeable changes and complicated scientific evidence. This has allowed courts and tribunals to assess seasonal changes to ice sheets and access to fish stocks; the status of coastal features; and feasibility of potential base points and delimitation methods. The jurisprudence is still developing but courts and tribunals already have legal precedents allowing them to delimit maritime boundaries with consideration for ongoing climate-related changes. It is submitted that foreseeable or ongoing changes affecting the essential basis of a maritime boundary should not be ignored as a matter of principle or due to evidentiary difficulties. Instead, they should be taken into account to prevent or mitigate any inequitable effects. Certainly, no two cases are alike and each decision will be shaped by the relief sought and arguments presented by disputing States. States can also delimit their maritime boundaries without any involvement of courts or tribunals and that paves the way for more creative solutions. Solutions that can help States adapt to, and even mitigate, adverse effects of climate change on the marine environment.

4

Maritime Delimitation and the Marine Environment

4.1 INTRODUCTION

The delineation and delimitation of maritime entitlements centres on coastal geography. UNCLOS establishes a sectoral approach to ocean governance and this sectoral division relies on the coastline as a point of departure. However, in reality, oceans are made up of complex, interconnected ecosystems that do not respect man-made lines of jurisdiction[1] and claims to maritime zones are largely driven by interests in the exploitation of marine living resources that make up these systems. Inadequate management of fish stocks has caused chronic over-fishing around the world and this impacts the ability of present and future generations to enjoy their maritime entitlements.[2] Maritime delimitation affects the management and conservation of marine ecosystems and therefore, the two are inherently linked. The delimitation of exclusive economic/fisheries zones and continental shelves shall result in equitable solutions and that arguably extends to intergenerational equity in the ability to exploit resources. If so, then environmental circumstances contributing to sustainable development of the marine environment should be among the objectives of maritime delimitation.

The sea can be viewed as an extension of land territory, an area subject to limited jurisdiction or a great void.[3] At any rate, it inhabits ecosystems that cannot be protected with individual efforts of coastal States within fixed boundaries. The international community is in the course of negotiating a binding instrument codifying new measures to promote marine biodiversity in areas beyond national jurisdiction.[4] Furthermore, as of December 2020, thirty-eight States have declared

1 See GAOR, 'Seventieth Session' (22 July 2015) UN Doc A/70/112, para 40.

2 Thomas Cottier, *Equitable Principles of Maritime Boundary Delimitation: The Quest for Distributive Justice in International Law* (Cambridge University Press, 2015) 161–163.

3 Andreas Østhagen, 'Maritime Boundary Disputes: What Are They and Why Do They Matter?' (2020) 120 Marine Policy, 1, 6 referring to Philip Steinberg, *The Social Construction of the Ocean* (Cambridge University Press, 2001) 18–25.

4 Intergovernmental Conference on an international legally binding instrument under UNCLOS on the conservation and sustainable use of marine biological diversity of areas beyond national jurisdiction 'Draft Text of an Agreement Under the United Nations Convention on the Law of the Sea on the

a State of Climate Emergency following the UNSG's call to action.[5] These developments demonstrate the growing need for urgent action to mitigate, and adapt to, the adverse effects of climate change on the marine environment, within and beyond national jurisdiction. These effects include loss of biodiversity and changing migratory patterns due to ocean warming and ocean acidification.[6]

The international community became aware of the threat of climate change and need for sustainable development around 1990, following the publication of the Brundtland Report[7] and the publication of the first IPCC report.[8] The 1992 Rio Declaration affirmed a global commitment to co-operation in the achievement of sustainable development and protection of the Earth's ecosystem.[9] A host of related commitments followed and the ecosystem approach has come to feature in relation to the management of marine resources. The year 2020 was anticipated as a critical year for drastic climate change action but the international community is still far from being on the necessary trajectory to meet the objective set forth in Article 2(1)(a) of the Paris Agreement.[10] This justifies a closer look at the feasibility of considering environmental circumstances in the delimitation process. After all, a majority of potential maritime boundary disputes remains unresolved;[11] States have a duty to conserve and manage living resources within their jurisdiction;[12] they must protect and preserve the marine environment;[13] and have the power to incorporate environmental considerations into the delimitation process.

Previous chapters explained that maritime boundaries are primarily delimited on the basis of coastal geography. Chapter 3 focused on the judicial process of maritime delimitation and only briefly referred to various other aspects that can affect negotiated boundaries. However, more than 90 per cent of maritime boundaries are effected by bilateral agreements and, unlike judicial decisions, these do not need to conform to the traditional delimitation methods described in Chapter 3. States can depart from the applicable law through bilateral agreements. Furthermore,

Conservation and Sustainable Use of Marine Biological Diversity of Areas Beyond National Jurisdiction' (17 May 2019) UN Doc A/CONF.232/2019/6.

5 António Guterres, 'Opening Remarks at Press Stakeout Following Climate Ambition Summit' (UN, 12 December 2020) available at: www.un.org/sg/en/content/sg/speeches/2020-12-12/remarks-press-stakeout-following-climate-ambition-summit accessed 16 December 2020.

6 See Section 1.3.

7 World Commission on Environment and Development, *Our Common Future* (Oxford University Press, 1987).

8 IPCC, *Climate Change: The IPCC 1990 and 1992 Assessment* (World Meteorological Organization, 1992).

9 Rio Declaration on Environment and Development (13 June 1992) 31 ILM 874, see particularly principles 1 and 7.

10 The Paris Agreement (adopted 12 December 2015, entered into force 4 November 2016) UN Doc FCCC/CP/2015/L.9/Rev/1; UNEP, *Emissions Gap Report 2019* (2020) and Universal Ecological Fund, *The Truth behind the Climate Pledges* (2019).

11 See Andreas Østhagen (n 3) 6.

12 UNCLOS article 56(1)(a).

13 UNCLOS articles 192 and 194.

courts and tribunals can be given the competence to decide on measures relating to environmental protection or management of transboundary resources when delimiting maritime entitlements. Thus, the delimitation process need not necessarily be limited to geographical circumstances, or even result in traditional boundaries. A large portion of the world's overlapping maritime entitlements has not been delimited and climate change may bring on a new generation of maritime boundaries as territory is submerged and Arctic waters become more accessible.[14] These future delimitations may consider environmental circumstances to a greater extent than their predecessors.

The status of the marine environment is not one of the legal criteria that generally qualify as relevant circumstances in maritime delimitation. In fact, the delimitation process is usually separated from issues concerning environmental protection or resource management, which are then reserved for subsequent agreements. States are often able to conclude agreements relating to the management of transboundary resources on the basis of geographically fixed boundaries. Indeed, this is envisioned by the FSA.[15] Still, the conclusion of supplementary agreements is not guaranteed when such considerations are ignored in the delimitation process. Consideration of transboundary management and environmental protection in the delimitation process can arguably pave the way to cooperation and better management of shared resources. In fact, Churchill explained in 1985 that it might be more practical and likely to result in an equitable solution if arrangements for the joint management of fish stocks and seabed resources were to affect the delimitation process, and not just dealt with in supplementary agreements.[16] This may be increasingly relevant now when the marine environment is faced with unprecedented threats and management thus made more challenging.

A host of obligations relating to the marine environment can be incorporated into the delimitation process to tackle the issues holistically. To that end, States can establish fixed or fluctuating boundaries by reference to environmental circumstances and even establish joint development zones or protected areas, instead of boundaries. This last proposition may be a feasible option to ensure appropriate management of vulnerable ecosystems and can potentially dissolve the need for traditional boundaries. As explained by Østhagen, co-operative management of transboundary resources and further development of management regimes 'make the exact location of the maritime boundary itself (if not the maritime domain) less important'.[17]

14 Thomas Cottier (n 2) 179; See also Clive Schofield, 'Parting the Waves: Claims to Maritime Jurisdiction and the Division of Ocean Space' (2012) 1 Penn State Journal of Law and International Affairs 48.

15 See articles 7 and 8.

16 Robin Churchill, 'Maritime Delimitation in the Jan Mayen Area' (1985) 9 (1) Marine Policy, 16, 27.

17 Andreas Østhagen (n 3) 7.

This chapter explores the relevance of environmental circumstances for the delimitation of maritime entitlements. It does so in the context of various obligations and approaches relating to conservation and management of the marine environment and is prompted by the need for adaptation to climate change. Environmental circumstances is a broad category but will, in the context of this chapter, refer primarily to fisheries but also to ecological circumstances relating to marine living resources and their sustainable development. This includes protection of vulnerable species and their habitats. The case law and boundary agreements that admit the relevance of environmental circumstances often relate to exploitation of fish stocks[18] and ongoing exploitation relates to healthy marine ecosystems. Furthermore, States are generally interested in, and obligated to ensure, sustainable development of fish stocks and associated species.

4.2 PROTECTION AND MANAGEMENT OF AREAS WITHIN NATIONAL JURISDICTION

The law governing maritime delimitation is set out in UNCLOS articles 15, 74 and 83. These provisions have come to entail clear rules, as described in Section 3.2. The judicial process of delimiting overlapping maritime entitlements can be a relatively straight forward process. However, it is intrinsically linked to numerous obligations that govern exploration; exploitation; conservation and management of marine resources within maritime zones; and protection of the marine environment, because the demarcation of ecosystems affects their management.[19]

UNSG António Guterres has discussed the dire need for action to combat climate change. Declarations and objectives will not suffice; concrete action is imperative.[20] The international community has adopted various soft law instruments, such as the UNESCO Declaration of Ethical Principles in relation to Climate Change,[21] which calls on States to promote transnational co-operation, implement policies to sustainably preserve ecosystems and apply a precautionary approach.[22] Furthermore, numerous pledges have been made to sustainable development, which commits

18 See, for example, *Maritime Delimitation in the Area between Greenland and Jan Mayen (Denmark v. Norway)* (Judgment) [1993] ICJ Rep 38,; Glen Herbert, 'Fisheries Relations in the Gulf of Maine: Implications of an Arbitrated Maritime Boundary' (1995) 19 (4) Marine Policy 301, 302; and Treaty between Australia and the Independent State of Papua New Guinea concerning sovereignty and maritime boundaries in the area between the two countries, including the area known as Torres Strait, and related matters (adopted 18 December 1978, entered into force 15 February 1985) 1429 UNTS 207.

19 See Aron Westholm, 'Delimiting Marine Areas: Ecosystem Approach(es?) in EU Marine Management' in David Langlet and Rosemary Rayfuse (eds) *The Ecosystem Approach in Ocean Planning and Governance: Perspectives from Europe and Beyond* (Brill Nijhoff, 2019) 117, 119–120, referring to Nathan Sayre, 'Ecological and Geographical Scale: Parallels and Potential for Integration' 29 Progress in human geography 276, 279.

20 António Guterres (n 5).

21 UNESCO, 'Declaration of Ethical Principles in Relation to Climate Change' in Resolution 15 adopted by the General Conference at its 39th session (30 October–14 November 2017) (UNESCO, 2018) Annex III, 129.

22 Ibid., articles 3 and 4.

States to manage natural resources, including those within jurisdiction, in a rational, sustainable and safe way that contributes to the protection of ecosystems.[23] Rio Principle 27 urges States to co-operate to achieve sustainable development and further develop international law in that field. Furthermore, the FSA obliges participating States to co-operate in 'the long-term conservation and sustainable use of straddling fish stocks and highly migratory fish stocks' and protection of marine biodiversity.[24]

The UN Framework Convention on Climate Change (hereinafter UNFCCC) commits States Parties to sustainable development.[25] Moreover, article 3(3) of the UNFCCC entails an obligation to 'take precautionary measures to anticipate, prevent or minimize the causes of climate change and mitigate its adverse effects'. Adverse effects refer, in this context, to environmental changes having 'significant deleterious effects on the composition, resilience or productivity of natural and managed ecosystems'.[26] Article 4(1)(f) further explains that States Parties shall take 'climate change considerations into account, to the extent feasible, in their relevant social, economic and environmental policies and actions'. Thus, the 197 States Parties to the UNFCCC are obligated to take precautionary action to mitigate the adverse effects of climate change, promote sustainable development, and, in particular, to incorporate climate change considerations in their environmental policies, which should extend to maritime zones. The UNFCCC encourages international and regional co-operation[27] and States must take action to prevent serious or irreversible damage, even when there is lack of full scientific certainty regarding those risks.[28] Additionally, States Parties to the Paris Agreement have agreed to shift the trend in global greenhouse gas emissions downward as soon as possible and rapidly reduce emissions.[29]

These general commitments could incentivize States to adopt new approaches to the management of marine resources and delimitation of overlapping maritime claims. Indeed, it seems reasonable to expect that States refrain from, or minimize, activities that emit greenhouse gases; take all appropriate measures to adapt to and mitigate the adverse effects of climate change; promote sustainable development; and incorporate these efforts into all relevant procedures. The following sections explore rules and approaches that are particularly relevant to the conservation and management of marine living resources.

23 ILA Committee on Legal Aspects of Sustainable Development, 'New Delhi Declaration of Principles of International Law Relating to Sustainable Development' (ILA, 2002).

24 FSA, preamble and articles 2 and 5.

25 United Nations Framework Convention on Climate Change (adopted 9 May 1992, entered into force 21 March 1994) 1771 UNTS 107, article 3(4).

26 UNFCCC article 1(1).

27 See, for example, UNFCCC articles 3(3), 3(5) and 4(1)(b).

28 UNFCCC article 3(3).

29 Paris Agreement article 4(1).

4.2.1 *Ecosystem Approach to Ocean Governance*

The ecosystem approach is a fairly new concept in international law. It has been adopted by the Conference of the Parties (hereinafter COP) to the Convention on Biological Diversity (hereinafter CBD)[30] and features in many ocean instruments.[31] The ecosystem approach received general recognition in 1995, when it was designated as the principal framework of action to be used under the CBD.[32] The States Parties to the CBD have described the ecosystem approach as 'a strategy for the integrated management of land, water and living resources that promotes conservation and sustainable use in an equitable way'.[33] This is further clarified by the Malawi Principles for the Ecosystem Approach, adopted in 1998 and presented at the Fourth Meeting of the COP to the CBD.[34] The principles are too many to recite here but they explain, inter alia, that under the ecosystem approach, '[m]anagement objectives are a matter of societal choice'[35] and '[m]anagement should be decentralized to the lowest appropriate level'.[36] It also provides that '[e]cosystem managers should consider the effects of their activities on adjacent and other ecosystems'[37] and recognizes that change is inevitable.[38] According to the States Parties to the CBD, the ecosystem approach does not operate to the preclusion of other management and conservation approaches but rather, integrates them to tackle complicated situations.[39]

The ecosystem approach has achieved general recognition as a guiding principle in various contexts, particularly for the management of marine resources.[40] In fact, Karmenu Vella, the European Commissioner for the Environment, Marine Affairs and Fisheries, recently explained that an ecosystem approach is necessary for ocean governance and that our future increasingly depends on it. According to him, it is now 'impossible to look into conservation and sustainable use of the oceans without taking an ecosystem approach to ocean management'.[41] The ecosystem approach

30 CBD (adopted 5 June 1992, entered into force 29 December 1993) 1760 UNTS 79, 143. See COP Decision V/6 'Ecosystem Approach' (Nairobi, 26 May 2000).

31 Philippe Sands and Jacqueline Peel, with Adriana Fabra and Ruth MacKenzie, *Principles of International Environmental Law*, 4th edition (Cambridge University Press, 2018) 457.

32 COP Decision II/8, 'Preliminary Considerations of Components of Biological Diversity Particularly under Threat and Action Which Could Be Taken under the Convention' (Jakarta, 17 November 1995), para 1.

33 CBD, COP Decision V/6 (n 30).

34 CBD, COP Decision IV/1B (Bratislava, Slovakia, 4–15 May 1998) referring to UNEP/CBD/COP/4/Inf.9 'Report of the Workshop on the Ecosystem Approach'.

35 Malawi Principle 1.

36 Malawi Principle 2.

37 Malawi Principle 3.

38 Malawi Principle 9.

39 CBD, COP Decision V/6 (n 30).

40 David Langlet and Rosemary Rayfuse (n 19) 2.

41 Ibid., 1 referring to a speech at a side-event to the UN Oceans Conference in June 2017, co-organized together with the United Nations Environment Programme, the UNEP/MAP, the Food and Agriculture Organization and the General Fisheries Commission for the Mediterranean.

was adopted in the 1980 Convention on the Conservation of Antarctic Marine Living Resources (hereinafter CCAMLR),[42] the OSPAR Convention,[43] the Helsinki Convention[44] and it features in the FSA, by implied terms.[45] The need for an ecosystem approach for coastal and ocean development was emphasized in the non-binding Plan of Implementation, resulting from the 2002 World Summit on Sustainable Development.[46] Furthermore, the 2001 Reykjavik Declaration on Responsible Fisheries in the Marine Ecosystem recognizes the interaction between species and the impact of human activities on ecosystems.[47] The Food and Agriculture Organization (hereinafter FAO) Code of Conduct on Responsible Fisheries adopts the ecosystem approach,[48] and so does the 2018 Agreement to Prevent Unregulated High Seas Fisheries in the Central Arctic Ocean (hereinafter CAOFA).[49] The FAO has also published technical guidelines regarding the ecosystem approach to fisheries[50] and the UNGA has regularly called for an ecosystem approach in its resolutions concerning sustainable fisheries and the law of the sea.[51]

The practical implementation of an ecosystem approach is highly complicated. The many variables involved make it challenging to specify any rules that make it operational. The OSPAR and Helsinki Commissions have jointly defined the ecosystem approach as 'the comprehensive integrated management of human activities based on the best available scientific knowledge about the ecosystem and its dynamics, in order to identify and take action on influences which are critical to the health of marine ecosystems, thereby achieving sustainable use of ecosystem

42 Convention on the Conservation of Antarctic Marine Living Resources (adopted 20 May 1980, entered into force 7 April 1982) 1329 UNTS 47, see article 2(3)(c) .

43 Convention for the protection of the marine environment of the North-East Atlantic (adopted 22 September 1992, entered into force 25 March 1998) 2354 UNTS 67, Annex V, article 3(1)(b)(iv).

44 Convention on the protection of the marine environment of the Baltic Sea (adopted 9 April 1992, entered into force 17 January 2000) 2099 UNTS 195, see article 15.

45 See FSA article 5 and the preamble.

46 Report of the World Summit on Sustainable Development Johannesburg, 'Adoption of the Plan of Implementation of the World Summit on Sustainable Development' (26 August–4 September 2002) UN Doc A/CONF.199/20, 139.

47 FAO, 'Reykjavik Declaration on Responsible Fisheries in the Marine Ecosystem' (1–4 October 2001) FAO Doc C200/INF/25, Appendix I.

48 FAO Code of Conduct for Responsible Fisheries, FAO COP Resolution 4/95 (31 October 1995). See, for example, articles 6, 9(2), 9(3)(1), 12(5) and 12(10)(11).

49 Agreement to Prevent Unregulated High Seas Fisheries in the Central Arctic Ocean (adopted 3 October 2018, entered into force 25 June 2021) available at: www.dfo-mpo.gc.ca/international/agreement-accord-eng.htm accessed 22 December 2020, see articles 2, 3(4) and 4(1) and 4(2).

50 FAO, *The Ecosystem Approach to Fisheries*, FAO Technical Guidelines for Responsible Fisheries No 4, Supplement 2 (2003).

51 See, for example, UNGA Res 75/89, 'Sustainable Fisheries, including through the 1995 Agreement for the Implementation of the Provisions of the United Nations Convention on the Law of the Sea of 10 December 1982 Relating to the Conservation and Management of Straddling Fish Stocks and Highly Migratory Fish Stocks, and Related Instruments' (8 December 2020), paras 16, 20, 163, 170 and 183; UNGA Res 75/239, 'Oceans and the Law of the Sea' (31 December 2020), paras 198–200.

goods and services and maintenance of ecosystem integrity'.[52] This joint statement further explains that the precautionary principle is an essential component of the ecosystem approach. Indeed, the instruments cited earlier in relation to the ecosystem approach generally also adopt the precautionary approach.[53]

Article 2(3)(c) of the CCAMLR indicates that application of the ecosystem approach should involve consideration of direct and indirect impacts of harvesting, other related activities and the presence of alien species. In the context of climate change, an ecosystem approach would particularly involve consideration of ongoing environmental changes, such as ocean warming and acidification, and anticipation of the consequences for marine living resources.

On 8 December 2020, the UNGA urged States to apply the ecosystem approach when designing measures aimed at, inter alia, overfishing and protection of vulnerable habitats.[54] This resolution also called upon regional fisheries management organizations to 'strengthen and modernise' their measures and approaches to fisheries management, taking the precautionary approach, the ecosystem approach and biodiversity considerations into account. The overall aim of this is to ensure conservation and sustainable development of marine resources.[55] The UNGA further asserted, on 31 December 2020, 'that continued environmental degradation in many parts of the world and increasing competing demands require an urgent response and the setting of priorities for management actions aimed at conserving ecosystem integrity'.[56] This UNGA Resolution goes on to explain that States must co-operate and take all appropriate measures when responding to the impacts on marine ecosystems in areas within and beyond national jurisdiction.[57]

UNCLOS was meant to solve all the problems of the oceans. In fact, following its adoption, there were hopes that it would allow for ecosystem management but the reality has been a piecemeal approach, due to lack of co-ordination between regimes.[58] Nevertheless, UNCLOS can, to a certain extent, be interpreted by reference to subsequent practice (as explained in Chapter 2).[59] Furthermore, 'any relevant rules of international law applicable in the relations between the parties' can affect the

52 Helsinki and OSPAR Commissions, 'Statement on the Ecosystem Approach to the Management of Human Activities "Towards an Ecosystem Approach to the Management of Human Activities"', First Joint Ministerial Meeting of the Helsinki and OSPAR Commissions (Bremen Germany 25–26 June 2003) Annex 5 Ref. §6.1. Available at: www.ospar.org/site/assets/files/1232/jmm_annex05_ecosystem_approach_statement.pdf accessed 12 February 2021.

53 See, for example, FSA article 6; FAO Code of Conduct for Responsible Fisheries article 7.5; CAOFA articles 2 and 5(1)(c).

54 UNGA Res 75/89 (n 51), para 20.

55 Ibid., para 163.

56 UNGA Res 75/239 (n 51), para 198(a).

57 Ibid., para 198(d).

58 Elizabeth Kirk, 'Maritime Zones and the Ecosystem Approach: A Mismatch?' (1999) 8 (1) Review of European Community & International Environmental Law, 67, 69.

59 See Section 2.5.3.3.

interpretation of UNCLOS.[60] This means that the rules on maritime delimitation might be informed by the many instruments referred to earlier. Indeed, a judicial decision has confirmed that the interpretation of UNCLOS can be impacted by other international law[61] and UNCLOS articles 74 and 83 explicitly refer to international law. Thus, while there is no direct legal basis for incorporating an ecosystem approach to maritime delimitation, or clear rules that would make it operational in this context, the ecosystem approach may still influence the delimitation process. After all, it is a guiding principle for the management of oceanic resources, its application is a matter of societal choice and it can take various shapes, depending on the context.

4.2.2 *Obligations to Protect and Manage Living Resources and the Environment*

UNCLOS entails several obligations relating to the marine environment and marine living resources. States must take measures, together and alone, that are necessary for conservation of the living resources of the high seas.[62] Moreover, coastal States must ensure proper conservation and management of the living resources within their exclusive economic zone and determine a total allowable catch to prevent over-exploitation.[63] They must also maintain or restore maximum sustainable yield, 'as qualified by relevant environmental and economic factors'. They are required to apply an ecosystem approach when doing this, that is, 'take into consideration the effects on species associated with or dependent upon harvested species with a view to maintaining or restoring populations of such associated or dependent species above levels at which their reproduction may become seriously threatened'.[64] It has been generally recognized that obligations to conserve and manage marine living resources are not just linked to utilization but to sustainable development.[65] Furthermore, the FSA, which aims to ensure 'long-term conservation and sustainable use of straddling fish stocks and highly migratory fish stocks',[66] commits States to the protection of marine biodiversity[67] and adopts an ecosystem approach.[68] These measures should be compatible with those taken within areas under national jurisdiction, as per FSA article 7.

All States have an 'obligation to protect and preserve the marine environment'.[69] UNCLOS article 194 obligates States to take positive action to prevent marine

60 VCLT article 31(3)(c).
61 *South China Sea (Philippines* v. *China)* (Merits) (2016) XXXIII RIAA 153, paras 956 and 959.
62 UNCLOS article 117.
63 UNCLOS article 61, paras 1 and 2.
64 UNCLOS article 61, paras 3 and 4.
65 Francisco Vicuña, *The Changing International Law of High Seas Fisheries* (Cambridge University Press, 1999) 145, 147.
66 FSA article 2.
67 FSA article 5(g).
68 FSA article 5(d) and (e).
69 UNCLOS article 192.

pollution from any source. Pollution of the marine environment extends, inter alia, to the indirect introduction 'of substances or energy into the marine environment' if it is likely to harm marine life and hinder activities, such as fisheries, and impair the quality of the oceans.[70] Boyle has explained that this includes pollution caused by greenhouse gas emission from land-based sources and from or through the atmosphere.[71] This means that CO_2 emissions qualify as marine pollution, which the international community must consequently address. The consequences of this pollution include ocean acidification, ocean warming and sea level rise, which results in, for example, 'economic loss to coastal communities resulting from depleted fish stocks, coral bleaching and loss of marine biodiversity'.[72]

UNCLOS article 194(1) specifies that States must take all necessary measures to 'prevent, reduce and control pollution of the marine environment from any source, using for this purpose the best practicable means at their disposal and in accordance with their capabilities, and they shall endeavour to harmonize their policies in this connection'. Moreover, UNCLOS emphasizes the applicability of these obligations in relation to 'rare or fragile ecosystems as well as the habitat of depleted, threatened or endangered species and other forms of marine life'.[73] The fact that greenhouse gas emission constitutes pollution within UNCLOS means that States have an obligation to take measures, individually or jointly, to prevent, mitigate or reduce the adverse effects of airborne pollution, including anthropogenic greenhouse gas emission, on the marine environment. That extends to the consequences of CO_2 emissions mentioned earlier. The obligations enshrined in UNCLOS articles 194 and 212 are phrased in general terms and do not require that States prevent all marine pollution. However, States must take some meaningful action towards the reduction of greenhouse gas emission and the UNFCCC may inform the content of these obligations.[74] Moreover, the Kyoto Protocol[75] and Paris Agreement can be useful for identifying benchmarks for the necessary reduction.

Boyle has explained that the environmental obligations of UNCLOS Part XII relate not only to fish stocks and marine mammals, or economic and private interests, but to marine biodiversity generally. This is supported by reference to UNCLOS articles 61 and 117, which outline the obligations to conserve living resources, and to the CBD.[76] Indeed, the tribunal in *Philippines* v. *China* recently confirmed the broad extent of these provisions. It explained, among other things,

70 UNCLOS article 1(1)(4).

71 Alan Boyle, 'Law of the Sea Perspectives on Climate Change' in David Freestone (ed) *The 1982 Law of the Sea Convention At 30: Successes, Challenges and New Agendas* (Martinus Nijhoff, 2013) 158.

72 Alan Boyle, 'Law of the Sea Perspectives on Climate Change' The International Journal of Marine and Coastal Law 27 (2012) 831, 832–833.

73 UNCLOS article 194(5).

74 Alan Boyle (n 72) 834.

75 Kyoto Protocol to the United Nations Framework Convention on Climate Change (adopted 11 December 1997, entered into force 16 February 2005) 2303 UNTS 148.

76 Alan Boyle (n 71) 158; see also Alan Boyle (n 72) 832.

that the content of the duty imposed by UNCLOS article 192 is informed by other relevant rules of international law, that it 'entails the positive obligation to take active measures', to protect the 'marine environment from future damage' and maintain or improve existing conditions.[77]

Obligations to protect the marine environment extend beyond an obligation to control pollution. ITLOS explained, in the *Fisheries Advisory Opinion*, that the reference to the 'marine environment' in Article 192 includes conservation of the living resources of the sea and other marine life.[78] The tribunal in *Philippines* v. *China* and the tribunal in *Chagos Marine Protected Area* also confirmed that UNCLOS article 194(5) 'is "not limited to measures aimed strictly at controlling marine pollution," which while "certainly an important aspect of environmental protection ... is by no means the only one."'[79] Furthermore, UNCLOS article 194 'extends to measures focused primarily on conservation and the preservation of ecosystems' and marine protected areas (hereinafter MPAs) qualify as such.[80] The CBD defines protected areas as geographically defined areas that are 'designated or regulated and managed to achieve specific conservation objectives'.[81] The designation of such areas is permissible under UNCLOS and customary international law but subject to a due diligence obligation of seeking harmonization with interested States.[82]

The *Chagos Marine Protected Area* dispute concerned the requirements attached to the establishment of MPAs. The United Kingdom, in its capacity as a coastal State, established an MPA, extending 200 nm around the baselines of the archipelago, covering over half a million square kilometres.[83] This affected the fishing rights held by Mauritius, which was an interested party because the Chagos Archipelago is meant to be, eventually, returned to Mauritius. The tribunal concluded that these significant rights of Mauritius had to be regarded by the United Kingdom before declaring the MPA.[84] The United Kingdom did regard the interests of the United States in this matter. That was demonstrated by timely consultation, exchange of information and balancing of rights and interests.[85] Yet, the same regard was not shown to Mauritius and that led to a finding that the designation of the MPA was incompatible with UNCLOS.[86]

Importantly, the tribunal explained that 'environmental considerations could potentially justify, for the purposes of Article 194(4), the infringement of Mauritian

77 *South China Sea (Philippines v. China)* (Merits) (2016) XXXIII RIAA 153, para 941.
78 *Request for an advisory opinion submitted by the Sub-Regional Fisheries Commission* (Advisory Opinion) [2015] ITLOS, 54 ILM 890, see paras 120 and 216.
79 *Philippines* v. *China* (n 77) para 945 referring to *Chagos Marine Protected Area (Mauritius* v. *United Kingdom)* (2015) XXXI RIAA 359, paras 320 and 538.
80 *Chagos Marine Protected Area* (n 79) para 538.
81 CBD article 2.
82 *Chagos Marine Protected Area* (n 79) para 539.
83 Ibid., para 5.
84 Ibid., para 521.
85 Ibid., para 528.
86 Ibid., para 536.

fishing rights in the territorial sea. Such justification, however, would require significant engagement with Mauritius to explain the need for the measure and to explore less restrictive alternatives'.[87] Consequently, measures to protect the marine environment, such as the proclamation of an MPA, may interfere with the rights of other States under the Convention but only if the requirements set out above are satisfied. This may be a significant point if coastlines recede to the extent that new rights are generated for third States.[88] Bilateral arrangement for the division of maritime entitlements might not be enforceable against third States in such scenarios, while an MPA might be.

States should endeavour to harmonize their policies when establishing MPAs.[89] Furthermore, States are generally obliged to co-operate on a global or regional basis when establishing rules for marine environmental protection.[90] In fact, ITLOS confirmed, in the *MOX Plant* case, that the obligation to co-operate is a fundamental principle in respect of protection of the marine environment.[91] The recently declared state of emergency further emphasizes the relevance of the principle of co-operation because it is particularly applicable in cases of environmental emergencies.[92] Thus, States are now, more than ever, urged to take active measures to protect the marine environment and co-operate to that end.

4.3 ENVIRONMENTAL CONSIDERATIONS IN THE DELIMITATION PROCESS

Maritime delimitation is often approached from the narrow perspective of coastal geography. Yet, it is essentially a question of ocean governance. It involves a plethora of ecosystems and can be essential to their well-being. Maritime delimitation is therefore linked to the numerous obligations States hold in relation to environmental protection, conservation and management of living resources. UNCLOS articles 15, 74 and 83 centre on coastal geography and taken alone, these provisions entail no obligation to sustainably manage fisheries or protect the marine environment subject to delimitation. However, addressing these issues separately may result in neglect of one or more factors. To achieve the overall objective of sustainable development, States must integrate environmental protection into all processes of development and not consider it in isolation therefrom.[93]

The following sections explore the interplay between marine ecosystems and the sectoral approach established under UNCLOS; the relevance of environmental circumstances to maritime delimitation; and the practical issue of identifying such circumstances.

87 Ibid., para 541.
88 See further discussion in Section 5.4.2.
89 Ibid., para 539; and UNCLOS article 194(4).
90 UNCLOS article 197.
91 *MOX Plant (Ireland* v. *United Kingdom)* (Provisional Measures) [2001] ITLOS 41 ILM 405, para 82.
92 Philippe Sands and Jacqueline Peel (n 313) 213.
93 Rio Declaration principle 4.

4.3.1 *Ecosystems and the Sectoral Approach*

The division of maritime entitlements establishes a sectoral approach. The delineation and delimitation of maritime zones creates man-made lines of jurisdiction and those lines determine the extent of coastal State sovereignty and sovereign rights. General UNCLOS provisions relating to the exploration, exploitation, conservation and management of natural resources follow this approach.[94] UNCLOS also adopts a species-specific approach to the management of certain species, that is, straddling, highly migratory, anadromous and catadromous stocks, sedentary species and marine mammals.[95] This sets a framework for the management of living resources under national jurisdiction, which is useful when paired with specialized multilateral agreements, such as the FSA or the 1946 Whaling Convention.[96] On that basis, bilateral arrangements can be concluded for the management of specific stocks, species or regions. However, the FSA and the Whaling Convention have a limited scope of application both in regard to species and number of States participants. Therefore, the two-tiered approach of UNCLOS and assumption of supplementary agreements have significant shortcomings. First, the fact that special safeguards are only afforded to specific fish stocks and marine mammals leaves numerous species vulnerable. Second, the sectoral approach and the species-specific approach do not require any consideration of the interdependence of different species.

More than twenty years ago, Kirk explained that traditional maritime zones take no account of migratory patterns. They were 'designed to give interested States control over what was deemed a suitable section of the ocean, not to ensure the sustainable use of ecosystems'.[97] The species-specific approach and the FSA were meant to supplement the sectoral approach by affording special consideration to certain species and the interdependence of fish stocks, wherever they were. In fact, the ecosystem approach is central to the FSA.[98] Even so, it does not ensure ecosystem management due to insufficient enforcement mechanisms and the fact that non-Parties are not obligated to belong to fisheries commissions if they conduct fisheries in areas controlled by such commissions (the free rider problem).[99] Moreover, although the FSA requires consideration for the effect of fishing on other species, agreements concluded under the FSA can focus solely on economically valuable fish stocks.[100] Still, the FSA has the benefit of creating mobile rules because agreements for the management of specific stocks apply to migratory

94 See UNCLOS articles 56(1)(a), 61, 62 and 77(1).
95 See UNCLOS articles 63–68.
96 International Convention for the Regulation of Whaling (adopted 2 December 1946, entered into force) 161 UNTS 72.
97 Elizabeth Kirk (n 58) 69.
98 See particularly FSA article 5.
99 Robin Churchill, 'Legal Uncertainties in International High Seas Fisheries Management' (1998) 37 Fisheries Research, 225, 229.
100 Elizabeth Kirk (n 58) 69.

resources, wherever they go; the scope of application is not determined by man-made lines.[101]

Traditional division of maritime entitlements leaves transboundary ecosystems vulnerable. It generally promotes exclusive, sectoral management, and cooperation only in regard to certain species. However, scientific evidence demonstrates that problems arising in the management of oceanic resources must be addressed in an integrated manner.[102] The notion of integrated management combines pollution prevention, management of fisheries and other species and protection of their habitats. It is practically very challenging to ensure integrated management of marine resources but at the heart of this notion sits the ecosystem approach.[103] In fact, the ecosystem approach may be able to bridge this gap between the sectoral division of maritime zones and ecosystems within, that is, if States cooperate and apply ecosystem management to transboundary resources. However, maritime boundaries will arguably form a more appropriate basis for ecosystem management if environmental circumstances are considered in the delimitation process.

When discussing the constraint of maritime delimitation to coastal geography in 1994, Charney stated that 'the conservation and management of marine resources may be made more difficult if maritime boundaries do not reflect natural boundaries or exploitation patterns'. He explained that maritime boundaries could be designed to co-ordinate with relevant ecosystems or social needs but concluded that this was untenable due to evidentiary difficulties and the changing nature of these factors.[104] However, as contemporaneous scientific evidence demonstrates, coastal geography is also prone to change. Procedural rules concerning scientific evidence, discussed in Section 3.3.2, are highly relevant here but will not be repeated. Instead, the following sections explore the relevance of environmental circumstances and methods of identifying relevant environmental circumstances, particularly the elusive relevant ecosystems.

4.3.2 *Relevance of Environmental Circumstances*

The law on maritime delimitation provides that environmental circumstances only affect the process if they qualify as 'relevant circumstances'. Courts and tribunals have almost entirely based their decisions on geographical circumstances, as explained in Chapter 3. Nonetheless, other factors can be relevant.[105] In fact, environmental circumstances have influenced a small

101 Ibid.

102 Philippe Sands and Jacqueline Peel (n 31) 457 referring to GESAMP, *A Sea of Troubles*, GESAMP Report No 70 (2001) 3.

103 Philippe Sands and Jacqueline Peel (n 31) 457.

104 Jonathan Charney, 'Progress in International Maritime Boundary Delimitation Law' (1994) 88 (2) American Journal of International Law 238–241.

105 Davor Vidas , 'Sea-Level Rise and International Law: At the Convergence of Two Epochs' (2014) 4 Climate law 77.

number of cases.[106] Moreover, States have been known to take non-geographical factors into account when negotiating maritime boundaries. In particular, environmental and economic circumstances have influenced maritime delimitation in a significant portion of maritime boundary agreements.[107] For example, maritime boundary agreements often take fisheries particularly into consideration and some boundaries are delimited by reference to the exploitation of minerals.[108]

The *Grisbådarna Arbitration* from 1909, the first landmark maritime boundary delimitation, took environmental circumstances into account. More specifically, the tribunal avoided the cutting up of discernible ecosystems when delimiting the territorial sea between Norway and Sweden. The parties agreed that the boundary should not cut across any important banks as this would cause a 'great inconvenience'.[109] The tribunal avoided this inconvenience by delimiting a boundary that would 'pass midway between the banks of Grisbådarna on one side, and the banks of Skjöttegrunde on the other'.[110] The banks of Grisbådarna were allotted to Sweden, as fishing activities there had been exercised more markedly and effectively by Swedish fisherman than by Norwegians. The banks of Skjöttegrunde fell on the Norwegian side despite a strong Swedish presence, but this was justified by reference to the insignificance of this part of the disputed territory, the fact that Norwegian fishermen had not been excluded from the Skjöttegrunde banks, and that they had been more influential there than at Grisbådarna.[111] It is clear that fisheries interests were deemed relevant for the delimitation of this maritime boundary but those interests were established by reference to historic use and dependency on the resource, rather than environmental concerns.

The Chamber of the ICJ assessed the impact of fisheries on the overall result in the *Gulf of Maine* case. The approach to environmental circumstances was unique in this case because it dealt with, not only the presence or access to fish and lobster, but also the location of ecosystems or recognizable limits in the marine environment. Canada and the United States emphasized the importance of biological and ecological circumstances in their arguments before the Chamber, identifying ecosystems, recognizable limits in the marine environment and oceanographic or ecological regimes in the area.[112] The Chamber explained that the water column should be 'taken into consideration not as some inert mass, but as the habitat of an exceptionally extensive

106 See *Denmark* v. *Norway* (n 18) para 78; *Delimitation of the Maritime Boundary in the Gulf of Maine Area (Canada/United States)* (Judgment) [1984] ICJ Rep 246, para 237. See also Victor Prescott and Clive Schofield, *The Maritime Political Boundaries of the World*, 2nd edition (Martinus Nijhoff, 2005) 239–241.

107 Barbara Kwiatkowska, 'Economic and Environmental Considerations in Maritime Boundary Delimitations' in Jonathan Charney and Lewis Alexander (eds) *International Maritime Boundaries, volume 1* (Martinus Nijhoff, 1993) 75.

108 Ibid., 76.

109 *Grisbådarna Arbitration* (n 64) 6.

110 Ibid.

111 Ibid., 7.

112 *Gulf of Maine* (n 106) paras 50–52.

wealth of fauna and flora'.[113] More specifically, it concluded that information and statistics regarding fisheries should be considered at the final stage of the delimitation process, when assessing the equity of the resulting boundary.[114] The Chamber indicated that the boundary might be adjusted if circumstances relating to fisheries made it 'radically inequitable' or 'likely to entail catastrophic repercussions for the livelihood and economic well-being of the population of the countries concerned'.[115] The threshold was not met in this case because, as the tribunal noted, the delimitation line afforded both States access to the locations that had traditionally been most important for their nationals.[116]

The possibility of avoiding fragmented management was discussed in the *Gulf of Maine*. The United States argued that the Georges Bank should not be divided and that the conservation and management of the fisheries there should be left to one State to avoid disputes. Still, the Chamber found no need to avoid this division of the Georges Bank or anticipate complications, even though the division clearly necessitated transboundary co-operation. Its decision did not endorse single management of the fisheries or conservation of the area but the Chamber expected the States to successfully co-operate in this regard, given their long tradition of amicable co-operation in maritime affairs.[117] However, what ensued were years of disputes and non-compliance across the boundary.[118]

An arbitral tribunal reached a similar conclusion a year later in *Guinea/Guinea Bissau*. In this case, the tribunal noted that a variety of circumstances could be relevant when delimiting maritime boundaries. These could include historic, political and economic circumstances but an exhaustive list could not be provided because each unique case might require consideration for different circumstances.[119] Both parties referred to the importance of access to fish stocks (and other resources) as part of their right to development and in the context of their economic dependency on such resources.[120] The tribunal acknowledged that economic factors were not completely irrelevant to its decision, although they were not sufficiently permanent to affect the location of the boundary. Instead, the tribunal found that the economic considerations should motivate the States to co-operate in the exploitation and management of the disputed resources to mutually further their economic interests.[121]

The ICJ confirmed the relevance of environmental circumstances in the Jan Mayen case of 1993. This decisions marked a shift in the jurisprudence as the Court

113 Ibid., para 48.
114 Ibid., para 237.
115 Ibid.
116 Ibid., para 238.
117 Ibid., para 240.
118 See further discussion in Section 4.4.1.
119 *Delimitation of the maritime boundary between Guinea and Guinea-Bissau (Guinea/Guinea-Bissau)* (1985) XIX RIAA 149 para 89.
120 Ibid., para 121.
121 Ibid., paras 122–123.

substantially adjusted the provisional median line to ensure equitable access to fisheries resources.[122] Still, the emphasis lay, like it did in the *Grisbådarna* case, with exploitation, rather than conservation of the resource. In this case, both Norway and Denmark emphasized their interests in fisheries in the disputed area.[123] The ICJ referred to earlier case law and found that it was obligated to consider whether any adjustments to the provisional median line was needed 'to ensure equitable access to the capelin fishery resources for the vulnerable fishing communities concerned'.[124] The provisional median line was, in the Court's opinion, 'too far to the west for Denmark to be assured of an equitable access to the capelin stock' and was, consequently, shifted eastwards.[125] The most important fish stock in the *Jan Mayen* case was capelin, which migrates, and the migration patterns are affected by climatic conditions.[126] The fact that the ICJ considered this migratory species to be relevant circumstances, calling for the adjustment of the provisional boundary, demonstrates that non-permanent environmental factors can be taken into account.

In the 1999 *Eritrea/Yemen* arbitration, the tribunal found that 'fish as a present and future potential resource is important for the general and local populations of each Party' and that 'interest in and development of fish as a food source is an important and meritorious objective'.[127] The tribunal rejected the relevance of all considerations relating to fisheries because neither party had shown that proposed lines would have catastrophic or inequitable effects on fishing activities, the fishing community or economic circumstances.[128] Still, the award arguably indicates that fisheries interests can be understood broadly, as relating to historic practice, economic dependency, location of fish stocks and food consumption.[129] The tribunal did not categorically reject the relevance of these different aspects of fisheries but found no significant reason to take them into account in this particular case because both States were equally affected.[130] Thus, the circumstances described earlier may only justify adjustment of the provisional boundary when having substantial impact on only one party to a dispute.[131]

The arbitral tribunal in *Barbados* v. *Trinidad and Tobago* also dealt with the relevance of dependency on fisheries. Barbados submitted that Barbadian fishermen were dependent on flying fish fisheries off the coast of Tobago for their livelihood

122 *Denmark* v. *Norway* (n 18) para 90.
123 Ibid., para 73.
124 Ibid., para 75.
125 Ibid., para 76.
126 Ibid., para 73.
127 *Second stage of the proceedings between Eritrea and Yemen (Maritime Delimitation) (Eritrea/Yemen)* (1999) XXII RIAA 335, para 71.
128 Ibid., para 72.
129 Ibid.
130 Ibid., paras 71 and 72.
131 See Stuart Kaye, 'Lessons Learned from the Gulf of Maine Case: The Development of Maritime Boundary Delimitation Jurisprudence since UNCLOS III' (2008) 14 (1) Ocean and Coastal Law Journal, 73, 93–94.

and had fished there for centuries with little or no interference. Barbados claimed that it would be catastrophic if its subjects were barred from fishing in these areas and provided several testimonies to that effect.[132] Barbados based its argument for the adjustment of the provisional boundary on three factors. First, the long history of artisanal fishing for flying fish off the coast of Tobago. Second, its dependency on these fisheries. Third, the lack of dependency of Trinidad and Tobago on these fisheries.[133] Trinidad and Tobago refuted all these arguments, describing them as fictional and explaining that the inability to harvest the disputed resource in recent years had produced no catastrophic consequences.[134] The tribunal neither affirmed nor rejected the contention that these fisheries interests could in principle qualify as relevant circumstances in the delimitation process. Such a decision was unnecessary because the tribunal found that Barbados had produced insufficient evidence for the submissions outlined earlier.[135] Thus, the tribunal set a high threshold for factually proving these circumstances. Moreover, the tribunal explained that geographical circumstances should normally prevail over fisheries interests because the former satisfied the 'quest for neutral criteria'.[136]

There are no recent examples of environmental circumstances affecting the delimitation line before courts or tribunals. Still, States have continued to reference environmental circumstances in judicial proceedings when maritime zones are delimited. For example, in *Bangladesh* v. *India*, Bangladesh raised arguments concerning the nation's dependency on fisheries and advocated for consequent adjustment of the delimitation line. India even agreed that economic considerations relating to fisheries could be relevant but only if entailing 'catastrophic repercussions'.[137] The tribunal did not reject the relevance of these circumstances as such but found that Bangladesh had not produced sufficient evidence of its dependence on fisheries in the Bay of Bengal to result in adjustment of the provisional equidistance boundary.[138] The tribunal referred to the tribunal's decision in *Barbados* v. *Trinidad and Tobago* where the fisheries interests of Barbados did not lead to adjustment of the provisional boundary because of insufficient proof of longstanding usage or catastrophic effects.[139] The tribunal in *Bangladesh* v. *India* did not give any further guidance on what might constitute necessary evidence but India submitted that a claim of economic dependency on fisheries should be supported by strong, documented evidence. It further noted that the report submitted by Bangladesh did not fully support the claim that fish production

132 *Delimitation of the Exclusive Economic Zone and the Continental Shelf (Barbados* v. *Trinidad and Tobago)* (2006) XXVII RIAA 147, paras 247 and 249.

133 Ibid., para 250.

134 Ibid., paras 254–257.

135 Ibid., para 265.

136 Ibid., para 228.

137 *Bay of Bengal Maritime Boundary Arbitration (Bangladesh* v. *India)* (2014) 167 ILR 1, para 394.

138 Ibid., para 424.

139 *Barbados* v. *Trinidad and Tobago* (n 132) paras 264–271.

was dependent on sovereign rights in the Bay of Bengal because it showed that inland waters were more important for those interests.[140]

The role of environmental circumstances may have diminished with the crystallization of the judicial process of maritime delimitation, exemplified by the *Black Sea* case.[141] This development of the law results from an emphasis on the need for transparency and predictability.[142] Meanwhile, the pressure to address the challenges of climate change and ensure sustainable development is reaching its pinnacle. The relevance of environmental circumstances in maritime delimitation depends on the objectives of each delimitation. Therefore, their relevance will be minimal as long as transparency, predictability and neutrality are emphasized, but can increase if environmental objectives are promoted.

The jurisprudence indicates that the relevance of environmental circumstances primarily relates to exploitation of resources. The environmental considerations emphasized in the cases discussed earlier mostly relate to equitable access to economically viable fish stocks, historic use or dependency on particular fish stocks. This dependency can flow from economic interests or interests in food security. These cases do not directly confirm the relevance of environmental circumstances in the context of ecosystem management or environmental protection. However, the *Gulf of Maine* case (and subsequent disputes) arguably demonstrate that such circumstances may have to be considered if the delimitation is to form a basis for fruitful transboundary co-operation. Furthermore, environmental considerations should arguably be integrated to the delimitation process to ensure ongoing access to marine resources. Indeed, ecosystem management and environmental protection may be prerequisites to long-term exploitation of relevant resources.

The case law demonstrates that environmental factors can influence the delimitation process if they radically affect States' ability to harvest marine resources or entail catastrophic repercussions. Moreover, the ICJ has shown that ongoing changes can be taken into account when assessing access to fish stocks. It considered seasonal changes and migration patterns in the *Jan Mayen* case and noted that the capelin was impacted by climatic factors.[143] Climate-related changes and the response to those changes, that is, ecosystem management and protection of vulnerable species, is relevant to the long-term exploitability of marine resources. Relevant environmental circumstances cannot extend only to immediate exploitation of fish stocks – that would make boundaries delimited on such a foundation obsolete or inappropriate when relevant resources relocate, for example, due to ocean warming. This is why environmental circumstances should now be considered in a broader context; the adverse effects of climate change make ecological circumstances and environmental protection increasingly relevant to sustainable utilization of relevant resources.

140 *Bangladesh* v. *India* (n 137) para 394.
141 See Section 3.2.2.3.1.
142 See, for example, *Bangladesh* v. *India* (n 137) para 339.
143 Ibid., paras 73 and 78.

The historical development of maritime delimitation demonstrates that changes occur gradually until landmark cases cement new methods. These changes have been influenced by circumstances existing in the international community and the various motives driving disputing States. As clearly articulated in Malawi Principle 1, '[m]anagement objectives are a matter of societal choice'. If the international society chooses to prioritize sustainable development when delimiting maritime entitlements, then the relevance of environmental circumstances becomes readily apparent. This change is easy to implement in delimitation agreements (as States have autonomy over their negotiations), but it will take a landmark case to change the law, as referred to in UNCLOS articles 74 and 83. States can accelerate this development by emphasizing environmental considerations in contentious delimitation cases and bilateral negotiations. That is a matter of choice.

4.3.3 *Identification of Relevant Environmental Circumstances*

The relevance of environmental circumstances is primarily tied to individual fish stocks. The identification of such stocks has not seemed particularly problematic. However, even if the relevance of environmental circumstances is limited to exploitation of commercially viable fish stocks, those stocks generally form part of bigger ecosystems, the circumstances of which can be relevant for ongoing access and sustainable use. In the same vein, relevant environmental circumstances may relate to the presence of a clearly defined MPA or protection of one particular species but those may also call for consideration of ecological circumstances. A broader consideration of relevant ecosystems or ecological circumstances is much more complicated than the identification of individual fish stocks. This was demonstrated by the *Gulf of Maine* case, where the location of discernible limits in the marine environment presented major challenges.[144] This section deals specifically with the identification of relevant ecosystems or practical units for ecosystem management.

It may be appropriate to identify the location of ecosystems or sub-units in the delimitation process if the protection or management of resources is deemed relevant. The purpose may be to avoid unnecessary division or inappropriate allocation of ecosystems; to lay a foundation for ecosystem management; or to establish protection measures. For example, the identification of ecosystems is relevant for the establishment of MPAs and for holistic protection of vulnerable species. Indeed, ecosystems should be defined before management and conservation measures are prescribed and such arrangements can be integrated in the delimitation process, as further explained in Section 4.4.[145]

An ecosystem is a unit of ecology that includes plants and animals that coincide, and the environment that they influence.[146] The CBD defines it as 'a dynamic

[144] *Gulf of Maine* (n 106) paras 54, 56 and 238.
[145] See particularly Sections 4.4.1.2 and 4.4.3.2.
[146] *Compact Oxford English Dictionary*, 2nd edition (Oxford University Press, 1991) 494.

complex of plant, animal and micro-organism communities and their non-living environment interacting as a functional unit'.[147] It can be difficult to identify and differentiate between ecosystems, even for experts. Kirk noted, more than twenty years ago, that a mechanism was needed for defining ecosystems to allow for holistic management of ecosystems.[148] This posed a significant challenge at the time but scientific advances are now making it practically feasible for States, courts and tribunals to define relevant ecosystems and evidentiary difficulties can be overcome as explained in Section 3.3.2. Indeed, it is worth repeating that the tribunal in the *Kishenganga Arbitration* clearly demonstrated the possibility of basing judicial decisions on, not only existing ecological circumstances, but potential changes in relevant ecosystems.[149]

Ecosystems can be defined in different ways and experts can disagree on their locations. This was evident in the *Gulf of Maine* case, when the United States and Canada acknowledged the existence of discernible oceano-biological boundaries separating distinct ecological communities, but disagreed on their location.[150] Canada identified an oceano-biological boundary at the extreme western limit of the delimitation area, east of the Great South Channel.[151] Meanwhile, the United States found three distinct ecological and oceanographic boundaries in the area and submitted that the most important one, separating most of the commercially exploitable fish stocks, ran along the Northeast Channel.[152] The Chamber of the ICJ confirmed that the 'great mass of water is taken into consideration not as some inert mass, but as the habitat of an exceptionally extensive wealth of fauna and flora'.[153] Yet, it was unable to identify a sure and stable boundary on this basis.[154]

Westholm has demonstrated how ecosystems are divided into manageable units of administrative ecosystems when applying the ecosystem approach.[155] This demarcation influences the area governed therein but the spatial scale also influences the identification of ecosystems[156] and consequently, implementation of the ecosystem approach. Westholm further explains that while nature must be divided into manageable units, '[a]ny attempt to delimit ecosystems geographically highlights the difficulty of interpreting nature in a human context'.[157] The following examples shed light on the process of legally defining ecosystems.

147 CBD article 2.
148 Elizabeth Kirk (n 58) 69.
149 *The Indus Waters Kishenganga The Indus Waters Kishenganga Arbitration (Pakistan* v. *India)* (2013) 150 ILR 311, para 100.
150 *Gulf of Maine* (n 106) paras 50–51.
151 Ibid., para 50.
152 Ibid., para 51.
153 Ibid., para 48.
154 Ibid., para 54.
155 Aron Westholm (n 19) 119–120.
156 Ibid., referring to Nathan Sayre, 'Ecological and Geographical Scale: Parallels and Potential for Integration' 29 Progress in Human Geography 276, 279.
157 Aron Westholm (n 19) 122.

The EU Water Framework Directive[158] extends to the territorial sea in relation to the achievement of good surface water chemical status.[159] For the purpose of managing these ecosystems, relevant waters are categorized as fresh water ecoregions or marine ecoregions and States Parties must establish river-basin management for their waters. This involves the demarcation of river basin districts and assigning management to competent authorities.[160] The waters within each district are categorized as river, lake, transitional water or coastal water and therein, different types of water are identified by, for example, ecoregion, salinity and mean depth. This process leads to the creation of management units, so-called 'water bodies'.[161] The division into water bodies is not an arbitrary process but one based on biological factors and the relevance of different factors depends on their significance under the directive's objectives and its provisions.[162] Similarly, the different interests in maritime delimitations could guide the identification of relevant 'ocean bodies'. For example, such bodies (or ecosystems) could be determined by reference to particularly relevant fish stocks and associated species.

Various factors can influence the identification of water bodies for the purpose of the Water Framework Directive. This includes man-made factors, such as the designation of protected areas and the Implementation Strategy stipulates that unmanageable fragmentation must be avoided.[163] Likewise, protected areas could be taken into account in the delimitation of maritime boundaries and efforts could be made to draw boundaries around, rather than through, ecosystem-units to avoid fragmented management.

Another EU directive, The Marine Strategy Framework Directive,[164] also requires the application of the ecosystem approach. The Directive aims to protect marine ecosystems and biodiversity, that is, to achieve good environmental status, and one of the key measures is the establishment of a network of MPAs.[165] The Directive divides marine waters into four 'marine regions' and eight 'subregions' for the purpose of management.[166] This division does not seem to centre on the location of ecosystems but builds on a report prepared by the International Council for the Exploration of the Sea about the marine regions of Europe.[167] However, States may divide the

158 Directive 2000/60/EC of the European Parliament and of the Council establishing a framework for Community action in the field of water policy [2000] OJ L327, article 1.

159 Aron Westholm (n 19) 123.

160 Ibid., 124, referring to Water Framework Directive article 3.

161 Ibid., referring to Water Framework Directive article 3, Annex II.

162 Ibid., referring to the Common Implementation Strategy for the Water Framework Directive (2000/60/EC) Guidance Document No 2, 5.

163 Aron Westholm (n 19) 124 and Common Implementation Strategy for the Water Framework Directive (2000/60/EC) Guidance Document No 2, 9.

164 Directive 2008/56/EC of the European Parliament and of the Council establishing a framework for community action in the field of marine environmental policy [2008] OJ L 164.

165 Ibid., articles 1 and 13(4).

166 Ibid., article 4.

167 Aron Westholm (n 19) 127, referring to ICES, 'Eco-Regions Advice to EC'.

subregions into 'subdivisions' for the purpose of implementing the Marine Strategy Framework Directive and it stipulates that States sharing a marine region or subregion must ensure concerted effort to meet the objectives of the Directive.[168] Such subdivision and co-operation could be useful when delimiting and managing overlapping maritime entitlements. Indeed, the delimitation process generally begins with broad strokes produced by the provisional equidistance line but the identification of subdivisions of ecosystems, for example, fishing banks, could influence the final result.

The Marine Strategy Framework Directive urges States Parties to use relevant 'existing regional institutional cooperation structures, including those under Regional Sea Conventions'.[169] This refers to the OSPAR Convention, the Helsinki Convention, the Barcelona Convention for the Protection of the Mediterranean Sea against Pollution[170] and the Bucharest Convention on the Protection of the Black Sea against Pollution.[171][172] These and other regional instruments could also be relevant when identifying ecosystems and making arrangements for transboundary resources in the delimitation process. They may in some instances establish large ecosystems that would either require the co-operation of several States or fragmented management, but it might be useful to establish subdivisions on the basis of the regions identified by these instruments.

The identification of relevant ecosystems is decidedly more complicated when it comes to migratory species, and it may not be practically feasible to assign all living beings to ecosystems. Still, scientists can keep track of the movements of migratory species and define the parameters of their ecosystems. A case in point is the process of describing 'Ecologically and Biologically Significant Areas' on the basis of the CBD.[173] The movement of marine species can be tracked with the help of pre-existing mechanisms, such as the 'Migratory Connectivity Project'.[174] In fact, modern technology can now enable real-time communication of the movements of marine species and associated boundaries and this is paving the way for dynamic area-based management tools in the marine environment, such as mobile MPAs.[175]

168 Marine Strategy Framework Directive articles 4(2) and 5(2).

169 Ibid., article 6(1).

170 Convention for the protection of the Mediterranean Sea against pollution (adopted 16 February 1976, entered into force 12 February 1978) 1102 UNTS 27.

171 Convention on the Protection of the Black Sea against Pollution (adopted 21 April 1992, entered into force 15 January 1994) 1764 UNTS 3.

172 See Aron Westholm (n 19) 127.

173 Sara Maxwell, Kristina Gjerde, Melinda Conners and Larry Crowder, 'Mobile protected Areas for Biodiversity on the High Seas' (2020) 367 (6475) Science (American Association for the Advancement of Science) 252, 253, referring to Daniel C Dunn et al, 'The Convention on Biological Diversity's Ecologically or Biologically Significant Areas: Origins, Development, and Current Status' (2014) 49 Marine Policy, 137.

174 Sara Maxwell, Kristina Gjerde, Melinda Conners and Larry Crowder (n 173) 253, referring to Daniel Dunn et al, 'The Importance of Migratory Connectivity for Global Ocean Policy' (2019) 286 (1911) Proceedings of the Royal Society B.

175 Sara Maxwell, Kristina Gjerde, Melinda Conners and Larry Crowder (n 173) 253.

The identification and monitoring of mobile ecosystems can entail different methods, for example, anchoring to environmental characteristics such as ocean temperature, visual or acoustic detection of species or modelling to forecast their presence.[176] These methods can result in the demarcation of ecosystems with geographic boundaries that are ambulatory, and not fixed.

4.4 ACHIEVING AN EQUITABLE SOLUTION WITH DUE REGARD FOR ENVIRONMENTAL CIRCUMSTANCES

Maritime delimitation is not extraneous to the living marine environment. It is closely related to various aspects of ocean management and can be applied in a way that is conducive of sustainable, ecosystem-based management, and promotes fulfilment of obligations concerning protection of the marine environment. Courts and tribunals may be reluctant to depart from established jurisprudence but as of 2015, more than 90 per cent of maritime boundaries were negotiated by disputing States,[177] and States can adopt novel approaches when delimiting this vast majority of overlapping maritime entitlements.[178] Thus, even if environmental considerations are rarely considered in the judicial process of maritime delimitation, they can still influence the negotiating process, and thereby, a large portion of the world's undelimited areas. Furthermore, State practice can affect the interpretation of UNCLOS articles 74 and 83, and States can explicitly extend the mandate in maritime delimitation cases to incorporate environmental considerations.

Environmental circumstances can affect the delimitation process in numerous ways. Under the traditional approach to maritime delimitation, one should first determine whether such circumstances qualify as 'relevant circumstances'. Once identified and deemed relevant, consideration for environmental circumstances could affect the location of a fixed or fluctuating boundary. Furthermore, as States are free to agree on any solution they deem equitable, they could come to an alternative arrangement and manage relevant areas without dividing boundaries.

4.4.1 *Fixed Boundaries*

The first, and most plausible, effect of environmental circumstances on maritime delimitation involves the drawing of a fixed boundary. A fixed maritime boundary would be consistent with traditional approaches to maritime delimitation and would promote the objectives of geographic stability, certainty and predictability. Environmental considerations can affect the location of a fixed boundary and maritime

176 Ibid., 253–254, referring to Sara Maxwell et al., 'Dynamic Ocean Management: Defining and Conceptualizing Real-Time Management of the Ocean' (2015) 58 Marine Policy 42.

177 Áslaug Ásgeirsdóttir and Martin Steinwand, 'Dispute Settlement Mechanisms and Maritime Boundary Settlements' (2015) 10 Review of International Organizations 119, 131.

178 Andreas Østhagen (n 3) 5.

delimitation can also result in specific arrangements applicable in conjunction with a fixed boundary. These different possibilities are discussed in the following sections.

4.4.1.1 Adjustment of Provisional Boundaries by Reference to Environmental Circumstances

Provisional maritime boundaries are generally adjusted by reference to all relevant circumstances, as explained in Chapter 3. Whether the delimitation process begins with a provisional equidistance or median line, or even an angle bisector, these provisional boundaries can be altered to account for relevant environmental circumstances, during the second stage of the delimitation process.[179] This adjustment can significantly alter the location of the boundary.

The equidistance/relevant circumstances method is ordinarily preferred in judicial delimitation.[180] Still, according to Cottier, equidistance only forms the basis of around 60 per cent of all maritime boundaries.[181] States can agree on a different starting point for maritime delimitation. Indeed, the equidistance method can be inappropriate under certain circumstances and replaced with other methods, such as the angle-bisector method,[182] or other more creative methods. The choice of delimitation methods and adjustment of provisional boundaries partly depends on the objective of each delimitation and the objectives can relate to a variety of factors, including environmental and economic factors. For example, States may wish to avoid fragmented ecosystem management or to ensure shared access to particular ecosystems. The following examples demonstrate how fixed boundaries have or could have been adjusted to account for relevant environmental circumstances.[183]

The *Grisbådarna* award established a fixed boundary by reference to environmental circumstances. In this case, the tribunal adjusted its provisional boundary to afford the fisheries at Grisbådarna to Sweden and avoid fragmentation.[184] The award demonstrates that States can agree to prioritize fisheries management and that such considerations can influence judicial delimitation of maritime boundaries. Here, the division of particular fishing banks was seen as a 'great inconvenience' and consequently, curtailed.[185]

The ICJ's delimitation of a single-purpose boundary in the *Jan Mayen* case of 1993 is a more recent example demonstrating how a fixed boundary can be adjusted by

179 See *Maritime Delimitation in the Black Sea (Romania v. Ukraine)* (Judgment) [2009] ICJ Rep 61, para 118.

180 See *Delimitation of the Maritime Boundary between Bangladesh and Myanmar in the Bay of Bengal (Bangladesh/Myanmar)* (Judgment) [2012] ITLOS, 51 ILM 844, para 238; and *Territorial and Maritime Dispute between Nicaragua and Honduras in the Caribbean Sea (Nicaragua v. Honduras)* (Judgment) [2007] ICJ Rep 659, para 272.

181 Thomas Cottier (n 2) 375.

182 Continental Shelf (Libyan Arab Jamahiriya/Malta) (Judgment) [1985] ICJ Rep 13, 44, para 56.

183 The cases are discussed in more detail in Section 4.3.2 and the *Gulf of Maine* case in Section 4.4.1.2.

184 *Grisbådarna Arbitration* (n 64) 6.

185 Ibid.

reference to relevant environmental circumstances. In this case, the Court delimited a fixed boundary, using the equidistance/relevant circumstances method, and adjusted the provisional boundary to ensure equitable access to capelin fisheries.[186]

The Chamber of the ICJ was confronted with potentially relevant environmental circumstances in the *Gulf of Maine* case. The environmental circumstances under discussion related to marine ecosystems and were eventually not considered relevant for the construction of a fixed maritime boundary.[187] This may have been a mistake because while the Chamber of the ICJ assumed that the States would co-operate amicably in the management of transboundary resources, they were unable to do so for a long time and that ultimately threatened the fish stocks.[188] The Chamber could have made provisions for co-operative management, as explained in the following section. Furthermore, it could have avoided this need for co-operation by establishing the boundary in a way that afforded the banks to one State.

4.4.1.2 Environmental Stipulations Accompanying Fixed Boundaries

It is not always appropriate to adjust a provisional boundary by reference to relevant environmental circumstances. Even if fisheries interests or other environmental circumstances are deemed relevant and sufficient evidence provided, it may still be inappropriate to adjust a fixed boundary by reference to such circumstances. The reason may be that those circumstances are expected to change or that the parties seek a single-purpose boundary and the adjustment is not feasible for delimitation of the continental shelf. Another approach to maritime delimitation that involves fixed boundaries and consideration for relevant environmental circumstances, involves the adoption of rules concerning ecosystem management or environmental protection across fixed boundaries. Indeed, Churchill has explained that States generally have to conclude agreements concerning the management of transboundary resources and rather than doing this in a piecemeal fashion, after the conclusion of a boundary, it would be logical to settle issues of transboundary co-operation in a combined effort.[189]

Mutual arrangements can be agreed upon when maritime entitlements are bilaterally delimited. In fact, maritime boundary agreements often include 'reciprocal fisheries arrangements' to ensure compatible management on either side of the boundary. In contrast, judicially decided maritime boundaries generally lack such provisions[190] but courts and tribunals can also make stipulations concerning transboundary arrangements. Provisions concerning reciprocal arrangements could actually eradicate the need for adjusting provisional boundaries and vice versa. Barbados

186 *Denmark* v. *Norway* (n 18) para 76.
187 *Gulf of Maine* (n 106) paras 237–238.
188 Ibid., para 240; See also Glen Herbert (n 18) 306–307.
189 Robin Churchill (n 16) 27.
190 Glen Herbert (n 18) 302–303.

contended, in *Barbados* v. *Trinidad and Tobago*, that 'the refusal by Trinidad and Tobago to conclude an agreement according renewed and continuing access for Barbadian fisherfolk to the waters off Tobago justifies adjusting the maritime boundary so as to place the waters in dispute within the EEZ not of Trinidad and Tobago but of Barbados'.[191] Thus, Barbados argued that the lack of agreement concerning fisheries should affect the location of the boundary. The opposite is also true; an assurance of mutual arrangements can eliminate the need for adjusting a provisional boundary.

There is a long tradition of States concluding arrangements concerning transboundary co-operation as a supplement to fixed boundaries. These agreements are often quite complicated and institutionalized and they can be agreed upon at the time of delimitation or whenever the need arises.[192] The tradition relates to non-living seabed resources, as well as living resources of the water column. For example, the 1981 Agreement between Iceland and Norway, which was concluded on the basis of recommendations of a Conciliation Commission, delimits a fixed, single-purpose boundary by reference to claims set forth based on fisheries interests. Moreover, it sets up a joint development zone for the exploration and exploitation of hydrocarbon resources.[193] Another example of a fixed boundary accompanied by stipulations concerning co-operative management is the Torres Strait treaty between Australia and Papua New Guinea.[194] It establishes two distinct boundaries, one for the continental shelf and another for the exclusive fisheries zone[195] and the latter covers 'all living natural resources of the sea and seabed'.[196] Furthermore, the treaty establishes a protected zone, the purpose of which is to protect the rights of traditional inhabitants and preserve the marine environment, indigenous fauna and flora.[197] The parties agree to share the allowable catch from commercial fisheries therein.[198] The treaty also sets up a Joint Advisory Council that can make recommendations concerning the Protected Zone or relating to the effective implementation of the treaty.[199]

It is by no means guaranteed that States are able to reach agreements supplementing fixed boundaries. The *Gulf of Maine* dispute is an example of a maritime boundary dispute involving critical overfishing where multiple attempts to negotiate failed. The Chamber of the ICJ established a permanent boundary in 1984 and yet, this did not solve the dispute. What followed were the creations of conflicting

[191] *Barbados* v. *Trinidad and Tobago* (n 132) paras 251.

[192] See Douglas Johnston and Mark Valencia, *Pacific Ocean Boundary Problems: Status and Solutions* (Martinus Nijhoff, 1991) 17.

[193] Agreement between Norway and Iceland on the continental shelf between Iceland and Jan Mayen (adopted 22 October 1981, entered into force 2 June 1982) 2124 UNTS 247.

[194] Treaty between Australia and Papua New Guinea (n 18).

[195] Ibid., article 4.

[196] Ibid., article 1.

[197] Ibid., article 10.

[198] Ibid., article 23.

[199] Ibid., article 19.

management policies and non-compliance across the boundary.[200] The delimitation took no account of environmental circumstances and so, it should come as no surprise that it did not form a good basis for joint management of transboundary fisheries.[201] It might have produced a better solution if either the location of the boundary took account of relevant environmental circumstances, or if the final decision made some stipulations toward co-operative management.

4.4.2 *Fluctuating Boundaries*

Fixed maritime boundaries are artificial lines designed to simplify management of the intricate marine environment. According to Kirk, these boundaries create a hyperreality that delimits the ocean into sections, but reality demands that the ocean is seen as a whole.[202] This sectoral approach is coupled with the species-specific approach, as explained in Section 4.3.1, which produces rules for specific species that transcend man-made boundaries.[203] These rules apply to organisms wherever they are and can supplement fixed boundaries. Nonetheless, this system does not ensure a holistic ecosystem approach to ocean management because States can focus their attention to individual stocks of commercially viable fish, to the detriment of other species.[204] These problems of fragmentation partly relate to the geographical scope of application for relevant rules and can in some instances be addressed with designation of large enough zones.[205] This may explain why the breadth of the exclusive economic zone covers the distance from shore where a vast majority of commercially viable fish stocks occurs and why MPAs often cover large areas. However, vast maritime zones, coupled with mobile rules, do not seem to suffice to ensure comprehensive ecosystem management.[206] A better solution, at least from an environmental standpoint, might be the establishment of fluctuating boundaries, that is, boundaries that change to reflect changes in the location of relevant ecosystems.

Scientists are promoting the use of dynamic ocean management. It is defined as 'management that changes rapidly in space and time in response to the shifting nature of the ocean and its users based on the integration of new biological, oceanographic, social and/or economic data in near real-time'.[207] Maxwell et al explain how this approach can serve to implement more traditional approaches, such as ecosystem management and adaptive ocean management.[208] Dynamic

200 Glen Herbert (n 18) 306–307.
201 Ibid., 308–309 and 316.
202 Elizabeth Kirk (n 58) 67.
203 The FSA sets the framework for such agreements concerning straddling and highly migratory fish stocks.
204 Elizabeth Kirk (n 58) 69.
205 Ibid.
206 Ibid.
207 See Sara Maxwell et al. (n 176) 43.
208 Ibid., 43–44.

ocean management enables rapid response to climatic changes and it can be used in conjunction with traditional techniques, such as marine spatial planning and quotas, to maximize management goals.[209] Technology has historically stood in the way of a dynamic ecosystem approach but the necessary technology is now readily available[210] and scientists are encouraging the use of fluctuating boundaries for MPAs.[211]

Dynamic management is increasingly applied to marine resources within national jurisdiction.[212] Mobile MPAs are among the management tools best suited to protect vulnerable migratory species in the changing ocean.[213] In fact, the negotiators of the new BBNJ Draft Agreement have been urged to promote the use of mobile MPAs as large MPAs with fixed boundaries cannot address significant seasonal and climate-related changes.[214] Scientists are stating that dynamic management tools, such as mobile MPAs, may be the only practical option offering sufficient protection for migratory species.[215] The feasibility of fluctuating boundaries for MPAs stems from the fact that MPAs are designed to regulate organisms that do not respect man-made boundaries[216] and the same can be said of exclusive economic and exclusive fisheries zones. Indeed, boundaries to maritime zones can also fluctuate by reference to ecosystems and this could bring them closer to the reality of the interests they serve.

Fluctuating boundaries, whether established by reference to coastlines or ecosystems, are closer to reality than the hyperreality established by fixed boundaries because they more resemble natural boundaries. Natural boundaries are widely applied on land but it is generally more difficult to identify such boundaries in the sea.[217] The 'neutral' or 'incontrovertible facts of coastal geography and offshore geomorphology' have historically been considered more relevant as a basis for natural maritime boundaries.[218] Yet, recent scientific advances and the growing need to respond to the adverse effects of climate change make environmental circumstances increasingly relevant as grounds for natural boundaries.

The notion of fluctuating boundaries was explored in Section 3.4.4. It explained how maritime boundaries can fluctuate in accordance with changing coastal geography, and the same rationale applies here. Maritime boundaries can fluctuate in accordance with environmental circumstances if deemed sufficiently relevant and if courts, tribunals or negotiating States anchor the boundaries to such circumstances

209 Ibid., 44.
210 Ibid., 43.
211 Sara Maxwell, Kristina Gjerde, Melinda Conners and Larry Crowder (n 173) 252.
212 See Sara Maxwell et al. (n 176) 43.
213 See Sara Maxwell, Kristina Gjerde, Melinda Conners and Larry Crowder (n 173) 254.
214 Ibid., 252.
215 Ibid.
216 Sara Maxwell et al. (n 176) 43.
217 Douglas Johnston and Mark Valencia (n 192) 22.
218 Ibid.

instead of coastal geography or geographic coordinates. Courts and tribunals have never established fluctuating boundaries by reference to environmental circumstances but the possibility was alluded to in the *Gulf of Maine* case.

The United States proposed a natural boundary in the *Gulf of Maine*.[219] However, the Chamber was not 'convinced of the possibility of discerning any genuine, sure and stable "natural boundaries" in so fluctuating an environment as the waters of the ocean, their flora and fauna'.[220] The Chamber was particularly hesitant to consider the oceano-biological boundary in the Georges Bank because it was tasked with the construction of a fixed, single-purpose boundary. Yet, an expert witness from the United States admitted upon cross-examination that relevant ecosystems were bound to change.[221] This suggests that the reasons for rejecting the relevance of the natural boundary were its irrelevance for the continental shelf delimitation and the impossibility of discerning *sure* and *stable* boundaries based on ecological circumstances. Thus, the decision might be different in a case where a court or tribunal was asked to delimit a separate exclusive fishery or exclusive economic zone boundary, and if geographic stability was not a principal objective.

It may not be practically feasible for States to have boundaries that fluctuate with dynamic ecosystems. Unlike the fluctuating boundaries discussed in Section 3.4.4, these would not correlate to ambulatory baselines. Nonetheless, they could to some extent be synchronized with mobile MPAs and could form an exemplary basis for ecosystem management.

4.4.3 *Alternative Arrangements*

Consideration for environmental circumstances can lead to alternative solutions. Instead of conventional boundaries (fixed or fluctuating), States can adopt cooperative arrangements, either involving joint management, environmental protection or decisions not to exploit resources. These arrangements are explored later, in Section 4.4.3.2, once the need for boundaries has been assessed.

4.4.3.1 Need for Boundaries?

The existence of overlapping entitlements does not necessitate a precisely defined maritime boundary. In fact, demarcation of territory on land only became prevalent in the thirteenth century,[222] and the first modern boundary treaty was concluded in

219 *Gulf of Maine* (n 106) para 52.
220 Ibid., para 54.
221 Ibid., C I/CR 84/16, 31.
222 John Ruggie, 'Territoriality and Beyond: Problematizing Modernity in International Relations' (1993) 47 (1) International Organization 139, 150.

1659.[223] Efforts to fix geographic boundaries around expanding territorial claims grew in the nineteenth and twentieth centuries but this development has since been a source of many international disputes.[224] Of all the wars fought between 1648 and 1990, at least 79 per cent relate to territory.[225] Still today, territorial disputes affect 41 per cent of sovereign States, and interstate friction is more likely to end in war if it relates to territory.[226] Territorialization of the oceans has resulted in clear dividing boundaries, but the notion of dividing ocean space with geographic boundaries is quite recent. Claims to sovereignty over an adjacent belt of sea were articulated in the seventeenth century[227] but there was no agreement on the breadth of maritime zones until 1958 (concerning the continental shelf and contiguous zone)[228] and 1982 (concerning the territorial sea and exclusive economic zone).[229] Thus, States have long held maritime entitlements without clearly defined boundaries.

UNCLOS articles 74 and 83 obligate States to delimit overlapping maritime zones. However, the articles do not refer explicitly to boundaries. In fact, the only reference to a bilateral line of delimitation is where UNCLOS article 15 refers to the median line as a default limit that neither State can extend its territorial sea beyond, unless otherwise agreed. UNCLOS articles 74 and 83 only obligate States to agree on equitable solutions on the basis of international law. Such solutions can entail demarcation of shared areas and joint management therein. Furthermore, States are encouraged to enter into practical arrangements for co-operation, pending delimitation agreements[230] and such arrangements need not involve dividing boundaries.

Churchill explained, in 1985, that the drawing of fixed boundaries could be a gamble where the location of resources was not fully known and that shared ventures could, under such circumstances, be preferable.[231] Modern technology certainly makes information on the location of resources more readily available

223 Friedrich Kratochwil, 'Of Systems, Boundaries, and Territoriality: An Inquiry into the Formation of the State System' (1986) 39 (1) World Politics 27, 33, referring to the 1659 Treaty of the Pyrenees between France and Spain.

224 Andreas Østhagen (n 3) 2.

225 Ibid., referring to John Vasquez, 'Why Do Neighbors Fight? Proximity, Interaction, or Territoriality' (1995) 32 (3) Journal of Peace Research 277, and David Carter, 'The Strategy of Territorial Conflict' (2010) 54 (4) American Journal of Political Science 969.

226 Andreas Østhagen (n 3) 2, referring to Krista Wiegand, *Enduring Territorial Disputes: Strategies of Bargaining, Coercive Diplomacy, and Settlement* (University of Georgia Press, 2011) and Paul Hensel, 'Charting a Course to Conflict: Territorial Issues and Interstate Conflict 1816–1992' in: Paul Diehl (ed) *The Road Map to War* (Vanderbilt University Press, 1999) 115, 137.

227 John Selden, *Of the dominion, or, Ownership of the sea* (*Mare Clausum*, 1635–1636) (translated into English and set forth with som [sic] additional evidences and discourses by Marchmont Nedham) (Lawbook Exchange, 2004).

228 See Convention on the Continental Shelf, article 1 and Convention on the Territorial Sea and the Contiguous Zone, article 24(2).

229 See UNCLOS articles 3 and 57.

230 UNCLOS articles 74(3) and 83(3).

231 Robin Churchill (n 16) 27.

today but climate-related changes can cause unforeseeable changes to migratory patterns of living resources. These changes can now make the drawing of fixed boundaries a gamble and alternative arrangements more feasible where ocean warming and ocean acidification is likely to impact marine ecosystems. Churchill also suggested that agreements on joint development might make the precise location of a boundary irrelevant and even make the boundary itself redundant.[232] Similarly, Østhagen suggested, in 2020, that the rise of co-operative management might eradicate the need for maritime boundaries.[233] Moreover, according to Dalby, 'traditional governance with its focus on boundaries and sovereignty is increasingly outdated'.[234]

4.4.3.2 Different Types of Alternative Arrangements

Section 4.4.1.2 explained how arrangements concerning joint management of resources can supplement fixed boundaries. Such arrangements can also function as alternatives to dividing boundaries. States can enter into co-operative arrangements for joint management of areas subject to national claims and these can eliminate the need for traditional boundaries.

Practical arrangements in areas subject to overlapping entitlements can take different forms, depending on the level of co-operation. States can establish joint development zones or even MPAs in areas subject to overlapping claims. These co-operative arrangements can form viable alternatives to traditional delimitation, particularly when negotiations are in a deadlock. It may seem unlikely that courts or tribunals will depart so extensively from the traditional methods described in Chapter 3. However, there are many examples of joint development zones from State practice and the adoption of such arrangements has also been proposed as part of formal dispute settlement. For example, the Conciliation Commission delimiting the continental shelf between Iceland and Jan Mayen urged the parties to agree on a co-operative arrangement for the production of hydrocarbon.[235] The Conciliation Commission also contemplated recommending co-operation in relation to other activities. It explained that such co-operation could involve, for example, training in the petroleum sector and ongoing access to petroleum at reasonable prices. The Commission concluded that it might not have the mandate to make all the recommendations that it explicitly referred to[236] but the mandate could of course be extended in future cases.

232 Ibid.

233 Andreas Østhagen (n 3) 7.

234 Simon Dalby, 'Bordering Sustainability in the Anthropocene' (2020) 8 (2) Territory, Politics, Governance 144, 145.

235 Report and Recommendations to the Governments of Iceland and Norway of the Conciliation Commission on the Continental Shelf Area between Iceland and Jan Mayen (June 1981) 20 ILM 826, 839 and 842.

236 Ibid., 840.

Schofield has recorded the recent rise of joint development zones as alternatives to maritime boundaries. He notes that these can accompany traditional maritime boundaries but more prevalent is the option to establish joint development in the absence of boundaries.[237] Such agreements generally demarcate geographic areas subject to joint development and define the applicable resources, rules and jurisdictions. Furthermore, they usually specify that the 'arrangements shall be without prejudice to the final delimitation', as also explicitly stated in UNCLOS articles 74(3) and 83(3).[238] Co-operative arrangements can be provisional and apply until a boundary is finally settled, as envisioned by UNCLOS articles 74(3) and 83(3). Yet, provisional arrangements can also become permanent, even after boundaries are settled. One example is the three-year agreement from 1989 between Denmark, Iceland and Norway concerning the management of capelin stocks.[239] This agreement has been extended several times, even though all the relevant boundaries have been agreed, so it is no longer a provisional arrangement in the sense of UNCLOS article 74(3).[240]

Joint development zones are usually established by neighbouring States in areas where no third States have competing claims. However, bilateral joint development arrangements have also been established in areas where third States have competing claims and this may call for negotiations with the third State.[241] Third States may become increasingly involved as changing coastlines generate new entitlements and altered migration patterns afford legitimate interests in fisheries management to new States. It may be easier to negotiate with such States and include them in joint development arrangements when there are no pre-existing boundary agreements.

Joint development can take many different forms.[242] There are countless variations of such arrangements but they broadly relate to the co-operative exploration or exploitation of particular resources within an area subject to overlapping maritime claims.[243] Johnston and Valencia refer to three categories of diplomatic solutions to maritime boundary disputes: 'Agreement to Designate Area in Dispute', 'Agreement on Some Limited Degree of Cooperation in Designated Area' and 'Arrangement for

237 Clive Schofield, 'Blurring the Lines? Maritime Joint Development and the Co-operative Management of Ocean Resources' (2009) 7 (1) Issues in Legal Scholarship, Article 3, 1, 4–5.

238 Ibid., 25.

239 Agreement between Denmark (on behalf of Greenland), Iceland and Norway on the stock of capelin in the waters between Greenland, Iceland and Jan Mayen (adopted 12 June 1989, entered into force 1 July 1989) 1548 UNTS 165.

240 The most recent agreement was concluded in 2018; see Framework Arrangement Between Greenland/Denmark, Iceland and Norway on the Conservation and Management of Capelin (adopted and entered into force 21 June 2018), Norwegian Government paper *Meld. St.* 15 (2018–2019), 43–44.

241 Clive Schofield (n 237) 26.

242 For a comprehensive overview of joint development zones, see J Tanga Biang, *The Joint Development Zone Between Nigeria and Sao Tome and Principe: A Case of Provisional Arrangement in the Gulf of Guinea. International Law, State Practice and Prospects for Regional Integration* (DOALOS, 2010).

243 Douglas Johnston and Mark Valencia (n 192) 36.

Integrated Joint Ocean Management'.[244] The substantive content of agreements concerning co-operative arrangement can also vary significantly. For example, States can establish joint zones for the purposes of managing shared resources: living, non-living or both. The arrangements can cover all rights subject to the exclusive economic/fisheries and/or continental shelf regimes and States can decide to establish MPAs in areas of overlapping claims or even cooperate in the mitigation of climate change, for example through ocean sequestration or ocean fertilization projects.

Developments in international environmental law will surely increase environmental considerations in future agreements concerning the exploitation and conservation of marine resources. States are already taking precautionary measures and applying the ecosystem approach to ensure sustainable development of fish stocks and long-term health of marine ecosystems. This has even resulted in a general ban on commercial fishing in the Central Arctic Ocean.[245] The CAOFA applies to the high seas and not an area subject to overlapping entitlements but it arguably represents the future of ocean governance. Furthermore, States Parties to the Paris Agreement have committed to 'reaching global peaking of greenhouse gas emissions as soon as possible' and rapid reductions thereafter.[246] This calls for drastic changes in the energy sector and reduction in the burning of fossil fuels. It is, in fact, imperative that States refrain from using mineral resources from their continental shelves to meet targets established under the Paris Agreement. Therefore, one can reasonably assume that international commitments made under the Paris Agreement change the approach to exploitation and conservation of the marine environment and encourage further co-operation in adaption to the adverse effects of climate change. For example, States might agree not to exploit oil and gas[247] in areas of overlapping maritime entitlements. Such agreements could dissolve the need for joint development zones concerning those resources and simplify the delimitation process. States could also agree on a reciprocal right to establish installations for the exploitation of renewable resources in areas of overlapping claims, regardless of whether a boundary is also concluded, and co-operate in the production of renewable energy. This could involve using areas of overlapping entitlements for projects that reduce or replace greenhouse gas emission, for example, artificial islands with wind turbines generating electricity for several States.[248] Furthermore, States could co-operate to establish means of protecting vulnerable ecosystems, such as mangrove swamps or saltmarshes, from rising seas.

244 Ibid., 24–27.

245 CAOFA article 3.

246 Paris Agreement article 4(1).

247 States are already making such pledges, see BBC, 'Denmark Set to End All New Oil and Gas Exploration' (4 December 2020) available at:www.bbc.com/news/business-55184580 accessed 23 February 2021.

248 Such a project is already underway, see BBC, 'Denmark to Build "first energy island" in North Sea' (4 February 2021) available at: www.bbc.com/news/world-europe-55931873 accessed 23 February 2021.

4.5 SUMMARY

UNCLOS carries various obligations relating to protection of the marine environment. States must take positive action to meet those obligations and they do not solely involve prevention and reduction of pollution. Special protection must be afforded to vulnerable ecosystems, and this may involve the establishment of MPAs. States shall co-operate in protecting the marine environment and they must also co-operate in the management of oceanic resources. The obligation to co-operate is fundamental to marine environmental protection and made more pressing by recent declarations of a Climate Change Emergency.

The sectoral division of maritime entitlements is not particularly useful as a basis for co-operative conservation and management of the oceans. States are obligated, under the FSA, to conclude agreements, on the basis of an ecosystem approach, concerning the management of straddling and highly migratory stocks. However, that leaves many species vulnerable because it is limited to straddling and highly migratory fish stocks on the high seas and also because those efforts are driven by economic interests. Sustainable management of ocean resources is too often an afterthought to the delimitation process and it is arguably more likely to result in sustainable development and fulfilment of these conservation and management obligations if maritime entitlements are delimited with due consideration for relevant environmental circumstances. That could facilitate subsequent co-operation concerning the protection and management of transboundary ecosystems.

Environmental circumstances have influenced the delimitation of a number of maritime boundaries but have mostly done so from an economic (and sometimes a social) perspective. This means that the most fundamental part of sustainable development has essentially been ignored. A broader consideration of environmental factors in maritime delimitation could promote sustainable development of the oceans for future generations, and consequently long-term exploitation of resources. Scientists are increasingly advocating for the use of ecosystem-based and dynamic ocean management and the ecosystem approach is increasingly prominent in legal instruments concerning the marine environment. Furthermore, international commitments relating to the mitigation of climate change necessitate general integration of environmental considerations to ocean management.

It is not a simple task, incorporating environmental concerns in the delimitation process. It demands the interweaving of ecological science with the law applicable to maritime delimitation. Still, the relevance of environmental circumstances should not be denied due to scientific uncertainty. Particularly not where there are risks of severe or irreversible harm to marine ecosystems. A preliminary step involves establishing the relevance of environmental circumstances for maritime delimitation. The theoretical relevance of environmental circumstances has been confirmed in the jurisprudence, as it relates to the presence and access to fish stocks, but has rarely affected the location of the boundary. Nonetheless, States can agree to take a broader approach to the relevance of environmental circumstances. The next step involves identification of relevant environmental circumstances and that challenge can be overcome as demonstrated by the examples discussed in Section 4.2.2. Finally, a decision must be made as to the effect given to relevant environmental circumstances. This presents three possibilities. First, fixed boundaries can be drawn with consideration for relevant environmental circumstances. Second, maritime boundaries can fluctuate to take account of dynamic ecosystems, in the same manner as mobile MPAs. Third, States can establish alternative, co-operative arrangements in areas of overlapping maritime entitlements. Such arrangements already exist and they can operate independently or as a supplement to traditional maritime boundaries.

The formidable effort of the international community towards marine biodiversity in areas beyond national jurisdiction should inspire States to take further action to ensure biodiversity in maritime zones under their jurisdiction. The BBNJ Draft Agreement relies on the ecosystem approach as a guiding principle and it emphasizes the use of MPAs as a management tool. Furthermore, the CAOFA bans commercial fishing in the Central Arctic Ocean in the name of the precautionary approach and also applies the ecosystem approach. These developments could also guide the delimitation of overlapping entitlements and promote sustainable development of ecosystems in areas of overlapping national claims. The climate crisis is inciting international recognition of the need for radical measures in environmental protection, and consideration of environmental factors in the delimitation process could be one small step in the right direction. Indeed, the international community is obligated, under the UNFCCC, to take precautionary action to mitigate the adverse effects of climate change, and States can work toward sustainable development and reduction of greenhouse gas emission through the delimitation process.

5

Fundamental Change of Circumstances

5.1 INTRODUCTION

Environmental changes will affect maritime entitlements as coastlines are engulfed by rising seas. Unilateral maritime limits fluctuate under existing international law and maritime boundaries can be established with consideration for the changing environment. Once established, maritime boundaries generally remain stable, regardless of subsequent changes. Agreed maritime boundaries are permanent under the pacta sunt servanda principle.[1] However, pacta sunt servanda does not provide that all agreements remain inviolable till the end of time.[2] Likewise, judicially decided maritime boundaries are permanent under the res judicata principle but decisions can be reviewed if new facts come to light.[3]

Treaties rely on the assumption that certain circumstances, essential to their conclusion, remain unchanged. It is on the basis of those circumstances that parties reach an agreement specifying their shared expectations and pacta sunt servanda aims to safeguard those shared expectations.[4] However, '[t]he pacta sunt servanda rule was intended to ensure the stability of law; not stability at any price, but stability based on justice'.[5] Thus, States can be freed from their contractual obligations through peaceful means, when circumstances leading to the conclusion of a treaty change and obligations under a treaty become 'unduly burdensome'.[6]

The doctrine of rebus sic stantibus provides that an unforeseen fundamental change of circumstances can be invoked as grounds for terminating a treaty if it affects the essential basis of the treaty and radically transforms obligations still to be

1 See *Frontier Dispute (Burkina Faso/Republic of Mali)* (Judgment) [1986] ICJ Rep 554, 573, para 46.

2 Rein Müllerson, 'The ABM Treaty: Changed Circumstances, Extraordinary Events, Supreme Interests and International Law' (2001) 50 International and Comparative Law Quarterly 509, 525.

3 Andreas Kulick, 'Article 60 ICJ Statute, Interpretation Proceedings, and the Competing Concepts of Res Judicata' (2015) 28 (1) Leiden Journal of International Law 73, 74.

4 Eric Stein and Dominique Carreau, 'Law and Peaceful Change in a Subsystem: "Withdrawal" of France from the North Atlantic Treaty Organization' (1968) 62 American Journal of International Law 577, 617.

5 United Nations Conference on the Law of Treaties 'First Session' (26 March -24 May 1968) UN Doc A/CONF.39/11, 150, para 56.

6 See Eric Stein and Dominique Carreau (n 4) 617.

performed. This customary rule has been codified in VCLT article 62. Treaties establishing boundaries are explicitly excluded from termination due to a fundamental change of circumstance,[7] but not all treaties delimiting maritime zones fall into this category. The co-chairs of the ILC's study group on sea level rise have indicated, after a preliminary study of the issue, that all maritime boundaries are exempt from termination due to fundamental changes.[8] However, this chapter suggests that a distinction should be made between territorial and non-territorial maritime boundaries and that the latter may be subject to the effects of VCLT article 62. At any rate, various boundary-related agreements may be affected by sea level rise, for example, those relating to exploitation of resources.[9] Additionally, the principle can have an effect on the interpretation and application of treaties establishing territorial boundaries, even if the treaties remain intact.

Maritime boundary agreements most commonly establish single-purpose boundaries at fixed coordinates. Some agreements make a clear distinction between different maritime zones, even where the boundaries are aligned.[10] There are also examples of separate boundaries for the exclusive economic or fisheries zone, and the continental shelf. The limits to these zones must not necessarily be aligned even if they fall within the 200 nm mark.[11] In addition to establishing maritime boundaries, maritime delimitation often entails provisions on co-operation between the parties relating to joint development zones, the exploitation and management of natural resources, or other issues such as protection of the marine environment.[12] Some of these agreements definitely fall outside the scope of the boundary exception.

This chapter is concerned with treaties that delimit maritime boundaries or alternative arrangements. It focuses primarily on the rebus sic stantibus rule, enshrined in VCLT article 62. However, it should be borne in mind that some maritime boundary agreements include provisions concerning dispute settlement.[13] Moreover, environmental changes may generate new rights for third States and existing boundary agreements will not be enforceable in such scenarios because treaties cannot create obligations or rights for third States without their consent.[14] Furthermore, judicial decisions can be challenged when environmental changes give rise to new claims. After all res judicata only prevents the revision of boundaries

7 VCLT article 62(2)(a).

8 ILC, 'Sea-Level Rise in Relation to International Law: First Issues Paper' (27 April–5 June and 6 July–7 August 2020) UN Doc A/CN.4/740, para 119.

9 Ibid., paras 179–180 and 190.

10 Cissé Yacouba and Donald McRae, 'The Legal Regime of Maritime Boundary Agreements' in David Colson and Robert Smith (eds) *International Maritime Boundaries, volume* 5 (Martinus Nijhoff, 2005) 3281, 3283–3285.

11 Ibid., 3287.

12 Ibid., 3291.

13 See Ibid., 3300; UN Doc A/CN.4/740 (n 8) para 134.

14 VCLT article 34.

insofar as the same relief is sought on the grounds advanced in previous proceedings between the same parties.[15]

This chapter provides a doctrinal analysis of VCLT article 62 to determine whether treaties delimiting maritime zones can be subject to termination or revision on the grounds of fundamentally changed circumstances. The origin and travaux préparatoires of VCLT article 62 are examined, and its application in relation to treaties establishing territorial and non-territorial boundaries as well as alternative arrangements. This analysis indicates that certain types of maritime boundaries and arrangements may be set aside by virtue of VCLT article 62 when relevant environmental circumstances have undergone drastic and unforeseen changes, leading to the radical transformation of rights and obligations.

5.2 ORIGIN OF VCLT ARTICLE 62

The ILC proposed to codify the law of treaties during its first session in 1949. At its thirteenth session in 1961, it decided to prepare draft articles for a subsequent convention on the law of treaties.[16] First, the members of the ILC and its Special Rapporteurs had to identify relevant rules of customary international law and determine if and how they should be codified. 'International law was like a great and ancient edifice the doors of which were being opened so that it could be put in order.'[17] This was a lengthy process of approximately twenty years and it resulted in the adoption of the VCLT on 22 May 1969 and subsequent entry into force on 27 January 1980.

Fitzmaurice, Special Rapporteur of the ILC, first presented a draft article implementing the clausula rebus sic stantibus to the law of treaties in his second report dated 15 March 1957.[18] The doctrine was heavily debated. Some members of the ILC raised objections to the existence of a customary rule justifying termination of a treaty due to changed circumstances, while others did not want to include it in the law of treaties since derogating from the pacta sunt servanda principle might cause friction in international relations. Eventually, rebus sic stantibus was codified in VCLT article 62. Therefore, the right to invoke a fundamental change of circumstances as grounds for terminating a treaty exists under VCLT and customary international law.[19]

15 Andreas Kulick (n 3) 74.

16 UN Doc A/CONF.39/11 (n 5) xi.

17 Yearbook of the ILC, 1949 'Summary Record of the First Session' (12 April 1949) UN Doc A/CN.4/SR.1, para 2.

18 ILC, 'Second Report on the Law of Treaties, by Mr GG Fitzmaurice, Special Rapporteur' (15 March 1957) UN Doc A/CN.4/107, 32.

19 Jeremy Waldron, 'F.W. Guest Memorial Lecture: August 22nd, 2005: The Half-Life of Treaties: Waitangi, Rebus Sic Stantibus' (2006) 11 Otago Law Review 161, 168

5.2.1 *Rebus Sic Stantibus*

Pacta sunt servanda is a fundamental principle of law. International co-operation relies on States honouring this principle and its importance cannot be overstated. Rebus sic stantibus presents an exception to the pacta sunt servanda principle. It can free States from treaty obligations that have become 'unduly burdensome' due to radically changed circumstances and, so, promotes peaceful change.[20] The clausula rebus sic stantibus was long considered to be an integral part of the pacta sunt servanda principle, tacitly attached to every treaty.[21] This changed over time as rebus sic stantibus achieved recognition as an independent rule in public international law with general scope, making it applicable regardless of whether express or implied consent could be derived from treaty provisions.[22]

Gentilis introduced the maxim *omnis conventio intelligitur rebus sic stantibus* in the sixteenth century. He is believed to have been the first legal scholar to discuss the principle. According to Pal of the ILC, the theory derives from canon law. It was affirmed by Suárez and Vattel but rejected by Grotius in the seventeenth century.[23] Grotius made a distinction between treaties and contracts and was reluctant to accept the termination of treaties due to changed circumstances because of derivative complications. Bynkershoek is also said to have rejected the theory of rebus sic stantibus in the eighteenth century, although he held that an impossibility of performance might allow for derogation from treaty obligations.[24] One might argue that such a contention does not necessarily reject the doctrine of rebus sic stantibus since, as will be discussed in subsequent sections, some members of the ILC did not distinguish between rebus sic stantibus and impossibility of performance while drafting the VCLT. Several members wanted to merge the two rules into one article while others suggested that even if dealt with under separate articles, they might apply in tandem.[25]

The existence of the customary rule rebus sic stantibus in public international law has been evidenced by State practice tracing back to the eighteenth century.[26] States have invoked the doctrine *eo nomine* or referenced a general principle allowing the termination or modification of a treaty due to changed circumstances.[27] Russia raised the principle in 1870 in order to withdraw from the 1856 Treaty of Paris

20 Eric Stein and Dominique Carreau (n 4) 617.

21 James Garner, 'The Doctrine of Rebus Sic Stantibus and the Termination of Treaties' (1927) 21 (3) American Journal of International Law 509, 509.

22 ILC, 'Summary Record of the 695th Meeting' (7 June 1963) UN Doc A/CN.4/SR.695, 148.

23 ILC, 'Summary Record of the 694th Meeting' (6 June 1963) UN Doc A/CN.4/SR.694, 136.

24 Ibid.

25 Ibid., 141.

26 Rein Müllerson (n 2) 526–527.

27 ILC, 'Second Report on the Law of Treaties, by Sir Humphrey Waldock, Special Rapporteur' (20 March, 10 April, 30 April and 5 June 1963) UN Doc A/CN.4/156 and Add.1–3, 81; Athanassios Vamvoukos, *Termination of Treaties in International Law: The Doctrines of Rebus Sic Stantibus and Desuetude* (Clarendon Press, 1985) 122–123.

concerning the neutralization of the Black Sea. The endeavour proved successful, despite some opposition; Russia was released from the treaty obligations at a London conference soon after declaring termination under rebus sic stantibus. Critics claimed that treaties could not be terminated without the acceptance of all parties but even if Russia's actions lead to a negotiated withdrawal rather than unilateral denunciation, the withdrawal was clearly a result of Russia invoking rebus sic stantibus.[28] In fact, some commentators have argued that the principle involves nothing more than the obligation to renegotiate.[29] However, the principle has developed over time and the rule codified in VCLT article 62 explicitly provides for termination, suspension and withdrawal from a treaty.

Rebus sic stantibus was advanced in several cases in the years and decades leading up to the codification of the VCLT. For example, in 1922, the Norwegian Government denounced its treaty with France, Germany, Great Britain and Russia without referring explicitly to the doctrine of rebus sic stantibus. Instead, Norway invoked altered circumstances prompted by changes in foreign politics and held that the foundations of the treaty were consequently lost.[30] The French Government also relied on rebus sic stantibus in 1922 to terminate a treaty in the *Nationality Decrees* case and proclaimed that the principle was applicable to all treaties of indefinite duration.[31] The USSR declared in 1924 that it wished to renegotiate and determine the status of old treaties with the United Kingdom since they were no longer enforceable according to the rebus sic stantibus principle due to changed circumstances generated by World War I.[32] Again, the Soviet Government invoked the rule of rebus sic stantibus to denounce a treaty of neutrality with the Japanese in 1945. The reasoning provided was that circumstances had changed fundamentally after the German invasion of the Soviet Union, Japan's alignment with Germany and Japan's war with the United States and United Kingdom, allies of the Soviet Union.[33]

Judicial decisions had never been based on the rule of rebus sic stantibus in 1963, when the Commission was in the midst of codifying the principle as an objective rule of law. Even so, it was 'regarded as one of the fundamental assumptions in public international law'.[34] The ICJ never rejected the existence of rebus sic stantibus before the implementation of VCLT article 62, although it was and still is reluctant to apply the doctrine. The same is true of municipal courts.[35] Still, the

28 Rein Müllerson (n 2) 527.

29 Ibid., 529–530; David Bederman 'The 1871 London Declaration, Rebus Sic Stantibus and A Primitivist View of the Law of Nations' (1988) 82 (1) American Journal of International Law 1, 29.

30 UN Doc A/CN.4/SR.695 (n 22) para 14.

31 *Nationality Decrees Issued in Tunis and Morocco (French Zone) on November 8th 1921 (Great Britain v. France)* (Advisory Opinion) (1923) PCIJ Series C, No 2: Speeches made and documents read before the court, 187–188.

32 Rein Müllerson (n 2) 527.

33 Ibid.

34 UN Doc A/CN.4/SR.695 (n 22) 147.

35 UN Doc A/CN.4/156 and Add.1–3 (n 27) 80.

European Court of Justice has upheld the principle's invocation on, at least, one occasion, which is discussed further in Sections 5.3.3 and 5.3.4.

Rebus sic stantibus has been called an 'odd corner' of the law of treaties.[36] As such, it was the object of substantial scrutiny by members of the ILC. Their opinions on the principle ranged from complete denial of its existence to regarding it as a rule of *jus cogens*.[37] The doctrine was referred to as 'one of the most controversial in the history of international law' and its implementation to the law of treaties, a matter of great responsibility.[38]

Yasseen, a member of the ILC, derived the existence of rebus sic stantibus from the nature of written law. He said that 'conventional rules could not be adapted ad infinitum', that rebus sic stantibus was a rule of jus cogens and, consequently, an inseparable part of the law of treaties.[39] Sir Humphrey Waldock, Special Rapporteur of the ILC, disagreed with Yasseen's contentions and advised that States should take changing circumstances into account when negotiating treaties, thereby preventing the need for rebus sic stantibus under given circumstances.[40] Amado, while promoting the implementation of the doctrine of rebus sic stantibus, called it the 'serpent of the law'.[41] According to him, the defensive opposition to the doctrine was based on believe in the sanctity of pacta sunt servanda, something that seems to have been an outdated view in his mind. Therefore, Amado encouraged other members of the ILC to abandon their defensive attitudes.[42]

Paredes asserted that:

> No one could enter into an undertaking for ever. That was why, under most systems of municipal law, contracts of service for life were prohibited. The same should apply even more strongly to States, because their life was much longer.[43]

On the opposite spectrum, Gros was of the view that 'anyone who cast doubt on the durability of treaties was contributing not to the progress of international law, but to its ruin'.[44] Despite this, Gros did not object to the inclusion of rebus sic stantibus in the VCLT.[45] Bartos agreed with Yasseen that rebus sic stantibus was a rule of jus cogens, although it was susceptible to criticism. He said that the principle of pacta sunt servanda could not apply without anomalies and that rebus sic stantibus provided a necessary countermeasure to deal with instances where the literal

36 Detlev Vagts, 'Review of Dahm et al., Volkerrecht' (2004) 98 American Journal of International Law 614, 615.
37 UN Doc A/CN.4/SR.695 (n 22) 144.
38 UN Doc A/CONF.39/11 (n 5) 367–368.
39 UN Doc A/CN.4/SR.694 (n 23) 141–142.
40 ILC, 'Summary Record of the 697th Meeting' (11 June 1963) UN Doc A/CN.4/SR.697, 157.
41 UN Doc A/CN.4/SR.694 (n 23) 142.
42 Ibid.
43 UN Doc A/CN.4/SR.695 (n 22) 147.
44 ILC, 'Summary Record of the 696th Meeting' (10 June 1963) UN Doc A/CN.4/SR.696, 153.
45 Ibid.

application of pacta sunt servanda would lead to injustice and, consequently, impair relations between States.[46]

Members of the ILC who objected to the implementation of a rebus sic stantibus clause did so because it represented a way to avoid a lawfully concluded treaty for the benefit of one of the contracting States. Despite those concerns, the Special Rapporteur and a majority of the ILC agreed that the doctrine had been established as a customary rule in international law.[47] According to Tunkin, the existence of the rule in international law had been made evident by State practice and scholarly review.[48] As he pointed out, States generally acknowledged this fact when confronted with the principle, even if its application to the case at hand was contested.[49] Special Rapporteur Waldock reached the conclusion that there was ample evidence of the principle's general acceptance in international law, which called for its codification. According to him, there existed 'a general belief in the need for a safety-valve of this kind in the law of treaties'.[50]

The Commission ultimately concluded that rebus sic stantibus was indispensable to the law of treaties because 'it would not be in the interest of the international order to maintain in being a treaty which had become anachronistic'.[51] It would provide legal means of terminating treaties and ensure that States would not be driven to take action outside the law.[52] Indeed, VCLT article 62 should function as 'an escape clause'.[53]

5.2.2 *Draft Articles*

Deciding to codify rebus sic stantibus in the law of treaties was only the beginning of an arduous process. What ensued were years of discussions and redrafting before the ILC could reach a compromise on what exactly the provision should entail and how to articulate it. The article was controversial from the very beginning. Yet, despite a clear desire for stability, members of the ILC and State representatives agreed that there had to be a lawful way to terminate or revise treaties when the essential basis for consent was radically affected.

VCLT article 62 is not an exact replica of the original customary rule. Members of the Commission decided, after lengthy discussions and with regard to State

46 UN Doc A/CN.4/SR.695 (n 22) 148.

47 Ibid 143; ILC, 'Draft Articles on the Law of Treaties' (18 July 1966) UN Doc A/CN.4/190, 258.

48 UN Doc A/CN.4/SR.695 (n 22) 144–145.

49 Ibid., 143.

50 UN Doc A/CN.4/156 and Add.1–3 (n 27) 82.

51 ILC, 'Summary Records of the Second Part of the Seventeenth Session' (3–28 January 1966) UN Doc A/CN.4/SER.A/1966, 84–85, para 77.

52 GAOR, 'Report of the International Law Commission on the Work of the Second Part of Its Seventeenth Session' (3–28 January 1966) UN Doc A/6309/Rev.1, 258.

53 Thomas Giegerich, 'Article 62. Fundamental Change of Circumstances' in Oliver Dörr and Kirsten Schmalenbach (eds) *Vienna Convention on the Law of Treaties: A Commentary* (Springer 2012) 1067, 1070.

commentary, to implement a modified version that constituted, in the words of the Commission, 'progressive development of customary international law'.[54] There are arguably two differences between the original customary rule and the rule codified in VCLT article 62. First, the latter applies to treaties of limited duration as well as perpetual treaties but a majority of scholars agreed that the customary rule only applied to perpetual treaties.[55] Second, the Commission decided to exclude treaties establishing boundaries from the scope of rebus sic stantibus to avoid dangerous frictions in international relations.[56] Some argued that this exception already existed but that is debatable. The Commission's decision to exclude treaties establishing boundaries was heavily criticized throughout the codification process and it seems to have been the primary reason why twelve State representatives, of 105, did not accept the article when it was finally put to a vote on 13 May 1969.[57]

The following sections give an account of the drafting history of VCLT article 62, with an emphasis on issues relating to fundamental changes to the environment and the exclusion of treaties establishing boundaries. The drafting history is highly relevant for subsequent sections of this chapter because it sheds light on how the article may operate in grey areas, particularly in relation to treaties establishing maritime boundaries. It explains why the boundary exception was introduced and how its scope was narrowed. Furthermore, the drafting history demonstrates that the concerns State often have in relation to termination, suspension or withdrawal from treaties are not limited to treaties establishing boundaries.

5.2.2.1 Draft Articles from 1957

Special Rapporteur Fitzmaurice presented his first report on the law of treaties on 14 March 1956.[58] This report not only focused on the framing and conclusion of treaties but also gave an overview of the arrangement of subsequent subject matters. Fitzmaurice proposed that the law of treaties should be divided into two chapters, the first dealing with validity of treaties and the second dealing with effects. The first chapter would include three parts: part I on formal validity, part II on essential validity and part III on temporal validity. Temporal validity included the topics of duration, termination, revision and modification of treaties;[59] a provision implementing the principle of rebus sic stantibus would belong to that category. On 15 March 1957, Fitzmaurice presented his draft articles on part III of the first

54 ILC, 'Summary record of the 833th meeting' (18 January 1966) UN Doc A/CN.4/SR.833, 77.
55 United Nations Conference on the Law of Treaties, 'First and Second Sessions' (26 March–24 May 1968 and 9 April–22 May 1969) UN Doc A/CONF.39/11/Add.2, 79.
56 Ibid.
57 United Nations Conference on the Law of Treaties, 'Second Session' (9 April–22 May 1969) UN Doc A/CONF.39/11/Add.1, 121–122.
58 ILC, 'Report on the Law of Treaties' (14 March 1956) UN Doc A/CN.4/101, 104.
59 Ibid., 106.

chapter.[60] This included the verbose draft article 22, a provisional codification of rebus sic stantibus.[61] Draft article 22 set out conditions and limitations concerning the application of the principle and explained that it primarily related to bilateral treaties. There were limitations on the invocation of fundamental breaches as grounds for termination. For example, a fundamental breach should not be invoked to terminate a multilateral treaty if the party invoking the breach had direct or proximate responsibility leading to the breach.

Draft article 22, paragraph 2, lists limitations regarding the type of change necessary for invocation of the principle. An essential change had to 'be an objective change in the factual circumstances relating to the treaty and its operation, and not merely a subjective change in the attitude towards the treaty of the party invoking the principle'. It should relate to facts or situations that were relevant to both parties giving their consent and jointly envisioned to continue. This expectation should have been a determining factor in the conclusion of the treaty. Furthermore, the change in question should either render the realization of the object and purpose of the treaty (or particular obligation) impossible, or destroy or completely alter the basis of the obligation relating to the facts referred to earlier. Changes in the motives of parties to enter into the treaty or continue performance would not suffice and the change would have to be unforeseeable. The rebus sic stantibus principle would be inapplicable if the treaty or other relevant agreement referred to the change in any way, because such stipulations would then prevail.

Draft article 22, paragraph 3, provided that parties would be precluded from invoking the principle under certain circumstances. Namely, if the treaty was of a limited duration, if the change was not invoked within a reasonable time after its occurrence and if the change was caused directly or proximately by the party invoking it.[62]

When discussing the juridical basis of rebus sic stantibus, Fitzmaurice built on a study proposing seven different theories and reduced them to three main theories.[63] According to the first, parties are assumed to have predicted that certain circumstances that were the foundation of their agreement would remain and to have intended its termination by virtue of an implied condition, in case of an essential change of said circumstances. The second theory presupposes the existence of a customary rule allowing contracting parties to request the termination of a treaty because of a fundamental change of circumstances. Fitzmaurice's third theory on the juridical basis of rebus sic stantibus combines the other theories by assuming that rebus sic stantibus is an objective rule of law, which imposes an implied condition to all treaties.[64]

60 UN Doc A/CN.4/107 (n 18) 16–70.

61 Ibid., 19.

62 Ibid., 18 32–33.

63 Ibid., 58–59 referring to Chesney Hill, *The Doctrine of 'Rebus sic stantibus' in International Law* (University of Missouri, 1934).

64 Ibid.

The Special Rapporteur noted that there was no substantial difference between the two latter theories since they both resulted in universal applicability of the rebus sic stantibus doctrine, regardless of contracting parties' intentions. There was one important difference though; termination of a treaty by virtue of an implied condition of the treaty would be automatic while invoking an objective rule of law would be up to the discretion of each party. The third theory would thus induce an automatic termination of a treaty which, in the view of Fitzmaurice, would be an incorrect use of the principle. He maintained that the doctrine of rebus sic stantibus could not result in automatic termination of treaties. Rather it operated by granting parties the right to invoke it by requesting termination or modification of a treaty. Therefore, the Special Rapporteur rejected the third theory and recommended basing the provision, implementing the doctrine of rebus sic stantibus, on the second theory.[65]

Fitzmaurice asserted that rebus sic stantibus would not allow denunciation of or withdrawal from a treaty if termination was expressly prohibited by treaty provisions or implied terms. Temporary agreements were excluded from the application of draft article 22 since agreeing on duration for a fixed number of years would imply prohibition on termination within the set time frame. This, however, would not affect the parties' right to agree on termination.[66] Treaties of infinite duration could be subject to withdrawal or denunciation if circumstances that formed an essential basis of the parties' consent had changed but this would not warrant an automatic termination, as explained earlier. Nonetheless, parties could, according to Fitzmaurice, suspend performance of the treaty obligations pending negotiated modification of the treaty, agreed termination, or an arbitral or judicial decision determining its fate. Suspension of a treaty could have dire consequences and, therefore, it should only be exercised when requirements of the provision were seemingly fulfilled.[67]

Fitzmaurice said that treaties containing provisions on termination could not be subject to the objective rule of rebus sic stantibus if the treaty provisions or implied terms could lead to termination of the agreement. The same would apply if the treaty incorporated the rule of rebus sic stantibus because in such a scenario, the termination would be governed by the terms of the treaty but not by operation of law, the objective rule of rebus sic stantibus being the residual ground of termination. Fitzmaurice further concluded that application of the principle would never result in the termination of a multilateral treaty unless all parties agreed to that eventuality. A fundamental change of circumstances affecting one or more of the parties could only be invoked to withdraw from or suspend the operation of a treaty in relation to the party invoking it.[68]

65 Ibid.
66 Ibid., 39.
67 Ibid., 32.
68 Ibid., 18.

The Special Rapporteur explained what could constitute an essential change of circumstances justifying the invocation of the rebus sic stantibus rule. First of all there would have to be an objective and genuine change of circumstances concerning the treaty and its operation; a subjective change in the parties perspectives towards the treaty would not suffice.[69] Second, the change would have to relate to circumstances that existed when the treaty was concluded and which led to the parties giving their consent to be bound by the treaty or the treaty obligation affected by the change. Furthermore, parties should have been relying on the continuance of those circumstances and not anticipating an essential change. Third, an essential change of circumstances under rebus sic stantibus should either prevent the realization of the treaty or specific treaty obligations[70] or destroy or seriously alter the basis on which parties acceded to the treaty. Fourth, a change in a party's motives or incentives to be bound by a treaty would not constitute an essential change of circumstances permitting withdrawal or denunciation of a treaty. Finally, parties to a treaty should not have foreseen the essential change of circumstances or have been reasonably expected to do so. If the anticipation of such change had been made evident by a treaty provision or subsequent agreement then those provisions would prevail over rebus sic stantibus.[71]

Special Rapporteur Fitzmaurice emphasized that even when all the aforementioned conditions were met, the rule could only be invoked in regards to treaties that were inherently indefinite and had no provisions governing termination. Moreover, it would have to be invoked within a reasonable time and the change could not be induced by the act or omission of the party invoking it.[72]

5.2.2.2 Draft Articles from 1963

The ILC continued its study of validity and duration of treaties at the fifteenth session. The new Special Rapporteur, Waldock, dealt with Fitzmaurice's draft article 22 in his second report on the law of treaties, which he submitted to the Commission on 20 March 1963.[73] Waldock's draft article 22, paragraph 1, provided that a fundamental change should not, as such, have an effect on the continuing validity of a treaty, although it could potentially affect its validity if all necessary conditions were met. Draft article 22, paragraph 2, stated that:

> An essential change in the circumstances forming the basis of a treaty occurs when:
>
> (a) a change has taken place with respect to a fact or state of facts which existed when the treaty was entered into;

69 Ibid.

70 This demonstrates the close link between the principle of *rebus sic stantibus* and the rule allowing termination of a treaty by virtue of impossibility of performance.

71 UN Doc A/CN.4/107 (n 18) 33.

72 Ibid.

73 UN Doc A/CN.4/156 and Add.1–3 (n 27) 38.

(b) it appears from the object and purpose of the treaty and from the circumstances in which it was entered into, that the parties must both, or all, have assumed the continued existence of that fact or state of facts to be an essential foundation of the obligations accepted by them in the treaty; and
(c) the effect of the change in that fact or state of facts is such as – (i) in substance to frustrate the further realization of the object and purpose of the treaty; or (ii) to render the performance of the obligations contained in the treaty something essentially different from what was originally undertaken.

Paragraph 3 specified that changes concerning policies, motives or attitudes of States seeking termination could not constitute an essential change. Paragraph 4 provided that States could not invoke essential changes that were caused by their acts or omissions; if the change was not invoked as grounds for termination within a reasonable time; or if the change was anticipated by express or implied terms or in a subsequent agreement between the same parties. Draft article 22, paragraph 5, introduced the boundary exception, stating that an essential change could not justify terminating:

(a) stipulations of a treaty which effect a transfer of territory, the settlement of a boundary, or a grant of territorial rights;
(b) stipulations which accompany a transfer of territory or boundary settlement and are expressed to be an essential condition of such transfer or settlement;
(c) a treaty which is the constituent instrument of an international organization.

Finally, paragraph 6 explained that termination or withdrawal from a treaty would only occur on the basis of an agreement or a procedure laid down in draft article 25.[74]

Waldock agreed with Fitzmaurice on the juridical basis for the rebus sic stantibus provision. He affirmed the doctrine's status as an objective rule of law that parties had the right to invoke in order to terminate a treaty when an essential change of circumstances had occurred.[75] The preceding theory that the doctrine of rebus sic stantibus applied to treaties by virtue of an implied condition was thereby rejected.[76]

Waldock changed the terminology of the draft article in a number of ways. Perhaps most notably, he expressed the rule in negative terms to emphasize that legitimate treaties should generally remain in force despite a change of circumstances. This was meant to prevent abuse, and ensure that the article would not be used 'as a pretext to escape from inconvenient obligations'.[77] Also, to this end, the rule was made subject to several procedural requirements.[78]

74 The entire draft article is available in UN Doc A/CN.4/156 and Add.1–3 (n 27) 79–80.
75 Ibid., 83.
76 Ibid., 59.
77 Ibid., 39.
78 Ibid., 39.

Fitzmaurice's draft article from 1957 was meant to exclude treaties of limited duration because provisions governing duration would imply the parties' understanding that the treaty could not be terminated earlier than expressly provided.[79] However, Waldock disagreed with Fitzmaurice on this issue and proposed that the provision implementing rebus sic stantibus could be applicable to treaties before their intended duration had lapsed – and also to perpetual agreements.[80] Waldock maintained that unilateral denunciation of treaties of limited duration was generally prohibited because fixing the duration of a treaty indicated the parties' will to exclude the right of termination within the relevant time frame.[81] However, the Special Rapporteur seems to have intended to exclude only the right of withdrawal or denunciation for treaties of limited duration when circumstances did not warrant extreme measures. After all, termination under the principle of rebus sic stantibus would constitute an exception to the general rule and be applied as lex specialis. The Commission seemed to unanimously support Waldock's innovation to include treaties of limited duration within the scope of the rebus sic stantibus provision.[82]

Paragraph 5 of Waldock's draft, providing that an essential change of circumstances could not be invoked for the purpose of terminating treaties or provisions concerning territorial rights or boundaries, was heavily criticized by several members of the ILC. Some asserted that sub-paragraph (b) was unnecessary or too thorough while others objected to paragraph 5 in its entirety.[83] Elias wished to delete the paragraph so as not to exclude treaties establishing boundaries or transferring territory from the application of rebus sic stantibus. He noted that the Permanent Court of International Justice (hereinafter PCIJ) in the case of the *Free Zones of Upper Savoy*[84] had not put forth such a requirement when addressing the substantive elements of rebus sic stantibus. Elias recognized the importance of respect for territorial rights and frontiers but suggested that courts should be entrusted with decision-making in individual cases rather than laying down a general rule in the VCLT.[85] Bartos was also reluctant to accept paragraph 5 of the Special Rapporteur‘s draft article, sub-paragraph (a), in particular because recent examples showed that boundary lines might be drawn precisely because of circumstances existing at the time of the conclusion of the treaty, which might later change. Therefore, Bartos proposed the removal of paragraphs 3, 4 and 5.[86]

79 UN Doc A/CN.4/107 (n 18) 39.

80 UN Doc A/CN.4/156 and Add.1–3 (n 27) 83.

81 Ibid., 65.

82 UN Doc A/CN.4/SR.696 (n 44) 156.

83 UN Doc A/CN.4/SR.697 (n 40) 157.

84 See *Case of the Free Zones of Upper Savoy and the District of Gex (Switzerland* v. *France)* PCIJ Rep Series A No 22.

85 UN Doc A/CN.4/SR.695 (n 22) 147.

86 Ibid., 149.

Ago did not wish to exclude the categories of treaties referred to in paragraph 5 entirely. He recommended leaving some latitude for exceptional instances[87] while admitting that certain dangers could ensue if boundary treaties were susceptible to termination under rebus sic stantibus.[88] De Luna and Verdross jointly submitted a revised draft of article 22 where no mention is made of treaties relating to frontiers or territories.[89] Castren doubted that the draft article proposed by De Luna and Verdross could prevent misuse of the rebus sic stantibus principle. Therefore, he also proposed an alternative, simplified version of the article excluding sub-paragraph (b) and rephrasing the requirements put forth in sub-paragraph (a).[90]

El-Erian was also unwilling to accept the exclusion of an entire category of treaties from the application of rebus sic stantibus.[91] El-Erian and the Chairman of the Commission, De Aréchaga, agreed that paragraph 5 should be omitted, but not so that boundary treaties could be terminated. Rather, because the situation created by treaties establishing territorial rights could not be reversed by termination of such treaties. They maintained that the issue was adequately dealt with by draft article 28, which stated that the termination of a treaty could not affect the validity of any act performed or of any right acquired under the provisions of the treaty prior to its termination.[92] Briggs also submitted that executed treaty provisions could not fall under the scope of rebus sic stantibus. However, unlike El-Erian and De Aréchaga, Briggs wished to include paragraph 5 in the article, presumably to emphasize the fact that a change of circumstances could not be invoked to invalidate already established boundaries or the completed transferral of territorial rights.[93]

The arguments advanced by El-Erian, De Aréchaga and Briggs, and the material content of draft article 28, are based on the doctrine of executed treaties, which provides that the termination of a treaty does not undo the legal situation that has been created through the rightful execution of treaty obligations. This may seem like a compelling reason to omit the exclusion of treaties relating to boundaries or territorial rights but even if provisions establishing boundaries would always be excluded under the doctrine of executed treaty provisions, some boundary treaties require continued performance inferring rights and obligations upon contracting parties. Without paragraph 5, these continuing rights and obligations could be denounced on the grounds of rebus sic stantibus.[94]

Waldock maintained that paragraph 5 of article 22 was of considerable significance. In formulating it, he had relied on the *Bremen* v. *Prussia* case from 1925, which demonstrated that treaties concerning the transfer of territory could entail

87 Ibid., 143.
88 UN Doc A/CN.4/SR.696 (n 44) 154.
89 Ibid., 152.
90 Ibid., 154. Mr Castren's draft article can be found in UN Doc A/CN.4/SR.694 (n 23) 136.
91 UN Doc A/CN.4/SR.695 (n 22) 144.
92 Ibid., 150.
93 UN Doc A/CN.4/SR.695 (n 22) 146.
94 See UN Doc A/CN.4/SR.697 (n 40) 158.

ongoing rights and obligations for contracting parties, such as exploitation of fishing ports.[95] In Waldock's view, the article implementing rebus sic stantibus should explicitly refer to stipulations of a treaty that affect a transfer of territory; the settlement of a boundary; or a grant of territorial rights, and stipulations that accompany a transfer of territory or boundary settlement and are expressed to be an essential condition of such transfer or settlement.[96] The reason for this was that otherwise parties could denounce obligations derived from a boundary treaty while retaining the territory they had acquired by virtue of the same treaty. This eventuality would be unjust, in the view of the Special Rapporteur. Therefore, he believed all treaties and treaty provisions relating to the transfer of territory or settlement of boundaries should be excluded from the application of rebus sic stantibus.[97]

Waldock accepted that referring to 'a grant of territorial rights' was unnecessary. He also deleted paragraph 5(c) from article 22 because another convention on the law of treaties in relation to international organizations was created: the Vienna Convention from 1986 on the Law of Treaties between States and International Organizations or between International Organizations (hereinafter 1986 Vienna Convention).[98] However, Waldock disagreed with members of the Commission who argued that article 28 was an adequate safeguard against denunciation of boundary treaties for the reason that the situation created by such treaties could not be undone by termination. The Special Rapporteur anticipated energetic attempts to invoke the principle of rebus sic stantibus in relation to such treaties if they were not specifically excluded and thus remained adamant on expressly referring to treaties relating to the settlement of a boundary.[99]

Members of the Commission disagreed in regards to whether changed circumstances should necessarily relate to an essential foundation of the agreement. Some members maintained that the rule could only apply if the change affected circumstances that constituted an essential basis of the treaty while others asserted that the rule was an overriding principle of law, applicable to all treaties following a change of circumstances, irrespective of the foundation of the treaty. This led to proposals to omit paragraphs 2(b) and 2(c).[100] Ago was among those members of the ILC who supported the inclusion of paragraph 2(b) since the requirement that the change affected circumstances essential to the agreement was an important element of the rebus sic stantibus rule. According to him, it should not be applicable unless the circumstances that existed at the time of the conclusion of the treaty and were affected by subsequent changes were so important to contracting parties that they

95 Ibid., 157; *Bremen* v. *Prussia* (29 June 1925) German Staatsgerichtshof, Annual Digest of Public International Law Cases, 1925–1926, case no 266.

96 UN Doc A/CN.4/SR.697 (n 40) 157.

97 Ibid.

98 Ibid., 157–158.

99 Ibid., 157.

100 Ibid., 156.

would not have entered into the treaty under the circumstances that later arose.[101] The Commission's final conclusion was to include the material requirements of paragraph 2(b), in what is now VCLT article 62(1)(a).

Waldock noted some disagreement as to whether the article should provide a right of denunciation or a right to seek revision of a treaty, obligating the other party to co-operate by renegotiating in good faith.[102] As demonstrated earlier by reference to precedents and State practice, the invocation of the principle often led to revision of treaties. Accordingly, the Commission decided that application of the codified rule would allow for termination, subject to procedural requirements. If the doctrine only granted the right of modification, the State seeking revision would be upon the mercy of other States Parties. However, the Special Rapporteur anticipated that invocation of the principle might also lead to modification of treaties since termination would only be a last resort and the threat of such extreme measures might induce amicable negotiations.[103]

Lachs suggested that the title of the article should be altered, omitting the term 'rebus sic stantibus' since it had, in his view, acquired a negative meaning among lawyers and the general public.[104] Tunkin supported the proposal[105] and it was evidently accepted by the Commission since later drafts do not expressly refer to the customary rule.

Waldock presented an alternative text for article 22 at the 710th meeting of the ILC in 1963.[106] That second draft article was much shorter than the previous version but substantially very similar. Members of the ILC generally agreed that this version was an improvement over previous draft articles and yet, some objections were raised. Again, Tabibi, Bartos, Paredes and Verdross agreed that treaties establishing a territorial settlement should not be excluded from the scope of the article and thus, proposed that paragraph 3(a) should be deleted.[107]

5.2.2.3 Draft Articles from 1965

The draft article was referred back to the drafting committee, which completed a revised version in 1965 and the article was then enumerated 44. It was submitted to States, who replied with written commentary, delegations in the Sixth Committee of the General Assembly gave their comments and Special Rapporteur Waldock made observations and amendment proposals in his Fifth Report on the Law of Treaties.[108] The article, as formulated by the drafting committee, read as follows:

101 UN Doc A/CN.4/SR.696 (n 44) 154.
102 UN Doc A/CN.4/SR.697 (n 40) 157.
103 Ibid.
104 ILC, 'Summary Record of the 693rd Meeting' (5 June 1963) UN Doc A/CN.4/SR.693, para 85.
105 UN Doc A/CN.4/SR.695 (n 22) 144–145.
106 ILC, 'Summary Record of the 710th meeting' (28 June 1963) UN Doc A/CN.4/SR.710.
107 Ibid., 251–252.
108 ILC, 'Fifth Report on the Law of Treaties by Sir Humphrey Waldock, Special Rapporteur' (15 November 1965–18 January 1966) UN Doc A/CN.4/183 and Add.1–4, 2

Article 44 – Fundamental change of circumstances

1. A change in the circumstances existing at the time when the treaty was entered into may only be invoked as grounds for terminating or withdrawing from a treaty under the conditions set out in the present article.
2. Where a fundamental change has occurred with regard to a fact or situation existing at the time when the treaty was entered into, it may be invoked as a ground for terminating or withdrawing from the treaty if:
   (a) The existence of the fact or situation constituted an essential basis of the consent of the parties to the treaty; and
   (b) The effect of the change is to transform in an essential respect the character of the obligations undertaken in the treaty.
3. Paragraph 2 above does not apply:
   (a) To a treaty fixing a boundary; or
   (b) To changes of circumstances which the parties have foreseen and for the consequences of which they have made provision in the treaty itself.
4. Under the conditions specified in article 46, if the change of circumstances referred to in paragraph 2 above related to particular clauses of the treaty, it may be invoked as a ground for terminating those clauses only.

Representatives of the United Kingdom had several reservations concerning this draft article. They submitted that the rule should only apply to treaties that had no provisions for denunciation or were at least of very long duration. Moreover, the British delegation endorsed a suggestion put forth by the Turkish Government, obliging States to negotiate before offering arbitral settlement.[109] The United States delegates were not convinced that the doctrine of rebus sic stantibus should be incorporated into the law of treaties because of difficulties related to preventing its abuse.[110] The Chinese delegation was concerned that the principle might be misused and advocated further study.

The Italian delegation suggested that the article should be made subject to compulsory jurisdiction[111] and Danish representatives promoted the idea of making the article subject to mandatory dispute settlement by submitting disagreements to an arbitral or judicial tribunal.[112] Waldock said that the issue of dispute settlements before independent tribunals related to several articles and would, thus, be dealt with in a separate article on procedural requirements.[113]

The Cameroonian delegation did not wish to exclude boundary treaties from the scope of the article because that would go against the principle of self-determination and be particularly unjust insofar as it related to boundaries that were forced upon

[109] Ibid., 40.
[110] Ibid.
[111] Ibid., 41.
[112] Ibid., 39.
[113] Ibid., 44.

States.[114] Canadian representatives suggested that paragraph 3(a) would be paraphrased in order to exempt boundary treaties in such cases where the boundary was based on a thalweg or other natural phenomena that subsequently moved. This would mean that treaties establishing boundaries by reference to fluctuating phenomena could be terminated under rebus sic stantibus.[115] The Australian Government wished to extend the scope of the exclusion found in paragraph 3(a) so that all treaties concerned with determinations of territorial sovereignty would be exempt. Representatives of the Netherlands also suggested widening the scope of paragraph 3(a) so as to include all treaties affecting a transfer of territory or the settlement of a boundary.[116]

Waldock addressed these issues relating to paragraph 3(a) and concluded that, even though several States opposed the exclusion of boundary treaties, a majority seemed to endorse it. He looked favourably upon the proposals put forth by the Australian and Dutch delegations and, consequently recommended that the paragraph should be redrafted to also refer to treaties transferring territory.[117] Waldock also addressed concerns raised by the Canadian Government, which envisioned a scenario where the location of natural phenomena, forming the basis of a boundary treaty, later changed (changing coastlines could be an example of such phenomena). He agreed that a natural catastrophe could possibly alter the location of a thalweg or other feature referenced in boundary delimitation but he doubted that such a change of circumstances should lead to the termination of a treaty under rebus sic stantibus. Instead, he believed that this type of a change in geographical circumstances should raise questions regarding the interpretation and application of the treaty.[118]

Bearing in mind the views expressed by participating governments, the Special Rapporteur proposed an alternative text to draft article 44. The following version was presented in his Fifth Report on the Law of Treaties, dated 15 November 1965:[119]

1. A fundamental change which has occurred with regard to a fact or state of facts existing at the time when a treaty was entered into may be invoked by a party as a ground for terminating or withdrawing from the treaty only if:
   (a) The existence of that fact or state of facts constituted an essential basis of the consent of the parties to be bound by the treaty;
   (b) The effect of the change is to transform in an essential respect the character of continuing obligations undertaken in the treaty; and

114 Ibid., 41.
115 Ibid., 39.
116 Ibid.
117 Ibid., 43.
118 Ibid., 44.
119 Ibid., 44.

(c) The change has not been foreseen by the parties and its consequences provided for in the treaty.

2. A fundamental change may not be invoked as a ground for terminating or withdrawing from a treaty provision fixing a boundary or effecting a transfer of territory.

The ILC considered both draft articles at its 833rd meeting on 18 January 1966.[120] Verdross stated that the provision excluding treaties fixing a boundary or affecting a transfer of territory was merely a reiteration of a general rule, namely, the doctrine of executed treaties. It provided that the termination of fully executed treaties could not affect a legal situation already created. Verdross said that the rebus sic stantibus rule could only be applicable to treaties that required further performance of treaty obligations. He, therefore, suggested that the article would exempt treaties that had been fully executed, instead of referring specifically to treaties fixing a boundary or affecting the transfer of territory.[121] Yasseen and Ruda agreed with Verdross that the principle of rebus sic stantibus could only apply to treaties that had not yet been fully executed.[122] However, Ruda was in favour of explicitly excluding treaties fixing a boundary because of their exceptional character.[123]

Ago said that a provision excluding treaties that had been fully executed might be meaningless since treaties generally ceased to exist once they were fully executed. He was of the opinion that treaties fixing boundaries were not automatically terminated when the frontier had been established, for example, a treaty fixing a boundary along the thalweg of a river had continuous effect and was continuously enforceable. Furthermore, Ago considered the reference to a treaty affecting transfer of territory unnecessary because such treaties would be covered by the provision excluding a treaty fixing a boundary.[124] This contention was echoed by Ruda.[125] De Aréchaga supported Verdros' proposal to exclude treaties that had been executed rather than boundary treaties, having suggested a similar provision in 1963.[126] The Special Rapporteur confronted and rejected the assertion that rebus sic stantibus would be inapplicable to boundary treaties on the grounds that they were fully executed. He said that the purpose of paragraph 2 was not to exclude all executed treaties but only treaties fixing a boundary or affecting the transfer of territory. The reason behind that exclusion was not that those treaties had ceased to exist but that they belonged to a category of treaties that required stability.[127]

120 UN Doc A/CN.4/SR.833 (n 54) 75–78.
121 Ibid., 76.
122 ILC, 'Summary record of the 834th meeting' (19 January 1966) UN Doc A/CN.4/SR.834, 80.
123 Ibid., 78.
124 Ibid., 82.
125 Ibid., 78.
126 Ibid., 83.
127 ILC, 'Summary Record of the 835th Meeting' (20 January 1966) UN Doc A/CN.4/SR.835, 86.

The Commission raised similar concerns as representatives of governments did before them concerning mandatory dispute settlement to prevent unilateral application of the principle. Again, Waldock emphasized the importance of making the article subject to procedural safeguards.[128]

5.2.2.4 *Final Draft Article from 1966 and the Ratified Provision*

The Commission referred the draft article from 1963 again to the drafting committee.[129] The final request for revision was accompanied by general remarks and suggestions of alternative wording.[130] The final draft article codifying the customary rule rebus sic stantibus was discussed during the Commission's 842nd meeting on 27 January 1966 and agreed upon with amendments, by 13 votes to 1, with 1 abstention.[131] Thereafter, the article became part of the draft articles on the law of treaties, adopted by the ILC on 18 July 1966, which prompted the Commission's recommendation to the General Assembly to convene an international conference with the aim to conclude a convention on the law of treaties.[132]

The draft article was presented as draft article 44 at the 842nd meeting but it was enumerated 59 after all the draft articles were joined together. It will be referred to as draft article 59 in the subsequent discussion.

Article 59 – Fundamental change of circumstances

1. A fundamental change which has occurred with regard to a circumstance existing at the time of the conclusion of a treaty and which was not foreseen by the parties may not be invoked as a ground for terminating or withdrawing from the treaty unless:
   (a) The existence of that circumstance constitutes an essential basis of the consent of the parties to be bound by the treaty; and
   (b) the effect of the change is radically to transform the scope of obligations still to be performed under the treaty.
2. A fundamental change of circumstances may not be invoked:
   (a) as a ground for terminating or withdrawing from a treaty establishing a boundary;
   (b) if the fundamental change is the result of a breach by the party invoking it either of the treaty or of another international obligation owed to the parties to the treaty.

128 Ibid., 85.
129 Ibid., 87.
130 UN Doc A/CN.4/SR.833 (n 54) 75–78; UN Doc A/CN.4/SR.834 (n 122) 78–85; UN Doc A/CN.4/SR.835 (n 127) 85–87.
131 ILC, 'Summary Record of the 842nd meeting' (27 January 1966) UN Doc A/CN.4/SR.842, 130.
132 ILC, 'Report of the International Law Commission on the Work of Its Eighteenth Session' (4 May–19 July 1966) UN Doc A/CN.4/191, 177.

The final draft article was considered at the conference convened by the General Assembly, by the Committee of the Whole during the 63rd, 64th and 65th meetings in May 1968. It was discussed in general terms and amendments, submitted by the Republic of Vietnam, Venezuela, Canada, Finland, the United States of America and Japan, were reviewed.

Thinh, a representative of Vietnam, stated that the rule of rebus sic stantibus was essential to the law of treaties due to constant changes in the international arena. His delegation proposed amendments to paragraphs 2(a) and 2(b) because these paragraphs were considered to limit the application of the rule more than necessary. The Vietnamese delegation did not wish to unconditionally exclude treaties establishing boundaries or application of the principle when the changed circumstances were induced by the party invoking the article since the application of rebus sic stantibus was particularly important in relation to political and perpetual treaties.[133] The delegation of Venezuela proposed that the rule should be stated in positive terms rather than negative.[134] The Canadian delegation was of the view that fundamentally changed circumstances should in some cases lead to suspension of a treaty and that this possible consequence should be explicitly provided for in the provision. Thus, it proposed an amendment to paragraph 1, adding the word 'suspending' before the word 'terminating'.[135]

The Finnish delegation proposed two amendments. First, it wished to incorporate the principle of separability so that application of the article could lead to termination of specific treaty provisions and not necessarily the entire treaty. Second, it suggested that paragraph 1 should refer to the possibility of suspending the operation of a treaty on the basis of changed circumstances.[136] Kearney, a representative from the United States, was of the view that the term 'treaty establishing a boundary' was too restrictive and failed to provide sufficient safeguard against unilateral termination of treaties that established territorial status or settled territorial disputes. He proposed that sub-paragraph 2(a) should be rephrased.[137] The Japanese delegation proposed an alternative text to paragraph 1(b) and endorsed the proposal submitted by the United States delegation.[138] Several other delegations supported the amendment proposed by the United States[139] but it was rejected by 43 votes to 14, with 28 abstentions.[140]

133 UN Doc A/CONF.39/11/Add.2 (n 55) 184.
134 Ibid., 183.
135 Ibid., 184.
136 Ibid., 184.
137 Ibid., 184.
138 UN Doc A/CONF.39/11 (n 5) 367.
139 See, for example, Ibid., 372.
140 Egon Schwelb, 'Fundamental Change of Circumstances Notes on Article 59 of the Draft Convention on the Law of Treaties as Recommended for Adoption to the United Nations Conference on the Law of Treaties by Its Committee of the Whole in 1968' (1969) 29 Zeitschrift für Ausländisches Öffentliches Recht und Völkerrecht 39, 57.

Stuyt of the Dutch delegation suggested combining articles 59 and 62, dealing with the procedure to be followed in cases of invalidity, termination, withdrawal from or suspension of the operation of a treaty. He commented on the ambiguity of several terms in article 59 and said that his delegation would not accept the article unless it was made subject to procedural requirements to prevent misuse of the principle.[141] The Ukrainian delegation expressly supported the Finnish and Canadian suggestions to allow suspension of the operation of a treaty under rebus sic stantibus.[142] So did the Indian delegation,[143] the Chilean delegation,[144] the Greek delegation,[145] the Hungarian delegation[146] and the delegation of the Union of Soviet Socialist Republics.[147] The delegation of Switzerland emphasized that the article should not allow unilateral denunciation unless subject to procedural safeguards and, consequently, withheld its consent.[148] The British delegation was also unwilling to approve the article until the content of article 62 had been decided.[149] Similar concerns were expressed by the Australian delegation.[150]

The Bolivian delegation rejected paragraph 2(a), considering it unreasonable to expect all boundary treaties to endure and be immune forever, despite changed circumstances. It considered the article indispensable to allow for peaceful modification of treaties. The Bolivian delegation maintained that there were no legal grounds for excluding treaties establishing boundaries from possible termination due to changed circumstances.[151] Tabibi, representing the delegation from Afghanistan, also promoted the deletion of paragraph 2(a) because the exclusion of boundary treaties would undermine the rule stated in paragraph 1 and compromise the right of self-determination and peaceful relations between States.[152]

The Moroccan representative also raised objections to paragraph 2(a), noting that the exclusion of boundary treaties had never been affirmed by legal theorists, judicial or arbitral decisions or State practice.[153] In this context, Tabibi referenced the *Free Zones of Upper Savoy* case from 1932, a case often cited when discussing whether boundary treaties should be excluded from the application of rebus sic stantibus. The case involved a treaty establishing customs zones. The French Government invoked rebus sic stantibus to terminate the treaty, but the argument

141 UN Doc A/CONF.39/11 (n 5) 368.
142 Ibid., 368.
143 Ibid., 373.
144 Ibid., 375.
145 Ibid., 378.
146 Ibid., 379.
147 Ibid., 374.
148 Ibid., 368.
149 Ibid., 369.
150 Ibid., 373.
151 Ibid., 370.
152 Ibid., 373.
153 Ibid., 379.

was rejected because merits of the case did not warrant the application of the doctrine – not because of an alleged exclusion of boundary treaties.[154]

The ILC agreed to include a provision allowing States to suspend the operation of a treaty, as suggested by the delegations of Canada and Finland, but other proposals were rejected. Thus, the draft article was referred back to the drafting committee,[155] which then produced the final version of the article:

> **Article 59 – Fundamental change of circumstances**
>
> 1. A fundamental change of circumstances which has occurred with regard to those existing at the time of the conclusion of a treaty, and which was not foreseen by the parties, may not be invoked as a ground for terminating or withdrawing from the treaty unless:
>   (a) The existence of those circumstances constituted an essential basis of the consent of the parties to be bound by the treaty; and
>   (b) The effect of the change is radically to transform the extent of obligations still to be performed under the treaty.
> 2. A fundamental change of circumstances may not be invoked as a ground for terminating or withdrawing from a treaty:
>   (a) If the treaty establishes a boundary; or
>   (b) If the fundamental change is the result of a breach by the party invoking it either of an obligation under the treaty or of any other international obligation owed to any other party to the treaty.
> 3. If, under the foregoing paragraphs, a party may invoke a fundamental change of circumstances as a ground for terminating or withdrawing from a treaty it may also invoke the change as a ground for suspending the operation of the treaty.[156]

Before finally approving the article, some objections were raised, mainly in regard to the exception found in paragraph 2(a). The Syrian delegation was among those that were reluctant to accept the exclusion of boundary treaties from the general scope of rebus sic stantibus and, therefore, rejected the provision.[157] Tabibi, of the Afghani delegation, expressed the view that paragraph 2(a) greatly weakened the principle enshrined in the article.[158] The Moroccan delegation agreed with Tabibi and suggested the deletion of paragraph 2(a).[159]

Fleischhauer, of the German delegation, pointed out a flaw in the wording of paragraph 1. The literal interpretation of the provision suggests that a fundamental change of circumstances may be invoked as a ground for terminating or withdrawing

154 *Switzerland* v. *France* (n 84).
155 (n 5) 382.
156 UN Doc A/CONF.39/11/Add.1 (n 57) 116–117.
157 Ibid., 117.
158 Ibid., 118.
159 Ibid., 120.

from a treaty, even if changes are foreseen, if all other requirements are met. This was clearly not the intended meaning of the article since all parties agreed that changes had to be unforeseen. Fleischhauer suggested an amendment for clarification[160] but to no avail.

The article was adopted at the 22nd plenary meeting on 13 May 1969, by 93 votes to 3, with 9 abstentions[161] and the VCLT was adopted by the Conference in Vienna, nine days later, on 22 May 1969.

5.3 ANALYSIS OF VCLT ARTICLE 62

The VCLT is limited to treaties between States[162] that are in written form and governed by international law.[163] Questions concerning State succession are not within the scope of the Convention[164] and the Convention is non-retroactive, making it inapplicable to treaties that were concluded before the entry into force of the VCLT.[165] Nonetheless, rules that are binding upon States under customary international law remain applicable, independently of the VCLT.[166] Therefore, rebus sic stantibus will apply to many instances not covered by the VCLT and its scope is somewhat broader than that of VCLT Article 62. For example, it applies to treaties concluded between international organizations under article 62 of the 1986 Vienna Convention.[167] This Convention is not yet in force but it suggests that the customary rule is applicable to treaties between non-State actors. Furthermore, the customary rule arguably applies to non-written agreements.

The terms of VCLT article 62 clearly set out the objective elements of the customary rule.[168] Indeed, the ICJ held, in the *Fisheries Jurisdiction* case, that VCLT article 62 'may in many respects be considered as a codification of existing customary law on the subject'.[169] Again, in the *Gabčíkovo-Nagymaros* case, the Court confirmed that the rule laid down in VCLT article 62 in many respects codifies existing customary international law.[170] However, the European Court of

160 Ibid., 118.

161 Ibid., 121.

162 VCLT article 1.

163 VCLT article 2(1)(a).

164 VCLT article 73. See also Ian Brownlie, *The Vienna Convention on the Law of Treaties* (Manchester University Press, 1984) 6.

165 VCLT article 4.

166 VCLT article 3(b).

167 See article 62 of the Vienna Convention on the Law of Treaties between States and International Organizations or between International Organizations (adopted 21 March 1986) 25 ILM 543.

168 See Athanassios Vamvaoukos, *Termination of Treaties in International Law: The Doctrines of Rebus Sic Stantibus and Desuetude* (Clarendon Press, 1985) 150–151.

169 *Fisheries Jurisdiction Fisheries Jurisdiction (Federal Republic of Germany* v. *Iceland)* (Jurisdiction) [1973] ICJ Rep 4, 63, para 36.

170 *Case Concerning the Gabčíkovo-Nagymaros Project (Hungary/Slovakia)* (Judgment) [1997] ICJ Rep 7, 64, para 46.

Justice has declared that the procedural requirements put forth in VCLT article 65 do not apply to the customary rule.[171]

Stuyt, a representative of the Dutch delegation, noted that VCLT article 62 was the only article in the draft convention that contained numerous concepts of ambiguous meaning and he warned that employing such terms in a legislative text might be dangerous.[172] The following sections will decipher these ambiguous meanings and provide an analysis of each requirement of VCLT article 62, all of which must be satisfied to justify its use.[173]

5.3.1 *A Fundamental Change of Circumstances*

The requirement that a change must be fundamental to justify the application of rebus sic stantibus has little significance as an independent requirement. The same can be deduced from other requirements of VCLT article 62. The change must affect the essential basis of the treaty and radically transform remaining obligations. Therefore, the reference to fundamentality can be understood as a safeguard ensuring that a change, justifying termination of a treaty, is severe or fundamental in character.[174]

A fundamental change should be objective, and it should affect the factual circumstances surrounding the treaty rather than the parties' attitudes towards the treaty.[175] The change should relate to circumstances, existing at the time of the conclusion of the treaty. The continuance of those circumstances should have been anticipated by both parties and motivated them to consent to the treaty or specific obligations affected by the fundamental change. The change should either render the performance of treaty obligations impossible or destroy or alter the foundation of the obligations under the treaty. Fitzmaurice noted two instances that would not suffice for the invocation of the principle. First, a change affecting the party's will to enter into a treaty or to continue performing treaty obligations and, second, a foreseeable change.[176]

To qualify as a fundamental change under VCLT article 62, a change must be of a qualitative and quantitative nature.[177] The qualitative element relates to the requirement that the change affects the facts that led both parties to give their consent to be bound by the treaty, as suggested in paragraph 2(1)(a). The quantitative element is embodied in paragraph 2(1)(b), which provides that the change must be

171 A *Racke GmbH & Co* v. *Hauptzollamt Mainz*, European Court of Justice: Racke C-162/96 [1998] European Court Reports I-3655, para 59.

172 UN Doc A/CONF.39/11 (n 5) 367.

173 Thomas Giegerich (n 53) 1078.

174 Ibid., 1085.

175 UN Doc A/CN.4/107 (n 18) 32–33.

176 Ibid.

177 Paul Reuter, *Introduction to the Law of Treaties* (Kegan Paul International, 1995) 189.

so extensive that it alters the conditions of the treaty and its *raison d'être*.[178] The drying up of a river or the silting up of a harbour would be examples of fundamental changes potentially justifying termination, withdrawal from, or suspension of a treaty, that is, if other requirements of VCLT article 62 were met.[179] Similarly, other geographical changes might qualify as fundamental changes, but only when they relate to the essential basis of a treaty.

A fundamental change of circumstances can affect almost any type of circumstances, for example, factual, political, legal, economic or social circumstances.[180] There are three exceptions to this otherwise general assumption: fundamental changes due to State succession, outbreak of hostilities and the severance of diplomatic relations cannot qualify as fundamental changes under VCLT article 62. The first two categories fall outside the scope of the 1969 Vienna Convention[181] and the severance of diplomatic or consular relations does not affect the legal relations established between the parties unless and insofar as such relations are indispensable, as per VCLT article 63.[182] Nonetheless, the European Court of Justice has confirmed that the outbreak of hostilities can amount to a fundamental change of circumstances under the customary rule rebus sic stantibus.[183] Therefore, as previously suggested, the scope of the customary principle may be somewhat broader than that of VCLT article 62.

Fundamental changes do not necessarily have to be factual. They can be political, legal[184] or economic, for example, changes relating to the costs derived from treaty obligations and changes in the fiscal situation of a contracting party.[185] However, the total extinction of one of the parties to a treaty, such as might result from the complete submergence of an island State, would not constitute a fundamental change in circumstances within the meaning of VCLT article 62. Rather, according to Waldock, it would qualify as an impossibility of performance and, consequently, be subject to VCLT article 61 or rules on State succession if there was a change in the identity of one of the States Parties.[186]

5.3.2 *Foreseeability*

Paragraph 1 of VCLT article 62 provides that a fundamental change of circumstances may not be invoked as a ground for terminating, suspending or withdrawing

178 Ibid.
179 Jeremy Waldron (n 19) 170.
180 Georg Dahm, Jost Delbrück and Rüdiger Wolfrum, *Völkerrecht: Die Grundlagen. Die Völkerrechtssubjekte* (De Gruyter, 2002) 751.
181 VCLT article 73.
182 Thomas Giegerich (n 53) 1081.
183 *A Racke GmbH & Co v. Hauptzollamt Mainz* (n 171) paras 53 et seq.
184 See Thomas Giegerich (n 53) 1081–1082.
185 Jeremy Waldron (n 19) 170.
186 UN Doc A/CN.4/156 and Add.1–3 (n 27) 78.

from a treaty if the change was foreseen by the parties at the conclusion of the treaty. When discussing draft articles, Fitzmaurice noted that parties to a treaty should not have been able to anticipate the fundamental change of circumstances with reasonable foresight.[187] This suggests that the evaluation of foreseeability should involve an objective test; an analysis of information generally available at the time of conclusion of the agreement. However, the terminology of VCLT article 62 indicates that the relevant criteria are what parties to an agreement actually foresaw ('foreseen by the parties'). Therefore, the principle should definitely not be invoked to withdraw from, suspend or terminate a treaty if the treaty provides for the change in any way. However, it is not entirely clear whether one can prove that a change was 'foreseen by the parties' if such a contention is not supported by stipulations of the treaty or the *travaux préparatoires*.

VCLT article 62 contains a flaw, relating to the condition of foreseeability. As previously mentioned, the literal interpretation of the provision suggests that an *unforeseen* fundamental change of circumstances may be invoked as a ground for terminating or withdrawing from a treaty. An amendment was proposed to correct this flaw, but only at a very late stage and it was not adopted.[188] Nonetheless, it seems quite clear that the ILC did not intend to allow termination in cases where parties had foreseen the fundamental change. Such interpretation would be manifestly unreasonable.[189] Consequently, any ambiguity relating to the foreseeability requirement would surely be interpreted in accordance with the clear intent of the parties, which makes this drafting mistake insignificant.

5.3.3 *Essential Basis of the Treaty*

The essential basis of a treaty refers to the circumstances that shaped the drafting process and the content of treaty provisions.[190] These are the circumstances that existed when the treaty was concluded and motivated the parties to give their consent.[191] A fundamental change cannot be invoked as grounds for terminating, suspending or withdrawing from a treaty unless it affects the essential basis of that treaty. In other words, a fundamental change of circumstances must directly affect the very obligation that States seek to terminate by invocation of the principle. For example, the fundamental change relied upon by Iceland in the *Fisheries Jurisdiction* case could not suffice because it related to fishing techniques and had no clear connection to the ICJ compromissory clause that Iceland sought to terminate.[192]

[187] UN Doc A/CN.4/107 (n 18) 33.

[188] UN Doc A/CONF.39/11/Add.1 (n 57) 118.

[189] Thomas Giegerich (n 53) 1086.

[190] Mark Villiger, Commentary on the 1969 Vienna Convention on the Law of Treaties (Martinus Nijhoff, 2009) 774.

[191] UN Doc A/CN.4/107 (n 18) 32–33.

[192] Thomas Giegerich (n 53) 1085, referring to *Fisheries Jurisdiction (United Kingdom of Great Britain and Northern Ireland* v. *Iceland)* (Jurisdiction) [1973] ICJ Rep 3, paras 38 *et seq*. See also Eduardo de Aréchaga, *International Law in the Past Third of a Century* (Sijthoff, 1978) 73 *et seq*.

The ICJ also addressed this condition in the *Gabčíkovo-Nagymaros* case when Hungary sought to terminate a treaty relating to the construction and operation of a system of dams due to a fundamental change of circumstances. Hungary argued that 'profound changes of a political nature, the Project's diminishing economic viability, the progress of environmental knowledge and the development of new norms and prescriptions of international environmental law' could cumulatively amount to a fundamental change of circumstances justifying termination.[193] The Court found that, although the political and economic circumstances had certainly been relevant for the conclusion of the treaty, they were not sufficiently linked to the object and purpose of the treaty to present an essential basis of the parties' consent.[194] This does not exclude the possibility of political and economic considerations forming an essential basis in other treaties. However, it demonstrates the importance of establishing a causal link between the specific circumstances that have undergone changes and the subject matter of the treaty.

The European Economic Community terminated The Cooperation Agreement between the European Economic Community and the Socialist Federal Republic of Yugoslavia (hereinafter Cooperation Agreement) in November 1991 due to the outbreak of hostilities in Yugoslavia. The Community's decision to terminate the agreement was challenged and brought before the European Court of Justice in *Racke* v. *Hauptzollamt Mainz*. VCLT article 62 was not directly applicable but the court proceeded to apply the customary rule. The agreement concerned trade concessions between the parties and the European Court found that an essential basis of the agreement was 'the maintenance of a situation of peace in Yugoslavia [...] and the existence of institutions capable of ensuring implementation of the cooperation envisaged by the Agreement throughout the territory of Yugoslavia'.[195] This was considered necessary to meet the broad objectives of the agreement, namely, the 'overall cooperation between the contracting parties with a view to contributing to the economic and social development of the Socialist Federal Republic of Yugoslavia and helping to strengthen relations between the parties'.[196]

5.3.4 *Radical Transformation of Ongoing Obligations*

The European Court of Justice, in *Racke* v. *Hauptzollamt Mainz*, considered whether the outbreak of hostilities constituted a change that radically transformed the extent of obligations still to be performed under the Cooperation Agreement. It found that the Council of Europe did not make a 'manifest error of assessment' when finding that the effects of the situation in Yugoslavia on economic and trade relations radically changed the conditions preceding the Cooperation Agreement and basis for its application.[197]

193 *Case Concerning the Gabčíkovo-Nagymaros Project* (n 170) para 104.
194 Ibid.
195 *A Racke GmbH & Co* v. *Hauptzollamt Mainz* (n 171) para 55.
196 Ibid., para 54.
197 Ibid., para 56.

Thus, the European Community could validly adopt a regulation suspending the effects of the Cooperation Agreement. The European Court of Justice did not discuss the requirement of radical change in any more detail but mentioned that it should not be confused with impossibility of performance. Indeed, the European Community could well have continued granting tariff concessions to Yugoslavia but 'there was no point in continuing to grant preferences, with a view to stimulating trade, in circumstances where Yugoslavia was breaking up'.[198]

This case, as previously mentioned, concerned application of customary international law. Still, VCLT article 62(1)(b) also provides that the effect of a change must be to radically transform the extent of obligations still to be performed under a treaty. Otherwise the change cannot justify termination, suspension or revision. The ILC did not explain how a radical transformation should be qualified but this requirement relates to the condition of a fundamental change and suggests that the change must affect ongoing obligations to a large extent.[199] The reference to obligations still to be performed aims to clarify that VCLT article 62 is not applicable to treaties that have been fully executed. There have to be obligations that have not yet been performed or a requirement of continuing performance.[200]

'The extent of obligations still to be performed can be radically transformed either directly or indirectly. Direct transformation means that the onerousness of the obligation is increased, whereas indirect transformation means that the value to be gained by further performance is diminished.'[201] The reference to obligations in plural does not seem to suggest that all obligations must be radically transformed but only the obligations of the party invoking a fundamental change of circumstances.[202]

The ICJ considered whether the alleged fundamental changes in the *Gabčíkovo-Nagymaros* case would satisfy the requirement of radically transforming ongoing obligations and while acknowledging that the agreement might have become less profitable, the Court asserted that the viability of the treaty had not diminished to such an extent that would justify invocation of rebus sic stantibus.[203] This suggests that a change affecting the economic viability of treaties may qualify as a fundamental change radically transforming ongoing obligations, but only where economic interests led to the conclusion of a treaty and those interests have been severely affected.

5.3.5 *Treaty Establishing a Boundary*

'There is hardly any theoretical reason why certain treaties should *a priori* escape a possible challenge due to a change of circumstances.'[204] Yet, treaties establishing

[198] Ibid., para 57.
[199] See Thomas Giegerich (n 53) 1085.
[200] UN Doc A/CN.4/183 and Add.1–4 (n 108) 43.
[201] Thomas Giegerich (n 53) 1089 referring to UN Doc A/CN.4/107 (n 18) 60, para 151.
[202] Thomas Giegerich (n 53) 1088.
[203] *Case Concerning the Gabčíkovo-Nagymaros Project* (n 170) para 104.
[204] Paul Reuter (n 177) 189.

boundaries are excluded from the application of the substantive rule embodied in VCLT article 62. The Commission noted that several ILC members and State representatives had reservations regarding the exclusion of treaties establishing boundaries, finding it too restrictive or incompatible with the principle of self-determination. Those arguing that it was contradictory to the principle of self-determination said that '[a]ny attempt to keep a treaty in force against the wishes of a people would involve a greater danger to peace than the application of the rebus sic stantibus doctrine'.[205]

Energetic attempts were made to eliminate the boundary exception and some States even tried to reduce its weight after it was implemented.[206] Yet, the Commission deemed it necessary and 'concluded that treaties establishing boundaries should be recognized to be an exception to the rule, because otherwise the rule, instead of being an instrument of peaceful change, might become a source of dangerous frictions'.[207]

The decision to exclude boundary treaties was supported by reference to the fact that most jurists, at the time of codification of the VCLT, assumed the existence of such an exception and so did France and Switzerland in the 1932 *Free Zones* case.[208] However, the *Free Zones* case was also referenced by those who opposed the exclusion of boundary treaties because, while upholding other points on the substantive elements of the principle, the PCIJ did not confirm the parties' contentions that boundary treaties were excluded from the application of rebus sic stantibus.[209] Instead of rejecting the rebus sic stantibus argument by reference to a boundary exception, it was rejected because of insufficient proof that the changed circumstances formed an essential basis of the treaty.[210]

The *Free Zones* case highlights that the term 'boundary' may refer to different lines of delimitation. This case involved a boundary which constituted a 'customs barrier' and a 'political frontier of the District of Gex, that is to say, of the Gex free zone.'[211] This was not a conventional land boundary but it did demarcate territorial rights between different States, which raises a fundamental but often overlooked

205 Egon Schwelb (n 140) 57.

206 The Government of the Syrian Arab Republic made a reservation to the VCLT upon ratification stating that it 'does not in any case accept the non-applicability of the principle of a fundamental change of circumstances with regard to treaties establishing boundaries, referred to in article 62, paragraph 2 (a), inasmuch as it regards this as a flagrant violation of an obligatory norm which forms part of general international law and which recognizes the right of peoples to self-determination' VCLT (with annex), 505–506.

207 UN Doc A/CONF.39/11 (n 5) 371.

208 UN Doc A/6309/Rev.1 (n 52) 259 referring to *Switzerland* v. *France* (n 84).

209 See UN Doc A/CONF.39/11/Add.1 (n 57) 121; UN Doc A/CN.4/SR.695 (n 22) 147. See *Switzerland* v. *France* (n 84) 158: 'As the French argument fails on the facts, it becomes unnecessary for the Court to consider [. . .] the question whether it would apply to treaties establishing rights such as that which Switzerland derived from the treaties of 1815 and 1816.'

210 *Switzerland* v. *France* (n 84) 157.

211 Ibid., 148.

question for the interpretation of VCLT article 62: What type of boundaries are excluded under paragraph 2(a)?

Subsequent sections provide an analysis of the boundary concept, in the context of VCLT article 62(2)(a); the object and purpose of the boundary exception; and, finally, the difference between territorial and non-territorial boundaries.

5.3.5.1 'Boundary' in the Context of VCLT Article 62(2)(A)

The ICJ has confirmed that treaty interpretation is based, primarily, on the text of a treaty.[212] The text must be interpreted in accordance with the ordinary meaning of the terms and the context they appear in.[213] The word boundary can be broadly construed for different purposes but the fact that a line qualifies as a boundary in some respects does not automatically make it a boundary within the meaning of VCLT article 62(2)(a).[214]

The ILC explained, when codifying the 1986 Vienna Convention, that the 'term "boundary" customarily denotes the limit of the land territory of a State, but it could conceivably be taken more broadly to designate the various lines that fix the spatial limits of the exercise of different powers'.[215] The ILC explained that lines could be boundaries for certain purposes and not others, for example, opposable to other States while not conferring exclusive jurisdiction.[216] The Commission asserted that territorial sea boundaries were 'true limit[s] of the territory of the State' but further noted that even if other maritime boundaries, and boundaries to air space, could also be categorized as 'true boundaries', they might not fall within the boundary exception of VCLT article 62(2)(a).[217]

When codifying VCLT article 62, the ILC explained that the phrase, 'treaty establishing a boundary', was broader than 'treaty fixing a boundary'; broad enough to encompass treaties of cession and delimitation.[218] Cession refers to '[t]he transfer of sovereignty over a territory by means of a treaty'[219] and delimitation can be described as 'marking off, or describing the limits or boundary line of a territory or country'.[220] The term clearly covers treaties delimiting land territory because the

212 See, for example, *Territorial Dispute (Libyan Arab Jamahiriya/Chad)* (Judgment) [1994] ICJ Rep 6, para 41; *Legality of the Use of Force (Serbia and Montenegro v. Belgium)* (Preliminary Objections) [2004] ICJ Rep 279, para 100.

213 VCLT article 31(1).

214 ILC, 'Report of the Commission to the General Assembly on the Work of the Thirty-fourth Session' (3 May–23 July 1982) UN Doc A/CN.4/SER.A/1982/Add.l (Part 2), 60–61. See also Thomas Giegerich (n 53) 1093.

215 Ibid., 60.

216 Ibid., 60–61.

217 Ibid., 61.

218 UN Doc A/6309/Rev.1 (n 52) 259.

219 'Cession' in Jonathan Law (ed) A *Dictionary of Law*, 8th edition (Oxford University Press, 2015) 95.

220 'Delimitation' in *Black's Law Dictionary: Free Online Legal Dictionary*, 2nd edition, available at: http://thelawdictionary.org/delimitation/ accessed 16 January 2021.

Commission only referred to such treaties when discussing the types of treaties encompassed by the boundary exception.[221] However, the reference to treaties of cession and delimitation leaves unclear whether the boundary exception extends beyond treaties that establish boundaries on land.

The only definition of a boundary ever advanced in the extensive drafting history of VCLT article 62 was Oppenheim's definition, defining State boundaries as 'the imaginary lines on the surface of the earth which separate the territory of one State from that of another, or from unappropriated territory, or from the open sea'.[222] This definition makes a distinction between boundaries between two or more States or between a State and unappropriated territory and boundaries where territory of a State meets the ocean. It implies that boundaries are either drawn between territory of different States or where territory ends, which must be at the baselines of coastal States or the outer limits of the territorial sea, depending on an interpretation of the word territory. It is unclear whether the reference to open sea covers all maritime zones or only maritime zones that do not fall within the first category, that is, qualifying as territory. The legal regime of the exclusive economic zone did not exist at the time of these discussions but the contiguous zone, fisheries zone and continental shelf were well-established legal regimes. Nonetheless, there was no category for boundaries delimiting the maritime zones of different States, except potentially the territorial sea boundaries. Just as the explanations referred to earlier, this definition rests on an interpretation of the word territory.

VCLT article 62(2)(a) extends to 'treaties establishing or modifying the territory of States'.[223] Still, treaties that establish territorial status are not excluded unless they also create boundaries. 'Treaties on territorial regimes such as those granting servitudes, long-term leases of territory, condominium agreements or other agreements on the exercise of territorial sovereignty are therefore not covered by the exception.'[224]

The United States delegation proposed an amendment to VCLT article 62, explicitly excluding treaties 'establishing territorial status' (specific regimes within territories), as well as treaties establishing boundaries. The delegation of Switzerland supported this proposal since it would mean that treaties concerning the joint utilization of rivers forming boundaries, freedom of navigation in rivers or rights of passage could not be terminated under rebus sic stantibus.[225] The delegation of the United States referred to the Antarctic Treaty as an example of a treaty that recognized a status quo or created a regime, a category of treaties that was not excluded under paragraph 2(a), but should be. The Australian delegation agreed with that contention and agreed that the Antarctic Treaty, which set up a system of scientific

[221] Except when inconclusively dealing with the *Free Zones* case: UN Doc A/6309/Rev.1 (n 52) 259; UN Doc A/CONF.39/11/Add.1 (n 57) 121; UN Doc A/CN.4/SR.695 (n 22) 147.

[222] UN Doc A/CONF.39/11 (n 5) 367. See Lassa Oppenheim, *Oppenheim's International Law, volume 1, Peace*, 8th edition (Longman, 1992) 531.

[223] UN Doc A/CN.4/SER.A/1982/Add.l (n 214) 60, para 4.

[224] Thomas Giegerich (n 53) 1093.

[225] Egon Schwelb (n 140) 56.

co-operation and demilitarization, would not be excluded under paragraph 2(a) as it did not establish boundaries.[226] Waldock contemplated widening the scope of paragraph 2(a) in accordance with the proposal put forth by the United States but the Commission was adamant on keeping the final wording of the article because it did not want to restrict the general rule of rebus sic stantibus too much.[227] Thus, the proposal to widen the scope of paragraph 2(a) was rejected.

The ICJ's decision in the *Aegean Sea* case is relevant to this discussion. It indicates that treaties delimiting the continental shelf should fall within the boundary exclusion of VCLT article 62(2).[228] However, the Court's *obiter dictum* regarding continental shelf boundaries does not definitively settle whether the provision covers all maritime boundaries. The *Aegean Sea* case dealt with the admissibility of a dispute concerning the delimitation of a continental shelf boundary between Greece and Turkey and involved a detailed analysis of the term 'territorial status'. Greece had accepted compulsory jurisdiction of the PCIJ through a unilateral declaration, submitted in 1929, which excluded 'disputes relating to the territorial status of Greece, including disputes relating to its rights of sovereignty over its ports and lines of communication'.[229] When subsequently acceding to the 1928 General Act on the Pacific Settlement of International Disputes in 1931,[230] Greece invoked article 39(2)(b), excluding '[d]isputes concerning questions which by international law are solely within the domestic jurisdiction of States'. The ICJ found that the earlier reservation had to be read into article 39(2)(b) and, consequently, both categories were excluded from compulsory jurisdiction, that is, disputes under the domestic jurisdiction of either State and disputes relating to territorial status.[231]

Turkey invoked Greece's reservation concerning disputes relating to territorial status and maintained that the case, consequently, fell outside the ICJ's jurisdiction. Greece asserted that references to 'territorial status', 'territorial situation' and 'territorial integrity' from the 1920s were 'to be given a restrictive interpretation limited to the maintenance of the *status quo* established by treaties, normally as the result of post-war settlement'.[232] The Court rejected this narrow approach and noted that reservations of disputes relating to territorial status should be interpreted broadly.[233] It found that the historical evidence presented by Greece confirmed 'that the expression "territorial status" was used in its ordinary, generic sense of any matters properly to be considered as relating to the integrity and legal régime of a State's territory'.[234] Furthermore, the

226 UN Doc A/CONF.39/11 (n 5) 372–373.
227 Ibid., 381.
228 *Aegean Sea Continental Shelf (Greece* v. *Turkey)* (Jurisdiction) [1978] ICJ Rep 3, para 85.
229 Ibid., para 57.
230 General Act (Pacific Settlement of International Disputes (adopted on 26 September 1928, entered into force 16 August 1929) 93 League of Nations Treaty Series 343.
231 *Aegean Sea Continental Shelf* (n 228) para 68.
232 Ibid., para 72.
233 Ibid., para 73.
234 Ibid., para 74.

generic nature of the term 'territorial status' led the Court to apply an evolutive interpretation, finding that the term covered the continental shelf, even though the concept was unknown to the Parties at the time of the conclusion of the 1928 General Act.[235]

The ICJ reached the conclusion that the dispute concerning the delimitation of the continental shelf between Turkey and Greece was excluded from mandatory jurisdiction under the Greek reservation.[236] However, this was not due to the continental shelf being classified as territory or having 'territorial status'. In the words of the Court, '[t]he question is not, as Greece seems to assume, whether continental shelf rights are territorial rights or are comprised within the expression "territorial status". The real question for decision is, whether the dispute is one which relates to the territorial status of Greece.'[237] This differs from the test applicable to VCLT article 62(2)(a) as it only excludes treaties that, in fact, establish (territorial) boundaries, and not those *relating* to such boundaries or otherwise creating 'territorial status'. The standard to be applied to treaties establishing boundaries under VCLT article 62(2)(a) must be stricter because 'territorial status' has a broader connotation than 'territory' or 'boundary', within the meaning of VCLT article 62(2)(a). This is supported by the drafting history discussed earlier, and the fact that the proposal to broaden the scope of the provision by referring to 'territorial status' was rejected.[238]

There is also an important difference between disputes *relating to* territorial status and those involving territorial status. Continental shelf delimitation certainly relates to territorial status.[239] Indeed, the continental shelf is a prolongation of land territory and the continental shelf entitlement exists by virtue of sovereignty over that land. Still, this does not justify an equation between a continental shelf boundary and a territorial boundary. The Court concluded, in the *Aegean Sea* case, that the delimitation of the continental shelf was not 'entirely extraneous to the notion of territorial status'[240] and, therefore, it was encompassed by the reservation of disputes relating to 'territorial status'.[241] Maritime boundaries are certainly not 'entirely extraneous' to treaties establishing territorial boundaries but that is not the standard to be applied when determining the scope of VCLT article 62(2)(a).

It was in this context and in support of its decision to categorize continental shelf delimitation as a 'dispute relating to territorial status' that the ICJ made the following statement: 'Whether it is a land frontier or a boundary line in the continental shelf that is in question, the process is essentially the same, and inevitably involves the same element of stability and permanence, and is subject to the rule excluding

235 Ibid., para 77.
236 Ibid., para 90.
237 Ibid., para 81. See also para 86.
238 See Section 4.3.5.1.
239 *Aegean Sea Continental Shelf* (n 228) paras 83–84.
240 Ibid., para 84.
241 Ibid., para 86.

boundary agreements from fundamental change of circumstances.'[242] This *obiter dictum* cannot suffice to conclude that VCLT article 62(2)(a) covers all maritime boundary treaties because the Court presented no analysis of the provision or the boundary concept and made no reference to other types of maritime boundaries. Moreover, the Court's finding was premised on the preceding conclusion that 'disputes relating to territorial status' encompass delimitation of the continental shelf and on the alleged need for permanence and stability for continental shelf boundaries. However, as previously explained, VCLT article 62(2)(a) cannot be interpreted so broadly as to cover all treaties relating to boundaries delimiting territorial status. At any rate, the desire for stable continental shelf boundaries has subsequently been addressed through UNCLOS articles 76(8) and (9), which, arguably, makes the categorical exclusion of continental shelf boundaries under VCLT article 62(2)(a) superfluous.

5.3.5.2 The Sanctity of Boundaries

This section will examine the object and purpose of the exclusion of boundary treaties from VCLT article 62. This is a prerequisite for determining what types of boundaries may be subject to termination. After all, the provision must be interpreted in accordance with the ordinary meaning of relevant terms and in light of the treaty's object and purpose.[243] The object and purpose of VCLT article 62(2)(a) is to safeguard the stability of boundaries, promote peace and security in the international spectrum[244] and avoid friction in international relations.[245] These declarations, put forth in the *travaux préparatoires*, are inconclusive on their own. However, it seems that certain types of boundaries enjoy a distinct level of sanctity in international law and this is arguably the rationale behind the boundary exception of VCLT article 62(2)(a). In fact, while States seem to view land boundaries as permanent, they often indicate an awareness of the potential need to revise or renegotiate treaties establishing maritime boundaries.[246] For example, the 2016 maritime boundary agreement between the Solomon Islands and the Republic of Vanuatu makes provisions for dispute settlement and future revision of the boundary.[247] Such provisions can also be found in treaties establishing land boundaries.[248]

242 Ibid., para 85.
243 VCLT article 31(1).
244 UN Doc A/CONF.39/11 (n 5) 371.
245 UN Doc A/CONF.39/11/Add.2 (n 55) 79.
246 Cissé Yacouba and Donald McRae (n 10) 3300.
247 Treaty between the Solomon Islands and the Republic of Vanuatu concerning their Maritime Boundaries of 7 October 2016, UNTS, articles 4–6.
248 See David Anderson, 'Negotiating Maritime Boundary Agreements: A Personal View' in Rainer Lagoni and Daniel Vignes (eds) *Maritime Delimitation* (Martinus Nijhoff, 2006) 121, 139.

Treaties establishing land boundaries are binding *erga omnes*. This characteristic is rooted in the principle of territorial integrity. '[A] State is by its very existence competent to consolidate its territory within the limits established by public international law.'[249] States are bound to respect the competence of other States to demarcate their own sovereign territory, and consequently, the territorial boundaries they establish.[250] According to this, the sanctity of boundaries may be traced back to title to territory and the principle of territorial integrity, which then safeguards only territorial boundaries. That arguably extends to boundaries delimiting territorial sovereignty at sea, that is, the territorial sea and internal or archipelagic waters. However, this highlights one relevant difference between land and maritime boundaries. Land boundaries are rooted in title to territory that is assumed to be infinite and binding *erga omnes*. This title may be lost when land territory is submerged but title over land cannot be transferred from one State to another through application of law. Conversely, title to maritime zones extends from, and fluctuates with, coastal geography and fluctuations can generate new rights for third States, that is, when areas become subject to the regimes of the high seas and the international seabed area due to coastline recession. Such changes can affect the validity of maritime boundaries and their opposability to third States.

Boundary treaties are generally said to constitute an exception to the *pacta tertiis* rule because they create obligations *erga omnes*.[251] The *erga omnes* validity of boundaries is based on the absence of competence for third States to regulate the issue.[252] However, this reasoning does not apply equally to maritime boundaries as it does to land boundaries because fundamental changes to coastal geography can generate new maritime entitlements and third States may challenge agreed maritime boundaries that infringe their lawful entitlements. In other words, bilateral maritime boundaries are not opposable to third States, the same way as land boundaries.[253] The sanctity of boundaries is, arguably, linked to this *erga omnes* effect and the lack of competence for third States in relation to sovereign territory. This does not apply to maritime boundaries if they can be challenged by third States. That suggests that boundaries only enjoy a distinct level of protection if, or as long as, they delimit sovereign title that no other State has the competence to delimit. The emergence of new claims to the area could alter this classification and make a boundary treaty subject to the *pacta tertiis* rule.[254]

249 Alexander Proelß, 'Article 34. General Rule Regarding Third States' in Oliver Dörr and Kirsten Schmalenbach (n 53) 605, 630–631.

250 Ibid.

251 Alan Boyle and Christine Chinkin, *The Making of International Law* (Oxford University Press, 2007) 239.

252 Alexander Proelß (n 249) 631.

253 See, for example, Nuno Sérgio Marques Antunes, 'The Pending Maritime Delimitation in the *Cameroon* v. *Nigeria Case*: A Piece in the Jigsaw Puzzle of the Gulf of Guinea' (2000) 15 (2) The International Journal of Marine and Coastal Law 163, 174.

254 See VCLT article 34.

VCLT article 62 was meant to reconcile the need for stability in treaty relations and 'principles of equity and justice calling for the adaptation of treaties to a profoundly changing environment'.[255] The stability of treaties is certainly important for international peace and security.[256] This applies to all treaties, whether they establish boundaries or not, and the object and purpose of boundary treaties is generally the creation of stable legal positions.[257] Indeed, as the ICJ explained in the *Temple of Preah Vihear* case, 'when two countries establish a frontier between them, one of the primary objects is to achieve stability and finality'.[258] Even so, when considering the underlying principles that inform the sanctity of boundaries, one can assume that VCLT article 62(2)(a) is only meant to safeguard the stability of boundaries delimiting territorial sovereignty.

5.3.5.3 Territorial and Non-Territorial Boundaries

The foregoing analysis leads to the conclusion that treaties establishing non-territorial boundaries can be subject to termination due to fundamentally changed circumstances. Consequently, this section seeks to explain how territorial boundaries can be distinguished from non-territorial boundaries.

Brownlie asserts that courts connote the term territory to the exercise of territorial jurisdiction.[259] 'State territory is that defined portion of the surface of the globe which is subjected to the sovereignty of a state.'[260] States have the right to exercise the functions of a State, within their sovereign territory, and to do so 'to the exclusion of any other State'.[261] This exclusive jurisdiction to exercise State functions only exists in regard to land, internal waters, archipelagic waters and the territorial sea, which suggests, that a treaty establishing a boundary, under VCLT article 62, is a treaty establishing a land or territorial sea boundary. In fact, Lando explicitly States that the continental shelf and exclusive economic zone must not be assimilated to territory.[262]

This interpretation corresponds to an entry made in the *Oxford Dictionary of Law* from 2015, which defines a boundary as:

> (in international law) An imaginary line that determines the territorial limits of a state. Such boundaries define the limitation of each state's effective jurisdiction. They are three-dimensional in nature in that they include the airspace and subsoil

255 Thomas Giegerich (n 53) 1068–1069.
256 UN Doc A/6309/Rev.1 (n 52) 260, para 13.
257 Thomas Giegerich (n 53) 1090.
258 *Temple of Preah Vihear (Cambodia* v. *Thailand)* (Merits) [1962] ICJ Rep 6, 34.
259 Ian Brownlie, *Principles of Public International Law* (Clarendon Press, 1998) 113.
260 'Territory' in John Grant and J Craig Barker (eds) *Encyclopaedic Dictionary of International Law, 3rd ed* (Oxford University Press, 2009).
261 *Island of Palmas case (Netherlands/USA)* (1928) II RIAA 829, 838.
262 Massimo Lando, *Maritime Delimitation as a Judicial Process* (Cambridge University Press, 2019) 32.

of the state, the *terra firma* within the boundary, and the maritime domain of the state's internal waters and territorial sea.[263]

According to this, boundaries do not comprise maritime boundaries beyond the territorial sea. Still, this is not entirely conclusively because another legal dictionary, also published by Oxford University Press (in 2009), States that boundaries are 'imaginary lines on the surface of the earth which separate the land territory or maritime zones (continental shelf and EEZ) of one State from that of another'.[264] This definition seems to classify territorial sea boundaries with those separating land territories (as does the first one) but also includes non-territorial maritime boundaries in the boundary concept. The former definition is narrower and sits better with the preceding discussions. It suggests that a boundary, in international law, defines a State's territory and delimits full sovereignty.

The ILC discussed the boundary concept when codifying the 1986 Vienna Convention.[265] The Commission explained that the term relates to the territory of a State[266] and that international organizations could not establish boundaries for themselves because they possessed no territory.[267]

The ILC noted that 'the outer limit of the territorial sea is a true limit of the territory of the State, which is not the case with other lines'.[268] Furthermore, it asserted that even if a line delimiting maritime entitlements might constitute a boundary in a general sense it might not fall under the scope of VCLT Article 62(2)(a): 'Lines of maritime delimitation (not to mention the delimitation of air space) may in fact have special features and it is possible that the stabilizing effect of article 62 does not extend to certain lines of maritime delimitation, even if, to all intents and purposes, they constitute true boundaries.'[269] This demonstrates that, although fundamental changes cannot be invoked to terminate territorial boundaries requiring stability, the opposite might be true of boundaries delimiting the exclusive economic/fisheries zone and continental shelf, that is, non-territorial maritime boundaries.[270]

The ICJ famously dealt with the boundary concept in the 1978 *Aegean Sea Continental Shelf* case and also, more recently, in 2002, 2008 and 2009. The Court addressed the classification of international agreements as boundary agreements in *Indonesia/Malaysia*[271] and in *Malaysia/Singapore*[272] and found that the

263 'Boundary' in Jonathan Law (ed) A *Dictionary of Law*, 8th edition (Oxford University Press, 2015) 73.
264 'Boundary/ies' in John Grant and J Craig Barker (n 260) 69.
265 UN Doc A/CN.4/SER.A/1982/Add.l (n 214) 61.
266 Ibid., 60–61.
267 Ibid., 61.
268 Ibid., here a reference was made, in a footnote, to continental shelf limits.
269 UN Doc A/CN.4/SER.A/1982/Add.l (n 214) 61.
270 Thomas Giegerich (n 53) 1093.
271 *Sovereignty over Pulau Ligitan and Pulau Sipadan (Indonesia/Malaysia)* (Judgment) [2002] ICJ Rep 625.
272 *Sovereignty over Pedra Branca/Pulau Batu Puteh, Middle Rocks and South Ledge (Malaysia/Singapore)* (Judgment) [2008] ICJ Rep 12.

question essentially depends on whether the agreement involves the transfer of territorial sovereignty.[273] As explained by Alvarez-Jimenez, agreements that allocate areas for administrative purposes cannot be assumed to delimit sovereignty. Therefore, such agreements do not qualify as boundary agreements.[274] Maritime boundaries that delimit sovereign rights arguably allocate areas for administrative purposes and similarly, should not be qualified as boundary agreements. Boundaries to the territorial sea delimit territorial rights and full sovereignty over the seabed and the superjacent waters and air column.[275] However, all other maritime boundaries must be categorized as non-territorial boundaries since they do not demarcate a State's territory and only delimit sovereign rights for specific purposes, that is, limited functional powers as opposed to full sovereignty. The ICJ confirmed this distinction in the *Black Sea* case, noting that agreements on 'State borders' cannot easily be understood as referring to 'areas beyond territory, including territorial seas'.[276] Thus, the Court concluded that an agreement delimiting the State borders of Romania and Ukraine, established a territorial boundary and not a boundary to the exclusive economic zone or continental shelf.[277]

5.3.6 *Not a Change Resulting from a Breach of the Party Invoking It*

VCLT article 62(2)(b) provides that a fundamental change of circumstances cannot be invoked as grounds for terminating a treaty if it 'is the result of a breach by the party invoking it either of an obligation under the treaty or of any other international obligation owed to any other party to the treaty'. This requirement is quite clear and, therefore, easily interpreted: States cannot be freed from contractual obligations by violating any international obligations owed to other parties to the treaty. This does not have to be a material breach, as referred to in VCLT article 60(3).[278]

Earlier versions of the provision used different terminology and were more explicit than VCLT article 62(2)(b). For example, under the draft article from 1957, a fundamental change could not be used to justify termination of a treaty when the change was 'caused, brought about, or directly or proximately contributed to, by the act or omission of the party invoking it'.[279] Similarly, the draft article from 1963 provided that the fundamental change could not have been 'caused, or substantially contributed to, by the acts or omissions of the party invoking it'.[280] No

273 Alberto Alvarez-Jimenez, 'Boundary Agreements in the International Court of Justice's Case Law, 2000–2010' (2012) 23 (2) EJIL, 495, 500–501, referring to *Indonesia/Malaysia* (n 271) and *Malaysia/Singapore* (n 272).

274 Ibid.

275 *Maritime Delimitation and Territorial Questions between Qatar and Bahrain* (*Qatar* v. *Bahrain*) (Merits) [2001] ICJ Rep 40, paras 173–174.

276 *Maritime Delimitation in the Black Sea* (*Romania* v. *Ukraine*) (Judgment) [2009] ICJ Rep 61, para 64.

277 Ibid., para 76.

278 Thomas Giegerich (n 53) 1094.

279 UN Doc A/CN.4/107 (n 18) 32–33.

280 Ibid., 33.

conscious decision was made to limit the scope of this provision so even though VCLT article 62(2)(b) is less detailed than earlier draft versions, it can be understood as covering both acts and omissions, as well as a substantial contribution to a breach that leads to a fundamental change. However, the breach must be attributable to the party invoking the breach, under article 2 of the ILC Draft Articles on State Responsibility for Internationally Wrongful Acts.[281]

Environmental changes, such as sea level rise, coastal erosion, volcanic and seismic activity, are generally not considered to be consequences of the conduct of individual States. The emergence of the Anthropocene and accelerated climate change has been attributed to greenhouse gas emissions and human impact on the Earth and, in that regard, some States have certainly been larger contributors than others. Even so, fundamental changes to the natural environment can generally not be attributed to single States or traced back to violations of public international law. Therefore, such changes should not be excluded as fundamental changes justifying termination under VCLT article 62, on the grounds that they are attributable to a contracting State as per VCLT article 62(2)(b).

5.3.7 *Procedural Requirements*

VCLT article 62 does not provide for the right of unilateral denunciation of a treaty even if all requirements put forth in the article are met. Rather, it gives a State the right to invoke the rebus sic stantibus principle before a court or a tribunal, requiring the relevant, independent organ to determine whether the conditions allow for termination or withdrawal from the treaty.[282] However, pending such a decision, a State invoking VCLT article 62 may suspend the operation of the treaty, as per VCLT article 62(3).[283] The article does not explicitly provide for the modification or revision of a treaty but States are free to negotiate such changes and negotiations can be triggered by the threat of termination.[284]

VCLT article 62 is subject to the procedural requirements of VCLT articles 65–67.[285] VCLT article 65 provides that a State invoking a fundamental change of circumstances to justify termination, suspension or withdrawal from a treaty shall notify other parties. 'The notification shall indicate the measure proposed to be taken with respect to the treaty and the reasons therefor.'[286] This notification must be in writing and 'signed by the Head of State, Head of Government or Minister for

281 Thomas Giegerich (n 53) 1094.

282 Herbert Briggs, 'Unilateral Denunciation of Treaties: The Vienna Convention and the International Court of Justice' (1974) 68 (1) American Journal of International Law 51, 66.

283 UN Doc A/CN.4/107 (n 18) 33.

284 See Thomas Giegerich (n 53) 1070.

285 ILC, 'Report of the International Law Commission on the Work of Its Eighteenth Session' (4 May–19 July 1966) UN Doc A/CN.4/SER.A/1966/Add. 1, 187–274.

286 VCLT article 65(1).

Foreign Affairs' or a representative who can produce full powers.[287] If opposing States raise no objections to said notification within three months, or less 'in cases of special urgency', the State seeking termination, withdrawal from or suspension of a treaty may carry out the proposed measure.[288] If objections are raised within the time frame determined in accordance with VCLT article 65(2), the States must 'seek a solution through the means indicated in Article 33 of the Charter of the United Nations'.[289] Those means are a solution by negotiation, enquiry, mediation, conciliation, arbitration, judicial settlement, resort to regional agencies or arrangements or other peaceful means of their own choice. Furthermore, a treaty cannot be terminated unless the State seeking termination, based on changed circumstances, has first sought consultation and negotiations in good faith.[290] Such consultations should be conducted by providing relevant information in a timely manner with sincere effort to balance the interests of opposing States.[291] Thus, a State may not withdraw from, or terminate a treaty, unless it has sought to engage in good faith negotiations or given the opposing party at least three months to react to the invocation of VCLT article 62.

5.4 VCLT ARTICLE 62 AND MARITIME BOUNDARIES

The co-chairs of the ILC's study group on sea level rise submit the First Issues Paper, in its preliminary paper, that VCLT article 62(2)(a) covers all maritime boundaries.[292] This may be a strong indicator of how the article should be interpreted. Nonetheless, the statement does not seem to rest on a thorough analysis. The conclusion is arrived at after short references to the *Aegean Sea Continental Shelf* judgment, the *Bangladesh* v. *India* award and a general desire for stability.[293] In accordance with the above analysis, this book proceeds by drawing a distinction between territorial and non-territorial maritime boundaries. First, invocation of the principle is considered in the context of non-territorial maritime boundaries and alternative arrangements. Second, the potential consequences for territorial maritime boundaries are considered. Section 5.4.2 concludes that territorial maritime boundaries are exempt from VCLT article 62 but discusses other rules potentially affecting the enforceability of such boundaries.

287 VCLT article 67.
288 VCLT article 65(2).
289 VCLT article 65(3).
290 Mark Villiger (n 190) 767.
291 See *Chagos Marine Protected Area (Mauritius* v. *United Kingdom)* (2015) XXXI RIAA 359, para 528.
292 UN Doc A/CN.4/740 (n 8) para 119.
293 Ibid., paras 118, 120–121.

5.4.1 *Treaties Establishing Non-Territorial Maritime Boundaries or Alternative Arrangements*

The following section applies the test enshrined in VCLT article 62(2)(a) to non-territorial maritime boundaries. Non-territorial maritime boundaries are arguably not all excluded from application of VCLT article 62 under the boundary exception. That finding leads to an analysis of other requirements of VCLT article 62 in the context of non-territorial maritime boundaries and climate change.

5.4.1.1 The Boundary Exception

Treaties that do not establish boundaries are obviously not subject to the boundary exception. The ICJ indicated in *Indonesia/Malaysia* that an agreement concerning administration on the disputed territory did not constitute a boundary agreement as it 'did not involve a transfer of territorial sovereignty'.[294] Furthermore, treaties delimiting maritime entitlements can establish territorial status without constructing boundaries.[295] Administrative agreements involve quota allocation, joint development and MPAs and such treaties are unequivocally susceptible to the effects of VCLT article 62. In fact, the ILC recently highlighted that the loss of maritime entitlements calls into question the continuation of various agreements relating to each maritime zone. For example, the loss of exclusive economic zone or continental shelf rights can affect agreements relating to fisheries, wind farms and mineral resources.[296]

Purcell submits that the term 'boundary' is used, in the law of the sea context, to refer to a line that separates two States.[297] However, the criteria laid out in Section 5.3.5 suggests that a 'boundary' within the meaning of VCLT article, is a line that separates the *territory* of two States.[298] Therefore, non-territorial maritime boundaries might not be considered 'boundaries' in the formal sense – even if some maritime boundary agreements employ the term.[299] Conversely, maritime boundaries might be 'true boundaries' without qualifying as boundaries in the context of VCLT article 62(2)(a).[300] At any rate, the terminology should not be decisive in the categorization of treaties because different expressions may be used to refer to the same legal

294 *Indonesia/Malaysia* (n 271) para 118.

295 Cissé Yacouba and Donald McRae (n 10) 3293.

296 UN Doc A/CN.4/740 (n 8) para 190.

297 Kate Purcell, *Geographical Change and the Law of the Sea* (Oxford University Press, 2019) 9, referring to *Delimitation of the maritime boundary between Guinea and Guinea-Bissau (Guinea/Guinea-Bissau)* (1985) XIX RIAA 149, 277.

298 See also Alberto Alvarez-Jimenez 'Boundary Agreements in the International Court of Justice's Case Law, 2000–2010' (2012) 23 (2) EJIL, 495.

299 See, for example, Agreement between Poland and Sweden concerning the delimitation of the continental shelf and fishing zones (adopted 10 February 1989, entered into force 30 June 1989) 1590 UNTS 361, article 1; Agreement between France and Belgium relating to the delimitation of the territorial sea (adopted 8 October 1990, entered into force 7 April 1993) 1728 UNTS 273, article 1.

300 UN Doc A/CN.4/SER.A/1982/Add.1 (n 214) 60–61. See also Thomas Giegerich (n 53) 1093.

concept[301] and the same expression may be used to refer to different legal concepts. The terms 'limits' and 'lines of delimitation' may be more appropriate for maritime boundaries[302] and some maritime boundary agreements refer to 'sea frontiers' or 'maritime frontiers'.[303] Johnston and Valencia have commented on the stability and revision of maritime boundaries and also made a distinction based on their territorial nature. They explain that 'co-operative arrangements, if not linear settlements, must be subject to review and revision, by agreement between the parties', even if the same does not apply to territorial maritime boundaries.[304]

As explained in Section 5.3.5, VCLT article 62(2)(a) applies to boundaries delimiting territorial sovereignty because the need for stable boundaries relates to sovereignty and territorial integrity. The exclusive economic/fisheries zone and continental shelf differ from the territorial sea in that they are zones of partial jurisdiction, limited to functional powers over clearly defined resources. They do not reflect the established territorial concepts of full sovereignty typical for *terra firma*[305] and may, therefore, be categorized as non-territorial boundaries. Still, not all boundary agreements can be neatly categorized as establishing either territorial or non-territorial boundaries. Treaties can delimit territorial boundaries as well as non-territorial boundaries and they can entail provisions unrelated to the construction of boundaries. It may, in some instances, be possible to separate provisions from a treaty and terminate only those that are affected by the fundamental change and not establishing territorial boundaries under VCLT article 44(2) and (3).[306] However, the principle of separability does not allow for termination of isolated provisions if the establishment of a territorial boundary forms an integral part of the treaty.[307] Thus, treaties that establish territorial boundaries may be excluded from termination under VCLT article 62(2)(a) in their entirety, even if they govern other issues as well, such as environmental protection, allocation of resources and delimitation of non-territorial boundaries.

One category of maritime boundaries is particularly difficult to categorize as permanent or subject to change and that concerns the continental shelf. There

301 *Aegean Sea Continental Shelf* (n 228) para 72.

302 Yoshifumi Tanaka, *Predictability and Flexibility in the Law of Maritime Delimitation* (Bloomsbury Publishing, 2006) 10 referring to Lucius Caflisch, 'The Delimitation of Marine Spaces between States with Opposite and Adjacent Coasts' in René-Jean Dupuy and Daniel Vignes (eds), *A Handbook on the New Law of the Sea, volume 2* (Martinus Nijhoff, 1991) 426 and *Delimitation of the Maritime Boundary in the Gulf of Maine Area (Canada/United States)* (Judgment) [1984] ICJ Rep 246, para 19.

303 See, for example, Agreement between the Royal Norwegian Government and the Government of the Union of Soviet Socialist Republics concerning the sea frontier between Norway and the USSR in the Varangerfjord (adopted 15 February 1957, entered into force 24 April 1957) 312 UNTS 289; Treaty concerning maritime delimitation between the Republic of Colombia and the Republic of Honduras (adopted 2 August 1986, entered into force 20 December 1999) 2093 UNTS 291.

304 Douglas Johnston and Mark Valencia, *Pacific Ocean Boundary Problems: Status and Solutions* (Martinus Nijhoff, 1991) 17.

305 Thomas Cottier, *Equitable Principles of Maritime Boundary Delimitation: The Quest for Distributive Justice in International Law* (Cambridge University Press, 2015) 67.

306 See Athanassios Vamvoukos (n 27) 205.

307 Thomas Giegerich (n 53) 1093.

should be no ambiguity that the continental shelf does not delimit territorial sovereignty and yet, it affords entitlements to submerged land territory and can be permanently described under certain circumstances. Treaties establishing continental shelf boundaries can be used as a basis for final and binding continental shelf delineation.[308] Therefore, the outer limits of the continental shelf may remain permanent and opposable to other States, even if a treaty, establishing the corresponding boundary, is terminated.

According to the arbitral tribunal of *Bangladesh* v. *India*, one of the principal objectives of continental shelf delimitation is the achievement of stability and finality because the exploration and exploitation of the continental shelf calls for 'important investments and the construction of off-shore installations'.[309] The tribunal further noted that stable continental shelf boundaries were necessary for 'development and investment' and that the very purpose of delimitation was to acquire such stability.[310] This economically motivated need for stability in relation to the continental shelf is adequately addressed by UNCLOS articles 76(8) and 76(9) (at least if the latter applies to all continental shelf limits, at and beyond 200 nm from baselines). Even if maritime boundaries are set aside, these limits will endure. There is no need to categorically exclude continental shelf boundaries from termination under VCLT article 62 if the outer limits to all continental shelf limits are permanently described. At any rate, the purpose of maritime boundary agreements cannot affect the general interpretation of VCLT article 62(2)(a) since it is the object and purpose of the VCLT that is relevant when interpreting that particular provision in accordance with VCLT article 31.

Having concluded that treaties establishing maritime boundaries and alternative arrangements beyond the territorial sea are not categorically excluded from termination under VCLT article 62(2)(a), the focus will be shifted to the general requirements of VCLT article 62. As explained in Chapters 1 and 2, coastal geography is expected to undergo significant changes in coming decades and this can have catastrophic effects on maritime entitlements worldwide. Such changes cannot justify the invocation of VCLT article 62 (or rebus sic stantibus) unless they were unforeseen at the conclusion of the treaty subject to termination; they affect the essential basis of the treaty and; alter the extent of ongoing obligations.

5.4.1.2 General Requirements of VCLT Article 62

First, it is necessary to identify the essential basis of treaties establishing non-territorial maritime boundaries. To justify termination of such treaties, a fundamental change must affect the circumstances that shaped treaty provisions

[308] Mexico used the Gulf of Mexico boundary between Mexico and the United States for its submission to the CLCS.

[309] *Bay of Bengal Maritime Boundary Arbitration (Bangladesh* v. *India)* (2014) 167 ILR 1, paras 216 and 218.

[310] Ibid.

and led to the conclusion of the treaty.[311] Lisztwan has noted that maritime boundary treaties generally contain no explicit reference to the essential basis or confirmation of the significance attached to relevant coastlines. This can make it difficult to prove that a change to coastal geography affects a maritime boundary's essential basis.[312] Still, it was made abundantly clear, in Chapters 2 and 3, that maritime entitlements are generated by land territory and that the delimitation of boundaries is based, primarily, on coastal geography. The fundamental obligation, in delimiting exclusive economic zone and continental shelf boundaries, is to achieve an equitable solution.[313] Therefore, it might be argued that the essential basis of such boundary agreements is that they delimit maritime entitlements in an equitable manner and it depends on the circumstances surrounding each treaty what the States deemed to be equitable at the time of its conclusion. The location of relevant coastlines is generally a determining factor when States accept to be bound by treaties establishing maritime boundaries and essential to their perception of an equitable boundary. However, circumstances relating to fisheries and ecosystems can also form an essential basis when States take untraditional approaches to maritime boundary delimitation, such as those discussed in Chapter 4.

Changes to the essential basis of a maritime boundary treaty have to be fundamental to justify invocation of VCLT article 62. This requirement is meant to ensure that a change, justifying termination of a treaty, is severe but that will generally be the case if a change affects the essential basis of the treaty and radically transforms obligations. Thus, it may be presumed that changes in the extent of territory, availability of natural resources or capacity to harvest fish can qualify as fundamental changes within VCLT article 62.[314] Environmental changes, such as drying up of a river or the silting up of a harbour, have been referred to as examples of fundamental changes that would justify termination if other conditions of article 62 were met.[315] The geographical location of a river can form an essential basis of a treaty and the fluctuation of a river channel can drastically change the rights and obligations of States as they lose or gain acres of land.[316] The drafting history also confirms that changes to the location of natural phenomena, such as the re-location of a river thalweg, can potentially qualify as fundamental changes. In fact, the Canadian Government suggested that boundary treaties should not be excluded from termination where the treaty was based on natural features that were relocated by virtue of such occurrences.[317] However, Special Rapporteur Waldock rejected this proposal and submitted that natural occurrences, altering the location of geographical

311 Mark Villiger (n 190) 774.
312 Julia Lisztwan, 'Stability of Maritime Boundary Agreements' (2012) 37 Yale Journal of International Law 191.
313 UNCLOS articles 74(1) and 83(1).
314 Thomas Giegerich (n 53) 1081.
315 Jeremy Waldron (n 19) 170.
316 UN Doc A/CN.4/183 and Add.1–4 (n 108) 39.
317 Ibid., 39.

features, might not lead to termination of boundary treaties but instead, affect the interpretation of treaties based on such features.[318]

Lisztwan submits that this demonstrates a conscious decision to exclude termination of boundary agreements on the basis of changes affecting the geographical features they depend upon. She further remarks that State representatives must have been aware that such features could undergo changes and that boundary agreements could be formulated and interpreted in such a way that boundaries could fluctuate in accordance with the natural phenomena they were based upon.[319] Indeed, fluctuating boundaries may be the alternative to termination of boundary treaties and this may suggest that boundary treaties are meant to be re-interpreted to reflect relevant natural occurrences. Still, States are not always content with fluctuating international borders (as demonstrated by the Chamizal dispute between the United States and Mexico) and invocation of VCLT article 62 remains available to treaties establishing non-territorial maritime boundaries. After all, changes affecting the location of natural phenomena are not categorically excluded from qualifying as fundamental changes. On the contrary, this part of the drafting history suggests that such changes even have an effect on treaties establishing territorial boundaries.

A fundamental change affecting a treaty's essential basis must also radically transform ongoing obligations to justify invocation of VCLT article 62. The change must affect entitlements to extensive maritime areas or significantly affect circumstances concerning the management of essential ecosystems. An obligation is transformed when it is made more onerous or 'the value to be gained by further performance is diminished'.[320] The reference to obligations still to be performed highlights that VCLT article 62 is not applicable to treaties that have been fully executed. There must be a requirement of continuing performance or certain obligations that have not been performed.[321] Obligations under a maritime boundary agreement certainly entail ongoing obligations and the 'value to be gained by further performance' is affected when there is considerable divergence between a State's entitlements under UNCLOS and rights afforded by the agreement.

Sea level rise and coastal erosion can have a drastic impact on maritime entitlements. 'Overall, third States stand to benefit from these changes, but at the expense of the coastal State.'[322] Archipelagic States are seriously vulnerable as they can lose the right to rely on archipelagic baselines.[323] However, sea level rise and coastal erosion can cause significant reduction of maritime entitlements for all coastal States. As explained by Soons, sea level rise of half a metre can move baselines at

318 Ibid., 44.
319 See Julia Lisztwan (n 312) 190.
320 Thomas Giegerich (n 53) 1089, referring to UN Doc A/CN.4/107 (n 18) 60, para 151.
321 UN Doc A/CN.4/740 (n 8) 43.
322 Ibid., para 190(g).
323 Ibid., paras 187–188.

gently shelving coasts inland by tens of kilometres.[324] Where islands are completely submerged, the consequences can be a decrease in the area of territorial sea by approximately 1,500 square kilometres and a decrease in the area of exclusive economic zone by up to 431,000 square kilometres.[325] These changes can affect the capacity to maintain various maritime limits and archipelagic status and can even threaten the existence of coastal States. Indeed, these changes can 'redraw the physical geographical reality of the world, radically altering coastlines, creating new ocean areas, and potentially inundating entire nation states.'[326] Hence, there can be no doubt that changes to coastal geography can be fundamental in character and that they can radically transform the extent of obligations still to be performed under treaties delimiting non-territorial maritime zones.

Fundamental changes cannot be invoked as grounds for terminating treaties if they are foreseen by States at the conclusion of the treaty. The changes cannot be anticipated by the treaty in any way.[327] Foreseeable environmental changes are generally not referred to in treaties establishing maritime boundaries, but there are exceptions.[328] States have even referred to the future emergence of new volcanic islands in their maritime boundary agreements.[329] A reference to such changes, by express or implied terms, prevents invocation of VCLT article 62.[330] Therefore, incorporation of foreseeable changes into delimitation agreements may promote legal stability.

It may prove impossible for States, international courts and tribunals to account for all future changes to coastal geography when delimiting maritime boundaries. Many maritime boundaries were delimited long before the effects of climate change were foreseeable. Moreover, even if certain changes have now become highly predictable, other changes take place with very little notice and have unpredictable consequences – for example, earthquakes and volcanic eruptions. The cause for change can also be unnatural and completely unforeseeable to the impacted State. For example, coastal features can suddenly become shooting targets for foreign navies (as was the case with the Icelandic Geirfugladrangur).[331]

324 Alfred Soons, 'The Effects of Sea Level Rise on Baselines and Outer Limits of Maritime Zones' in Tomas Heidar (ed) *New Knowledge and Changing Circumstances in the Law of the Sea* (Brill Nijhoff, 2020) 364.

325 Ibid., 366.

326 Rosemary Rayfuse, 'W(h)ither Tuvalu? International Law and Disappearing States' (2009) 9 University of New South Wales Faculty of Law Research Series 2.

327 UN Doc A/CN.4/107 (n 18) 33.

328 See, for example, Treaty between Romania and Ukraine on the Romanian-Ukrainian State border regime, collaboration and mutual assistance on border matters (adopted 17 June 2003, entered into force 27 May 2004) 2277 UNTS 3.

329 See Agreement between the Socialist Republic of the Union of Burma and the Republic of India on the Delimitation of the Maritime Boundary in the Andaman Sea, in the Coco Channel and in the Bay of Bengal (adopted 23 Dec 1986, entered into force 14 September 1987) 27 ILM 1144.

330 UN Doc A/CN.4/107 (n 18) 33.

331 British and American soldiers used the Icelandic rock, Geirfugladrangur, as a shooting target around 1940, contributing to its dissolution. See Morgunblaðið 'Geirfugladrangur telst enn flæðisker' (2012) available at: www.ruv.is/frett/drangurinn-sem-er-bara-blindsker accessed 16 January 2021.

In particular, the consequences of climate change can be unforeseeable as these are dependent on many factors and predictions regularly change. States can rely on the IPCC assessment reports, which produce the most reliable data predicting climate-related changes on the marine environment.[332] These reports cannot predict the consequences of all climate-related changes for coastlines or individual features. In particular, the consequences of extreme weather events are difficult to predict. The arbitral tribunal in *Bangladesh* v. *India* actually went as far as calling 'all predictions concerning the amount of coastal erosion or accretion unpredictable'.[333] This is of course debatable and States can also seek to exclude environmental changes in general terms, for example, by referencing 'objective modifications due to natural phenomena'.[334]

VCLT article 62 seems to have limited practical relevance.[335] The reluctance of courts and tribunals in employing the principle makes the termination of non-territorial boundaries, on these grounds, unlikely.[336] Still, unless VCLT article 62 has become a dead letter, it can be invoked to terminate, suspend or withdraw from treaties establishing non-territorial maritime boundaries when all the necessary requirements are satisfied. The principle may also incite mutual revision of treaties establishing such boundaries or affect their interpretation. VCLT article 62 can serve as 'a lever to induce a spirit of compromise in the other party'[337] and enable termination as a last result in the most extreme cases.[338] After all, the 'natural remedy (and the one best compatible with the rule of pacta sunt servanda) would be a revision of the treaty so as to adapt it to the new circumstances'.[339]

5.4.2 *Treaties Establishing Territorial Maritime Boundaries*

Treaties delimiting territory, or territorial maritime zones, are typically not subject to revision. States can still renegotiate such treaties.[340] A fundamental change of circumstances cannot justify termination, suspension or withdrawal from a territorial maritime boundary treaty under VCLT article 62. This excludes direct application of VCLT article 62 but does not necessarily mean that all territorial maritime boundaries are fixed in place to the end of time. Indeed, Special Rapporteur Waldock explained that VCLT article 62(2)(a) did not indicate that

332 Navraj Ghaleigh, 'Science and Climate Change Law – the Role of the IPCC in International Decision-making' in Cinnamon Carlarne, Kevin Gray and Richard Tarasofsky (eds) *The Oxford Handbook of International Climate Change Law* (Oxford University Press, 2016) 61.
333 *Bangladesh* v. *India* (n 309) para 399.
334 Treaty between Romania and Ukraine (n 328).
335 See Thomas Giegerich (n 53) 1070.
336 Julia Lisztwan (n 312) 184.
337 See UN Doc A/6309/Rev.1 (n 52) 258, para 6.
338 Thomas Giegerich (n 53) 1070 referring to Georg Dahm, Jost Delbrück and Rüdiger Wolfrum (n 180) 753.
339 Thomas Giegerich (n 53) 1070.
340 Douglas Johnston and Mark Valencia (n 304) 17.

boundaries should be immutable. Rather that termination of boundary treaties should be achieved through other means than the application of VCLT article 62.[341] Some of these alternative means are addressed later.

First, it should be noted that the situation may arise where maritime boundaries are inviolable but stipulations concerning fishing rights, environmental protection, joint development zones and so on, are subject to termination under VCLT article 62. Waldock specifically warned against this type of situation where States could escape obligations concluded on the basis of a boundary agreement while the boundary remained stable.[342] This potentially unjust situation will only arise if the stipulations are found in separate treaties or if the principle of separability allows for termination of individual provisions, that is, if the entire agreement is not characterized as a boundary treaty. Therefore, this supports the proposal presented in Chapter 4 concerning the incorporation of environmental considerations into the delimitation process and combining the provisions in a single instrument. If such an instrument qualifies as a treaty establishing a boundary, subject to VCLT article 62(2)(a), then the entire treaty should be exempt from termination.

As previously discussed, fundamental changes can lead to fluctuating boundaries or incite revision of territorial boundaries. States can always negotiate new boundaries and revision can affect not only the geographic location of maritime boundaries but also their nature and function.[343] In fact, maritime boundary treaties commonly contain provisions governing the settlement of disputes. According to Anderson, '[i]t would require some unusual reason [. . .] to prompt the negotiators to include in the terms of a boundary treaty a provision for its denunciation or termination.'[344] However, such provisions exist in maritime boundary treaties and they would be unnecessary if the treaties were meant to remain permanent regardless of subsequent developments.[345] Judicial decisions can also be reviewed if new facts come to light;[346] this general rule has no caveat relating to boundaries.

Whether agreed upon or by judicial decision, maritime boundaries do not create obligations for third parties. Treaties cannot create obligations for States without their consent[347] and decisions of the ICJ are only binding between the parties and in respect of each particular case.[348] The ICJ has noted that 'in continental shelf delimitations, an agreement between the parties which is perfectly valid and binding on the treaty level may, when the relations between the parties and a third State are taken into consideration, prove to be contrary to the rules of international law

341 UN Doc A/CONF.39/11 (n 5) 381.

342 See Section 5.2.2.2.

343 See Douglas Johnston and Mark Valencia (n 304) 17.

344 See David Anderson (n 248) 132–133.

345 Cissé Yacouba and Donald McRae (n 10) 3300. See also DOALOS, *Handbook on the Delimitation of Maritime Boundaries* (UN, 2000) para 308.

346 Andreas Kulick (n 3) 74.

347 VCLT article 34.

348 Article 59 of the ICJ Statute.

governing the continental shelf'.[349] Thus, maritime boundaries can be contested by third States if their rights are violated.[350] Even if negotiating States take full account of such rights at the time of delimitation, subsequent changes may affect the enforceability of settled maritime boundaries if circumstances change and new rights emerge for third States.[351] Indeed, some maritime boundary agreements specify that the parties will negotiate with third States in the future concerning potentially overlapping entitlements.[352]

The ICJ has dealt specifically with maritime boundaries and their effects on third States. It confirmed, in the *North Sea Continental Shelf* cases, that pre-existing boundary agreements would not be binding *erga omnes* without a clear legal basis.[353] The decision concerned an agreement establishing a continental shelf boundary between Denmark and the Netherlands and potential implications for the German continental shelf. Germany submitted that the boundary treaty was res inter alios acta and that it had no bearing on the delimitation of Germany's continental shelf.[354] The alleged legal basis for the delimitation agreement between Denmark and the Netherlands was the customary equidistance-special circumstances rule[355] but the States admitted that it would not be binding on Germany if it could show special circumstances justifying departure from the equidistance line.[356] Thus, even the parties to this agreement agreed that it could not have the effect of depriving a third State of its lawful claim to an area. This means that delimitations, based on UNCLOS article 74, 83 or customary international law, may become unenforceable against third States if baselines recede and competing claims emerge.

'It is [...] not uncommon in maritime boundary agreements for the parties to agree that they will negotiate with third parties in the future on potential overlapping jurisdiction.'[357] Such provisions are no prerequisite and maritime boundaries can always be contested by third States if their rights are infringed[358] but this arguably demonstrates an awareness of the effects of the pacta tertiis and res inter alios acta principles. Disputes concerning newly generated entitlements may be subject to the compulsory dispute settlement of UNCLOS Part XV.[359] This is true even if boundaries have previously been constructed by courts and tribunals because res judicata only prevents the revision of boundaries insofar as the same relief is sought on the grounds advanced in previous proceedings between the same

349 *Burkina Faso/Republic of Mali* (n 1) para 47.
350 Cissé Yacouba and Donald McRae (n 10) 3297.
351 See Section 2.4.
352 Cissé Yacouba and Donald McRae (n 10) 3298.
353 See *North Sea Continental Shelf (Federal Republic of Germany/Netherlands) (Federal Republic of Germany/Denmark)* (Judgment) [1969] ICJ Rep 3, paras 35–36.
354 Ibid., para 9.
355 Ibid., para 37.
356 Ibid., para 14.
357 Cissé Yacouba and Donald McRae (n 10) 3298.
358 Ibid., 3297.
359 Unless they are excluded under UNCLOS article 298(1)(a)(i).

parties.[360] Furthermore, a judicial decision might be revised in light of new facts or subsequent developments[361] and the opposability of maritime boundaries could be affected by the extinction of a party (submergence of an island State), triggering impossibility of performance.[362]

The case of the fluctuating territorial boundary along the Rio Grande was thoroughly discussed in Section 3.4.4. It demonstrates how territorial boundaries may change when affected by natural occurrences and is a good example of the need that arises for negotiating new treaties and resorting to judicial settlement when natural phenomena that forms an essential basis of a boundary undergoes significant changes. Changes in the Rio Grande incited many disputes, even after a concrete wall was built to fix the river in place. Fundamental changes, such as those affecting the Rio Grande, cannot be ignored. They cannot lead to termination, suspension or withdrawal from treaties establishing territorial boundaries but the disputes still find their course.

Members of the ILC seem to have been aware of the effect VCLT article 62 might have on boundaries based on natural phenomena when discussing draft article 11 of the Vienna Convention on Succession of States in respect of Treaties in 1972. The article, as adopted in 1978, provides that boundaries established by treaties will not be affected by State succession. Yet Kearney, chairman of the 1194th meeting of the Commission, supported the notion to refer to boundary settlements rather than boundaries. Explaining his position, Kearney explicitly referred to the boundary between the United States and Mexico in the Rio Grande and said that it was an uncertain boundary because of changes in the river's location. He indicated that safeguarding the boundary itself might not provide the coveted stability of international boundaries but the Special Rapporteur and other members of the ILC did not respond to his proposal, which was ultimately rejected.[363] Indeed, the Rio Grande disputes, and the analysis of this chapter, demonstrate that treaties establishing territorial boundaries will generally remain opposable following a fundamental change of circumstances while their location changes. Thus, it is not geographic stability but, rather, legal stability that is guaranteed by VCLT article 62(2)(a).

5.5 SUMMARY

International courts and tribunals have not definitively decided whether the term 'boundary' encompasses all maritime boundaries. The ICJ stated, in the *Aegean Sea* case, that continental shelf boundaries fall within the scope of VCLT article 62(2)(a). However, the Court's *obiter dictum* was arguably premised on the fact that the

360 Andreas Kulick (n 3) 74.
361 See article 61 of the Statute of the ICJ.
362 UN Doc A/CN.4/156 and Add.1–3 (n 27) 78
363 ILC, 'Summary Records of the Twenty-Fourth Session' (2 May–7 July 1972) UN Doc A/CN.4/SER.A/1972, 259.

continental margin is less susceptible to change than other maritime zones, and the fact that investments in the continental shelf require stability. This stability is now ensured with UNCLOS article 76(8) and (9), but does not apply to other maritime zones.

The question, whether the term 'boundary' in VCLT article 62(2)(a) encompasses maritime boundaries, has been disputed by scholars but even those who argue that maritime boundaries are generally exempt from the application of rebus sic stantibus are unsure when it comes to the complete submergence of islands. Such a scenario might justify invocation of principles such as res inter alios acta, impossibility of performance and rebus sic stantibus, and they could apply in tandem. In fact, the travaux préparatoires of VCLT and the 1986 Vienna Convention suggest that VCLT article 62(2)(a) only excludes boundaries delimiting the territory of a State.

The object and purpose of the boundary exception is rooted in the idea that boundaries are inviolable. That stems from the principle of territorial integrity and lack of competence for third States to interfere with territorial boundaries. However, boundaries outside the territorial sea do not delimit territorial sovereignty and maritime boundaries are only opposable to other States insofar as they delimit areas that third States have no entitlement to. This indicates that the boundary exception of VCLT article 62(2)(a) only extends to territorial boundaries, which means that a fundamental change to the essential basis of a treaty may be invoked to justify termination of non-territorial maritime boundaries. Furthermore, a fundamental change, affecting the natural phenomena that territorial boundaries are based upon, can alter the interpretation and application of such treaties. Thus, territorial boundaries can also be affected by environmental changes, even if the treaties remain enforceable.

The strict requirements attached to VCLT article 62 may only be satisfied on very rare occasions. Nonetheless, the principle can induce willingness to compromise and renegotiate. In fact, it has been argued that the principle involves an obligation to renegotiate rather than a right of termination. It certainly follows the spirit of pacta sunt servanda for States to mutually revise or reinterpret their treaties to adapt to fundamental changes. Still, it may seriously strain international relations if States are dependent on each other's willingness to renegotiate and rebus sic stantibus is a vital escape clause. VCLT article 62 was meant to promote peace and stability and prevent friction in international relations. Its application should enable mutual revision of outdated and inequitable maritime boundaries. If interpreted broadly, the boundary exception may hamper the peaceful settlement of such disputes and drive States to take action outside the law.

Conclusion

AMBULATORY MARITIME LIMITS

All baselines are ambulatory de lege lata. So too are the outer limits measured from baselines, with the exception of permanently described continental shelf limits. Straight baselines drawn under UNCLOS article 7(2) along highly unstable coastlines enjoy a distinct level of stability, but they must also be adjusted when they depart, to an appreciable extent, from the general configuration of the coastline, or the internal waters are no longer closely linked to the land domain. Consequently, the stability provided under UNCLOS article 7(2) is conditional, which means that all baselines are ambulatory and subject to ongoing adherence to UNCLOS. Maritime zones generally have no legal existence without the coastal front and they fluctuate with ambulatory baselines. Outer limits of the continental shelf can be permanently fixed, but only if the requirements of UNCLOS articles 76(8) and 76(9) are satisfied.

The growing instability of maritime entitlements, caused by climate-related changes, has raised concerns regarding increased international conflicts and wasted resources. Indeed, challenges to outdated maritime limits may increase as coastal geography changes more drastically and the resources poured into artificial conservation may be better spent on climate change mitigation. Proposals have been put forth to permanently fix all maritime limits in order to minimize the effects of climate change and promote stability in the distribution of maritime entitlements. However, a new rule, permanently fixing the location of baselines and/or zonal limits, would call for a revision of UNCLOS, an implementing agreement or uniform subsequent practice leading to the development of new customary rules or revised interpretation of existing rules. The most viable option to stabilize maritime limits is to change the interpretation of relevant UNCLOS provisions, through subsequent practice, so as to allow coastal States to permanently describe their limits to the UNSG. State practice is still, at the time of writing, far from being uniform.

As an alternative solution, States can maintain their most important entitlements through artificial conservation of the coastline. This is costly but conforms to the applicable international law. Low-lying developing States will certainly need assistance in addressing the threats ahead, but the freezing of maritime limits offers no protection against depletion of oceanic resources and destruction of human habitation or freshwater supply. The willingness to help threatened States by securing their maritime entitlements in a time of need is not a compelling argument for changing the law of the sea because more general coping strategies are needed. Stability of the legal order of the oceans should not be sacrificed since it only addresses one aspect of a much bigger problem.

EQUITABLE DELIMITATION OF FLUCTUATING MARITIME ENTITLEMENTS

Once agreed upon, maritime boundaries enjoy a distinct level of stability because they are safeguarded by the pacta sunt servanda principle and res judicata, in the case of judicially decided maritime boundaries. This creates a discrepancy between maritime limits and maritime boundaries because maritime limits fluctuate to continuously adhere to the basis for title while boundaries generally do not. Maritime boundaries are delimited by reference to coastal geography and, consequently, there is a clear link between the boundary and relevant coastlines. However, this link is broken when coastlines, and maritime limits, fluctuate and related boundaries remain in place.

UNCLOS articles 74 and 83 provide that maritime boundaries must represent equitable solutions. Equity enables law to adapt to changed circumstances and respond to new challenges, such as those arising from climate change. Maritime boundaries can be delimited in a way that makes them less dependent on unstable base points and more continuously equitable. Selection of base points and adjustment of provisional boundary lines can take account of coastal instability and imminent coastal changes to strengthen the link between coastal geography and maritime boundaries. The angle-bisector method is also appropriate for unstable coastlines as it reflects the general direction of the coast. Furthermore, maritime boundaries can be based on fluctuating phenomena such as baselines or median lines, as opposed to fixed coordinates, to ensure continued correlation between the basis for title and resulting maritime boundary.

The ICJ has confirmed, on several occasions, that there is a difference between base points for the purpose of drawing unilateral maritime limits and bilateral boundaries. Base points that are appropriate for delineation of ambulatory maritime limits may be inappropriate for the construction of permanent maritime boundaries. This seems logical, given the fact that the fixing of bilateral boundaries does not stabilize ambulatory maritime limits. Maritime limits may be established on the basis of unstable coastal features because the limits can be altered as soon as relevant coastal geography changes. However, the same coastal features may be inappropriate for the construction of permanent maritime boundaries because they are binding on both parties, notwithstanding subsequent changes to relevant coastal geography. Therefore, maritime boundaries should not be based on coastal features unless they are appropriate, in view of the permanence of the boundary. Base points on the coastline are preferable to base points on low-tide elevations and the same logic must apply to all unstable coastal features, whether they are low-tide elevations or disappearing points attached to the mainland.

Courts and tribunals have primarily relied on coastal geography when establishing bilateral maritime boundaries. This results from the land dominates the sea principle. However, a majority of maritime boundaries is settled through negotiations and negotiated boundaries can be delimited on whatever basis the negotiating States see fit. Environmental circumstances are particularly relevant, even if often disregarded in the case law, because natural resources subject to delimitation are seriously threatened by ocean warming and acidification. States are obligated to take active measures to protect the marine environment, including the habitats of vulnerable ecosystems, and to sustainably manage living resources under their jurisdiction.

The traditional, mathematical approach to maritime delimitation, completely disregards the ecosystems that make up the oceans. States are expected to conclude separate agreements concerning the management of certain resources but the boundaries are not always a feasible basis for such arrangements, nor does this system promote sustainable development. The idea that delimitation should happen in isolation from the many obligations States hold in regard to environmental protection and sustainable development, enforces the piecemeal approach that UNCLOS has been criticized for. However, the integration of environmental considerations in the delimitation process could improve co-operation between neighbouring States concerning conservation and management of marine resources; sustainable development; and protection of the marine environment. Efforts to ensure sustainable use of marine resources could present equitable solutions for future generations and their ability to enjoy maritime entitlements. Furthermore, the incorporation of broad environmental considerations in the delimitation process could help the international community mitigate and adapt to climate change by addressing commitments to reduce the emission of greenhouse gases, for example, by agreeing not to exploit oil and gas in areas subject to delimitation.

States, courts and tribunals should consider environmental circumstances and related obligations in the delimitation process. The relevance of such circumstances depends on the objective of each delimitation and is essentially a matter of choice for the States concerned. Consideration of environmental factors could have various consequences for the delimitation process. It could affect the adjustment of provisional boundaries or lead to fluctuating boundaries. Furthermore, it could lead to co-operative arrangements, such as joint development zones or the establishment of protective areas.

SETTLED MARITIME BOUNDARIES AND FUNDAMENTAL CHANGES

Predictions relating to climate change are still not precise enough to account for all the effects it may have on coastal geography or the marine environment. There are many variables and volatile changes often have unforeseeable effects. Nonetheless, such changes can be taken into account at the time of delimitation through the construction of ambulatory boundaries, but where they have been ignored, unforeseeable changes can lead to the termination, suspension, withdrawal from or revision, of certain agreements delimiting maritime entitlements.

The ILC's First Issues Paper on sea level rise in relation to international law has indicated that maritime boundaries are subject to the boundary exception of VCLT article 62. However, this book concludes that States can invoke an unforeseen fundamental change of circumstances as grounds for discontinuing treaties that establish non-territorial maritime boundaries, as such treaties are not excluded under VCLT article 62(2)(a). Furthermore, agreements concerning exploitation and management of maritime zones may be subject to change due to unforeseen, fundamental, environmental changes. Such changes must affect the essential basis of the treaty, radically transform ongoing obligations and must not result from a breach of the party invoking it.

Coastal geography is usually an essential basis of treaties establishing non-territorial boundaries and the environmental changes that now seem inevitable may have catastrophic effects on coastal geography and the exercise of sovereign rights in relevant maritime areas. Yet, all the necessary requirements of VCLT article 62 will only be satisfied on rare occasions and the motivation to maintain good political relations with neighbouring States may act as a deterrent for invocation of the principle. Furthermore, courts and tribunals have shown a reluctance to employ VCLT article 62 and rebus sic stantibus, not just in relation to treaties that might be classified as boundary treaties, but in general. Therefore, it seems unlikely that a fundamental change of coastal geography or environmental circumstances will lead to the revision, suspension or termination of a maritime boundary treaty, without the consent of both parties. However, the possibility is of great significance for this study because it demonstrates that international law has the means to address the serious repercussions that may ensue from future changes to coastal geography.

The submission that changes to coastal geography or the marine environment may affect the application of maritime boundaries may seem destined to ignite friction in international relations. That is not the intention. It is well understood that many international disputes relate to territory and it is in the collective interest of the international community that these disputes be firmly settled. However, climate-related changes that now seem inevitable will disrupt the geographic stability that public international law has long taken for granted and maritime boundaries will be affected, whether by virtue of rebus sic stantibus or other principles of law. Territorial disputes are known to escalate into war more often than any other types of disputes. One reason for this may be that States do not have the escape clause of rebus sic stantibus to settle such disputes through legal means. Indeed, rebus sic stantibus is a necessary safety-valve in international relations and this is not the time to restrict its application. We may be at the brink of a new world order, one characterized by instability, and this calls for a re-evaluation of traditional views relating to stability.

FINAL WORDS

Global warming has widespread and various implications for ocean governance. It stands to affect the extent of maritime entitlements and the living conditions of all natural beings. Entire ecosystems are at risk as a consequence of ocean acidification, thermal expansion of the oceans, melting glaciers and sea level rise. Furthermore, coastal geography is undergoing significant changes due to sea level rise, coastal erosion, extreme weather events and deforestation. Such physical changes will affect States' capacity to continuously generate maritime entitlements, the basis for which is the coastal front, and the loss of a coastal front will eventually impact statehood.

VCLT article 62 was intended to strike a balance between two essential components of treaty relations: stability of treaties and the need to respond to profound changes. The same principles of equity and justice that call for adaptation to fundamental changes may also encourage States to delimit maritime entitlements in a way that anticipates the changes. Thus, States may increasingly incorporate foreseeable changes into the delimitation process. This can lead to consideration of coastal instability and environmental changes, such as ocean warming. It can also result in provisions in boundary agreements saying that parties intend to negotiate revision (among themselves or with a third party if necessary) in case of relevant natural occurrences. Additionally, anticipation of the increasing impacts of environmental changes may prompt negotiating States to include clauses, alluding to foreseeable changes, if only to prevent future invocation of VCLT article 62. Indeed, consideration of future changes can eradicate the need for the principle and result in more permanently equitable solutions, making States less inclined to seek revision.

International law is flexible enough to govern the division of maritime entitlements in an era of instability, even though it is based on the assumption that coastal geography provides a stable basis for title. The changing environment may justify new approaches and interpretations of international law, but this can be accomplished with respect for legal stability. Disputes will inevitably arise as treacherous seas dismantle entitlements that coastal States have long relied upon. However, disputes can be settled through peaceful means under UNCLOS Part XV and, instead of resorting to measures outside the law, States arguably have a legal basis for revision of outdated maritime boundaries.

The ILC's preliminary discussion of the potential effects of sea level rise on maritime limits and boundaries is characterized by a strong desire for peace, stability and equity. The international community is faced with unprecedented instability and the general instinct seems to be to herald the principle of stability and resist change. However, it seems illogical that proposals to change the law be driven by the principle of stability. Furthermore, the principle of stability has no capacity to mitigate the effects of climate change or address climate-related issues such as greenhouse gas emission or loss of biodiversity. In contrast, principles of co-operation, precaution and the ecosystem approach can tackle even the gravest threats at their source.

Bibliography

UN DOCUMENTS

CLCS, 'Fifth Session' (3–14 May 1999) UN Doc CLCS/11.

CLCS, 'Eleventh Session' (24–28 June 2002) UN Doc CLCS/34.

CLCS, 'Fourteenth Session' (30 August–3 September 2004) UN Doc CLCS/42.

CLCS, 'Twenty-fourth Session' (1 October 2009) UN Doc CLCS/64.

CLCS, 'Twenty-sixth Session' (2 August–3 September 2010) UN Doc CLCS/68.

CLCS, 'Thirty-fourth Session' (27 January–14 March 2014) UN Doc CLCS/83.

FAO, 'Reykjavik Declaration on Responsible Fisheries in the Marine Ecosystem' (1–4 October 2001) FAO Doc C200/INF/25.

FAO, 'Code of Conduct for Responsible Fisheries' (31 October 1995) FAO COP Resolution 4/95.

GAOR, 'Fifty-seventh Session' (8 October 2002) UN Doc A/57/57/Add.1.

GAOR, 'Report of the International Law Commission, Sixty-eighth Session' (2 May–10 June and 4 July–12 August 2016) UN Doc A/71/10.

GAOR, 'Report of the International Law Commission Fifty-eighth Session' (1 May–9 June and 3 July–11 August 2006) UN Doc A/61/10.

GAOR, 'Report of the ILC on the Work of Its Seventy-first Session' (29 April–7 June and 8 July–9 August 2019) UN Doc A/74/10.

GAOR, 'Report of the International Law Commission Covering the Work of Its Eighth Session' (23 April–4 July) UN Doc A/3159.

GAOR, 'Report of the International Law Commission on the Work of the Second Part of Its Seventeenth Session' (3–28 January 1966) UN Doc A/6309/Rev.1.

GAOR, 'Seventieth Session' (22 July 2015) UN Doc A/70/112.

GAOR, 'Summary Record of the 20th Meeting' (28 November 2017) UN Doc A/C.6/72/SR.20.

ILC, 'Report of the International Law Commission on the Work of Its Eighteenth Session' (4 May–19 July 1966) UN Doc A/CN.4/191.

ILC, 'Second Report on the Law of Treaties, by Sir Humphrey Waldock, Special Rapporteur' (20 March, 10 April, 30 April and 5 June 1963) UN Doc A/CN.4/156 and Add.1–3.

ILC, 'Fifth Report on the Law of Treaties by Sir Humphrey Waldock, Special Rapporteur' (15 November 1965–18 January 1966) UN Doc A/CN.4/183 and Add.1–4.

ILC, 'Draft Articles on the Law of Treaties' (18 July 1966) UN Doc A/CN.4/190.

ILC, 'Summary Record of the 693rd Meeting' (5 June 1963) UN Doc A/CN.4/SR.693.

ILC, 'Summary Record of the 694th Meeting' (6 June 1963) UN Doc A/CN.4/SR.694.

ILC, 'Summary Record of the 695th Meeting' (7 June 1963) UN Doc A/CN.4/SR.695.

ILC, 'Summary Record of the 696th Meeting' (10 June 1963) UN Doc A/CN.4/SR.696.
ILC, 'Summary Record of the 697th Meeting' (11 June 1963) UN Doc A/CN.4/SR.697.
ILC, 'Summary Record of the 335th Meeting' (27 April 1956) UN Doc A/CN.4/SR.335.
ILC, 'Summary Record of the 710th Meeting' (28 June 1963) UN Doc A/CN.4/SR.710.
ILC, 'Summary Record of the 842nd Meeting' (27 January 1966) UN Doc A/CN.4/SR.842.
ILC, 'Summary Record of the 3016th Meeting' (7 July 2009) UN Doc A/CN.4/3016.
ILC, 'Summary Record of the 833th Meeting' (18 January 1966) UN Doc A/CN.4/SR.833.
ILC, 'Summary Record of the 834th Meeting' (19 January 1966) UN Doc A/CN.4/SR.834.
ILC, 'Summary Record of the 835th Meeting' (20 January 1966) UN Doc A/CN.4/SR.835.
ILC, 'Report of the International Law Commission on the Work of Its Eighth Session' (4 July 1956) UN Doc A/CN.4/104.
ILC, 'Sea-Level Rise in Relation to International Law: First Issues Paper' (27 April–5 June and 6 July–7 August 2020) UN Doc A/CN.4/740.
ILC, 'Ninth Report on Unilateral Acts of States' (6 April 2006) UN Doc A/CN.4/569 and Add.1.
ILC, 'Report on the Law of Treaties' (14 March 1956) UN Doc A/CN.4/101.
ILC 'Summary Record of the First Session' (12 April 1949) UN Doc A/CN.4/SR.1.
ILC, 'Summary Records of the Twenty-fourth Session' (2 May–7 July 1972) UN Doc A/CN.4/SER.A/1972.
ILC, 'Summary Records of the Second Part of the Seventeenth Session' (3–28 January 1966) UN Doc A/CN.4/SER.A/1966.
ILC, 'Documents of the Fourth Session Including the Report of the Commission to the General Assembly' (6 June 1952) UN Doc A/CN.4/SER.A/1952/Add.l.
ILC, 'Report of the International Law Commission on the Work of Its Eighteenth Session' (4 May–19 July 1966) UN Doc A/CN.4/SER.A/1966/Add. 1.
ILC, 'Second Report on the Law of Treaties, by Mr GG Fitzmaurice, Special Rapporteur' (15 March 1957) UN Doc A/CN.4/107.
ILC, 'Report of the Commission to the General Assembly on the Work of the Thirty-fourth Session' (3 May–23 July 1982) UN Doc A/CN.4/SER.A/1982/Add.l (Part 2).
Intergovernmental Conference on the BBNJ Agreement, 'Revised Draft Text of an Agreement Under the United Nations Convention on the Law of the Sea on the Conservation and Sustainable Use of Marine Biological Diversity of Areas Beyond National Jurisdiction' (23 March–3 April 2020) UN Doc A/CONF.232/2020/3.
Third United Nations Conference on the Law of the Sea, '171st Plenary Meeting' (16 April 1982) UN Doc A/CONF.62/SR.171.
UNCLOS: Meeting of States Parties, 'Decision Regarding the Date of Commencement of the Ten-year Period for Making Submissions to the Commission on the Limits of the Continental Shelf Set Out in Article 4 of Annex II to the United Nations Convention on the Law of the Sea' (29 May 2001) UN Doc SPLOS/72.
UNCLOS: Meeting of States Parties, 'Decision Regarding the Workload of the Commission on the Limits of the Continental Shelf and the Ability of States, Particularly Developing States, to Fulfil the Requirements of Article 4 of Annex II to the Convention, as well as the Decision Contained in SPLOS/72, paragraph (a)' (20 June 2008) UN Doc SPLOS/183.
UNCLOS, Official Records, Volume III, 'Summary Records of Meetings and Annexes' (24 February–27 April 1958) UN Doc: A/CONF.13/39.
UNESCO, 'Declaration of Ethical Principles in Relation to Climate Change' in Resolution 15 adopted by the General Conference at its 39th session (30 October–14 November 2017) (UNESCO 2018) Annex III, 129.

UNGA Res 72/249, 'International Legally Binding Instrument Under the United Nations Convention on the Law of the Sea on the Conservation and Sustainable Use of Marine Biological Diversity of Areas Beyond National Jurisdiction' (19 January 2018).

UNGA Res 73/202, 'Subsequent Agreements and Subsequent Practice in Relation to the Interpretation of Treaties' (20 December 2018).

UNGA Res 73/265, 'Report of the International Law Commission on the Work of Its Seventieth Session' (22 December 2018).

UNGA Res 75/89, 'Sustainable Fisheries, Including through the 1995 Agreement for the Implementation of the Provisions of the United Nations Convention on the Law of the Sea of 10 December 1982 Relating to the Conservation and Management of Straddling Fish Stocks and Highly Migratory Fish Stocks, and Related Instruments' (8 December 2020).

UNGA Res 75/239, 'Oceans and the Law of the Sea' (31 December 2020).

United Nations Conference on the Law of Treaties 'First Session' (26 March–24 May 1968) UN Doc A/CONF.39/11.

United Nations Conference on the Law of Treaties, 'Second Session' (9 April–22 May 1969) UN Doc A/CONF.39/11/Add.1.

United Nations Conference on the Law of Treaties, 'First and Second Sessions' (26 March–24 May 1968 and 9 April–22 May 1969) UN Doc A/CONF.39/11/Add.2.

United Nations Conference on the Law of the Sea, 'Summary Records of the 31st to 35th Meetings of the Fourth Committee' (24 February –27 April 1958) UN Doc A/CONF.13/C.4/SR.31–35, 93.

World Summit on Sustainable Development, 'Adoption of the Plan of Implementation' (26 August–4 September 2002) UN Doc A/CONF.199/20, 139.

ILA DOCUMENTS

ILA, 'Conference Resolution Sydney' (2018) ILA Res 5/2018.

ILA Baselines Committee, 'Conference Report Sofia 2012' (ILA, 2012).

ILA Baselines Committee, 'Conference Report Washington 2014' (ILA, 2014).

ILA Baselines Committee, 'ILA Straight Baselines Study-Protests' (ILA, 2016).

ILA Baselines Committee, 'Johannesburg Conference' (ILA, 2016).

ILA Committee on International Law and Sea Level Rise, 'Johannesburg Conference' (ILA, 2016).

ILA Committee on International Law and Sea Level Rise, 'Minutes of the Lopud Intersessional Meeting' (ILA, 2017).

ILA Committee on International Law and Sea Level Rise, 'Sydney Conference' (ILA, 2018).

ILA Committee on Legal Aspects of Sustainable Development, 'New Delhi Declaration of Principles of International Law Relating to Sustainable Development' (ILA, 2002).

ILA Committee on the Outer Continental Shelf, 'Conference Report Toronto 2006' (ILA, 2006).

ILA Committee on the Outer Continental Shelf, 'Berlin Conference (2004)' (ILA, 2004).

Roach A, 'Archipelagic States Practice: Update on Article 47 in Committee's Final First Report Archipelagic States Practice' (ILA Baselines Committee, 2017).

BOOKS AND CHAPTERS

Aréchaga E, *International Law in the Past Third of a Century* (Sijthoff, 1978).

Anderson D, 'Negotiating Maritime Boundary Agreements: A Personal View' in Lagoni R and Vignes D (eds) *Maritime Delimitation* (Martinus Nijhoff, 2006) 121.

Andreone G, 'The Exclusive Economic Zone' in Rothwell D, Oude Elferink A, Scott K and Stephens T (eds) *The Oxford Handbook of the Law of the Sea* (Oxford University Press, 2015) 159.

Aust A, *Modern Treaty Law and Practice*, 2nd edition (Cambridge University Press, 2007).

Boyle A, 'Law of the Sea Perspectives on Climate Change' in Freestone D (ed) *The 1982 Law of the Sea Convention At 30: Successes, Challenges and New Agendas* (Martinus Nijhoff, 2013) 157.

Boyle A and Chinkin C, *The Making of International Law* (Oxford University Press, 2007).

Brown E, *The International Law of the Sea, volume 1* (Dartmouth, 1994).

Brownlie I, *Principles of Public International Law* (Clarendon Press, 1998).

Brownlie I, *The Vienna Convention on the Law of Treaties* (Manchester University Press, 1984).

Byers M, *International Law and the Arctic* (Cambridge University Press, 2013).

Caron D, 'Climate Change, Sea Level Rise and the Coming Uncertainty in Oceanic Boundaries: A Proposal to Avoid Conflict' in Hong S-Y and Dyke JV (eds) *Maritime Boundary Disputes, Settlement Processes and the Law of the Sea* (Martinus Nijhoff, 2008) 1.

Churchill R, 'The Impact of State Practice on the Jurisdictional Framework Contained in the LOS Convention' in Oude Elferink A (ed) *Stability and Change in the Law of the Sea: The Role of the Los Convention* (Martinus Nijhoff, 2005) 91.

Churchill R, 'The 1982 United Nations Convention on the Law of the Sea' in Rothwell D, Oude Elferink A, Scott K and Stephens T (eds) *The Oxford Handbook of the Law of the Sea* (Oxford University Press, 2015) 24.

Churchill R and Lowe A, *The Law of the Sea*, 2nd revised edition (Manchester University Press, 1988).

Churchill R and Lowe A, *The Law of the Sea*, 3rd edition (Juris Publishing, 1999).

Colson D and Smith R (eds), *International Maritime Boundaries VI* (American Society of International Law, Martinus Nijhoff, 2011).

Cottier T, *Equitable Principles of Maritime Boundary Delimitation: The Quest for Distributive Justice in International Law* (Cambridge University Press, 2015).

Crawford E and Rayfuse R, 'Chapter 10: Climate Change and Statehood' in Rayfuse R and Scott S (eds) *International Law in the Era of Climate Change* (Edward Elgar Publishing, 2012) 243.

Dahm G, Delbrück J and Wolfrum R, *Völkerrecht: Die Grundlagen. Die Völkerrechtssubjekte* (De Gruyter, 2002).

DOALOS, *Handbook on the Delimitation of Maritime Boundaries* (UN, 2000).

Dolliver L and Nelson M, 'Claims to the Continental Shelf beyond the 200-Mile Limit' in Götz G, Selmer P and Wolfrum R (eds) *Liber Amicorum Günther Janicke – Zum 85 Geburtstag* (Springer, 1998) 573.

Dörr O, 'Article 31. General Rule of Interpretation' in Dörr O and Schmalenbach K (eds) *Vienna Convention on the Law of Treaties: A Commentary* (Springer, 2012) 521.

Evans M, 'Maritime Boundary Delimitation: Where Do We Go from Here?' in Freestone D, Barnes R and Ong D (eds), *The Law of the Sea: Progress and Prospects* (Oxford University Press, 2006) 137.

Foster C, *Science and the Precautionary Principle in International Courts: Expert Evidence, Burden of Proof and Finality* (Cambridge University Press, 2011).

Freestone D and Pethick J, 'Sea Level Rise and Maritime Boundaries: International Implications of Impacts and Responses' in Blake G (ed) *Maritime boundaries: World Boundaries, volume 5* (Routledge, 1994) 73.

Frost R, *The Mending Wall* (David Nutt, 1914).

Gardiner R, *Treaty Interpretation*, 2nd edition (Oxford University Press, 2015).

Ghaleigh N, 'Science and Climate Change Law – the Role of the IPCC in International Decision-making', in Carlarne CP, Gray KR and Tarasofsky R (eds) *The Oxford Handbook of International Climate Change Law* (Oxford University Press, 2016) 56.

Giegerich T, 'Article 62. Fundamental Change of Circumstances' in Dörr O and Schmalenbach K (eds) *Vienna Convention on the Law of Treaties: A Commentary* (Springer, 2012) 1067.

Grant J and Barker JC (eds), *Encyclopaedic Dictionary of International Law*, 3rd edition (Oxford University Press, 2009).

Harrison J, *Making the Law of the Sea: A Study in the Development of International Law* (Cambridge University Press, 2011).

Hayashi M, 'Sea Level Rise and the Law of the Sea: Future Options' in Vidas D and Schei P (eds) *The World Ocean in Globalisation* (Martinus Nijhoff, 2011) 187, 188–190.

Heiðar T, 'Legal Aspects of Continental Shelf Limits', in Nordquist M, Moore J and Heiðar T (eds) *Legal and Scientific Aspects of Continental Shelf Limits* (Martinus Nijhoff, 2004) 19.

Hill C, *The Doctrine of 'Rebus sic stantibus' in International Law* (University of Missouri, 1934).

International Hydrographic Organization, *Hydrographic Dictionary*, 5th edition (IHO, 1994).

International Hydrographic Organization, International Oceanographic Commission, International Association of Geodesy and Advisory Board on the Law of the Sea, *A Manual on Technical Aspects of the United Nations Convention on the Law of the Sea – 1982: Special Publication No 51*, 4th edition (International Hydrographic Bureau, 2006).

Houghton J, Jenkins G, Ephraums J (eds), *Climate Change: The IPCC Scientific Assessment* (Cambridge University Press, 1990) chapter 9.

Ibler V, 'Jus Cogens and the Law of the Sea' in Kohen M (ed) *Promoting Justice, Human Rights and Conflict Resolution through International Law* (Brill, 2007) 747.

IPCC, '2019: Summary for Policymakers' in Pörtner H-O, Roberts D, Masson-Delmotte V, Zhai Panmao, Tignor M, Poloczanska E, Mintenbeck K, Alegría A, Nicolai M, Okem A, Petzold J, Rama B, Weyer N (eds) *IPCC Special Report on the Ocean and Cryosphere in a Changing Climate* (World Meteorological Organization, 2019).

IPCC, '2018: Summary for Policymakers' in Masson-Delmotte V, Zhai P, Pörtner H-O, Roberts D, Skea J, Shukla P, Pirani A, Moufouma-Okia W, Péan C, Pidcock R, Connors S, Robin Matthews JB, Chen Y, Zhou X, Gomis M, Lonnoy E, Maycock T, Tignor M and Waterfield T (eds) *Global Warming of 1.5°C. An IPCC Special Report on the impacts of global warming of 1.5°C above pre-industrial levels and related global greenhouse gas emission pathways, in the context of strengthening the global response to the threat of climate change, sustainable development, and efforts to eradicate poverty* (World Meteorological Organization, 2018).

IPCC, *Climate Change: The IPCC 1990 and 1992 Assessment* (World Meteorological Organization, 1992).

Jesus J, 'Rocks, New-Born Islands, Sea Level Rise and Maritime Space' in Frowein J, Scharioth K, Winkelmann I and Wolfrum R (eds) *Verhandeln für den Frieden – Negotiating for Peace: Liber Amicorum Tono Eitel* (Springer, 2003) 579.

Johnston D and Valencia M, *Pacific Ocean Boundary Problems: Status and Solutions* (Martinus Nijhoff, 1991).

Kapoor D, and Kerr A, *A Guide to Maritime Boundary Delimitation* (Carswell, 1986)

Karl W, *Vertrag und spätere Praxis im Völkerrecht* (Springer, 1983).

Kwiatkowska B, 'Economic and Environmental Considerations in Maritime Boundary Delimitations' in Charney J and Alexander L (eds) *International Maritime Boundaries, volume 1* (Martinus Nijhoff, 1993) 75.

Lando M, *Maritime Delimitation as a Judicial Process* (Cambridge University Press, 2019).
Langlet D and Rayfuse R (eds), *The Ecosystem Approach in Ocean Planning and Governance: Perspectives from Europe and Beyond* (Brill Nijhoff, 2019) 117.
Lathrop C, 'Baselines' in Rothwell D, Oude Elferink A, Scott K and Stephens T (eds) *The Oxford Handbook of the Law of the Sea* (Oxford University Press, 2015) 69.
Law J (ed) *A Dictionary of Law*, 8th edition (Oxford University Press, 2015).
Lee K, *The Demise of Equitable Principles and the Rise of Relevant Circumstances in Maritime Boundary Delimitation*, submitted for the Degree of PhD School of Law (The University of Edinburgh, 2012).
Marston G, 'The Stability of Land and Sea Boundary Delimitations in International Law' in Blake G (ed) *Maritime boundaries: World Boundaries, volume 5* (Routledge, 1994) 144.
Meyer T, 'Institutions and Expertise: The Role of Science in Climate Change Lawmaking' in Carlarne CP, Gray KR and Tarasofsky R (eds) *The Oxford Handbook of International Climate Change Law* (Oxford University Press, 2016) 442.
McColl R (ed) *Encyclopedia of World Geography, volume 1* (Facts on File, Inc, 2005).
Mcdougal M and Burke W, *The Public Order of the Oceans* (Yale University Press, 1962).
Murphy S, 'The Relevance of Subsequent Agreement and Subsequent Practice for the Interpretation of Treaties' in Nolte G (ed) *Treaties and Subsequent Practice* (Oxford University Press, 2013) 82.
Nordquist M (ed) *United Nations Convention on the Law of the Sea 1982 – A Commentary, volume 2* (Martinus Nijhoff, 1993).
Nordquist M, Nandan S og Rosenne S, *United Nations Convention on the Law of the Sea 1982, volume 2, A Commentary* (Brill Nijhoff, 1982).
Noyes J, 'The Territorial Sea and Contiguous Zone' in Rothwell D, Oude Elferink A, Scott K and Stephens T (eds) *The Oxford Handbook of the Law of the Sea* (Oxford University Press, 2015) 91.
O'Connell D, *The International Law of the Sea, volume 2* (Clarendon Press, 1984).
Oppenheim L, *Oppenheim's International Law, volume 1, Peace*, 8th edition (Longman, 1992).
Oppenheimer M and Glavovic B (coordination lead authors), '2019: Sea Level Rise and Implications for Low-Lying Islands, Coasts and Communities' in Pörtner HO, Roberts D, Masson-Delmotte V, Zhai P, Tignor M, Poloczanska E, Mintenbeck K, Alegría A, Nicolai M, Okem A, Petzold J, Rama B and Weyer N (eds) *IPCC Special Report on the Ocean and Cryosphere in a Changing Climate*.
Oude Elferink A, 'The Continental Shelf beyond 200 Nautical Miles: The Relationship between the CLCS and Third Party Dispute Settlement' in Oude Elferink A and Rothwell D (eds) *Oceans Management in the 21st Century: Institutional Frameworks and Responses* (Martinus Nijhoff, 2004) 107.
Platzöder R (ed) *Third United Nations Conference on the Law of the Sea: Documents, volume 4* (Oceana Publications, 1983).
Platzöder R (ed) *Third United Nations Conference on the Law of the Sea: Documents, volume 12* (Oceana Publications, 1987).
Prescott V and Schofield C, *The Maritime Political Boundaries of the World*, 2nd edition (Martinus Nijhoff, 2005).
Proelß A, 'Article 34. General Rule Regarding third States' in Dörr O and Schmalenbach K (eds) *Vienna Convention on the Law of Treaties a Commentary* (Springer, 2012) 605.
Purcell K, 'Maritime Jurisdiction in a Changing Climate' in Gerrard M and Fischer Kuh K (eds) *The Law of Adaptation to Climate Change: U.S. and International Aspects* (The American Bar Association, 2012) 729.

Purcell K, *Geographical Change and the Law of the Sea* (Oxford University Press, 2019).

Rayfuse R, 'Chapter 6: Climate Change and the Law of the Sea' in Rayfuse R and Scott S (eds) *International Law in the Era of Climate Change* (Edward Elgar Publishing, 2012) 147.

Reed M, *Shore and Sea Boundaries, volume 3* (United States Government Printing Office, 2000).

Reisman W and Westerman G, *Straight Baselines in International Maritime Boundary Delimitation* (MacMillan Press, 1992).

Reuter P, *Introduction to the Law of Treaties* (Kegan Paul International, 1995).

Roach A and Smith R, *Excessive Maritime Claims*, 3rd edition (Martinus Nijhoff, 2012).

Sands P and Peel J, with Fabra A and MacKenzie R, *Principles of International Environmental Law*, 4th edition (Cambridge University Press, 2018).

Sands P and Peel J, *Principles of International Environmental Law*, 3rd edition (Cambridge University Press, 2012).

Schofield C and Freestone D, 'Options to Protect Coastlines and Secure Maritime Jurisdictional Claims in the Face of Global Sea Level Rise' in Gerrard M and Wannier G (eds) *Threatened Island Nations: Legal Implications of Rising Seas and a Changing Climate* (Cambridge University Press, 2013) 141.

Schofield C and Warner R, *Climate Change and the Oceans Gauging the Legal and Policy Currents in the Asia Pacific and Beyond* (Edward Elgar Publishing, 2012).

Shaw M, *International Law*, 6th edition (Cambridge University Press, 2008).

Simma B, 'Miscellaneous Thoughts on Subsequent Agreements and Practice' in Nolte G (ed) *Treaties and Subsequent Practice* (Oxford University Press, 2013) 46.

Sinclair I, *The Vienna Convention on the Law of Treaties*, 2nd edition (Manchester University Press, 1984).

Sohn L and Noyes J, *Cases and Materials on the Law of the Sea* (Transnational, 2004).

Song Y-H, 'Okinotorishima: A "Rock" or an "Island"? Recent Maritime Boundary Controversy between Japan and Taiwan/China' in Hong S-Y and Jon VD (eds) *Maritime Boundary Disputes, Settlement Processes, and the Law of the Sea* (Martinus Nijhoff, 2009) 145.

Soons A, 'An Ocean under Stress: Climate Change and the Law of the Sea': Addendum to 'Climate Change: Options and Duties under International Law' (2018) 145 Mededellingen van de Koninklijke Nederlandse Verenigling voor International Recht, 71.

"Soons A, 'The Effects of Sea Level Rise on Baselines and Outer Limits of Maritime Zones' in Tómas Heiðar (ed) *New Knowledge and Changing Circumstances in the Law of the Sea* (Brill Nijhoff, 2020) 358."

Sorel J-M and Eveno V, '1969 Vienna Convention, Article 31: General Rule of Interpretation' in Corten O and Klein P (eds) *The Vienna Conventions on the Law of Treaties: A Commentary* (Oxford University Press, 2011) 804.

Stephens T, 'Warming Waters and Souring Seas: Climate Change and Ocean Acidification' in Rothwell D, Oude Elferink A, Scott K and Stephens T (eds) *The Oxford Handbook of the Law of the Sea* (Oxford University Press, 2015) 777.

Tanaka Y, *Predictability and Flexibility in the Law of Maritime Delimitation* (Bloomsbury Publishing, 2006).

Treves T, 'Historical Developments of the Law of the Sea' in Rothwell D, Oude Elferink A, Scott K and Stephens T (eds) *The Oxford Handbook of the Law of the Sea* (Oxford University Press, 2015) 1.

UN Office of Ocean Affairs and Law of the Sea, *Baselines: An Examination of Relevant Provisions of the United Nations Convention on the Law of the Sea* (UN, 1989).

Vamvoukos A, *Termination of Treaties in International Law: The Doctrines of Rebus Sic Stantibus and Desuetude* (Clarendon Press, 1985).

Vicuña F, *The Changing International Law of High Seas Fisheries* (Cambridge University Press, 1999).
Villiger M, *Commentary on the 1969 Vienna Convention on the Law of Treaties* (Martinus Nijhoff, 2009).
Weil P, *The Law of Maritime Delimitation – Reflections* (Cambridge University Press, 1989).
Westholm A, 'Delimiting Marine Areas: Ecosystem Approach(es?) in EU Marine Management' in Langlet D and Rayfuse R (eds) *The Ecosystem Approach in Ocean Planning and Governance: Perspectives from Europe and Beyond* (Brill Nijhoff, 2019) 117.
World Commission on Environment and Development, *Our Common Future* (Oxford University Press, 1987).
Yacouba C and McRae D, 'The Legal Regime of Maritime Boundary Agreements' in Colson D and Smith R (eds) *International Maritime Boundaries, volume 5* (Martinus Nijhoff, 2005) 3281.
Zalasiewicz J, Crutzen P, and Steffen W, 'The Anthropocene' in Gradstein FM et al (eds) *The Geologic Time Scale 2012, volume 2* (Elsevier, 2012).

JOURNAL ARTICLES

Ásgeirsdóttir Á and Steinwand MC, 'Dispute Settlement Mechanisms and Maritime Boundary Settlements' (2015) 10 Review of International Organizations 119.
Alexander L, 'Baseline Delimitations and Maritime Boundaries' (1983) 23 Virginia Journal of International Law 503.
Alvarez-Jimenez A, 'Boundary Agreements in the International Court of Justice's Case Law, 2000–2010' (2012) 23 (2) European Journal of International Law 495.
Ananthaswamy A, 'Going, Going . . .' (2009) 202 (2715) New Scientist 26.
Anderson D, 'Recent Boundary Agreements in the Southern North Sea' (1992) 41 (2) International and Comparative Law Quarterly 414.
Antunes N, 'The Pending Maritime Delimitation in the Cameroon v Nigeria Case: A Piece in the Jigsaw Puzzle of the Gulf of Guinea' (2000) 15 (2) The International Journal of Marine and Coastal Law 163.
Beckman R and Schofield C, 'Moving Beyond Disputes Over Island Sovereignty: ICJ Decision Sets Stage for Maritime Boundary Delimitation in the Singapore Strait' (2009) 40 (10) Ocean Development and International Law 1.
Bederman D, 'The 1871 London Declaration, Rebus Sic Stantibus and a Primitivist View of the Law of Nations' (1988) 82 (1) American Journal of International Law 1.
Bostica H and Howey M, 'To Address the Anthropocene, Engage the Liberal Arts' (2017) 18 Anthropocene 105.
Bowden J, 'The Texas-New Mexico Boundary Dispute along the Rio Grande' (1959) 63 The Southwestern Historical Quarterly 225.
Boyle A and Harrison J, 'Judicial Settlement of International Environmental Disputes: Current Problems' (2013) 4 (2) Journal of International Dispute Settlement 245.
Boyle A, 'Further Development of the Law of the Sea Convention: Mechanisms for Change' (2005) 54 International and Comparative Law Quarterly 563.
Boyle A, 'Law of the Sea Perspectives on Climate Change' (2012) 27 The International Journal of Marine and Coastal Law 831, 832.
Briggs H, 'Unilateral Denunciation of Treaties: The Vienna Convention and the International Court of Justice' (1974) 68 (1) American Journal of International Law 51.

Carleton C and Schofield C, 'Developments in the Technical Determination of Maritime Space: Charts, Datums, Baselines, Maritime Zones and Limits' (2001) 3 (3) International Boundaries Research Unit Maritime Briefing 1.

Caron D, 'When Law Makes Climate Change Worse: Rethinking the Law of Baselines in Light of a Rising Sea Level' (1990) 17 (4) Ecology Law Quarterly 621.

Chapman G and Johnson E, 'The Limits of Anchoring' (1994) 7 Journal of Behavioural Decision Making 223.

Charney J, 'Progress in International Maritime Boundary Delimitation Law' (1994) 88 (2) American Journal of International Law 227.

Chin A, Gillson L, Quiring S, Nelson D, Taylor M, Vanacker V and Lovegrove D, 'An Evolving Anthropocene for Science and Society' (2016) 3 Anthropocene 1.

Churchill R, 'The Persisting Problem of Non-Compliance with the Law of the Sea Convention: Disorder in the Oceans' (2012) 27 (4) The International Journal of Marine and Coastal Law 813.

Churchill R, 'The Greenland-Jan Mayen Case and Its Significance for the International Law of Maritime Boundary Delimitation' (1994) 9 The International Journal of Marine and Coastal Law 1.

Churchill R, 'Legal Uncertainties in International High Seas Fisheries Management' (1998) 37 Fisheries Research, 225.

Churchill R, 'Maritime Delimitation in the Jan Mayen Area' (1985) 9 (1)Marine Policy, 16.

Committee of Experts for the Progressive Codification of International Law, 'Report of the Subcommittee on Territorial Waters, League of Nations' Legal Questions 10, reprinted in (1926) 20 American Journal of International Law 62.

Dalby S, 'Bordering Sustainability in the Anthropocene' (2020) 8 (2) Territory, Politics, Governance, 144.

D'Aspremont J and Mbengue M, 'Strategies of Engagement with Scientific, Fact-Finding in International Adjudication (2014) 5 Journal of International Dispute Settlement 240.

Dyke J V, 'Legal Issues Related to Sovereignty over Dokdo and Its Maritime Boundary' (2007) 38 Ocean Development and International Law, 157.

Garner J, 'The Doctrine of Rebus Sic Stantibus and the Termination of Treaties' (1927) 21 (3) American Journal of International Law 509.

Herbert G, 'Fisheries Relations in the Gulf of Maine: Implications of an Arbitrated Maritime Boundary' (1995) 19 (4) Marine Policy 301.

Hirst W and Robertson D, 'Geographic Information Systems, Charts and UNCLOS – Can They Live Together?' (2004) 136 Maritime Studies 1.

Hodgson R and Smith R, 'The Informal Single Negotiating Text (Committee II): A Geographical Perspective' (1976) 3 Ocean Development and International Law 225.

Kaldunski M, 'A Commentary on Maritime Boundary Arbitration between Bangladesh and India Concerning the Bay of Bengal' (2015) 28 (4) Leiden Journal of International Law 799.

Kaye S, 'The Law of the Sea Convention and Sea Level Rise after the South China Sea Arbitration' (2017) 93 International Law Studies Series, US Naval War College, 423.

Kaye S, 'Lessons Learned from the Gulf of Maine Case: The Development of Maritime Boundary Delimitation Jurisprudence since UNCLOS III' (2008) 14 (1) Ocean and Coastal Law Journal, 73.

Khadem A, 'Protecting Maritime Zones from the Effects of Sea Level Rise' (1998) 5 (3) IBRU Boundary and Security Bulletin 76.

Kimball L, 'Treaty Implementation: Scientific and Technical Advice Enters a New Stage' (1996) 28 Studies in Transnational Legal Policy 177.

Kirk E, 'Maritime Zones and the Ecosystem Approach: A Mismatch?' (1999) 8 (1) Review of European Community & International Environmental Law 67.

Kratochwil F, 'Of Systems, Boundaries, and Territoriality: An Inquiry into the Formation of the State System' (1986) 39 (1) World Politics 27.

Kulick A, 'Article 60 ICJ Statute, Interpretation Proceedings, and the Competing Concepts of Res Judicata' (2015) 28 (1) Leiden Journal of International Law 73.

Kulp S and Strauss B, 'New Elevation Data Triple Estimates of Global Vulnerability to Sea-Level Rise and Coastal Flooding' (2019) 10 Nature Communications,1.

Lisztwan J, 'Stability of Maritime Boundary Agreements' (2012) 37 Yale Journal of International Law 153.

Lusthaus J, 'Shifting Sands: Sea Level Rise, Maritime Boundaries and Inter-state Conflict' (2010) 30 Politics 113.

Magnússon B, 'Outer Continental Shelf Boundary Agreements', (2013) 62 (02) International and Comparative Law Quarterly 345.

McDorman T, 'The Role of the Commission on the Limits of the Continental Shelf: A Technical Body in a Political World' (2002) 17 International Journal of Marine and Coastal Law 301.

Müllerson R, 'The ABM Treaty: Changed Circumstances, Extraordinary Events, Supreme Interests and International Law' (2001) 50 International and Comparative Law Quarterly 509.

Olorundami F, 'Objectivity versus Subjectivity in the Context of the ICJ's Three-Stage Methodology of Maritime Boundary Delimitation' (2017) 32 The International Journal of Marine and Coastal Law 36.

Oude Elferink A, 'Article 76 of the LOSC on the Definition of the Continental Shelf: Questions concerning Its Interpretation from a Legal Perspective' (2006) 21 (3) The International Journal of Marine and Coastal Law 269.

Oude Elferink A, 'The Continental Shelf in the Polar Regions: Cold War or Black-Letter Law?' (2009) 40 Netherlands Yearbook of International Law 121.

Oxman B, 'The Third United Nations Conference on the Law of the Sea: The Ninth Session' (1980) 75 (2) American Journal of International Law 211.

Rayfuse R, 'International Law and Disappearing States: Maritime Zones and the Criteria for Statehood' (2011) 41 (6) Environmental Policy and Law 281.

Rayfuse R, 'W(h)ither Tuvalu? International Law and Disappearing States' (2009) 9 University of New South Wales Faculty of Law Research Series 1.

Rhee S-M, 'Sea Boundary Delimitation between States before World War II' (1982) 76 American Journal of International Law 555.

Roach A and Smith R, 'Straight Baselines: The Need for a Universally Applied Norm' (2000) 31 Ocean Development and International Law 47.

Ruddiman W, Ellis E, Kaplan J, Fuller D, 'Defining the Epoch We Live in' (2015) 348 (6230) Science 38.

Ruggie J, 'Territoriality and Beyond: Problematizing Modernity in International Relations' (1993) 47 (1) International Organization 139.

Schofield C, 'Rising Waters, Shrinking States: The Potential Impacts of Sea Level Rise on Claims to Maritime Jurisdiction' (2011) 53 German Yearbook of International Law 189.

Schofield C, 'Parting the Waves: Claims to Maritime Jurisdiction and the Division of Ocean Space' (2012) 1 Penn State Journal of Law and International Affairs 40.

Schofield C, 'Shifting Limits?: Sea Level Rise and Options to Secure Maritime Jurisdictional Claims' (2009) 4 Carbon and Climate Law Review 405.

Schofield C, 'Departures from the Coast: Trends in the Application of Territorial Sea Baselines Under the Law of the Sea Convention' (2012) 27 (4) The International Journal of Marine and Coastal Law 723.

Schofield C and Arsana I M A 'Closing the Loop: Indonesia's Revised Archipelagic Baselines System' (2009) 1 (2) Australian Journal of Maritime and Ocean Affairs 57.

Schofield C, 'Blurring the Lines? Maritime Joint Development and the Co-operative Management of Ocean Resources' (2009) 7 (1) Issues in Legal Scholarship, Article 3, 1.

Schwelb E, 'Fundamental Change of Circumstances Notes on Article 59 of the Draft Convention on the Law of Treaties as recommended for Adoption to the United Nations Conference on the Law of Treaties by Its Committee of the Whole in 1968' (1969) 29 Zeitschrift für Ausländisches Öffentliches Recht und Völkerrecht 39.

Song Y-H, 'The Application of Article 121 of the Law of the Sea Convention to the Selected Geographical Features Situated in the Pacific Ocean' (2010) 9 Chinese Journal of International Law 663.

Soons A, 'The Effects of a Rising Sea Level on Maritime Limits and Boundaries' (1990) 37 (2) Netherlands International Law Review 207.

Stein E and Carreau D, 'Law and Peaceful Change in a Subsystem: "Withdrawal" of France from the North Atlantic Treaty Organization' (1968) 62 American Journal of International Law 577.

Stoutenburg J, 'Implementing a New Regime of Stable Maritime Zones to Ensure the (Economic) Survival of Small Island States Threatened by Sea-Level Rise' (2016) 26 The International Journal of Marine and Coastal Law 263.

Suarez S, 'The Outer Limits of the Continental Shelf: Legal Aspects of their Establishment' (2009) 199 Beiträge zum ausländischen öffentlichen Recht und Völkerrecht 239.

Truman H, '150 – Proclamation 2667 – Policy of the United States with Respect to the Natural Resources of the Subsoil and Sea Bed of the Continental Shelf' (September 28, 1945).

Vagts D, 'Review of Dahm et al., Volkerrecht' (2004) 98 American Journal of International Law 614.

Vidas D, 'Sea-Level Rise and International Law: At the Convergence of Two Epochs' (2014) 4 Climate Law 5.

Waldron J, 'F.W. Guest Memorial Lecture: August 22nd, 2005: The Half-Life of Treaties: Waitangi, Rebus Sic Stantibus' (2006) 11 Otago Law Review 161.

Walker M, Johnsen S, Rasmussen S, Popp T, Steffensen J, Gibbard P, Hoek W, Lowe J, Andrews J, Björck S, Cwynar L C, Hughen K, Kershaw P, Kromer B, Litt T, Lowe D, Nakagawa T, Newnham R, Schwander J, 'Formal Definition and Dating of the GSSP (Global Stratotype Section and Point) for the Base of the Holocene Using the Greenland NGRIP Ice Core, and Selected Auxiliary Records' (2009) 24 Journal of Quaternary Science 3.

Zalasiewicz J, Williams M, Steffen W and Crutzen P J, 'The New World of the Anthropocene' (2010) 44 (7) Environmental Science and Technology 2228.

WEBSITES

Australian Government (Geoscience Australia), 'Australian Maritime Boundaries (AMB)' available at: <www.ga.gov.au/webtemp/image_cache/GA7675.pdf> accessed 16 January 2021, section 2.5.

BBC, 'Denmark to Build "First Energy Island" in North Sea' (4 February 2021) available at: <www.bbc.com/news/world-europe-55931873> accessed 23 February 2021.

BBC, 'Denmark Set to End All New Oil and Gas Exploration' (4 December 2020) available at: <www.bbc.com/news/business-55184580> accessed 23 February 2021.

Cochrane J, 'Indonesia, Long on Sidelines, Starts to Confront China's Territorial Claims' (New York Times, 2017) available at: <www.nytimes.com/2017/09/10/world/asia/indonesia-south-china-sea-military-buildup.html> accessed 16 January 2021.

'Delimitation' in *Black's Law Dictionary: Free Online Legal Dictionary 2nd ed* available at: <http://thelawdictionary.org/delimitation/> accessed 16 January 2021.

DOALOS, 'Deposit of Charts and/or Lists of Geographical Coordinates and DOALOS Geographic Information System (GIS)' (UN, 2016) available at: <www.un.org/depts/los/doalos_activities/about_doalos.htm#GIS> accessed 16 January 2021.

DOALOS, 'Submissions, through the Secretary-General of the United Nations, to the Commission on the Limits of the Continental Shelf, pursuant to article 76, paragraph 8, of the United Nations Convention on the Law of the Sea of 10 December 1982' (UN, 2021) available at: <www.un.org/Depts/los/clcs_new/commission_submissions.htm> accessed 16 January 2021.

DOALOS, 'The United Nations Convention on the Law of the Sea (A Historical Perspective)' (UN, originally prepared in 1998) available at: <www.un.org/Depts/los/convention_agreements/convention_historical_perspective.htm#-Key%20provisions> accessed 7 January 2021.

DOALOS, 'Chronological Lists of Ratifications of, Accessions and Successions to the Convention and the Related Agreements' (UN, 2020) available at: <www.un.org/Depts/los/reference_files/chronological_lists_of_ratifications.htm> accessed 27 November 2020.

Dorst L and Elema I, 'The Effects of Changing Baselines on the Limits of the Netherlands in the North Sea' Conference Paper for ABLOS, 2008 available at: <www.researchgate.net/publication/265167053> accessed 16 January 2021.

Helsinki and OSPAR Commissions, 'Statement on the Ecosystem Approach to the Management of Human Activities "Towards an Ecosystem Approach to the Management of Human Activities"', First Joint Ministerial Meeting of the Helsinki and OSPAR Commissions (Bremen Germany 25–26 June 2003) Annex 5 Ref. §6.1 available at: <www.ospar.org/site/assets/files/1232/jmm_annex05_ecosystem_approach_statement.pdf> accessed 12 February 2021.

IPCC, 'The role of the IPCC and key elements of the IPCC assessment process' (IPCC, 2010) available at: <www.ipcc.ch/2010/02/04/the-role-of-the-ipcc-and-key-elements-of-the-ipcc-assessment-process/> accessed 16 January 2021.

IPCC, 'Organization' available at: <www.ipcc.ch/organization/organization.shtml> accessed 13 January 2021.

Ísleifsson A, 'Kolbeinsey nú tuttugu metrar frá vestur- og að austurodda' (Vísir, 2021) available at: <www.visir.is/g/20212102115d/kol-beins-ey-nu-tuttugu-metrar-fra-vestur-og-ad-austur-odda?fbclid=IwAR2ZHicSbiB5CVoeoL9K9ihsDFqC3SSLuTRSZQdUMYjOtVoor-GNhc3xDIQ> accessed 27 April 2021.

Lean G, 'Disappearing World: Global Warming Claims Tropical Island' (The Independent, 2006) available at: <www.independent.co.uk/environment/climate-change/disappearing-world-global-warming-claims-tropical-island-5331748.html> accessed 13 January 2021.

Morgunblaðið 'Geirfugladrangur telst enn flæðisker' (2012) available at: <www.ruv.is/frett/drangurinn-sem-er-bara-blindsker> accessed 16 January 2021.

Nagano Y, 'Growing Coral to Keep a Sea Claim Above Water' (The New York Times, 2014) available at: <www.nytimes.com/2014/11/19/business/energy-environment/growing-coral-to-keep-a-sea-claim-above-water.html?_r=0> accessed 17 January 2021.

Note verbale, Permanent Mission of the People's Republic of China to the United Nations, notification regarding Japan's submission on the continental shelf beyond 200 nautical miles to the Commission on the Limits of the Continental Shelf, No. CML/2/2009 available at: <www.un.org/depts/los/clcs_new/submissions_files/jpn08/chn_6feb09_e.pdf> accessed 9 January 2021.

Pieters J, 'Schiphol Expansion Would Move Miles into North Sea in New Proposal' (NL Times, 12 March 2018) available at: <https://nltimes.nl/2018/03/12/schiphol-expansion-move-miles-north-sea-new-proposal> accessed 16 January 2021.

Roy E, '"One Day We'll Disappear": Tuvalu's Sinking Islands' (The Guardian, 2019) available at: <www.theguardian.com/global-development/2019/may/16/one-day-disappear-tuvalu-sinking-islands-rising-seas-climate-change> accessed 20 April 2021.

Shears R, 'The World's First Climate Change Refugees to Leave Island due to Rising Sea Levels' (Dailymail, 2007) available at: <www.dailymail.co.uk/news/article-503228/The-worlds-climate-change-refugees-leave-island-rising-sea-levels.html> accessed 13 January 2021.

Working Group on the Anthropocene, 'What is the "Anthropocene"? – current Definition and Status' (2019) available at: <https://quaternary.stratigraphy.org/working-groups/anthropocene/> accessed 13 January 2021.

Index

For EU product safety concerns, contact us at Calle de José Abascal, 56–1°,
28003 Madrid, Spain or eugpsr@cambridge.org.

www.ingramcontent.com/pod-product-compliance
Ingram Content Group UK Ltd.
Pitfield, Milton Keynes, MK11 3LW, UK
UKHW020005151225
466041UK00009B/304

* 9 7 8 1 0 0 9 0 4 8 6 2 0 *